*Land Reform,
American Style*

Land Reform, American Style

Edited by

Charles C. Geisler

and

Frank J. Popper

ROWMAN & ALLANHELD
PUBLISHERS

ROWMAN & ALLANHELD

Published in the United States of America in 1984
by Rowman & Allanheld
(A division of Littlefield, Adams & Company)
81 Adams Drive, Totowa, New Jersey 07512

Library of Congress Cataloging in Publication Data
Main entry under title:

Land reform, American style.

    Includes bibliographical references.
    1. Land use — Government policy — United States.
2. Land tenure — United States.   I. Geisler, Charles C.
II. Popper, Frank J.
HD205.L35   1983   333.3'1'73   83-13725
ISBN 0-86598-016-0

HD
205
.L35
1984

84 85 86 / 10 9 8 7 6 5 4 3 2 1

Printed in the United States of America

To Barbara and Deborah

Contents

Tables and Figures

TABLES

FIGURES

Preface

The idea that scholars have overlooked American land reform occurred to us in 1980. We asked ourselves if there had been many domestic insurgencies among tenants and dispossessed rural people in a nation that prides itself on immense land reserves and widely distributed private property. We wondered how much American land reform resembled land reform abroad. We decided to look at contemporary American land reform as undertaken by minority and mainstream citizens in both cities and countrysides. It was the beginning of a long-distance, long-term collaboration greatly satisfying to both of us.

Matthew Held of the publishing firm of Rowman & Allanheld expressed interest that was especially encouraging because it came early in the project. Cornell University gave research support for Geisler, and Popper benefited from colleagues at the Environmental Law Institute and Resources for the Future. Arlo Woolery of the Lincoln Institute of Land Policy kindly invited William Doebele of Harvard University, Neal Roberts of York University, and Gene Wunderlich of the U.S. Department of Agriculture to help us bring the many tributaries of American land reform into a coherent stream of thought. Holly Ladra, Francene Signor, Helene Vigorita, and Elaine Emling ably typed and edited the manuscript. Charles Popper put us up (and put up with us) when we worked in Cambridge, Massachusetts. Our contributors performed nobly.

C.C.G., Ithaca, New York
F.J.P., Washington, D.C.

PART ONE

Overview

1

Introduction

CHARLES C. GEISLER AND FRANK J. POPPER

Americans have historically looked upon land reform as an issue in developing nations and an irrelevancy at home. The United States has no landless peasantry or landed aristocracy, its plantation economies dissolved shortly after the Civil War, and its domestic land endowment is so vast that free land was still available into the 1960s for Alaskan homesteading. In the American context, land reform has seemed superfluous, if not a contradiction in terms.

Today this complacent double standard is fading. Americans are becoming more concerned about the fairness and efficiency of domestic patterns of land distribution. The U.S. Department of Agriculture has extensively documented inequities in land ownership that in Third World countries would prompt the State Department to recommend land reform. Third World-style approaches that nationalize land or sweep aside oligarchies are unlikely in the United States. Yet incremental efforts to improve the competitive position of small farmers, preserve land resources, and protect the property rights of disadvantaged and minority groups are increasingly evident — efforts that in varying degrees combine conservative, liberal, and radical impulses.

The American concern over land reform is most noticeable in rural areas, but also appears in urban ones. Its manifestations include:

- the controversy, in California and elsewhere in the West, over the enforcement of the 1902 Reclamation Act's 160-acre limit on the size of farms receiving water from federal irrigation projects
- the mounting concern over large corporate and other absentee land-ownership, domestic and foreign
- the Sagebrush Rebellion, where states are seeking greater control over federal landholdings within their borders
- initiatives by the Department of Agriculture, state and local governments, public interest groups, the Catholic church, and grass-

roots coalitions to probe the structure of American agriculture, defend the family farm, and preserve prime agricultural land
- the long-dormant land claims of minorities—Indians, Mexican-Americans, and Southern Blacks—that have recently been sustained by the courts
- fears that the middle-class return to inner cities and the accompanying condominium conversions are displacing the poor, minorities, elderly, and renters
- the exercise at all levels of government of new land-use planning and regulatory tools to preserve social settings and natural resources.

These diverse American conflicts show the importance of landownership, and especially its distribution. "Land reform," both as a phrase and as a concrete policy, has increasingly claimed the attention of planners, politicians, lawyers, conservationists, community activists, and property owners. We believe it deserves their attention. This book examines the origins, effects, implications, and prospects of land reform in the United States.

There is today no politically unified, self-aware American land reform movement. What exists instead, and seems likely to persist in the future, is a set of insurgent groups that share two characteristics with their Third World counterparts: they are economically disadvantaged, and they are trying to gain power over what they consider their land. They believe they have been unfairly deprived of their rights in land and wish to reclaim them. American land reform groups, like those abroad, seek more influence over the ownership, use, and regulation of land. They justify their claims in terms of social equity, economic efficiency, community control, and the quality of local life. Both here and abroad, government support varies from enthusiastic to absent.

Yet American land reformers are not always like their counterparts abroad. Domestic land reformers have often sought partial, incremental change rather than massive social reconstruction. They have relied on precedent, legal or otherwise, rather than a wholly new order. Their efforts have increasingly had an environmental thrust missing in the Third World. Organized labor abroad supports land redistribution schemes that give peasants alternatives to urban slums and unemployment; American labor has supported land reform in the past when the country was less developed, but ignores land reform today. Another difference is that foreign advisors or funding agents have not given counsel, exerted political leverage, or acted as models for American land reform.

American land reform groups differ enormously in their roots, methods, goals, and results. One cannot even draw the seemingly obvious Third World analogy and say that American reformers uniformly seek more dispersed landownership. For instance, many American reformers no longer seek to break up large agricultural holdings and redistribute them; instead they emphasize increasing the productivity of existing farm units. Some land reformers want to open the public domain to further private ownership and use; others want to close it. Some seek more centralization of planning; others seek less centralized, more local planning.

As social scientists — a rural sociologist and a political scientist — we view the land reform movement as an economic struggle over land-based power. Other disciplines see it differently. Lawyers, for instance, often see it as a bold attempt to transfer ownership rights or shift authority between different levels or branches of government. Economists see it as an injection of non-market mechanisms into land markets. Historians may see much of it as the latest stage in the disposal of the public domain. These conceptions indicate the variety of changes land reformers are trying to achieve.

We believe that the American land reform movement is best conceived as a set of skirmishes that is part of a larger battle over the American allocation of land resources. The system used to be primarily economic — buyers and sellers essentially determined land uses and values. But the system is becoming more political: society at large and key groups within it — who are not necessarily buyers or sellers — are coming to have greater influence over land uses and values. Thus owners now have less control over their holdings than they once had. They are, voluntarily or involuntarily, sharing their control — with neighbors, nonowners, advocates of new value systems and new material interests, or government. Once-sovereign owners must take into account the many concerns of the larger community.

The land reform movement is only one aspect of the increasingly political allocation of land. Others are local land-use regulations such as zoning and its alternatives, as well as the recent attempts at state and federal land-use regulation. So are broader environmental regulations and the legal controversies surrounding alleged public takings of private property.

Yet the land reform movement illustrates the political nature of American land allocation more starkly. It emphasizes redistribution of landownership rather than regulation of land use. It represents a direct, frontal challenge to established interests. Unlike environmentalism or state land-use regulation, land reform's different facets draw support from across the ideological continuum rather than primarily from the liberal center. The Sagebrush Rebellion, for instance, springs from the Western right, while many of the attempts to defend the family farm come from the populist center and left. The movement's concern over large corporate and absentee ownership touches the concerns of much of the political spectrum.

The land reform movement cuts deep into American life and raises problems of profoundly long standing. The revival of the land claims of Indians, Mexican-Americans, and Blacks is perhaps the most obvious example. Yet the land reform movement raises even more basic questions: Is the American distribution of landownership fair? Is it efficient? Can it be both? Does it lead to desirable outcomes for most of us? In what sense can owners now be said to own their land? In what ways are nonowners coming to have claims upon it? How is the movement altering the balance of land power? Under what conditions is it succeeding, and with what results? What are land reform's unintended social consequences? These are the issues that inspire this book.

The chapters of this book were written specially for it. The authors come from around the country and across the political spectrum, are activists and academics, have optimistic and pessimistic views of land reform's future. The next chapter's historical survey precedes others dealing with the current relation between land reform and agriculture, natural resources, minorities, rural communities and urban ones. The authors do not always agree with each other, nor we with them, but we believe that they are helping land reform enter the political and moral agenda of the nation.

2

A History of Land Reform in the United States: Old Wine, New Battles

CHARLES C. GEISLER

...the man who settles on the land in the right way is, with the rarest exceptions, likely to become a good American, as are all his children.

> Richard T. Ely (1921)

"Some day," old Jamie had said, "there will come a reckoning and the country will discover that farmers are more necessary than traveling salesmen, that no nation can exist or have any solidity which ignores the land. But it will cost the country dear. There'll be hell to pay before they find out."

> Louis Bromfield (1933)

Many believe that to inhabit a nation which is no longer "agrarian" is to inhabit a nation no longer in need of land reform — that is, of redistributive policies intended to eradicate grossly unequal landownership and oppressive tenancy patterns. Americans are schooled in the fact that their 2.3 billion acres are a bountiful endowment by world standards. Over 70 percent of the United States' population inhabits less than 2 percent of the land, and the farming population has been reduced to caretaker proportions. New generations of technology appear to offset land losses by permitting greater production from less land. Roughly three-fifths of the United States' land mass is privately owned, suggesting broad ownership opportunities. If the country needs land reform, the logic continues, it is in the area of land-use planning and the redistribution of control rather than in the redistribution of ownership.

But such logic has its limitations. From a social and a political standpoint, the distribution of ownership is at least as significant as total or average acreage figures. A recent report on eighty-three countries by the World Bank (1975) showed that just over 3 percent of the people own or control 80 percent of the agricultural land — countries presumably in need of land reform. In 1978, a federally sponsored study of landownership in the United States concluded that domestic ownership was almost equally concentrated.[1] The top 5 percent of all landowners owned 75 percent of the land, but the bottom 78 percent owned 3 percent (Lewis, 1980). Agricultural land was less concentrated: the top 5 percent own 51 percent. But the level of concentration would be much more apparent if, as in the World Bank survey, the comparison were with the population as a whole rather than just owners, and if control (for instance, through loans and credit) as well as ownership were considered. By the year 2000, the largest 50,000 U.S. farms are expected to operate half of the nation's farmland (Schertz and Wunderlich, 1981).

So, notwithstanding Jefferson's vision that Americans possessed "a chosen country, with room enough for our descendants to the thousandth and the thousandth generation" (Richardson, 1897:323), land reform in America is not an idle concern. Despite its accelerated economic growth, its vanishing agrarians, and its high technologies, the United States remains a rural nation with unfinished rural agendas. Much poverty in America is rural and intertwined with land tenure. Some of the nation's poorest people inhabit portions of its richest lands. Private efforts to improve property impoverish some owners through higher taxation or gentrification, while public improvements create windfalls for many who are already wealthy. Despite its place in the nation's value system, widespread private ownership was a myth by 1880 — barely twenty years after the Homestead Act released millions of acres to the landless. In the twentieth century, the dream of home ownership is slipping from the grasp of the average citizen and is unlikely soon to be retrieved. In both centuries federal lands have become the preserve of private grazing, mining, timber, and recreation interests. Although the United States encourages land reform abroad based on private ownership (Boxley, 1977), private property in America is not equitably distributed, nor is it an inalienable right (Cribbet, 1978).

Over the past two decades considerable ferment has arisen over land concentration and absenteeism, foreclosure and disclosure issues, and the poverty and powerlessness resulting from patterns of landownership, control, and taxation in America. This ferment has occasioned grass-roots conferences on national land reform, an outpouring of research, journalism, and bibliographies on domestic land reform issues,[2] and numerous insurgencies among urban and rural citizens in search of landownership and its assumed benefits.[3] The failing of this ferment lies neither in its aspirations nor in its lack of mass appeal, but in the foreshortened sense of history it must overcome. Basic to the misconception that America needs no land reform is that it has had none in the past.

The objective of the present chapter is to demonstrate that, historically, numerous land reform episodes have occurred in America, both in the name of broad private ownership and as alternatives to this prevailing property model. Land reform was not unusual in nineteenth-century America, nor were the insurgencies that carried it to every part of the nation. These insurgencies spilled forcefully into the twentieth century as well. This chapter carries the story through the New Deal, after which domestic land reform in ownership rights has been, until the new ferment of the 1970s, obscured by a misplaced apprehension that land reform is alien to America.

POST-INDEPENDENCE EFFORTS IN DOMESTIC LAND REFORM

Land reform has been a perennial American theme. Americans fought the War for Independence in part to terminate colonial manorial systems, feudalistic quitrents, socage, and other institutions protecting landed privilege (Bennett, 1956). Shortly after independence, the new nation confiscated many hundreds of square miles of Tory estates in Maine, New Hampshire, New York, Pennsylvania, Massachusetts, Georgia, South Carolina, and Virginia (Nevins and Commager, 1945). Such land reform found its rationale among French Encyclopedists and Physiocrats (Eisinger, 1947) as well as British and Scottish radicals like William Blackstone, John Locke, Thomas Spence, William Ogilvie, and Thomas Paine (Sakolski, 1957).

Land policies during the nation's first century were based on an overriding objective — the orderly establishment of domestic empire. The goal meant displacing the indigenous inhabitants, colonizing the land as rapidly as possible to prevent settlement claims by the French, English, Spanish, Mexicans, and Russians, and imposing what we would now term a national land-use plan so as to guide the continent's development and implant agrarian democracy. The plan, emerging from a congressional committee chaired by Thomas Jefferson and embodied in both the Land Ordinance of 1785 and the Northwest Ordinance of 1787, proposed extensive federal surveys and the division of public and private lands. At first the subdivisions were ten miles on a side with 100 internal units, following the land-division pattern used in Roman colonies two thousand years earlier.[4] These subdivisions were later modified to the six-mile-square township with 36 segments, the bulwark of much local government in the United States today. It was a new empire in the making, with widespread private ownership as its cornerstone.

In England, agrarian society flourished before industrialization; in the United States, agrarian society grew along with nascent capitalism (Wiley, 1969). The ideology and fact of widely held private property fitted the youthful nation's economy well. As in most developing countries today, capital was in chronic shortage during the nation's takeoff phase of development. In keeping with the wish expressed in Hamilton's 1790

Report on the Public Lands, the nation pursued a general policy of substituting abundant land for scarce capital for almost a century (Robbins, 1942; Hurst, 1961).[5] The result was a powerful industrial order which would transform the agrarian property system as it matured (Lerner, 1957).

The social engineering of Jefferson and the fiscal engineering of Hamilton distributed people and infrastructure across the land. According to Madison, good government's chief object was the protection of men in their "different and unequal faculties for acquiring property" (U.S. Government, 1927:489–90). Yet the new owners were often not landless immigrants, Eastern tenants or factory workers, or other aspiring landowners of limited means. Instead, they were speculators (Sumner, 1913; Sakolski, 1932; Gates, 1968), entrepreneurs and politicians (Scheiber, 1975; Scott, 1977), and other relatively privileged people. With exceptions—e.g., soldiers who were awarded land in lieu of cash payments for their services (Bogue, 1969)—land concessions to poorer persons came only with struggle or even armed insurrection, such as tenant revolts (Ellis, 1944; Lynd, 1967); farmer protests against tight credits, tariffs, and towering interest rates (Shannon, 1957); political agitation by squatters on the frontier that led to no less than sixteen preemption acts (Webb, 1931); and a series of insurgencies among the working classes of the East that, after thirty years, convinced Congress to pass the Homestead Act of 1862 (Zahler, 1941).

Thus, monetizing the nation's land provoked a "running war between the ideal of an independent agrarian society of small holders and the reality of freewheeling speculators who accumulated vast blocks of the best farm, timber and mineral lands" (Green, 1973:20). Frontier land was the stock market of the day. Washington himself, as well as many legislators who passed federal land laws in the 1800s, speculated heavily in Western lands (Beard, 1949). They seemed oblivious to the tenure disparities such practices introduced and the land monopolies they fostered. For instance, the notorious Yazoo land fraud involved the Georgia legislature's sale of thirty million acres in what is today Mississippi and Alabama. It created fortunes for a few insiders at the expense of a far greater number of later settlers (McGrath, 1966).

Thus nineteenth-century American land reformers such as George Henry Evans, Thomas Skidmore, Gerrit Smith, George W. Julian, and Horace Greeley declared the unequal division of land the basis for social injustice (Riddleberger, 1955; Sakolski, 1957). In books, pamphlets, and newspapers aimed at Eastern working classes, they proclaimed that the cure to chronically low wages was the Western migration of excess labor—an excess "that depressed wages, kept the working day long, jobs insecure, and weakened the bargaining power of labor" (Gates, 1968:391). Greeley's *New York Tribune* popularized such epigrams as "Go west, young man" and "Vote yourself a farm." Some 600 newspapers allegedly followed the *Tribune* in supporting free Western homesteads.[6] American land reformers formed the National Reform Association which opposed land mo-nopolization on the basis of every person's natural right to own land. Its three tenets were: freedom of public lands to the landless and bona fide settler; limitation of the amount of land a single person might own; and exemption of homesteads from execution of debt (Zahler, 1941).[7] The Free Soil Party, with substantial support from the land reformers, polled 10 percent of the popular vote in the presidential elections of 1848.

Wage slavery motivated Eastern land reformers, but so did the Southern enslavement of Blacks. Free soil was a heresy among landed in-terests in the South, who attacked the constitutionality of free soil legis-lation and vigorously supported the Kansas-Nebraska Act of 1854 abol-ishing the Missouri Compromise that had forbidden slavery north of 36°31'. Yet land reformers such as Gerrit Smith and George Julian were elected to Congress in this period on tickets of antislavery and land reform. In 1852, Northern Democrats secured a plank in their party platform asserting the "natural right" of men to the soil (Webb, 1931), and four years later the platform of the incipient Republican party linked slavery to the need for land reform in its own party platform. Abraham Lincoln, newly elected, said of pending homestead legislation, "I am in favor of settling the wild lands into small parcels so that every poor man may have a home" (Robbins, 1942:206).

THE HOMESTEAD ACT AND NEW SUITORS ON THE LAND

Republicans supported free soil, Southern Democrats were absent from Congress during the Civil War, and land reformers such as Greeley shaped an East-West alliance based on mutual agrarian-industrial in-terests. In 1862 the Homestead Act became the law of the land. Historians repeatedly identify it as the consummation of antebellum land reform agi-tation; some have heralded the act as the greatest democratic measure of all history (Robbins, 1942:209). Yet to the former slave, the Native American, the landless immigrant, or even the fourth-generation white American trying to secure a farm, the act's munificence was doubtful.

The Homestead Act entitled heads of families or persons twenty-one years of age who were citizens or who had filed to become citizens, to acquire 160 acres of surveyed public lands at no cost other than a nominal filing fee (Gates, 1973). The law embodied three fundamental concepts—residency on land would lead to ownership, ownership was affirmed by labor invested in the land, and residency and labor would be rewarded by a reduced purchase price as well as low-interest loans and reasonable terms of payment. In 1862, over a billion acres of public domain remained in the nation, although two-thirds was not arable and large portions re-mained unsurveyed. Over the next twenty years there would be 552,000 original land entries. Less than half of these would qualify as final entries (Robbins, 1942).

Southern Blacks seeking farmland in their states of origin were intimidated and discouraged, leading to a Southern Homestead Act in 1866 that applied to some 48 million acres in five Southern states. This act was repealed ten years later, with not more than four thousand Blacks gaining title under its auspices. At the same time, one of the more radical (and ephemeral) land reforms known in United States history was performed in the name of freed slaves immediately after the war by John Eaton, President Grant's Superintendent of Negro Affairs. Eaton leased abandoned plantations on the Sea Islands, along the Georgia coast and inland (including that of Jefferson Davis) to Blacks on a communal basis, or partitioned them into private 40-acre parcels. Some forty thousand freedmen were settled in this classic land reform. Later, however, these plantations were leased to entrepreneurs who employed former slaves as wage labor. W. E. B. DuBois and others have suggested that the racial history of the nation might have changed dramatically had the Eaton experiments not been aborted (Bennett, 1972).

Speculators had consolidated much of the choicest and easily accessible public domain before 1862. After 1862 it was commonplace for individuals and corporations to file land claims fraudulently and to thereby strip the land of resources without concern for final entry. In the decades following, most homesteads were created from land that had long since passed from federal ownership into private hands (Gates, 1973). Of the 1,145 million federal acres outstanding in 1867, 125 million acres were reserved for railroads and 140 million more were destined for states at whatever prices they chose to offer. And, since two-thirds of the original federal base was not arable and another 175 million acres were held apart in Indian reservations, the Homestead Act was something less than a land cornucopia.

With Western land hunger now at a feverish pitch, the federal government turned to Indian lands as a remedy. Says Robbins (1942:279):

> If the prodigious grants of land to railroad corporations forced many actual settlers to take lands unfavorably located, it is likely that it was this same lack of available good lands that led the settler to break in upon the Indian reservations....[I]t was this pressure upon Indian lands that led to most of the Indian wars between 1862 and 1877.

In the 1870s, under pressure from mineral corporations and speculators, Congress placed a moratorium on future Indian treaties and terminated some existing ones (Kelly, 1979). The General Allotment (Dawes) Act of 1887 was ironically described as an Indian "homestead act"; reservations were broken up and American citizenship conferred upon those accepting allotments. By 1892, 26 million acres of Indian land had been "restored" to the public domain; by 1906, some 75 million acres — about three-fourths of the whole amount of Indian land released by the Dawes Act — had been appropriated by whites.

Nature itself conspired against the Homestead Act to pervert its redistributive purposes. Easterners had underestimated the acreage needed for sustainable settlement of arid Western lands; farm sizes practical in Virginia and Illinois proved unworkable in Utah or Montana (Hibbard, 1924:409). The 160-acre maximum was gradually doubled and then in some states redoubled many times. Land monopolization had again appeared, now in the guise of antimonopoly. Western water law hastened this trend by allowing speculators to obtain lands most accessible to water — an advantage over other landholders who wished to irrigate their lands. "In the arid country," according to Walter Prescott Webb (1931:352), "the homestead law was of little avail; thousands of these homesteads reverted to the government yearly, while others passed into the hands of large landowners, speculators and stockmen."

In sum, the Homestead Act was the product of regional politics and free soil innocence rather than reform. In the forty years between 1860 and 1900, some 600,000 homestead patents were issued. Yet it is estimated that only one in six acres went directly from the government to farmer-settlers as intended (Gates, 1936; Cochran, 1979). By the 1880 census, the first in which statistics on tenancy, mortgages, and size of land-holdings were published, landlordism had become entrenched, farm indebtedness among owners was on the rise, and farmland concentration showed the deficiencies of the Homestead Act. As Robbins summarizes (1942:268):

> The actual settler by the eighties was not in a favored position; in fact, corporations and speculators were definitely in the ascendancy. This was not only the situation with regard to the agricultural lands of the country, but with regard to other kinds of lands as well. The actual settler, the placer miner, the hand logger, and the individual grazer were all at a disadvantage in competing with the corporation and moneyed interests on the last American frontier. . . . Legal regulations were evaded, the honest settler was thwarted; in fact, a system of landlord-tenant and land concentration was growing up on American soil. . . .

POST-HOMESTEAD EFFORTS AT RETRIEVAL

Land reformers a century ago sought to retrieve the public domain from what Bryant (1972:72) has termed the "predators on the public patrimony." A variety of land reform insurgencies attracted supporters ranging from the dignified to the destitute. Extraordinary land wealth was accumulating in America beyond the reach of common citizens. Thus the insurgencies tried to redistribute land to the small holder for whom it had been intended or back to the federal government for safe and perpetual keeping.

Indignation over the coexistence of monumental wealth and dismal poverty in this period aroused the considerable reform powers of Henry George, a newspaper columnist from California. George's friends in that state organized a Land Reform League to propagate the message of his seminal work, *Progress and Poverty* (1879). George advocated (1975:327) neither the forced redistribution of land nor its nationalization:

> Let us abandon all attempts to get rid of the evils of land monopoly by re-
> stricting landownership. An equal distribution of land is impossible, and
> anything short of that would be only a mitigation, not a cure, and a miti-
> gation that would prevent the adoption of a cure.

By 1890, roughly ten years after *Progress and Poverty* appeared, property
taxes provided 72 percent of all state and 92 percent of all local tax
revenues; at least three-fourths of these amounts were drawn from taxes on
realty (Andrews, 1979:35). George proposed a land tax that distinguished
between land and its improvements. By not taxing land improvements,
growth would advance without penalty, creating work and wealth. By
capturing the increasing value of land for public rather than private
benefit, speculation would cease, the commonwealth would be enriched,
and land would pass to those who would use it most efficiently (Sakolski,
1957).

In the same year *Progress and Poverty* appeared, the federal government
proposed its own remedial land reform strategy to counter the failures of
homestead legislation. One year earlier, Major John Wesley Powell had
written in his famous *Report on the Lands of the Arid West* (1878:30):

> Monopoly of land need not be feared. The question for legislators to solve is
> to devise some practicable means by which water rights may be distributed
> among individual farmers and water monopolies prevented.

Powell proposed his own plan for effective settlement of the West based on
irrigation districts tied to natural watersheds rather than arbitrary survey
boundaries (Webb, 1931).

In 1879 the National Academy of Sciences recommended the reorganization and consolidation of the country's land and scientific surveys,
Congress authorized "a commission to investigate the whole land system,"
and the United States Geological Survey was established to carry out the
mission (Robbins, 1942:288). Congress also authorized a Public Lands
Commission to classify the remaining public domain and recommend its
wisest use and disposal. Many policymakers believed that old land reform
programs had foundered for technical reasons. Scientific management of
resources could revive them. But in 1880 the land commissioner of the
Department of Interior released a report on the failure of public land distribution programs due to fraud and corruption.[8] The Public Land Commission, appointed the year before, came to the same conclusion and
called for not only a thorough classification and survey of remaining
public lands, but also forfeiture of the extensive railroad lands not used in
accordance with their grants (Robbins, 1942). By the late 1880s land
reform again loomed large in the political platforms of both major parties.
Democrats demanded the restoration of 100 million acres of public
domain to be "sacredly held as homesteads for our citizens" (Ellis,
1928:73).

The consummate land reform of the late nineteenth century was the
little-known Revision Act of 1891. According to Andrews (1979:36), it

"symbolized the final victory of the agrarian land reformers over the speculators, repealing or restricting many of the earlier laws that had permitted widespread land speculation." Its reform content lay in its massive repeal of much former United States land law. Sections of the Timber Culture Act, the Desert Land Act, the Preemption Law, and the Homestead Act — all abused in the extreme — were amended or repealed in the name of the common man and conservation. Unused railroad lands were confiscated and restored to the public domain,[9] and the president was given authority to set aside large forested areas as national parks. Under the Forest Reserve Act of 1891, for example, Presidents Harrison, Cleveland, McKinley, and Roosevelt restocked the nation with 283 million acres of forest reserves — the beginning of the contemporary national forests (Cochran and Miller, 1961). By 1900, both major political parties were officially on record favoring conservation, and agricultural land was no longer the single focus of attention among land reformers.

The conservation movement — personified by John Muir, John Wesley Powell, Gifford Pinchot, and Theodore Roosevelt — conveyed two land reform messages to a nation seeking to reconcile further growth and expansion with the husbanding of resources. Some have portrayed it as a mass movement intent on restraining the privileged access of the rich and powerful to the public domain. For instance, writes Allin (1936:16):

> To keep greed and special privilege from getting an increasingly unfair share of land, mineral, forest, and other resources was a part of Theodore Roosevelt's "trust busting" efforts. This redistribution-of-wealth motive was the real spark that arrayed public support behind the efforts of the conservationists.

For many conservationists, land reform meant disseminating an enlightened land ethic that would protect the beauty, diversity, and integrity of the land. Reformers such as Muir redignified wastelands and wilderness. No longer were wild places solely to be assaulted and tamed.

Yet others have portrayed the conservation movement more cautiously, suggesting that it promoted privilege rather than checking it. In practice, conservation meant administrative centralization, scientific management, and top-down planning (Hays, 1959). It meant displacing the market as prime arbiter of distributing and valuing land. It meant, particularly to Pinchot, resource rationalization, waste reduction, efficiency, and sustained-yield management — conserving land as a form of future capital. Good conservation was good business. For a century, United States land policy had been ostensibly conducted in the name of the small holder; now lands were being reclaimed and reserved in the name of future generations and aesthetic abstractions formulated by elites.

American land reform prior to the Civil War echoed the concerns of the Eastern working class and abolitionists concerned with social welfare. Both thrusts required western expansion and settlement. By the latter part of the century, domestic land reform mirrored rather different class values. On the one hand, affluent Easterners sought to restore large areas of the public domain. This meant restrictions on settlement and on the exploitation of Western lands. It meant, therefore, a rupture in the agrarian-industrial alliance that brought the Republican party and the Homestead Act into being in the 1860s. On the other hand, there was a resurgence of agrarian values among Southern and Western small holders bitterly opposed to land monopoly and to the corrupt federal land policies into which the Homestead Act had devolved.

Unlike the conservation land reform, which gained allegiance among Easterners, this grass-roots Populist movement for rural reform was indigenous. Led by farmers and miners, it was less a settler reaction to the closing of the frontier in the final decades of the century[10] than a mass insurgency among people losing their land as a result of foreclosures, fluctuations in market prices, and endemic crop liens. Tenancy continued to rise in official census figures, as did farm debt. Bondage and peonage were revived in the land (Woodward, 1951; Goodwyn, 1980). Discontent and disillusionment among farmers spawned regional and national organizations—the Grange, the National Farmers' Alliance, the People's Party, and the Farmers' Union—dedicated to restoring "land to the tiller" and the tiller to an agrarian democracy.

Despite divergent class interests, the grass-roots insurgents and conservationists agreed that without massive institutional reform, land reform was in vain. Agrarian radicals sought a fundamental recasting of relationships between city and countryside. "The great cities," thundered William Jennings Bryan in his famous Cross of Gold speech, "rest upon our broad and fertile prairies. Burn down your cities and leave our farms, and your cities will spring up by magic; but destroy our farms, and the grass will grow in the streets of every city in the country" (Bogue, et al., 1970:251). Though supporters of laissez-faire, the bulk of radical agrarians called for currency reform, free silver, government ownership of the railroad and telegraph lines, the recapture of excessive railroad land grants, the abolition of foreign landowning, abandonment of protective tariffs, a graduated income tax, and assorted labor reforms (Shannon, 1957).

Most daring was the Populist proposal for a massive bank reform, the Sub-Treasury Land and Loan Systems, by which a decentralized U.S. Treasury would replace the private banking system, terminating its stranglehold on agricultural debtors. According to this plan, the federal government would establish a subtreasury, warehouse, and grain elevator in each county with an annual production of $500,000 in certain crops. The U.S. Treasury would become the principal source of rural capital and give viability to the large-scale farm cooperatives pioneered in the 1880s (Goodwyn, 1980). Although the private banking system prevailed, along with systemic debt and insecurity that had provoked Populist unrest, the warehouse component of the reform was not widely different from the Warehouse Act of 1916 and its later amendments (Shannon, 1957).

It should now be clear that the more venerable land reform traditions in America at the turn of the century served very different interests. Followers of George sought tax reforms that allowed the full development of property, the reallocation of land to those who would use it productively, and the redistribution of wealth as the unearned value of land was restored to government and its wards. Eastern conservationists sought restoration of land to the public domain with an eye toward long-term resource planning and economic efficiency — hallmarks of the emerging Progressive movement. Agrarian radicals sought government protection from monopolies, speculators, merchant bankers, and business interests that plundered the freehold system upon which they depended.

THE TWENTIETH CENTURY: REFORM AND COUNTERREFORM

Congress passed the National Reclamation Act of 1902 to open arid lands for widespread ownership and family farming by encouraging regulated water development. The chairman of the House committee drafting the legislation reassured Congress:

> In order that no such lands may be held in large quantities or by non-resident owners, it is provided that no water right for more than 160 acres shall be sold to any landowner, who must also be a resident or occupant of his land. This provision was drawn with a view to breaking up any large land holdings . . . in the vicinity of government works and to insure occupancy by the owner of the land reclaimed (cited in Taylor, 1973:21).

Other twentieth-century homestead laws followed — the Kincaid Act of 1904, the Enlarged Homestead Act of 1909, the Three Year Homestead Act of 1912, and the Stock Raising Homesteading Act of 1916 — but none were as sweeping as the 1902 law. It provided public financing for irrigation and drainage improvements. It established reclamation districts that could possess and then sell improved land to settlers. It provided free, long-term credit for land improvement. It made ability-to-pay arrangements to assure that lower-income applicants could gain access to the land. It stated conditions of residency to deter absenteeism, and set acreage limitations to foster homesteading in place of speculation. It created cooperatives to handle the land transactions and the development to follow. During the next two decades the law led to the reclamation of roughly 1,600,000 acres of arid Western land (Beard and Beard, 1927).

Yet the land reform potential of the reclamation law was eventually eroded. Large landowners sought to eliminate both the acreage and residency requirements, despite numerous congressional hearings, objections by reclamation administrators, and protests by diverse grass-roots and religious organizations. Exemptions from the 160-acre limitation have gradually crippled the law, despite research demonstrating the penalties small holders and rural communities suffer because of absenteeism and land concentration (Goldschmidt, 1978; Fujimoto, 1977). In the middle 1970s a grass-roots coalition known as National Land for People sued the federal government over what it termed illegal enforcement of the 1902 act. Though a federal court upheld these charges and ordered the Department of the Interior to prepare new regulations ensuring enforcement, large landowners obtained an injunction against these until an environmental impact report was prepared. While this was in preparation, major amendments were lobbied through Congress setting a 960-acre limit in the House, and in the Senate a maximum of over 2,000 acres (LeVeen, 1978). Today, major agribusiness firms such as Superior Oil, Tenneco, and Chevron USA have many thousands of acres within the water districts, and federal water subsidies range as high as $800 per acre (Sinclair, 1982).

Other conservation and homesteading laws, passed at the turn of the century, also generated counterreform. Despite a trust-busting president and a growing Progressive movement, water laws often accelerated the land monopoly in the West despite their redistributive mandates (the Carey and National Reclamation Acts); forestry legislation permitted the transfer of valuable timber tracts to large corporations (the Forest Lieu and Timber and Stone Acts); Western rangelands were overstocked and overgrazed (the Kincaid Act); and mineral lands were reserved for selected private interests through reinterpretation of Progressive legislation (the General Leasing Act). Using 1897 legislation, the Secretary of the Interior permitted power-generating plants in new federal forest reserves (Robbins, 1942).

These abuses did not go unnoticed. The National Conservation Commission, appointed by Roosevelt in 1907, riveted public attention on the nation's ailing land laws and produced the first national resource inventory in 1908. In 1909, Roosevelt's Country Life Commission submitted a report to the president noting the "disregard of inherent rights of land workers." This resulted from concentrated landownership, tenancy and absenteeism, from "waterlordism" (the concentrated private control of waterways), the unrestricted private harvesting of forests, and discriminatory practices by private railroad companies (Jacobs, 1984). Yet Westerners perceived a double standard. They argued with some justification that the East had capitalized its eighteenth- and nineteenth-century development by opening the frontier for settlement, exploitation, and markets. Many Westerners felt entitled to similar policies in the present century, in the name of regional fairness if not states' rights and local control. This early sagebrush rebellion was advanced by the anticonservation policies of two Westerners who became Interior Secretaries — Ballinger under Taft, and Wilbur under Hoover.[11]

FROM POPULISM TO AGRARIAN SOCIALISM

Utopian and religiously motivated socialism made its mark on early land reform efforts in America only occasionally. Important exceptions were intentional communities such as Brook Farm, the Oneida Community,

New Harmony, the Hutterites in South Dakota, and the Amana Society in Iowa (Eaton, 1943). LeWarn (1978) documents a series of utopian socialist experiments in the Puget Sound region during the present century, and Shepperson (1966) tells of socialists retreating to Nevada to live on the land during red scares in this century. Other socialist land reforms gained a vast farm following between 1900 and World War II—a marriage of Populist remnants and socialists who believed that the more likely converts in America were rural, not urban.[12]

In the late nineteenth century the Populists threw their support to the Democrats but, with the Democrats' defeat in 1896, lost their independent identity. Yet the conditions against which they struggled persisted and even worsened. Crop liens and farm debt were intractable, as were the foreclosures and land centralization they hastened (Goodwyn, 1980). The agricultural census showed that tenancy rose dramatically between 1880 (25 percent of all farms) and 1925 (35 percent), and continued to climb for the next fifteen years. By 1935 some 6.8 million people inhabited America's farmland in seeming fulfillment of the Jeffersonian ideal. Yet nearly half were tenants. Where the twin faces of tenancy and landlordism appeared, so did socialist ferment.

The land reform policies of the socialists had roots in the National Farmers Alliance in the 1880s. A decade later, the hero of the 1894 Pullman strike, Eugene Debs, tried to establish a utopian colony in the West (Buhle, 1980). Due to doctrinal insistence on land collectivization, Debs's socialist commonwealth did not materialize. But, as Goodwyn (1980:20) notes, this was to change:

> The party's early militants of 1898–1901 were still confined to the kitchen in 1902. But they understood the economic realities on the American land and thus the political drives of their potential smallholder-tenant constituency: Both groups wanted freedom from the usurious credit system and both wanted land. The Socialist party, perforce, would have a clear-cut farm program: no absentee landlords, no hired hands for resident landlords, no speculators in the public domain, no tenants, no sharecroppers, "for occupancy and use only."

By 1912 the socialist solution to the land question had legitimacy (Lipset, 1970). America's largest socialist movement was, in the final analysis, agrarian (Goodwyn, 1980). By 1913, the Kansas-based socialist weekly, *Appeal to Reason,* outsold the *Saturday Evening Post* and was the nation's best-selling weekly (Klein, 1979).

Jeffersonian socialism had several facets. Some socialist reformers still wished to collectivize land—for example, the Western "bonanza" farms owned by well-endowed corporations. In the Southwest, socialists established large-scale marketing and purchasing cooperatives much like the Populists' subtreasury vision (Green, 1978). By 1919, the Farmers' Non-partisan Political League of North Dakota captured a clear electoral mandate. The North Dakota state legislature enacted the entire League program, consisting of an industrial commission, a bank of North Dakota,

the North Dakota Mill and Elevator Association, the Home Building As-
sociation of North Dakota, and a comprehensive insurance program
(Shannon, 1957; Lipset, 1970). Like the land reformers of nearly a century
before, League members struck important alliances with urban laborers.
Nonpartisan League reforms surfaced in fifteen states, mostly in the
Midwest, but waned with the agricultural depression that followed.

Another facet of socialist land reform united various religious leaders
with agrarians in the 1920s and 1930s.[13] Typical of this union were books
such as *Revolt of the Sharecroppers* by Howard Kester, a Vanderbilt Divinity
School graduate who acquired the support of Reinhold Niebuhr and
Norman Thomas for various cooperative farms of displaced tenant farmers
and sharecroppers. Kester also served as Southern secretary of the Fellowship of Reconciliation, ran for Congress as a Socialist, organized the
Fellowship of Southern Churchmen, and was among the leaders of the
Southern Tenant Farmers' Union (STFU). In 1935 STFU drafted a New
Homestead Act calling for a national agricultural land authority that
would nationalize all farmland except that belonging to working farmers
with less than 160 acres or to cooperative farms. Compensatory land
payments would be made through twenty-year bonds with an upper limit
of $100,000 per person. Long-term leases would replace outright own-
ership. Central planning would govern productivity, assure conservation,
assist with credit, and give land to the landless.[14] The New Homestead
Bill, called by STFU cofounder H. L. Mitchell (1979:216) the organization's most significant contribution, failed to gain congressional
support.

Not all land reform proposals of the 1930s were socialist. The Southern
Agrarians were a group of intellectuals centered around Vanderbilt University who contributed over two hundred essays critical of corporate
America and produced a neo-Jeffersonian manifesto entitled *I'll Take My
Stand* (1930). One land reform proposed by John Crowe Ransom (later an
eminent literary critic) advocated a massive return to subsistence homesteads as a solution to the Depression's privation. Ransom argued that
government financing and technical assistance for indigent farmers,
combined with tax and pricing penalties for large operators, would
eliminate unemployment. Another proposal, by Frank Owsley, involved
public purchase of lands owned by insurance companies and absentee
owners for redistribution in eighty-acre parcels to qualified tenant
farmers—at the rate of 500,000 farmers per year. He also proposed that
soil rehabilitation and crop diversification be accomplished through strict
land-use controls, and sought an equilibrium between industry and agriculture through tariffs—that is, parity pricing of different sectors'
products.

NEW DEAL LAND REFORMS

How, one wonders, did official New Deal reforms affect people on the
land? What became of the tillers and tenants immortalized in Erskine
Caldwell and Margaret Bourke-White's *Have You Seen Their Faces?* (1937),

in John Steinbeck's *The Grapes of Wrath* (1939), and in James Agee and Walker Evans's *Let Us Now Praise Famous Men* (1941)? Goodwyn (1980:16) attempts to describe their numbers:

> Simple tenancy figures grandly understate the extent of immiseration of Americans who worked the land. By 1940 not only were half the people on the land reduced to tenancy throughout the South, but most of the remaining landowners had been locked into permanent indebtedness. If one adds in the vast tide of tenants and smallholders adrift in "America's Granary" on the Western plains, one is dealing with tens of millions of people. . . .

For American farmers, the Great Depression began in 1917, at the end of World War I. As the 1921 Congressional Joint Commission of Agricultural Inquiry reported, United States agriculture suffered "an avalanche of descending prices" (Genung, 1944:294). The issues of land productivity and tenure immobility were thrust before the federal government for many years to come and set the stage for extended debates on national land policy in subsequent years. The government's response was foreshadowed in the 1923 *Agricultural Yearbook*. It pointed to the relative abundance of arable land and room for rural resettlement, so long as there was administrative integration of previously uncoordinated land policies (USDA, 1923:506). It soon became apparent that, much in contrast to the insurgent land reforms just reviewed, "administrative integration" meant centralized authority and expanded public interests in private land.

Government land policies of the 1920s and 1930s were at once revolutionary and eclectic. They deliberately mingled employment, conservation, production, and redistribution objectives — as, for instance, in Franklin Roosevelt's 1932 campaign speech in Topeka, Kansas, where he outlined a program for agricultural relief including conservation and "a definite policy looking to the planned use of land" (Gaus and Wolcott, 1940:142). Many of FDR's policies sought to alter American faith in unchecked private landownership.

Some have suggested that the revolution in property rights began with the conservation movement (e.g., Gates, 1968). Certainly the Revision Act of 1891, as its name suggests, was a rebuke of private property abuses by the federal government (Gaus and Wolcott, 1940), and economists such as Richard T. Ely were questioning traditional property institutions early in their careers.[15] Federal land policy in the first third of the twentieth century went beyond protection of the public domain, however. As one member of the U.S. Forest Service stated in the 1920 *Yearbook of Agriculture* (pp. 155–56), "valuable resource lands should be treated as public utilities."

Land reform redefined as national land-use planning began to appear in 1926. Soon after the Supreme Court upheld the constitutionality of local zoning, Cyrus Kehr released his pioneer work, *A National Plan* (1926), and the Committee on the Bases of a Sound Land Policy produced its final report, *What About the Year 2000?* (1929). Both stressed the need for a comprehensive national land-use plan. The latter report precipitated a national mapping inventory of farm-area types in conjunction with the 1930 Census, a National Conference on Land Utilization held in 1931, the National Advisory and Legislative Committee on Land Use and the National Land Use Planning Committee. . . . In 1927, the American Law Institute began its monumental *Restatement of the Law of Property* which, published nearly a decade later, distinguished various interests in property which had evolved in common law as the United States accelerated on its course of urban-industrial development (Geisler, 1980:501).

In the early 1930s, the tide of private scholarship and government reports promoting national land-use planning crested. It was a time of upheaval for traditional concepts of ownership. The Forest Service released *A National Plan for American Forestry* (1933), which concluded that practically all the major forestry problems grew out of private ownership (Gaus and Wolcott, 1940:141). In 1933 the newly created Tennessee Valley Authority ignored small holder concerns by launching government ownership, conservation, and hydroelectric generation on a scale unparalleled in U.S. history, at the expense of several thousand rural families living on the land and aspiring to own it (McDonald and Muldowny, 1982). In 1934 the Taylor Grazing Act removed Western rangeland from homesteading and therefore from traditional ownership. The 1934 Indian Reorganization Act, to the relief of many tribes, ended government efforts to force their members to become small-scale landowners and farmers.

Among the most controversial New Deal agricultural policies was the Agricultural Adjustment Administration (AAA) of 1933. In his *Agricultural Reform in the United States* (1929), Harvard economist John D. Black set the intellectual stage for the AAA, which granted farm operators payment and tax benefits in exchange for voluntary acreage limitations for soil-depleting crops (Finegold, 1981). But instead of sharing benefits with tenants and sharecroppers, as the law intended, landlords frequently helped themselves to the entire government largesse (U.S. Department of Agriculture, 1940; Myrdal, 1944). Tenants and croppers were left to fend for themselves as rural wage laborers or to leave the land entirely, which hundreds of thousands did. The displacement, sometimes considered an unavoidable side-effect of farm mechanization, was an American "enclosure movement" (Abrams, 1939:68) that doomed large numbers of small holders and tenants in the wake of class-conscious public policy (Fligstein, 1978; James, 1981). The STFU judged the resulting rural poverty and insecurity "more frightful than at any time since the Civil War" (Gilbert and Brown, 1981:5).

By the middle 1930s, some AAA supporters viewed reform as moving people off rather than onto the land (Rasmussen, 1960). But not all 1930s' federal programs contributed to the exodus. The Subsistence Homesteads program relocated unemployed laborers to twenty-six new communities where they could operate farms while holding industrial jobs in project factories (Conkin, 1959). Under the 1935 Emergency Relief Appropriations Act, Washington established the Resettlement Administration, perhaps the most radical of the New Deal reforms. Together with its successor, the Farm Security Administration, it purchased nearly two million acres of land in 200 locales — 141 being largely agricultural and designed to equip thousands of sharecroppers and tenants with technical skills they would need as farm owners or operators (Salamon, 1974). Project settlers signed lease-purchase agreements with an option to buy that were assisted by long-term, low-interest mortgages. Private land, leased land, and a lesser amount of land run as cooperative farms were highly supervised. Other lands went to new-community experiments to house, employ, and rehabilitate the urban poor. Though some have criticized the actual accomplishments of the Farm Security Administration — it originally sought ten million acres to resettle 20,000 families (Holley, 1975) — others have praised it as an unusual experiment in American land reform (Baldwin, 1968; Salamon, 1974).[16]

In the election year 1936, President Roosevelt's newly appointed Committee on Farm Tenancy concluded that farm tenancy was the basic cause of the nation's rural poverty. It recommended the federal purchase of land for resale to tenant farmers through long-term contract to overcome absenteeism, speculation, and the squandering of resources. Despite the authority of these findings and the historical opportunity for a pervasive land reform (Gray, 1937), a weakened piece of legislation emerged from Congress in 1937, the Bankhead-Jones Farm Tenant Act. It was supported by most of the Southern Agrarians, though largely condemned by the STFU. The Farm Security Administration was supposed to carry out the act's tenant-aid and rural-rehabilitation mandates, but was hampered by the American Farm Bureau Federation, the federal Extension Service, state agricultural colleges, and corporate interests. All had an aversion to experiments in cooperative farming, land leasing, purchasing associations, migrant-labor assistance, subsidized credit, debt adjustment, and tenure improvement (Gaus and Wolcott, 1940). Large areas of submarginal land were finally purchased, but usually for conservation rather than redistribution.[17]

Conservation played an ambiguous role in the land reform efforts of the New Deal. Years of land abuse by both rich and poor alike left portions of the nation's agricultural lands severely stripped of topsoil. Yet conservation policies were uneven, particularly from the standpoint of social equity. The *Farm Tenancy Report* of 1937, the 1938 *Yearbook of Agriculture,* and scholarly research of the period viewed tenancy as the source of soil erosion. Such blaming the victim, though later abandoned (Fast, 1981), may explain why New Deal land reformers in Washington saw tenants, rather than the prevailing tenure system, as the problem. Soil conservation, it should be recalled, partially motivated the acreage allotment policies of the AAA.

The late Depression years saw the demise of the Farm Security Administration through red-baiting and conservative assaults on its budget

(McConnell, 1969). Its replacement, the Farmers Home Administration, embodied new federal priorities. Rural landownership as a national concern was supplanted with urban and particularly suburban home-ownership expansion—a shift that can be traced to President Hoover's Conference on Home Building and Home Ownership in 1931, foreclosure moratorium laws (such as the 1934 Frazier-Lemke Act), and a revolution in credit fostering the illusion of home ownership and fulfillment of the American dream. Between 1900 and 1929 residential nonfarm mortgage debt grew from $2.9 billion to $29 billion; by 1965 it would grow to $260 billion—the largest single item of credit in America's new debt-based economy (Stone, 1977).

CONCLUSION

The 1940 *Yearbook of Agriculture* was one of the last government documents acknowledging that land reform was needed in the United States. Thereafter, others have argued that land redistribution in the United States was not in itself an effective solution to inequitable agricultural incomes (Heady, 1953), and that population pressure, land monopolization, and even extensive tenancy were no longer matters of great domestic concern. According to Corty (1963:271), "forces identified as leading to land reform are not developing very rapidly in the United States." He continues, "the reverse appears to be true. . . . there is less need for land reform in the United States now than there was 50 years ago." Ten years later economist Richard Milk (1972:239) explained that although foreigners might see a need for land reform in the United States, "there is a vast difference between a country where the major stream of income is derived from the land . . . and a nation where less than 10 percent of either the income stream or the agricultural employment is involved."

As the beginning of this essay indicates, this perspective has not gone unchallenged. Erik Eckholm (1979) has drawn explicit parallels between soil erosion problems in the United States and Third World nations, and has encouraged land reform as a remedy to both situations. In 1979 a World Congress on Agrarian Reform and Rural Development was held in Rome and attended by delegates from developed as well as developing nations. Ambassador Andrew Young, who headed the American delegation, echoed the Southern Agrarians of the New Deal in the concluding words of his plenary address to the gathering (Young, 1979:7):

> Our people, whether they have been slaves, migrant workers, poor farmers, or part of the agro-business empire, have all been part of a loyalty and a patriotism, a security and prosperity that has made peace and development possible for over two centuries. . . . We have the audacity to think that the people of the land are the power of any nation.

But perhaps more telling at the Rome congress was the virtual absence of any mention of land reform in the document prepared for the occasion by the United States Department of Agriculture (Jordan et al., 1979). The perception that land reform is exclusively a foreign problem, shared by many Americans, may be a consequence of unsuccessful attempts at domestic reform or of the tensions between the United States and Communist powers after World War II. The American tenure ideal of equitably distributed full ownership was far from realized at mid-century (Hammon, 1943; Kloppenburg and Geisler, 1983), and the loss of family farms was unrelenting (Higbie, 1963). During this Cold War era, it was widely intimated that land reform was un-American unless done abroad to end feudalism or avert communism. Thus Washington used its considerable influence to promote land reforms in Japan, South Korea, Taiwan, and elsewhere to discourage rural insurrection. According to Warriner (1957:3–4):

> The United States first made advocacy of land reform part of its official foreign policy in 1950, when it supported a Polish resolution in favour of land reform in the General Assembly of the United Nations, and thereby challenged the Communist claim to leadership in the use of land reform as a political warfare weapon.

American land reformers, mindful of the political and practical difficulties in land redistribution, have altered the meaning of domestic land reform. Just as official land reformers earlier in the century deemphasized land for tenant farmers and instead stressed higher incomes and living standards (Salter, 1934), policymakers in later years emphasized efficiency of production rather than land distribution and spoke of "agrarian reform" rather than "land reform" (Tuma, 1965). Perhaps this shift in emphasis sealed the defeat of domestic land reform efforts, despite the efforts of presidents, both political parties, grass-roots insurgencies, and Jefferson's priestly visions. Alternatively, there exists a new awareness that land redistribution in a vacuum — without credit, technical assistance, infrastructure, and flexible property institutions — cannot succeed. America has these resources. Thus an historical irony surrounds the unfinished business of the nation's land reform; few societies are as capable of meeting the requirements for full-fledged agrarian reform. Nowhere else but in the United States are the conditions for land reform as promising.

NOTES

1. The top 5 percent of landowners hold at least 90 percent of private land in Hawaii, Florida, Wyoming, Oregon, and New Mexico, and at least 80 percent in Washington, Utah, New York, Nevada, Maine, Louisiana, Idaho, California, and Colorado (Davis and Geisler, 1983).

2. This work is summarized in Devereaux (1970), Meyer (1979), and Geisler (1983), and in bibliographies compiled by Conant (1972), Smith (1975), and Fisher (1980).

3. Land proprietorship is, among other things, believed to positively affect personality, family life, and citizenship (Grissette, 1923; Stacy, 1972); health and self-esteem (Woofter et al., 1930); access to credit (Raper, 1936); economic security (Briggs, 1943; McGee and Boone, 1976); and individual freedom (Brannon, 1950), as well as equality between the sexes (Raup, 1976).

4. Marschner (1959:17) conjectures that Jefferson was aware of the Roman system, since he referred to the subunits in his draft survey ordinance as *centuriae* (Latin "hundreds"), a system also propounded by William Penn (for Pennsylvania), by John Locke (for Carolina), and by others in Europe (where Jefferson had just spent several years). See Gates (1968) for further detail on the Land Ordinance of 1785.

5. Hamilton's report was not adopted, but did serve as a basis for ensuing federal land policies. This principle of treating land as capital was overturned by the Homestead Act of 1862 but remained a guiding principle in government policy at least until 1875 (see Land Office Report of 1875, cited in Webb, 1931:404).

6. See Gates (1968:390–93) for more detailed discussion.

7. The ideas of Tom Paine, Thomas Spence, and other English reformers were evident in American writings of the day, and the National Reform Association shared certain things in common with the National Land Company of the English Chartists (for details, see to Zahler, 1941).

8. This "Report of the Land Commissioner, 1880" is briefly summarized in Robbins (1942:288).

9. The railroads successfully contested such forfeitures in the courts, leaving only one-fiftieth of the amount of land demanded by the Democrats in 1888 to be returned (Hibbard, 1924:250). Lumber companies gained unlimited free access to national forests, as did ranchers to public rangelands. Hardrock mining companies, under the Mining Law of 1872 (still in effect today), could extract minerals from 87 percent of all federal lands outside of Alaska without permit or royalty.

10. See, for example, Hicks (1931) as discussed in Hofstadter (1955:49). Hofstadter takes the view, contrary to that presented here, that the large industrial and small agricultural sector continued to be mutually compatible in this period (1955:120 ff). This contrasts with the views of more Marxist scholars such as Beard and Beard (1927), Down (1978), Zinn (1980), and Mann and Dickinson (1980), but also with more conventional interpretations such as those of Schumpeter (1942).

11. An early statement similar to that of the contemporary Sagebrush Rebellion is found in the Denver Lands Commission of 1907 (Robbins, 1942:353).

12. Theodore Roosevelt viewed Populism "as a class struggle which would destroy the nation through internal struggle" (Hays, 1972:267). Though probably inaccurate in his characterization of the Populists, Roosevelt was prophetic with regard to the new direction agrarian radicalism was to take in the wake of the Populist insurgency. Useful sources on agrarian socialism in America include Daniels (1978), Burbank (1974), Ameringer (1940), Quint (1964), Dyson (1981), and Green (1979).

13. The Catholic church showed interest in the plight of settlers and small farmers at least as far back as the 1890s (Brandfon, 1967), as did other denominations; see, for example, Vecsey (1979), Marejka (1980), and Lutz (1981), in addition to the Hart contribution appearing later in this volume. The descriptive material prepared for the Delta Farm declared its intention "to exemplify the return of Christianity to its prophetic mission of identification with the dispossessed, of bearing witness of the judgement of God in history upon the injustices of the existing economic and political order, and of aiding men to enter into the possibilities of a more abundant life with which God has endowed his creation" (Franklin, 1980:2).

14. Under the provisions of the bill, no landowner would receive over $100,000 as compensation for land; the authority planned to issue loans for tools and livestock, which in time would become personal property, and to provide machinery and storage facilities. The plan involved land rationalization — retiring submarginal lands and conservation reclamation of superior lands. In preparation for the bill, STFU polled its members as to the type of tenure system they preferred. Over half hoped to eventually own their own farms, and long-term leases were more popular than cooperative and short-term leases (Gilbert and Brown, 1981).

15. For discussion of Ely's ideas and influence, see Geisler (1980).

16. McConnell (1969) considers the pros and cons of the FSA in some detail and in historical context. For an extensive bibliography on land settlement strategies and experiences of the New Deal period, see Bercaw, Hannay, and Colvin (1934).

17. Among the Agrarians, H. C. Nixon was the most critical of Bankhead-Jones, claiming that it would perhaps reach only 5 percent of the nation's landless farmers, although he actively supported the bill's passage (see Gilbert and Brown, 1981). Grubbs (1971) offers a most candid indictment of Bankhead-Jones. Its deficiencies can be inferred from the still needed reform suggestions made in USDA (1940:81–100).

REFERENCES

Abrams, Charles. 1939. *Revolution in Land.* New York: Harper.

Agee, James, and Evans, Walker. 1941. *Let Us Now Praise Famous Men.* Boston: Houghton-Mifflin.

Allin, Bushrod W. 1936. "Soil conservation—its place in national agricultural policy." Washington, DC: U.S. Department of Agriculture.

Ameringer, Oscar. 1940. *If You Don't Weaken.* New York: Holt.

Andrews, Richard N. L. 1979. "Land in America: a brief history." In *Land in America.* Edited by Richard N. L. Andrews. Lexington, MA: Lexington Books. Pp. 27–40.

Anonymous. 1930. *I'll Take My Stand: The South and Agrarian Land Tradition by 12 Southerners.* New York: Harper.

Baldwin, Sidney. 1968. *Poverty and Politics: The Rise and Decline of the Farm Security Administration.* Chapel Hill: University of North Carolina Press.

Beard, Charles A. 1949. *An Economic Interpretation of the Constitution of the United States.* New York: Macmillan.

Beard, Charles A., and Beard, Mary. 1927. *The Rise of American Civilization.* New York: Macmillan.

Bennett, Henry C. 1956. "Land and independence—America's experience." In *Land Tenure.* Edited by Kenneth Parsons, Raymond Penn, and Philip Raup. Madison: University of Wisconsin Press. Pp. 36–44.

Bennett, Lerone, Jr. 1972. "The making of Black America." *Ebony* (February).

Bercaw, Louise O., Hannay, A. M., and Colvin, Esther M. 1934. *Bibliography on Land Settlement.* Misc. Publ. No. 172. Washington, DC: U.S. Department of Agriculture.

Black, John D. 1929. *Agricultural Reform in the United States.* New York: McGraw-Hill.

Bogue, Allan. 1969. "Senators, sectionalism, and the 'Western' measures of the Republican party." In *The Frontier in American Development.* Edited by E. M. Willis. Ithaca, NY: Cornell University Press. Pp. 20–46.

Bogue, Allan, Phillips, Thomas D., and Wright, James E. (eds.). 1970. *The West of the American People.* Itasca, IL: F.E. Peacock Publishers.

Boxley, Robert F. 1977. *Landownership Issues in Rural America.* ERS–655. Washington, DC: Economic Research Service, U.S.D.A.

Brandfon, Robert L. 1967. *Cotton Kingdom of the New South.* Cambridge, MA: Harvard University Press.

Brannan, C. F. 1950. *Hope, an American Export.* Washington, DC: U.S Department of Agriculture.

Briggs, F. A. 1943. "Security in owning land." *Farm & Ranch* 62 (September): 6.

Bromfield, Louis. 1933. *The Farm.* Leyden, MA: Aeonian Press.

Bryant, R. W. G. 1972. *Land: Private Property, Public Control.* Montreal: Harvest House.

Buhle, Paul. 1980. "The rise and fall of Socialist electoral politics in the 1900s." *In These Times* (October 1–7): 12.

Burbank, Garin. 1974. "The political and social attitudes of some early Oklahoma Democrats." *Chronicles of Oklahoma* 52 (Winter): 439–55 .

Caldwell, Erskine, and Bourke-White, Margaret. 1937. *Have You Seen Their Faces?* New York: Viking Press.

Cochran, Thomas C., and Miller, William. 1961. *The Age of Enterprise.* New York: Harper Torchbooks.

Cochrane, William W. 1979. *The Development of American Agriculture.* Minneapolis: University of Minnesota Press.

Conant, Florence. 1972. *Land Reform: A Bibliography.* Cambridge, MA: Center for Community Economic Development.

Conkin, Paul K. 1959. *Tomorrow a New World: The New Deal Community Program.* Ithaca, NY: Cornell University Press.

Cooker, Francis W. (ed.). 1947. *Democracy, Liberty and Property.* New York: Macmillan.

Corty, Floyd L. 1963. "Are we headed for land reform in the United States?" *Land Economics* 38 (August): 270-73.

Cribbet, John E. 1978. "Property in the twenty-first century," *Ohio State Law Journal* 39: 671-78.

Daniel, Cletus E. 1978. *Bitter Harvest.* Berkeley: University of California.

Davis, John E., and Geisler, Charles C. 1983. "The role of alternative land institutions in employment and local economic development." Paper presented at the annual meetings of the Rural Sociological Society, Lexington, KY (August).

Devereux, Don. 1970. "New approaches to land reform." *New Mexico Review* (April): 5-6.

Dowd, Douglas. 1978. *The Twisted Dream.* Cambridge, MA: Winthrop.

Draper, James L. 1973. "Land reform: difficult yet essential." *Antipode* 7 (December): 43-45.

Dubossky, Melvin. 1969. *We Shall Be All.* New York: Quadrangle-New York Times Books.

Dyson, Lowell K. 1982. *The Red Harvest.* Lincoln, NB: University of Nebraska Press.

Eaton, J. W. 1943. *Exploring Tomorrow's Agriculture: Cooperative Group Farming, A Practical Program for Rural Rehabilitation.* New York: Harper.

Eckholm, Erik, 1979. *The Dispossessed of the Earth: Land Reform and Sustainable Development.* Worldwatch Paper 30. Washington, DC: Worldwatch Institute.

Eisinger, Chester E. 1947. "The influence of natural rights and physiocratic doctrines on American agrarian thought during the revolutionary period." *Agricultural History* 21: 13-23.

Ellis, G. D. 1928. *Platforms of Two Great Political Parties, 1856-1928.* Washington, DC: U.S. Government Printing Office.

Ellis, David M. 1944. "Land tenure and tenancy in the Hudson Valley, 1790-1860." *Agricultural History* 18: 75-82.

Ely, Richard T. 1921. "Introduction." In *A Stake in the Land.* Edited by P. A. Speck. New York: Harper Bros.

Fast, Sarah E. 1981. "An historical analysis of the impact of land tenure on soil erosion, 1930-1980." Unpublished manuscript. Department of Natural Resources, Cornell University, Ithaca, NY.

Finegold, Kenneth. 1981. "From agrarianism to adjustment: the political origins of New Deal agricultural policy." *Politics and Society* 11: 1-27.

Fisher, Steve. 1983. "Annnotated bibliography." In *Who Owns Appalachia? Landownership and Its Impact.* By the Appalachian Land Ownership Task Force. Lexington, KY: University Press of Kentucky. Pp. 178-217.

Fligstein, Neil D. 1978. "Migration from counties of the South, 1900-1950." Ph.D. dissertation, University of Wisconsin, Madison.

Foner, Eric. 1980. "Ante-bellum labor and the slave system." *In These Times* (August 27–September 2).

Franklin, Samuel H., Jr. 1980. *Early Years of the Delta Cooperative Farm and the Providence Cooperative Farm.* Alcoa, TN: Lamar Copy Service (unpublished manuscript).

Fujimoto, Isao. 1977. "The U.C. Davis story." In *The Family Farm in California.* Sacramento: State of California. Pp. 13-26.

Garin, John B. 1974. "The social origins of agrarian socialism in Oklahoma, 1910-1920." Ph.D. dissertation, University of California, Berkeley.

Gates, Paul Wallace. 1936. "The Homestead Law in an incongruous land system." *American Historical Review* 41: 652-81.

———. 1953. "From individualism to collectivism in American land policy." In *Liberalism as a Force in History: Lectures on Aspects of the Liberal Tradition.* Edited by Chester M. Destler. New London: Connecticut College. Pp. 15-28.

———. 1968. *History of Public Land Law Development.* Washington, DC: U.S. Public Land Law Review Commission.

Gaus, John M., and Wolcott, Leon O. 1940. *Public Administration and the United States Department of Agriculture.* Chicago: R.R. Donnelley & Sons.

Geisler, Charles C. 1980. "The quiet revolution in land use control revisited." In *The Rural Sociology of the Advanced Societies*. Edited by F. H. Buttel and H. Newby. Montclair, NJ: Allanheld, Osmun. Pp. 489–526.

———. 1983. "The new lay of the land." Introduction to *Who Owns Appalachia? Landownership and Its Impact*. Appalachian Land Ownership Task Force. Lexington, KY: University Ppress of Kentucky.

Genung, A. B. 1940. "Agriculture in the World War." In *Farmers in a Changing World*. 1940 Yearbook of Agriculture. Washington, DC: U.S Department of Agriculture. Pp. 227–96.

George, Henry. 1975. *Progress and Poverty*. New York: Robert Schalkenbach Foundation.

Gilbert, Jesse, and Brown, Steve. 1981. "Alternative land reform proposals in the 1930s: the Nashville Agrarians and the Southern Tenant Farmers' Union." *Agricultural History* 55 (October): 351–69.

Goldschmidt, Walter. 1978. *As You Sow*. Montclair, NJ: Allanheld, Osmun.

Goodwyn, Lawrence. 1980. "The cooperative commonwealth & other abstractions: in search of a demccratic premise." *Marxist Perspectives* 3 (Summer): 8–42.

Gray, L. C. 1937. *Basic Elements of a National Program of Land Reform*. Washington, DC: Resettlement Administration.

Green, James. 1978. *Grass-Roots Socialism: Radical Movements in the Southwest*. Baton Rouge: Louisiana State University Press.

Grissette, F. A. 1923. *The Effects of Home and Farm Ownership*. North Carolina State University Extension Bulletin 2(9): 99–108.

Grubbs, D. 1971. *Cry from the Cotton: The Southern Tenant Farmer's Union and the New Deal*. Chapel Hill: University of North Carolina Press.

Hays, Samuel P. 1959. *Conservation and the Gospel of Efficiency*. New York: Atheneum.

Heady, Earl O. 1953. "Fundamentals of resource ownership policy." *Land Economics* 29 (May): 44–56.

Hibbard, Benjamin H. 1924. *A History of the Public Land Policies*. New York: Macmillan.

Hicks, J. O. 1931. *The Populist Revolt*. Minneapolis: University of Minnesota Press.

Higbee, Edward C. 1963. *Farms and Farmers in an Urban Age*. New York: Twentieth Century Fund.

Hofstadter, Richard. 1955. *The Age of Reform*. New York: Vintage Books.

Holley, Donald. 1975. *Uncle Sam's Farmers*. Urbana: University of Illinois Press.

Home Missions Council. 1940. *The Church and Land Tenure*. Report of Conference, Land Tenure Committee (October). Chicago: Home Missions Council.

Hurst, Willard J. 1961. *Law and Economic Growth: The Legal History of the Lumber Industry of Wisconsin, 1836–1915*. Cambridge, MA: Harvard University Press.

James, David R. 1981. "The transformation of local state and class structure and resistance to the civil rights movement in the South." Ph.D. dissertation, University of Wisconsin, Madison.

Jacobs, Harvey M. 1984. "Localism and rural land policy: toward progressive rural land planning." Ph.D. dissertation, Cornell University, Ithaca, NY.

Jordan, Max F., et. al. 1979. *Agrarian Reform and Rural Development in the United States: A Country Review Paper*. Working Paper No. 7814. Washington, DC: U.S. Department of Agriculture, Economics, Statistics, and Cooperative Service.

Kehr, Cyrus. 1926. *A National Plan: A Basis for Coordinated Physical Development of the United States of America with a Suggestion for World Plan*. New York, London: Oxford University Press.

Kelly, K. B. 1979. "Federal Indian land policy and economic development in the United States." In *Economic Development in American Indian Reservations*. Albuquerque, NM: University of New Mexico Development Series No. 1, Native American Studies. Pp. 30–42.

Kester, Howard. 1936. *Revolt of the Sharecroppers*. New York: Covici, Friede.

Kloppenburg, Jack R., Jr., and Geisler, Charles C. 1983. "The agricultural ladder revisited: Which way is up?" Paper presented at the annual meetings of the Midwest Sociological Society, Kansas City.

LeVeen, E. Phillip. 1978. "Reclamation policy at a crossroads." *Public Affairs Report* 19 (October): 1–11.

LeWarn, Charles. 1978. *Utopias of Puget Sound: 1885–1915*. Seattle: University of Washington Press.

Lewis, James A. 1980. *Landownership in the United States, 1978.* Agriculture Information Bulletin No. 435. Washington, DC: U.S. Department of Agriculture, Economiics, Statistics, and Cooperative Service.

Lipset, Seymour M. 1970. *Agrarian Socialism.* Berkeley: University of California Press.

Lutz, Charles P. 1981. "Lutherans study land theology." *Catholic Rural Life* 31 (December): 21-23.

Lynd, Staughton. 1967. *Class Conflict, Slavery and the United States Constitution.* Indianapolis: Bobbs-Merrill.

McClaughry, John. 1972. *Expanded Ownership.* Newark, NJ: Medic Press.

McConnell, Grant. 1969. *The Decline of American Democracy.* New York: Atheneum.

McDonald, Michael J., and Muldowny, John. 1982. *TVA and the Dispossessed.* Knoxville: University of Tennessee.

McGee, Leo, and Boone, Robert. 1977. "Black rural land ownership: a matter of economic survival." *Review of Black Political Economy* 8(Fall): 62-69.

McGrath, Peter C. 1966. *Yazoo: The Case of Fletcher* v. *Peck.* New York: Norton.

Madison, James. 1927. *Documents Illustrative of the Formation of the Union.* 177. Washington, DC: U.S. Government Printing Office.

Mann, Susan A., and Dickinson, J. A. 1980. "State and agriculture in two eras of American capitalism." In *The Rural Sociology of the Advanced Societies.* Edited by F. H. Buttel and H. Newby. Montclair, NJ: Allanheld, Osmun. Pp. 283-325.

Maris, Paul V. 1940. "Farm tenancy." In *Farmers in a Changing World.* 1940 Yearbook of Agriculture. Washington, DC: U.S. Department of Agriculture. Pp. 887-906.

Marshner, Fred J. 1959. *Land Use and Its Patterns in the United States.* Agricultural Handbook No. 153 (April). Washington, DC: U. S. Department of Agriculture.

Meyer, Peter. 1979. "Land rush." *Harper's* (January): 45-60.

Milk, Richard G. 1972. "The new agriculture in the United States: a dissenter's view." *Land Economics* 48 (August): 228-39.

Mitchell, H. L. 1979. *Mean Things Happening in This Land.* Montclair, NJ: Allanheld, Osmun.

Moomaw, I. W. 1951. "Land reform: a Christian challenge." *Social Action* 17(6): 4-18.

Myrdal, Gunnar. 1962. *An American Dilemma: The Negro Problem and Modern Democracy.* New York: Harper and Row.

Nelson, W. E., Jr. 1979. "Black rural land decline and political power." In *The Black Rural Land Owner — Endangered Species.* Edited by L. McGee and R. Boone. Westport, CT: Greenwood Press.

Nevins, A., and Commager, H. S. 1945. *A Short History of the United States.* New York: Modern Library.

Nixon, Herman C. 1938. *Forty Acres and Steel Mules.* Chapel Hill: University of North Carolina Press.

Owsley, Frank. 1935. "The pillars of agrarianism." *American Review* 4 (March): 530-41.

Quint, Howard. 1964. *The Forging of American Socialism: Origins of the Modern Movement.* Columbia: University of South Carolina Press.

Ransom, John Crowe. 1932. "Land." *Harper's* (July): 216-24.

Raper, Arthur F. 1936. *Preface to Peasantry: A Tale of Two Black Belt Counties.* Chapel Hill: University of North Carolina Press.

Rasmussen, Wayne D. (ed.) 1960. *Readings in the History of American Agriculture.* Urbana: University of Illinois Press.

Raup, P. M. 1976. "Land reform and economic development." In *Agricultural Development and Economic Growth.* Edited by H. M. Southworth and B. F. Johnson. Ithaca, NY: Cornell University Press. Pp. 267-326.

Richardson, J. D. 1897. *Messages and Papers of the President.* Washington, DC Vol. I.

Riddleberger, Patrick W. 1955. "George W. Julian: abolitionist land reformer." *Agricultural History* 29: 108-115.

Robbins, Roy M. 1942. *Our Landed Heritage.* Princeton, NJ: Princeton University Press.

Sakolski, Aaron M. 1932. *The Great American Land Bubble: The Amazing Story of Land-Grabbing, Speculations and Booms from Colonial Days to the Present Times.* New York: Harper.

————. 1957. *Land Tenure and Land Taxation in America.* New York: Robert Schalkenbach Foundation.

Salamon, Lester P. 1974. "The time dimension in policy evaluation: the case of the New Deal land reform experiments." Paper presented for the annual meetings of the American Political Science Association (August). Chicago.

Salter, Leonard, A., Jr. 1943. "Farm property and agricultural policy." *Journal of Political Economy* 51 (February): 13–22.

Schertz, L. P., and Wunderlich, Gene. 1981. "Structure of U.S. farming and landownership in the future: implications for soil conservation." Paper presented at NCR-II Symposium on Policy, Institutions and Incentives for Soil Conservation (May 19–21), Zion, Illinois.

Schumpeter, Joseph A. 1942. *Capitalism, Socialism and Democracy.* New York: Harper.

Shannon, Fred. 1957. *American Farmers Movements.* New York: Anville Press.

Shepperson, W. 1966. *A Retreat to Nevada: A Socialist Colony of World War I.* Reno: University of Nevada Press.

Sinclair, Ward. 1982. "Congress about to pump up subsidies to irrigation-water users." *Washington Post* (May 16): A2.

Smith, Charles L. 1975. *A Bibliography on Land Reform in Rural America.* San Francisco: Center for Rural Studies.

Stacey, W. A. 1972. *Black Home Ownership: A Sociological Case Study of Metropolitan Jacksonville.* New York: Praeger.

Steinbeck, John. 1939. *The Grapes of Wrath.* New York: P.F. Collier.

Stone, Michael. 1978. "Gimme shelter!" In *U.S. Capitalism in Crisis.* Edited by Bruce Steinberg and associates. New York: Union for Radical Political Economics. Pp. 182–93.

Taylor, Paul S. 1973. "The law says 160 acres." *People and Land* 1 (Summer): 21–22.

Tuma, Elias H. 1965. *Twenty-Six Centuries of Agrarian Reform.* Berkeley: University of California Press.

U.S.D.A. 1920. Yearbook of Agriculture. Washington, DC: U.S. Department of Agriculture.

————. 1923. Yearbook of Agriculture. Washington, DC: U.S. Department of Agriculture.

U.S. Government. 1940. *Technology on the Farm.* Special Report by an Interbureau Committee and the Bureau of Agriculture Economics of the United States Department of Agriculture (August). Washington, DC: U.S Government Printing Office.

————. 1927. Documents Illustrative of the Formation of the Union. Washington, DC: U.S. Government Printing Office.

U.S. Special Committee on Farm Tenancy. 1937. *Farm Tenancy.* Message from the President of the United States transmitting the report of the Special Committee on Farm Tenancy. Seventy-fifth Congress, First Session, House Document 149.

Vecsey, George. 1979. "Catholic church backing debates on land reform." *New York Times* (July 22): 1.

Warriner, Doreen. 1957. *Land Reform and Economic Development.* Cairo, Egypt: National Bank of Egypt.

Webb, Walter P. 1931. *The Great Plains.* Toronto: Blaisdell Publishing Company.

Wehrwein, Carl F. 1958. "An analysis of agricultural ladder research." *Land Economics* 34: 329–37.

Wiley, Norman. 1969. "America's unique class politics: the interplay of the labor, credit and commodity markets." In *Recent Sociology,* No. 1. Edited by Hans Peter Dreitzel. London: Macmillan. Pp. 188–213.

Woodward, C. Vann. 1951. *Origins of the New South, 1877–1913.* Baton Rouge: Louisiana State University.

World Bank. 1975. *Assault on Poverty.* Washington, DC: The World Bank.

Young, Andrew. 1979. Statement by Ambassador Andrew Young, U.S. Representative to the United Nations, at the World Conference on Agrarian Reform and Rural Development, Rome (July 13).

Zahler, Helene S. 1941. *Eastern Working Men and National Land Policy.* New York: Columbia University Press.

Zinn, Howard. 1980. *A People's History of the United States.* New York: Harper Colophon.

PART TWO

Land Reform and Agriculture

3

The Social Costs of Large-Scale Agriculture: The Prospects of Land Reform in California

DEAN MacCANNELL AND JERRY WHITE

The Westlands Water District in the Central Valley of California receives irrigation water from a joint state-federal project that supplies some of the nation's largest and most productive farming operations. The area has a history of social problems resulting from misdirected federal subsidies. The Westlands District is covered by the 1902 Reclamation Act, which restricts federally subsidized irrigation water to farms of less than 160 acres. Nonetheless, large farms averaging over 2,000 acres have obtained the subsidy for themselves and have prevented small operators from receiving it. They have achieved these distortions by legal maneuvering, lobbying, and direct participation on district, state, and local boards. The peculiar way that the Reclamation Act has been interpreted in the Westlands has contributed to the great local disparity between the rich and the poor. Some government analysts have begun to study land reform as a possible corrective.[1] This paper will first examine in detail the social inequities produced in the Westlands by the current implementation of the Reclamation Act, and then consider their implications for land reform.

OVERVIEW

Farm owner/operators in the Westlands tend to live in substantial homes on their properties, leaving the towns to the workers. These towns are as physically deteriorated, impoverished, and lacking in services as any in the United States and are worse off in some respects than rural communities in Third World countries. Rodriguez and Johnson report that during the 1979 harvest, over 6,000 people were sharing 575 housing units in one Westlands community (Rodriguez and Johnson, 1979). They found people, including many undocumented workers from Mexico, living in garages and tool sheds that lacked beds, windows, floors, running water, and sewage disposal facilities. The squatters' settlements are near the growers' estate-size homes that have private ticker-tapes, airstrips, and research labs.

The potential need for land reform measures in future rural development programs has been recognized by the United States Department of Interior in a recent *Draft Environmental Impact Statement on Acreage Limitation.* The report contains economic and other projections based on adoption of a "small farm alternative" that would require farm owners to sign over some property rights to the Interior Department in exchange for continued use of subsidized irrigation water (USDI, 1981:2–4). The new contracts would give the owners five years to sell their properties in 160-acre parcels. At the end of five years, growers continuing to receive subsidized irrigation water on properties exceeding 320 acres (for a husband-wife operation) would have their excess land sold for them by the Interior Department. This proposal is consistent with those portions of United States agricultural policy that are oriented toward small- to moderate-scale resident owner-operators. It is radical in terms of traditional American values about private ownership and free enterprise.

But the small farm alternative is only one of several possibilities projected by the Interior Department. Others ranged from less radical reforms to legalizing current arrangements. The department rules would affect seventeen Western states, not just California. But the impact of any reform would be concentrated in California's Central Valley, where noncompliance with acreage limitations is greatest.

RECLAMATION THEORY AND RECLAMATION PRACTICE

In the American West the debate over agricultural subsidies has focused on the pros and cons of enforcing the acreage-limitation provisions of the Reclamation Act. A recent report of the Interior Department's Bureau of Reclamation summarizes these provisions and their intent:

> The Reclamation Act of 1902 (43 U.S.C. 431), as amended, limited the acreage of public land that a person could acquire, and section 5 of the Act provided that: "No right to the use of water for land in private ownership shall be sold for a tract exceeding 160 acres to any one land owner, and no such sale shall be made to any land owner unless he be an actual bona fide resident on such land, or occupant thereof, residing in the neighborhood of said land. . . ." The legislative history of the above provision indicates that the Congress wanted to
>   — provide opportunity for a maximum number of settlers on the land and to promote home building;

— spread the benefits of the subsidized irrigation program to the maximum number of people; and

— promote the family size farm as a desirable form of rural life. (U.S. Bureau of Reclamation, 1978:193-194)

The original language of the law, as well as its legislative reinterpretations in 1914, 1924, and 1926, makes clear that Congress wanted to create a partnership between the federal government and resident small holders that would lead to a populous, politically stable, and economically self-sustaining rural sector. This position was plainly stated in 1959 by Senator Paul Douglas of Illinois:

> The people of Illinois are paying taxes, and have paid taxes, to build these CVP (Central Valley Project) dams, reservoirs, conduits, and irrigation systems. They have paid taxes against their own economic interests, because they believed it was in the national interest; and are ready to continue to do so, but on condition that the money which we contribute shall be used to maintain agrarian democracy, and not huge agrarian estates. We are willing to have money spent for a democratic . . . farm system, but we do not want to have it spent to build up the power and strength of huge landowners. . . . We do not want a system with a big manor house on the hill, and farm laborers living in hovels. We want a system in which the owner is the cultivator. That is the basis of American agrarian democracy.[2]

Rural sociological studies, especially the California work by Walter Goldschmidt and Isao Fujimoto, suggest that the thinking behind the legislation was sound. Had the Reclamation Act given a competitive advantage to small holders, as was intended, we would now have viable rural communities in the water districts of the American West.[3]

The large landowners opposed to the Reclamation Act petitioned the courts and lobbied Congress in 1944, 1947, 1959, 1960, and 1982 for exemptions from the acreage limitations and residency requirements.[4] Legislation now pending in Congress would repeal the Reclamation Act entirely and legalize existing arrangements. The growers have argued that farming on the scale required by the Reclamation Act is not sufficiently profitable to attract aggressive management and investment into Western agriculture:

> "This is certainly not the time to disrupt successful practices by imposing unrealistic limitations on farm size served by federal reclamation water," said Republican Assemblyman Gordon Duffy, one of a five-member panel of Central Valley state legislators who testified [at a Congressional hearing]. "What is an economic unit of land? That can best be determined by testimony from settlers who developed and worked the land and not those wild-eyed social planners who all of a sudden profess great knowledge of how we can best feed our people." (*Sacramento Bee,* 1980:A10)

Critics of the Reclamation Act minimize the social harm to rural society done by large business operations. And they argue, against evidence to the contrary,[5] that any scale-down would have disastrous economic effects on the region and the nation. The large farmers of the West have developed a broad political base and a strong solidarity with their cause among elected public officials, members of water boards, and agents of the Bureau of Reclamation.

The support for continued subsidy of western farming operations extends into the local administration of federal policy. An Interior Department report states flatly: "That some Bureau of Reclamation employees played down large landowners' fears about [the imposition of the] acreage limitation in the early days of the project seems almost certain" (USDI, 1981:3–61). This is probably an understatement. The local support for large-farm interests has prevailed over every federal initiative to enforce the Reclamation Act, including a 1958 unanimous decision of the United States Supreme Court that upheld acreage limitation at the 1902 level of 160 acres.

Every petition of the large Western growers for relief from the Reclamation Act has been denied, and yet there has never been a scale-down of agricultural operations to the level required by law. In its 1958 decision, the Supreme Court stated:

> It is a reasonable classification to limit the amount of project water available to each individual in order that benefits may be distributed in accordance with the greatest good to the greatest number of individuals. The limitation insures that this enormous expenditure will not go in disproportionate share to a few individuals with large land holdings. Moreover, it prevents the use of federal reclamation service for speculative purposes. In short, the excess acreage provision acts as a ceiling, imposed equally on all participants, on the federal subsidy that is being bestowed.[6]

In sum, the Reclamation Act, as stated by Congress and upheld by the Supreme Court, was not intended to contribute to massive social inequity and the breakdown of democratic institutions in the rural sector. But in practice the large growers have subverted the act for their own benefits. The best illustration of the distinction between reclamation theory and practice and between rich and poor is the Westlands Water District.

THE WESTLANDS CASE

During the 1960s there was a substantial amount of construction activity in the Westlands as a result of the building of the San Luis unit and the local surface-water delivery system. After completion of the water delivery system in 1968, the value of agricultural products grown in the district increased to a 1978 level of $300 million a year.

The San Luis unit of the Central Valley Water Project consists of the San Luis dam twenty miles north of the Westlands Water District and a large concrete-lined canal extending 100 miles south. The canal enters the Westlands at the Mile Eighteen pumping station at the extreme north end of the district, and ends at Kettleman City in the extreme south. In addition to supplying the farms in the Westlands with surface irrigation water, the San Luis unit is an important link in the California aqueduct. The unit was constructed beginning in 1958, at an eventual cost of over $600 million. The state of California provided $175 million, and $160 million is eventually repayable by the Westlands Water District and other users. The remaining $265 million came from the federal government. The 1978 Bureau of Reclamation *Special Task Force Report on the San Luis Unit* estimates that when all the bills are paid by the water users over the next fifty years, the users will have received a subsidy of $1,540 per acre — a figure representing the difference between actual costs of water delivery and the amount users will pay for it (USBR, 1978). This figure, which has not been contested by the farming community, amounts to an average subsidy of over $3 million for a 2,000-acre farm.

The Westlands Water District contains about 600,000 acres of irrigable land (USBR, 1978). According to a recent statement of the WWD, there are no 160-acre farms in the Westlands. In 1977, according to WWD records, there were 216 farms in the Westlands, averaging 2,200 acres (USBR, 1978). The current scale of operations does not necessarily mean that the Reclamation Act has been violated. A provision of the act allows for farming to continue temporarily on its former scale if the farmer agrees to sell his land to small holders. The current scale of operations in the Westlands is not illegal; it reflects a successful effort by large owners to hold onto their land while simultaneously accepting subsidized water and working for a change in the law which will permit them to keep their land and continue to receive water. The reason the 160-acre limit and residency requirement of the reclamation law have recently become important political issues is because the term is almost up on many of the Westlands farmers' promises to sell. A recent court-ordered moratorium on the sale of excess lands has only served to put off the day of reckoning and intensify the politics surrounding irrigation water.

In addition to the prevalence of large farms, less than twenty percent of the total farmland in the Westlands is owned by individuals or corporations that have home addresses in or near (within fifteen miles of) the district.[7] The highest proportion of acreage in the Westlands (22.8 percent) is held by individuals and corporations based in San Francisco; most of this land is owned by Southern Pacific Railroad. More acreage in the Westlands is owned by persons and corporations in Los Angeles than by those with addresses in the local towns of Coalinga, Five Points, Tranquillity, or Huron. Thus, the Westlands is an area of small, poor towns surrounded by more than half a million acres of rich farmland held in 200 farming units owned by local farmers and by wealthy investors living in distant cities. Even though the Westlands is in full technical compliance with the Reclamation Act, the current operating scale, residency patterns, and social conditions are precisely those the act was passed to prevent.

Some Social Features of the Westlands

The Westlands Water District (WWD) is located on the west side of Fresno County and is 70 miles long, eight to fifteen miles wide, and almost perfectly flat. The San Luis Canal, Interstate Highway Five, and a Southern Pacific Railroad line run through the district. The canal, the highway, and the massive plantings of cotton, grains, and other crops often extending as far as the eye can see are the most evident man-made features of the area. The largest town in the vicinity of the WWD is Coalinga, with a 1978 population of 6,375. Coalinga is located in an oil field about fifteen miles from the southwest end of the district.

We examined five Fresno County census tracts that overlap the WWD and the largest community within each tract (see figure 3.1). The name of each tract matches the name of the largest community in it. The names of the five tracts and communities are Coalinga, Firebaugh, Huron, Mendota, and San Joaquin/Tranquillity. Mendota touches the east boundary of the WWD, and Coalinga lies in some hills several miles west of the WWD, but the others are lined up along a north-south axis about three miles from the eastern boundary of the WWD. San Joaquin/ Tranquillity, as the name implies, is actually two small centers, 5.1 miles apart along the same highway and rail lines. Huron falls entirely within the WWD. The only other named places that fall entirely within it are Three Rocks, Cantua Creek, and Five Points. Three Rocks, a community of 350 that attracted statewide attention because of its poverty,[8] is in the Mendota census tract, Cantua Creek in the San Joaquin/Tranquillity tract. Five Points, which has a current estimated population of 100 persons, is in three enumeration districts (Coalinga, Huron, and San Joaquin/Tranquillity), so any data specific to it are beyond retrieval.

Table 3.1 gives current and recent population sizes of communities and census tracts in the district. During the last twenty years, there has been a movement off the land and into the towns of the district, producing substantial increases in the size of the communities, with little or no gain in the total region. The movement of people off the land, which seems the result of increasing mechanization of agricultural production during the period, is in precisely the opposite direction from that intended by the Reclamation Act.

Mexican-Americans are an absolute and growing majority of the population in the district (see table 3.2). The population is less than 4 percent black, and representation of other races and nationalities is negligible, although there are some Orientals.

Housing Conditions

A stated goal of the Reclamation Act is to promote home building, and we examined the quality of housing in and near the district. Data from the 1970 census provide a reasonable baseline shortly after completion of the

FIGURE 3.1. MAP OF THE WESTLANDS STUDY AREA

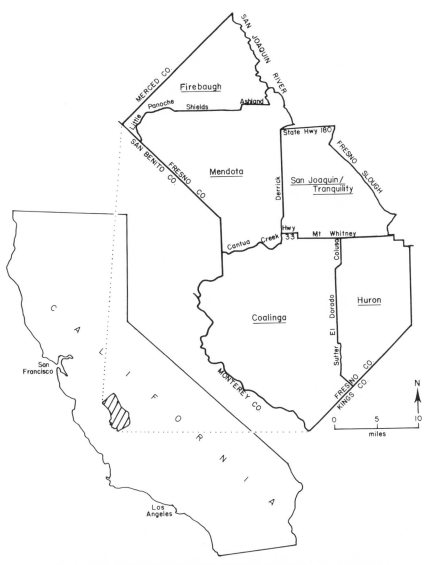

Source: U.S. Bureau of the Census. Census of Population and Housing: 1970. Census Tracts. Final Report PHC (1) – 75 Fresno, California, SMSA

TABLE 3.1. POPULATION OF THE WESTLANDS STUDY AREA

Community	1960	1970	1978*
Huron	1,269	1,525	2,540
Remainder of tract	3,606	1,999	
Coalinga	5,965	6,161	6,375
Remainder of tract	2,010	1,196	
San Joaquin/ Tranquillity	879	1,506	1,630
Remainder of tract	4,061	3,024	
Mendota	2,099	2,705	4,040
Remainder of tract	3,621	2,927	
Firebaugh	2,070	2,517	3,940
Remainder of tract	5,210	3,883	
TOTALS	30,790	27,443	

Source: U.S. Bureau of the Census, 1970
*State of California estimate based on tax returns

TABLE 3.2. PROPORTION OF WESTLANDS
POPULATION WITH SPANISH SURNAMES

Community	1960	1970
Huron	48%	61%
Coalinga	11%	—
San Joaquin/ Tranquillity	30%	35%
Mendota	48%	71%
Firebaugh	35%	48%

Source: U.S. Bureau of the Census, 1970

construction of the San Luis unit and delivery of the subsidized surface irrigation water (see table 3.3). The two decades before 1970 saw extensive removal of substandard migrant labor housing from the district. Thus the figures are for a recently reduced housing stock, with some of the worst conditions eliminated.

Yet housing conditions for the Westlands are inferior to other rural areas of the valley; conditions for the Mexican-American population of the district are even worse. There is little evidence here that the Reclamation Act has fostered home building. Over half the homes in the area were built before 1950. During the period of construction of the San Luis unit, more homes were removed from the area than were built. The housing stock in rural areas of Fresno County not affected by reclamation is newer and in better condition. Ten percent of the homes in the Westlands lacked plumbing in 1970, as compared to 3.4 percent for other rural and small town areas of Fresno County. Almost 20 percent of the homes in the rural area around Firebaugh lacked plumbing.

Figures on crowding reveal a similar disparity between the Westlands and other rural and small town areas of Fresno County (see table 3.4).[9] Over 12 percent of the population of the Westlands lived in housing with more than 1.5 persons per room. The same figure for rural Fresno County as a whole was 5 percent. Also, Mexican-Americans paid substantially greater rents than the rest of the population of the Westlands, perhaps in an attempt to obtain larger homes for their larger families. But they did not succeed. Over 18 percent of the Mexican-American population lived in homes with more than 1.5 persons per room, and the figures were as high as 43 percent in the Coalinga tract.

TABLE 3.3. QUALITY OF HOUSING STOCK IN THE WESTLANDS, 1970

Housing Indicator	Rural Fresno County	Huron	Coalinga	San Joa- quin/Tran- quillity	Mendota	Fire- baugh Comm.	Rural Fire- baugh
Percent of households lacking plumbing	3.4	9.7	9.1	7.0	—	16.7	19.3
Percent of housing units built before 1949	44.3	44.6	56.6	50.5	50.8	53.6	68.6
Median value of owner-occupied units	$15,400	$13,200	$12,200	$12,000	$12,800	$14,300	$10,000

Source: Census table H-1, U.S. Bureau of the Census, 1970

TABLE 3.4. CROWDING AND COSTS OF HOUSING BY ETHNICITY IN THE
WESTLANDS COMPARED TO RURAL FRESNO COUNTY AS A WHOLE, 1970

	Rural Fresno County	Huron	Coalinga	San Joa-quin/Tran-quillity	Mendota	Fire-baugh Comm.	Rural Fire-baugh
All Families: Percent living in houses with >1.5 persons per room	5.4	14.3	14.1	9.0	16.3	—	12.3
Spanish Sur-name Families: Percent living in houses with >1.5 persons per room	17.2	18.4	43.0	19.3	23.0	—	18.4
Median rent, all rental units	--	—	--	$58	$54	$56	$58
Median rent, Spanish sur-name renters	--	—	--	$81	$63	$69	$58
Median rent, Spanish sur-name families below poverty level	--	$44	--	$60	$51	$47	$52

Source: Census table H-1, U.S. Bureau of the Census, 1970

The crowded situation of the Mexican-American population of the Westlands appeared to be not much more severe than the rest of rural Fresno County (approximately 18 to 43 percent vs. 17.2 percent). However, when we looked at the other end of the scale—that is, at the availability of larger homes to Mexican-Americans—the picture shifted in favor of other rural areas. Over 60 percent of the Mexican-American families in rural Fresno County lived in homes with fewer than one person per room. The same figures for the Westlands were 10 to 20 percent lower.

Poverty and Inequality

The Reclamation Act is intended to promote family farming and to provide for a maximum distribution of benefits from federal water projects. Yet Fresno County as a whole is one of the poorest in California. The proportion of the population living at or below the federal poverty standard in rural Fresno County was twice that for the state of California in 1970 (15.1 percent vs. 7 percent). The proportion of the population of the Westlands living in a state of poverty ranged from two to thirteen percentage points higher than in rural Fresno County (see table 3.5). If we examine the figures at 1.5 times the federal poverty standard, we find the Westlands to have been fifteen points higher than the rest of rural Fresno County. In other words, the people of the Westlands were among the poorest of the poor in the state of California. The only area of the state of comparable size with poverty figures as high as those found in the Westlands was the Imperial Water District.

Poverty in the Westlands falls most heavily on the Mexican-American majority. In some census tracts the proportion of the Mexican-American population living below the federal poverty standard in 1970 ran as high as 35 to 53.7 percent. Almost 84 percent of the Mexican-American population in the rural Firebaugh tract lived at or below 1.5 times the federal poverty standard.

The median family size of the Mexican-American population living below the poverty line in the Westlands was about six persons in 1970 (see table 3.6). These families were subsisting on about $3,000 a year. Less

TABLE 3.5. POVERTY AND ETHNICITY IN THE WESTLANDS
COMPARED TO RURAL FRESNO COUNTY AS A WHOLE, 1970

	Rural Fresno County	Huron	Coalinga	San Joa- quin/Tran- quillity	Mendota	Fire- baugh Comm.	Rural Fire- baugh
All Families:							
Percent at or below federal poverty level	15.1	17.3	17.4	18.8	26.3	20.9	28.9
Percent at 1.5 x federal poverty level	28.0	43.7	36.0	39.4	49.7	44.4	48.6
Spanish Sur- name Families:							
Percent at or below federal poverty level	—	24.6	37.7	29.2	29.7	35.1	53.7
Percent at or below 1.5 x federal pov- erty level	—	55.7	55.7	53.7	56.0	62.0	83.8

Source: Census tables P-8, P-1, U.S. Bureau of the Census, 1970

TABLE 3.6.   CHARACTERISTICS OF SPANISH FAMILIES BELOW
POVERTY LEVEL IN THE WESTLANDS, 1970

	Huron	Coalinga	San Joa-quin/Tran-quillity	Mendota	Fire-baugh Comm.	Rural Fire-baugh
Mean family income below poverty level	$2,722	$3,675	$3,790	$2,859	$2,428	$2,982
Median family size below poverty level	6.0	6.3	6.2	5.5	4.6	7.0
Percent below poverty level receiving public assistance	42.9	—	33.3	29.4	33.1	—
Below poverty level, percent of family heads in labor force	100.0	100.0	76.8	88.3	100.0	100.0
Percent of families below poverty level with female head of household	29.5	—	14.8	16.1	23.7	8.6

Source: Census tables P-8, P-1, U.S. Bureau of the Census, 1970
[Rural Fresno data not available.]

than half of them were receiving any form of public assistance. Virtually
all the heads of poverty households were in the labor force. The great majority (about 85 percent) were whole families, with husband-wife teams as
heads of households.

Income, Employment, and Affluence

Median family income for the rural areas of Fresno County was about
$4,000 lower than for the rest of the state, and income in the Westlands
was about $2,500 lower than for the rest of rural Fresno County. The fam-
ily income of the Mexican-American population of the Westlands was another $1,000 lower (U.S. Bureau of the Census, 1970).

During the 1960s, all families in the WWD registered gains in income
ranging from 37.6 to 67.5 percent. But this growth in family income compared to a gain of 95.7 percent for Fresno County and 106 percent for the
state of California during the same period (Security Pacific Bank, 1973).

This was the decade when more than 600 million tax dollars were spent in and near the Westlands to construct irrigation facilities.

Employment statistics, especially in agricultural areas, are difficult to interpret. Table 3.7 indicates comparatively little unemployment in the WWD. The district thus presents a paradox: high employment combined with high poverty. We can only assume that most of the poor in the Westlands are working poor. The data also indicate that the majority of all employed persons (and the great majority of Mexican-American employees) are farm workers. The proportions of the labor force classed as farm workers — including Spanish surname farmworkers — in the Westlands (from 34 to 91 percent) ranged from two to three times greater than that for other rural areas of Fresno County. It is a minority of employed people in the region — those who exist on the margins of the agribusiness system — who do not experience poverty and inequality, the lot of the majority of the region's employed, those directly involved in agricultural production.

We have seen that there are proportionally more poor families in the Westlands than in rural Fresno County and the rest of the state. Table 3.8 gives the results of an examination of the other end of the income scale and reveals that there are also proportionally fewer families that are moder-

TABLE 3.7.   EMPLOYMENT AND ETHNICITY IN THE
WESTLANDS, 1970

	Rural Fresno County	Huron	Coalinga	San Joa- quin/Tran- quillity	Mendota	Fire- baugh Comm.	Rural Fire- baugh
Percent of labor force employed	92.8	93.3	100.0	95.7	91.2	93.6	77.3
Percent of Spanish sur- name labor force employed	—	91.0	100.0	96.6	89.0	96.3	89.1
Percent of labor force occupied as farm workers	16.4	55.7	50.2	55.6	50.6	34.0	57.5
Percent of Spanish sur- name labor force occu- pied as farm workers	—	64.1	91.4	77.5	55.0	46.6	75.3

Source: Census table P-3, U.S. Bureau of the Census, 1970

TABLE 3.8. AFFLUENCE AND ETHNICITY IN THE WESTLANDS
COMPARED TO RURAL FRESNO COUNTY AS A WHOLE, 1970

	Rural Fresno County	Huron	Coalinga	San Joa- quin/Tran- quillity	Mendota	Fire- baugh Comm.	Rural Fire- baugh
All Families:							
Percent with incomes greater than $10,000/yr.	39.9	20.9	30.4	28.1	19.8	21.4	15.4
Spanish Surname Families:							
Percent with incomes greater than $10,000/yr.	n.d.	12.6	11.4	18.0	20.8	18.7	8.7

Source: Census table P-3, U.S. Bureau of the Census, 1970

ately well-off. The proportion of all families with incomes greater than $10,000 a year in 1970 lagged about twenty percentage points behind the rest of rural Fresno County.

Education

Even though they are poorer and live in inferior houses, the people of the Westlands are better educated than other rural peoples in Fresno County. It is hard to know what to make of this finding. There may exist a good base of human knowledge and capacity on which to build stronger communities. On the other hand, the combination of relatively greater education and depressed social conditions suggests the presence of a structural obstacle to development. The possibility of such an obstacle is also suggested by the changing educational levels of the Mexican-American population of the Westlands.

The only dramatic social change that we were able to find that occurred during the period of the building of the San Luis unit was the gain in median years of education for the Spanish-surname population of San Joaquin/Tranquillity, Huron, and Mendota (see table 3.9). The increases ranged from about 18 to 43 percent, and were much greater than those for the rest of the population during the same period (about 3 to 16 percent). By contrast, only in Mendota were the Mexican-Americans able to close the income gap between themselves and the rest of the population (see table 3.10). In San Joaquin/Tranquillity, the greater educational gains of the Mexican-Americans permitted them merely to keep up with the

TABLE 3.9. MEDIAN YEARS OF EDUCATION (MYE) AND ETHNICITY IN THE WESTLANDS, 1960–1970

	Rural Fresno County*	Huron		Coalinga		San Joaquin/ Tranquillity		Mendota		Rural Firebaugh	
	MYE 1970	MYE '70	Percent Change 60–70	MYE '70	Percent Change 60–70	MYE '70	Percent Change 60–70	MYE '70	Percent Change 60–70	MYE '70	Percent Change 60–70
All individuals	7.4	7.8	16.4	9.6	12.9	9.6	2.9	7.0	2.9	8.5	4.9
Spanish surname	—	5.3	43.2	4.6	−19.2	6.2	17.7	5.3	17.7	4.9	−3.9
Difference		2.5		5.0		3.4		1.7		3.6	

Source: Census table P–2, U.S. Bureau of the Census, 1970
*1960–1970 percent change for Rural Fresno County cannot be reconstructed from available data.

TABLE 3.10. MEDIAN FAMILY INCOME AND ETHNICITY IN THE WESTLANDS, 1970

	Rural Fresno County* 1970 income	Huron 1970 income	Huron Percent Change 60-70	San Joaquin/ Tranquillity 1970 income	San Joaquin/ Tranquillity Percent Change 60-70	Mendota 1970 income	Mendota Percent Change 60-70	Firebaugh 1970 income	Firebaugh Percent Change 60-70
All families	$8,626	$6,150	67.3	$6,505	37.6	$6,138	67.5	$5,596	45.0
Spanish surname families	—	5,105	58.4	5,609	38.2	5,847	99.5	4,648	37.8
Difference		1,045		956		291		948	

Source: Census table P-3, U.S. Bureau of the Census, 1970
*1960-1970 percent change for Rural Fresno County cannot be reconstructed from available data.

income of the rest of the population. And in Huron, where the educational gains of the Mexican-Americans were greatest, they lagged behind in income.

Infrastructural Changes, 1958–1978

We have measured changes in the service, institutional, and commercial sectors before and after the building of the San Luis unit. These measures should show any changes produced by the introduction of subsidized irrigation water. By means of comprehensive searches of community telephone and other directories published for the years 1958, 1968, and 1978, we enumerated service facilities such as grocery, hardware, and other stores; personal services, including beauty and barber shops; banks and credit unions; transportation-related businesses and services, including bus stations and auto repair shops; voluntary organizations and churches; recreational facilities; schools; medical services; and government offices. The overall picture that emerges is one of little or no growth as a result of the building of the irrigation system and the delivery of water (see table 3.11). Moreover, the aggregate finding disguises declines of particular services in several communities. There was a loss of five doctors from the entire study area. San Joaquin/Tranquillity lost its only doctor and a pharmacy. Four local newspapers disappeared from the area and were not replaced. Four taxi services went out of business, leaving none in the entire study area in 1978. The number of businesses serving agriculture increased in Firebaugh and Huron, but declined in the other communities. The only sectors that showed consistent growth in all

TABLE 3.11. DECLINE OF SERVICES IN THE WESTLANDS DURING AND AFTER BUILDING THE SAN LUIS UNIT, 1958–1978

	1958		1968		1978	
	Total Services	Services per Capita	Total Services	Services per Capita	Total Services	Services per Capita
Huron	60	.047	69	.045	77	.030
Coalinga	245	.041	279	.045	274	.043
San Joaquin/Tranquillity	75	.085	104	.069	107	.066
Mendota	86	.041	80	.029	100	.024
Firebaugh	122	.059	155	.061	148	.037

Source: U.S. Bureau of the Census, 1970
[Rural Fresno data not available.]

communities were banking and, ironically, government agencies, including welfare. We conclude that communities' capacity for self-sufficiency has not been improved and may have been damaged by the introduction of federally subsidized irrigation water.

CONCLUSION

In 1959, at the time of the debate over building the San Luis unit, Congressman Sisk of California, a legislator of evident goodwill who also assumed compliance with the Reclamation Act, described the benefits he expected to see:

> If the San Luis Unit is built . . . the present population of the area will almost quadruple. There will be . . . in all 87,500 people sharing the productivity and the bounty of fertile lands blossoming with an ample supply of San Luis water. Why will this land support four times as many people if this project is built? Because it is inevitable and historic that under the impact of reclamation laws, as well as the economics of farm management and operation, these lands will break down into family-sized units, each cultivated by individual owners and their families. . . . We are seeking to make our greatest land resources available to provide more and better living for more people. This, I believe, is the real and ultimate goal of the reclamation policy laid down by Congress more than a half-century ago — not merely to irrigate land and produce crops. (U.S. House, 1959:13–15)

The assumptions of such statements were clearly faulty; the unit had precisely the opposite effects. Growing recognition of the failure of reclamation to achieve its own goals is leading to serious consideration of land reform policies both inside and outside government.

The structural preconditions for land reform have already been reached. Briefly, these conditions are (1) regional dependence on a single industry — agriculture; (2) a dualized class system with a few landowning elites at the top and large numbers of landless workers at the bottom; and (3) a rigid status structure in which there are no institutional or other means (e.g., education or moral turpitude) for movement between the classes, either upward or downward.[10] The Westlands case is further exacerbated by an ethnic division which perfectly coincides with the class structure; the owners of farms are white, and over 95 percent of the workers are brown, black, and East Indian. Only an apartheid society can maintain this pattern in a population where nonwhites are rapidly becoming the majority.

With the possible exception of its ethnic pattern, the Westlands case is far from unique. Wherever there is a single-industry region rigidly organized into two social classes, one typically finds the same: poverty; ignorance; occupationally related and other diseases; destabilization of individuals, families, and communities; the breakdown of democratic forms of government; and degradation of the physical environment. There are only two ways to modify this structure: one way is to introduce a successful competing industry, and the other is land reform. It was precisely this choice that Congress was trying to avoid by inserting social provisions into the Reclamation Act of 1902. It is the choice that has again been thrust upon us by failure to enforce the law.

NOTES

1. See the "Small Farm Alternative" and "Proposed Rules" sections of USDI (1981).

2. *Congressional Record,* 105 (1959), pp. 7496-97. Also quoted in part in USDI (1981), pp. 3-66.

3. See, for example, Goldschmidt (1978); Fujimoto (1977), pp. 13-26; Ray (1968); United States Senate (1971), Ninety-Second Congress, *Hearings,* part two, p. 479; Prof. Philip M. Raup as quoted in Berry (1978), pp. 171-72; Peterson (1977), pp. 2-13; Michaels and Marousek (1978). Much of this literature has been nicely summarized in a recent helpful paper by Nuckton, Rochin, and Gwynn (1982).

4. For discussion of the legislative history of the Reclamation Act and the growers' attempts to change it, see Taylor (1968), pp. 24-29 and 68-72. See also USDI, pp. 3-61.

5. For a helpful study of the probable effect of a scale-down in the Westlands on crop mix and production levels, see LeVeen and Goldman (1978), pp. 929-34.

6. *Ivanhoe Irrigation District* v. *McCracken,* 357 U.S. 1958, p. 1329.

7. The source for this and other residency statistics used in this report is Echoe Map Publishing Company (1978 and 1979).

8. A recent (August 19, 1980, p. 1) news item:

FRESNO (UPI) Three Rocks residents lost their power May 22 after Fresno County Superior Court Judge Hollis Best upheld a Board of Supervisors decision to disband the community because of unsafe and unsanitary living conditions. Three Rocks residents argue that the denial of electricity is making those very problems all the worse.

The 51 families who, in the eyes of San Joaquin Valley farm workers, have become symbols of the fight against poverty, have until Aug. 31 to get out of town.

Fresno County supervisors ordered the community broken up after health officials found the housing substandard, the sewer and water systems inadequate and makeshift electrical connections unsafe.

The town of Three Rocks is only an example of a type of community that can be found embedded in the system of large-scale agriculture throughout the state of California. In "Second Thoughts," *The Nation* (October 6, 1979, p. 293) Carey McWilliams wrote:

Ripley, California—two square miles of squalor set amid some of the richest agricultural land in the world, near the prosperous town of Blythe. The town is bordered by soybeans on the south, alfalfa on the east, cotton and cantaloupes on the west, and tomatoes on the north. Some 450 people, farm laborers and their families, live in Ripley in run-down frame houses, tar paper shacks and aging trailers. Ripley has no street lights, no public telephones, no curbs, no gutters and no sewer system. Garbage is thrown into a ditch. The elementary school was closed in 1971 to save funds; two years ago an arsonist set fire to it. . . . At night the teen-agers hang around a gutted gas station drinking beer and smoking marijuana.

9. Throughout this report, "other rural areas of Fresno" refers to the small communities and farm and nonfarm populations of the county, not including the data for the city of Fresno. Perhaps a better usage would be "nonmetropolitan Fresno county." The data presented underestimate the difference between the Westlands and the rest of the county because the figures for the Westlands census tracts are included in the balance of county data. This pattern of double counting of the Westlands pushes the averages closer together than would be the case if they could be disaggregated. Note also that the data for other rural areas of

Fresno include the communities on the east side of the valley famous for their small-scale farming and relatively high quality of community life.

10. For an excellent discussion of the structural preconditions for land and agrarian reform, see Tuma (1965).

REFERENCES

Berry, Wendell. 1978. *The Unsettling of America.* New York: Avon Books.

Davis (California) *Enterprise. 1980. "Residents defy order to vacate." (August 19): 1.*

Echoe Map Publishing Company. 1978. AGRI-Land: Fresno County West of Highway 99. San Mateo, CA: Echoe Map Publishing Co.

Echoe Map Publishing Company. 1979. AGRI-Land: Kings County. San Mateo, CA: Echoe Map Publishing Co.

Fujimoto, Isao. 1977. *"The U.C. Davis story." In The Family Farm in California.* Sacramento: State of California. Pp. 13–26.

Goldschmidt, Walter F. 1978. *As You Sow.* Montclair, NJ: Allanheld, Osmun.

LeVeen, E. Phillip, and Goldman, George E. 1978. "Reclamation policy and the water subsidy: an analysis of the distributional consequences of an emerging policy choice." *American Journal of Agricultural Economics* 60 (December): 929–34.

McWilliams, Carey. 1979. "Second thoughts." *The Nation* (October 6): 293.

Michaels, Gregory H., and Marousek, G. 1978. *Economic Impact of Farm Size Alternatives on Rural Communities.* Moscow, ID: University of Idaho, Agricultural Economic Experiment Station, Bulletin No. 582, May.

Nuckton, Carole, Rochin, Refugio, and Gwynn, Douglas. 1982. "Farm size and rural community welfare: an interdisciplinary approach." *Rural Sociology* 47(1): 32–46.

Peterson, Steve. 1977. "Community services task force report." In *The Family Farm in California.* Sacramento: State of California. Pp. 2–13.

Ray, Victor K. 1968. *The Corporate Invasion of American Agriculture.* Washington, DC: National Farmers Union.

Rodriguez, Rich, and Johnson, John. 1979. "They call it Tortilla Flats." *Fresno Bee* (September 9).

Sacramento (California) *Bee. 1980. (March 1): A10.*

Security Pacific Bank. 1973. The Central Valley Report. Los Angeles: Security Pacific Bank.

Small Farm Viability Project. 1977. *The Family Farm in California.* Sacramento: State of California.

Taylor, Paul S. 1968. "Water, land and people in the Great Valley." *American West* 5 (March): 24–29, 68–72.

Tuma, Elias. 1965. *Twenty-six Centuries of Agrarian Reform: A Comparative Analysis.* Berkeley: University of California Press.

United States Bureau of the Census. 1960 and 1970. *Census of Population and Housing.* Census Tracts. Final Report PHC (1) – 75, Fresno, CA, SMSA.

United States Bureau of Reclamation. 1978. *Special Task Force Report on the San Luis Unit.* Washington, DC: U.S. Bureau of Reclamation.

United States Congress. 1959. *Congressional Record* 105, pp. 7496–97. Eighty-sixth Congress.

United States Department of the Interior. 1981. *Acreage Limitation: Draft Environmental Impact Statement.* Washington, DC: U.S. Department of the Interior.

United States House of Representatives. 1959. *San Luis Unit of the Central Valley Project,* H.R. 301. Hearings before the House Subcommittee on Irrigation and Reclamation, March 16–17, 19. Eighty-sixth Congress, First Session.

United States Senate. 1971. *"Who owns the land?" Hearings before the Subcommittee on Migratory Labor of the Committee on Labor and Public Welfare.* November 5, 1971. Ninety-second Congress, First and Second Sessions.

United States Supreme Court. 1958. *Ivanhoe Irrigation District* v. *McCracken.* 357 U.S.

4

Agricultural Land Reform in America

FREDERICK H. BUTTEL

There is an irony in discussions of land reform in American agriculture. Agricultural development planners during the late 1950s and early 1960s saw the Western path of agricultural development, epitomized by the rural social structure and agricultural technology of the United States, as the most desirable — if not the only possible — strategy for Third World development. Thus they advocated land reform and agricultural research as cornerstones of agricultural growth. In effect, they attempted to replicate American dispersed family farms that rapidly adopt new agricultural technologies while they compete to maintain their positions in product markets.

Recently, land reform literature has shifted in focus from the Third World to the First. Land reform in underdeveloped countries proved to be politically difficult and spatially constrained; land concentration in the Third World is generally greater now than it was before World War II (Griffin, 1978). The ultimate rationale for agricultural land reform — that small farms were more productive than large farms (Dorner, 1972; Berry and Cline, 1979) — is no longer considered universally valid (Crouch and de Janvry, 1979). The problems and failures of the Green Revolution cast further doubt on the applicability of the Western experience (Griffin, 1974; Pearse, 1980). American intellectuals and activists even began to question whether our own country's path of agricultural development was socially desirable. American agriculture, once the model for progressive land reform, was itself in need of reform.

The American land reform movement has altered agricultural politics (see, for example, Guither, 1980; Paarlberg, 1980), but has had little impact on agricultural structure up to the present. This does not mean that land reform has failed, for it is just beginning. Nevertheless, this diverse land reform movement — consisting in fact of several overlapping movements concerned with relieving hunger, reforming state and local government, preserving farmland, conserving rural resources, and upholding the family farm (Guither, 1980) — now finds itself without a sympathetic federal government. It also faces a growing internal debate as to what types of strategies or policies to pursue.

This paper will explore the meaning of agricultural land reform in advanced industrial-capitalist societies. Reform could consist of transferring ownership and/or control of farmland from large farmers and landowners to small ones. But this is too simple. It ignores the complexities of formulating long-term strategies or short-term policies for specific problems — for instance, federal irrigation policy, agricultural research priorities, or retention of prime agricultural land.

The basic dilemma is that agricultural land reform in America has become intimately bound up with protecting the family farmer. American family farming is still prominent, but family or household production in agriculture in the advanced industrial societies is probably destined for slow but certain extinction. Economies of scale and the inexorable laws of capitalist development — the concentration and centralization of capital — may make family farming an anachronism. Family farming would therefore give way to industrial or corporate farming based primarily on hired labor. This development, similar to that of other large sectors in advanced industrial societies, would thus undermine a land reform strategy based on the family farm — similar to trying to preserve craft production in the textile industry. Accordingly, protecting a class of independent household producers destined for extinction would be a waste of reformist energy. The remainder of this paper builds to this conclusion and suggests alternative reformist strategies.

THE STATUS OF FAMILY FARMING

The high concentration of inequality in agricultural sales and assets is well recognized. According to the most recent (1978) Census of Agriculture, there were 81,307 farms in the United States with sales of $200,000 or more. This handful of large farms represented 3.3 percent of U.S. farms, yet accounted for 44.2 percent of gross agricultural sales and averaged $589,278 in annual sales per farm (U.S. Department of Agriculture, 1981:46). Again, according to USDA, there were 1,761,000 farms with annual sales of less than $20,000, representing 65.9 percent of U.S. farms but only 8.6 percent of gross sales. These farmers were by no means in poverty, for the average off-farm income per farm family was several times larger than net farm income. The smallest farms — ones with annual sales of less than $2,500, also had nonfarm income which averaged over $17,000 per family. Such farms, many of which since 1974 have no longer been considered farms by Bureau of the Census criteria, represented 34.1 percent of farms by USDA count. Including net farm income placed these farms, on average, well above the national median family income of $17,640.

If agriculture is conceived primarily as a production sector, our attention should probably be confined to the 200,000 largest farms. They account for roughly two-thirds of American agricultural production, but less than ten percent of American farms. Most depend on hired labor and thus are larger-than-family farms, even if they are not necessarily corporate or industrial ones. But if agriculture is conceived as a combination of a production sector and residence of families who live on farmland, our evaluation would change. We would conclude that the vast majority of farms are operated primarily with the use of family labor. The family farm would dominate.

But what is a family farm? Vogeler (1981:9) declares it a myth, using a classical definition including family ownership of most or all land and other capital items; family provision of most or all labor; family entrepreneurial or managerial control over production decisions; and most or all family livelihood deriving from farm income and farm-produced commodities. The U.S. Department of Agriculture (1976:28), declaring the family basis of U.S. agriculture, employed a much broader definition—one based on operation of a family-owned farm business. Vogeler's restrictive definition of family farming would thus exclude several types of farmers that clearly fall within the U.S. Department of Agriculture's definition. Farms excluded under this more restrictive definition would include tenant farmers who surrender entrepreneurial control of production decisions through contracts, farms where the majority of labor is provided by hired workers, and farm families who derive the majority of their income from nonfarm sources. Using the USDA definition, 95 percent of farms can be classified as family farms.

The late 1930s and early 1940s brought several changes to American agriculture that accelerated until the 1970s—tractor and tractor-related technologies, biochemical technologies, and federal commodity programs that boosted farm prices and reduced instability in agricultural income. Mechanization, along with the Agriculture Department's decision not to require landlords to distribute government commodity payments to tenants or sharecroppers, facilitated consolidation of farms and eviction of tenants. Mechanical and biochemical technologies placed a premium on farmers' access to credit, which in turn benefitted large farmers. The overall result was a spectacular decline in the number of farms, especially small ones.

The postwar period also saw a dramatic shift in tenancy and land rental. Tenant farmers had relatively small farms that yielded correspondingly low incomes. But by 1974 tenant farms—ones where the operator leases all land from others—averaged 468 acres, compared to 252 acres per farm for full owners and 852 acres per farm for part owners (Hottel and Harrington, 1979:99). Sixty-two percent of American farms were operated by full owners, but they accounted for only 35 percent of total cultivated land. Part-owner and tenant farms accounted for 27 and 11 percent, respectively, of all farms and for 53 and 12 percent, respectively, of cultivated land (Hottel and Harrington, 1979:98).

Such figures suggest that for short-term profits and favorable cash flows, returns from rented land are higher than those from owned land, producing a separation of ownership and operation. The most dynamic of farmers, part-owner farmers, combine rentals and ownership to take advantage of technological and financial economies of scale. Ownership, leveraged by profits from rented lands and appreciation of the value of owned lands, provides the part owner with the long-term capital gains benefits associated with rising land values. Thus landowners, especially those who diversify through land rental, are in a superior position to buy increasingly expensive farmland and to benefit from continuing inflation in land prices.

Are these family farms? Table 4.1, derived from Rodefeld's (1979) research, sheds light on the role of hired labor and absentee ownership among the largest and most rapidly growing of U.S. farms. This table reports selected size and labor characteristics of U.S. commercial farms — farms with sales of $2,500 or more in 1974 — divided into five size categories. The figures indicate the importance of rented land and hired labor on farms with sales of $100,000 or more, which accounted for roughly 54 percent of agricultural sales. The results are especially striking on the employment of agricultural wage labor. Farms with sales of $500,000 or more averaged 22.8 hired workers per farm, farms with sales of $200,000 to $499,999 averaged 4.4 workers per farm, and farms with sales of $100,000 to $199,999 averaged 2.5 workers per farm. American agriculture is shifting toward concentration of production and sales among a handful of relatively large farms based on hired labor. The observation is confirmed by census data showing that among all farms with sales of $2,500 or more, the number of hired workers has increased from 712,715 in 1974 to 953,323 in 1978 (U.S. Department of Commerce, 1980). Since the mid-1960s, there has been a general growth in the number of worker-days of farm wage work, with temporary wage work (by workers employed less than 75 days per year) showing a slight absolute decline and full-time wage work (by workers employed 150 days or more per year) accounting for most of the increase in the total number of worker-days. The numbers of full-time wage laborers and of total worker-days have become increasingly concentrated on fewer and larger farms, along with cash receipts and amounts of land cultivated (Rodefeld, 1978, 1979, 1980).

It is unclear whether large nonfamily farms are organized as industrial or corporate farms or simply as larger-than-family ones. Industrial or corporate farms are managed by a hired employee, while larger-than-family ones are managed by the owner. The distinction could be crucial for land reform policy. If, for example, the bulk of dynamic large farms are industrial or corporate ones, legislation restricting the operation of corporate

TABLE 4.1. SELECTED SIZE AND LABOR CHARACTERISTICS OF COMMERCIAL U.S. FARMS, 1974

	Value of 1974 Sales					
	$500,000 or more	$200,000 -499,000	$100,000 -199,000	$ 40,000 -99,000	$ 2,500 -39,000	Total
Number and Percent of Farms	11,412 0.7%	40,034 2.4%	101,153 6.0%	324,310 19.1%	1,121,138 71.9%	1,695,047 100%
Size Characteristics						
Total Acres Operated (million acres, percent total)	53.8 5.9%	91.5 10.1%	131.4 14.5%	246.6 27.2%	382.2 42.4%	905.6 100%
Percent of Acres Owned by Operator*	57.6%	52.1%	51.2%	59.9%	65.4%	59.4%
Average Acres Operated/Farm	4,718	2,287	1,209	761	314	534
Labor Characteristics						
Farms Employing Hired Labor (number, percent)	10,934 95.8%	34,450 86.0%	72,104 71.3%	179,247 55.3%	404,206 33.2%	700,941 41.3%
Farms Employing Full-time Workers (number, percent)	10,611 93.0%	29,535 73.8%	47,657 47.1%	77,304 23.9%	57,986 4.8%	223,093 13.2%
Number and Percent of Full-time Workers	242,384 34.0%	131,193 18.4%	117,659 16.5%	136,667 19.2%	84,812 11.9%	712,715 100%
Average Number of Workers/Farm	22.8	4.4	2.5	1.8	1.5	3.2
Total Labor Expenditures (dollars, percent)	$1,704,561 37.3%	$860,200 18.8%	$709,710 15.5%	$756,487 16.6%	$535,041 11.7%	$4,566,000 100%
Average Labor Expenditure/Farm	$155,895	$ 24,969	$ 9,843	$ 4,220	$1,324	$ 6,514

Source: U.S. Bureau of the Census, 1974 Census of Agriculture, as reported in Rodefeld (1979):53

*Acres owned by business owner, minus acres rented or leased to others, divided by total acres operated.

farming operations may be useful. On the other hand, the predominance of family proprietorships among large, expanding farms would likely render anticorporate legislation ineffective in preserving small, traditional family farms.

Most estimates place the number of corporate or large-scale industrial farms at about 32,000, or slightly over 1 percent of all U.S. farms. These farms account for approximately 10 percent of gross agricultural sales (Rodefeld, 1978). Larger-than-family farms represented 4 percent of all farms and accounted for 25 percent of gross sales in 1964 (Rodefeld, 1979). The relative number and sales of these larger-than-family farms probably have increased considerably in the past seventeen years (Raup, 1978a). Larger-than-family farms are therefore more significant in U.S. agriculture than are corporate or industrial farms, although the latter are extremely important in California, Arizona, New Mexico, Texas, Florida, and Hawaii.

The growing predominance of nonfamily forms of production in U.S. agriculture may mean that the role of the small farm is slowly diminishing. The trend was visible from roughly 1940 to 1975, but since then the number of relatively small farms has been stable or has even grown. For instance, the 1978 Census of Agriculture (U.S. Department of Commerce, 1980) indicated an increase in the number of farms with sales of less than $20,000 from 1,514,137 in 1974 to 1,585,065 in 1978.

There are several reasons for the turnaround. Many small-farm families have significant off-farm income that allows them to remain in agriculture despite low farm returns. Small farmers tend to have lower debt-to-asset ratios and lower levels of cash expenditures as a percentage of cash receipts than do large farmers — thus insulating them from instability in factor and product prices (U.S. Department of Agriculture, 1981). Small farmers increasingly appear to be settling into less competitive niches in the agricultural economy — for example, producing for local markets rather than for national or international ones. Thus, small farms may have become more viable at a time of increasing concern about their annihilation.

At the same time, during the late 1970s, a "disappearing middle" phenomenon has harmed medium-sized, full-time family farms. The 1978 Census of Agriculture (U.S. Department of Commerce, 1980), for example, indicated that farms with sales of $20,000 to $39,999 composed the most vulnerable sales class group in agriculture during the late 1970s. The number of farms in this category declined from 322,046 to 306,886 from 1974 to 1978, while farms with annual sales of less than $20,000 and greater than $100,000 exhibited significant growth.

American agriculture is thus moving toward a two-tier or dualistic structure where large nonfamily farms and, to a lesser degree, small — often "subfamily" farms — grow in prominence, while the middle range of medium-sized, full-time family farms declines. The transformation is ongoing, as yet incomplete. Family farms still dominate in many regions and commodities. Nevertheless the transformation will be the prime force with which the agricultural land reform movement must contend.

ISSUES IN AGRICULTURAL LAND REFORM

The foregoing discussion raises a number of critical questions for agricultural land reform groups whose activities focus directly or indirectly on preserving the family farm. This section will explore a number of issues associated with preservation of the family farm and assess prevailing strategies of reform.

Public Assistance to Small and Family Farms

The most immediate means for helping family farmers is to direct public resources toward them. A number of mechanisms for public assistance to small and family farms have been pursued — expansion of federal supervised credit programs for small and beginning farmers; government programs for the purchase, lease, and (concessionary) sale of land to young farmers otherwise unable to buy land; and expansion of off-farm employment opportunities in rural regions.

Our review of the emerging dualistic pattern of agriculture has suggested that retention of small farms is unlikely to be a crucial issue in coming decades. Roughly two-thirds of American farm families operate low-sales-volume farms where gross income does not yield a net income comparable to the median nonmetropolitan family income. Small farms are likely to increase slightly or remain constant as a proportion of the total number of farms, without major public policy changes. Access to off-farm income, in addition to some of the economic advantages enjoyed by small-scale producers, will ensure the persistence of modestly prosperous small farmers.

Yet not all small farmers can earn substantial off-farm income; these essentially full-time small farmers often represent a significant poverty class (see, for example, Madden and Baker, 1981). Targeting public assistance to full-time, poverty-level, small farmers will be difficult. Supporting farm product prices through commodity programs — the traditional mechanism to increase farm income — will result in few benefits for poverty-level, small-scale farmers. Stimulation of industrial employment opportunities in rural regions has limitations. The programs tend to involve significant transfers of public subsidies to private capital and thus may be inequitable (Hill, 1980). The local employment benefits of rural industrialization tend to be overemphasized, particularly because the more attractive jobs tend to be taken by persons outside the rural community or region (Summers et al., 1976). Poverty-level small farmers tend to be relatively old and to have low educational backgrounds, making them poor competitors for the nonfarm jobs created.

Moreover, the ongoing trend toward two-tier agriculture suggests that the most formidable task for the land reform movement will be to stem the tide of the disappearing middle range of full-time, medium-scale, family farms. Taking the aggregate sales class of $40,000 to $99,999 as a proxy measure for this group, 1978 data indicate that it now represents only 14.9

percent of all farm operators (U.S. Department of Agriculture, 1981:43). Such farmers tend to share many of the problems of larger-than-family farmers, especially high debt-to-asset ratios (U.S. Department of Agriculture, 1981:54). Yet they are also disadvantaged in comparison to larger-than-family farmers because of tax laws and other public policies. The demands of on-farm work on the time of family members also tends to lead to relatively low off-farm incomes. Most significantly, however, the agricultural land reform movement has ignored these medium-sized, generally full-time, family farmers while concentrating on small farmers, some of whom are not socioeconomically disadvantaged. Continued pursuit of this strategy is likely to harm the movement.

A final dilemma is that small and family farmers may have declined so much in terms of total agricultural production that their collective land and capital assets represent an inadequate base from which to compete with larger nonfamily farms. Farms with sales of less than \$100,000 annually now account for less than 44 percent of total agricultural sales (U.S. Department of Agriculture, 1981:43). While family farmers are hardly an extinct social class, they have experienced such a long decline that alteration of public subsidies to various classes of farms — an outcome which, as we shall discuss below, seems unreachable in itself — may be ineffective in achieving the democratization or reform of agriculture. Family farms once seemed destined to predominate in numbers, but the growing domination by large, nonfamily producers appears difficult to stem.

Restrictions on Corporate Farming

Much of the effort of the agricultural land reform movement has assumed that corporate farms, partly because of massive public subsidies (e.g., tax laws and irrigation subsidies), are unfairly competing with and displacing family farms. Thus restrictions or the banning of corporate farming operations might help the family farm — an assertion that may be true for several regions and commodities. Corporate farms have clearly contributed to the near-demise of family farms in the Southwest and the Southeast, especially those producing lettuce, tomatoes, grapes, and citrus (Friedland et al., 1980).

The national picture is different. Corporate organization does not neatly coincide with large-scale industrial farming, since the majority of corporate farms in U.S. agriculture are family proprietorships (Reimund, 1979). Large-scale industrial farms are a minority in terms of numbers and sales when compared with large nonfamily farms in the U.S. Studies of local agricultural land markets indicate that when family farmers sell their lands, the lands are most likely to be purchased by neighboring larger-than-family farmers, rather than by nonfarm corporations engaged in agriculture (U.S. Department of Agriculture, 1981, chapter 4; Raup, 1978a). There is emerging evidence that the rapid growth of farming by nonfarm corporations during the 1960s has slowed or reversed because such corporations have suffered cash-flow problems and have slowly begun to liquidate their farm assets (Buttel, 1981).

Thus the agricultural land reform movement may have overestimated the significance of corporate or large-scale industrial farming and underestimated the role of larger-than-family farms. Efforts to reduce the influence of corporate/industrial farms may have merit. But restrictions on corporate farming may be less fruitful than anticipated if they cause the agricultural land reform movement to ignore larger-than-family farms. For both political and ideological reasons, controlling the growth of larger-than-family farms may be considerably more difficult than curbing corporate agriculture.

Agricultural Land Preservation

Agricultural land preservation has tended to be a "motherhood" goal, despite the conflicts that have typically surrounded implementation. Agricultural land preservation has usually meant preferential assessment or taxation of agricultural land (see, for example, Roberts and Brown, 1980). Such measures are intended to reduce the pressure on urban-fringe farmers to sell their land because of competition for farmland for urban uses and the concomitant high property taxes. Arguments for preserving agricultural land by tax measures almost invariably center on protecting the status of the family farmer (see, for example, Belden et al., 1979). Raup (1980), however, presents evidence suggesting that the massive loss of agricultural land to urban uses after World War II may be approaching an end and that agricultural land preservation may not be a key issue in the 1980s. Raup notes that the major sources of "land withdrawals" — the interstate highway system, water impoundments, and construction of homesites and industrial parks — are now essentially completed.

There is also the question of the actual beneficiaries of preferential assessment and taxation. The studies edited by Roberts and Brown (1980) suggest that land speculators, rather than farmers, are often the major recipients of tax advantages. Also, preferential taxation, if it causes farmers to bid up land prices in local land markets, may confer disproportionate advantage on large and absentee landowners. It is unclear that agricultural land preservation primarily benefits family farmers. It may instead confer disproportionate benefits on larger owners, both farm and nonfarm.

One may question the purpose of agricultural land preservation. Most arguments for agricultural land preservation suggest that prime agricultural land is "running out" and that land must be saved to feed a growing American and world population. In the abstract the point has some truth, but it must be evaluated against the realities of present American productive capacity and the destination of food exports. Approximately 40 percent of the value of U.S. agricultural commodities is exported annually; short- and even long-term needs for agricultural land do not really affect domestic consumption. Most food exports go to relatively affluent industrial countries, especially in Western Europe, Eastern Europe, and Japan. The bulk of agricultural exports sold to Third World nations goes to the most privileged ones — countries such as Brazil that are often expanding their own agriculture. As a result, only a small amount of U.S. food exports goes to hungry people in poor countries (see, for example, George, 1977). The long-term necessity for feeding the hungry in the United States and abroad as a rationale for agricultural land preservation may not be persuasive.

Altering the Research and Extension Priorities of the Land-Grant Colleges

American agriculture is among the most capital-intensive in the world, and considerable attention has recently been focused on the role of the land-grant college system in promoting this capital-intensiveness. Beginning with the penetrating critique by Hightower (1973) of the land-grant college complex, there has been an emerging consensus in the agricultural land reform movement that the public research and extension system has hurt the family farmer and helped corporate farmers (see, for example, Vogeler, 1981). Accordingly, the movement has emphasized altering the research and extension priorities of the land-grant system, especially as they affect small farmers.

Have research and extension priorities indeed been biased toward larger farmers? This question can be answered largely in the affirmative. Land-grant college research in agronomy and economics has often been conducted with the needs of "progressive" — that is, relatively large — operators in mind. There is some evidence that most land-grant college research is equally applicable to farms regardless of size (ESCOP, 1981). But a great deal of mechanization research is designed for large farm applications, and most research in the plant and animal sciences has focused on capital-intensive practices more suitable for larger operators with superior access to credit and the benefits of the tax system. The biases of land-grant research may be due less to the technologies it develops than to the institutional settings where they are deployed.

But would more research and extension for small farmers promote agricultural land reform? The answer is likely to be no. Many "appropriate" technologies advocated most strongly by agricultural land reform proponents — for instance, organic farming and on-farm biomass energy production — tend to have significant economies of scale. That is, these technologies will generally not help the small farm operator. Moreover, the fact that massive technological change has accompanied the decline of the family farmer does not mean it has caused it. The key socioeconomic changes in U.S. agriculture — the decline of small farms, the concentration of agricultural land and sales — were in motion well before the major surge of public agricultural research during the 1940s and 1950s (Cochrane, 1979). Research was at most a contributing cause of these changes. It is doubtful that agricultural technology developed specifically for small and family farmers would stem the tide of agricultural transformation. Moreover, an increasing proportion of agricultural research is conducted privately by agribusiness firms. Thus a shift in public agricultural research priorities would not necessarily decrease research on the technical problems of large farmers. The locus of the research would merely change from public institutions to private ones, with a corresponding loss of public accountability.

Consequently, there are grounds for skepticism about the effectiveness of altering land-grant college research to promote agricultural land reform. The development of appropriate technologies can make a difference for many farmers, and the land-grant colleges should shift in this direction. But such changes will not enable small farmers to outperform large ones.

Tax and Commodity Policies

Tax and commodity policies are probably the single most important forces producing agricultural dualism. The policies tend to subsidize larger operations directly and create indirect benefits for large landowners by means of an inflationary land market where public subsidies raise land values. But can these policies be changed?

The features of the tax codes that subsidize capital-intensity and large farms are not specific to agriculture, but result from long-standing policies designed to stimulate capital investment and growth in industry in general (Robinson, 1980). Tax incentives for industrial expansion, especially regarding capital gains, have been sharpened by the Reagan administration, and change in the opposite direction will be extremely difficult. Barry and Baker (1977), for example, have argued that a significant capital gains tax should be levied on farmers who use unrealized capital gains on their currently owned land as equity to leverage the purchase of additional land. Such a proposal would reduce the demand for land by established large farmers and improve the acquisition chances of small and entering farmers. However, as Robinson (1980) points out, farmers—even smaller operators—tend to resist public policies that reduce public subsidies to any part of the agricultural industry.

Another barrier is the disguised regressiveness of commodity price support programs. It is disguised since it tends to work primarily through the land market. To reduce regressiveness, the schedule of benefits must be sharply progressive—that is, it must penalize scale in each supported commodity. Some limited progress has been made by setting payment ceilings, which are usually a maximum of $50,000 per farm. But such a high payment ceiling reduces payments for only the very largest of farms; it usually does not hurt the financial position of most larger-than-family farms. Still, groups such as the American Farm Bureau Federation and major commodity organizations will dependably direct their great political clout against penalties to large-scale farmers in commodity programs.

The difficulties of the agricultural land reform movement's predominant strategies imply that the movement faces a crisis of theory and strategy. The crisis springs from outdated assumptions about the dynamics of agriculture and from a near-religious adherence to stereotyped arguments about agricultural transformation — for instance, that corporate farm operations and the land-grant colleges have been largely responsible for the demise of the small family farmer. I would like to offer several suggestions for a revision of the movement's theory and practice.

RESOLVING THE DILEMMAS OF AGRICULTURAL LAND REFORM

The future struggle for agricultural land reform must take into account some dramatic new realities of the late 1970s and early 1980s which the recent outpouring of "neopopulism" (de Janvry, 1980) cannot address. Hightower, who best summarizes the current agenda of the movement, notes in closing that

> these are just a few of the elements of a program that would help us to restore the family farm to a position of national resource. There is nothing radical or even new about them. They require no major wrenching of the existing economic order. If we want to have family farms, even small family farms, we can have them. It is not that we lack solutions, but that we have lacked the will. (Hightower, 1975:249)

One must disagree. The options now available for agricultural land reform are much different from those available before World War II. The great exodus of people from the farm is now largely complete; the victims are firmly rooted in nonfarm sectors outside the arena of agricultural politics. Medium-sized family farmers, the historic bulwark of Progressive agrarian protest (Rogin, 1966), are a distinct minority. Large-scale, nonfamily forms of agriculture are entrenched and in a superior position to increase their dominance. While downward redistributions of agricultural property have occurred in the past, they have usually taken place because of massive changes in world markets or agricultural technology rather than as a result of political action (Friedland, 1981). The Eden of independent family farming in reality features long hours of work, income instability, exploitation of women and children, and occupational hazards on the family farm.

Hightower's argument is a historical half-truth, an invitation to cling to imagined past utopias. The family farm in advanced capitalism, even in a politically supportive setting, faces serious problems. We must therefore consider alternatives to large-scale, nonfamily production which do not depend on returning to small farms. Agriculture can be democratized through public control over agriculture instead of by dispersal of farm ownership and operation. The three dominant priorities for agricultural land reform in the present decade should be undoing the biases in the tax system, public intervention in the rural land market, and improvement in the conditions of agricultural labor.

Reversing Tax Biases toward Concentration in Agriculture

Taxation is of necessity a major plank in any land reform agenda. According to USDA economist Thomas A. Miller,

> by giving advantages to high-income farmland buyers, such [federal and state tax] laws have created incentives for farmers to shift their attention from efficiency and productivity to farm expansion, agglomeration, and appreciation of land value. A progressive tax on farm real estate, a shift to accrual accounting, a limit on the deductibility of interest on borrowed funds, a repeal of the investment tax credit, and tough inheritance laws would all have the opposite effect. These proposals, along with strict commodity program payment limits, are opposed by family farmers and larger farmers alike. (Miller, 1979:113)

Miller argues that farm expansion does not increase efficiency and that it may lead to excessive capital-intensity, debt, overvaluing of asset values, and the formation of a "landed aristocracy" (Miller, 1979:114; see also U.S. Department of Agriculture, 1981, chapters 6 and 8). Existing tax policies tend to benefit agriculture in relation to other sectors at the same time that they benefit some farmers more than others.

Miller's observations suggest a more general dilemma: the structural policies necessary for land reform tend to be opposed not only by large nonfamily farmers, but also by small and family farmers — the policies' intended beneficiaries. Should the agricultural land reform movement pursue measures largely opposed by those who are to be helped? The long-term impacts of government policies that harm small and family farmers are not well understood by the victims, and the land reform movement has an obligation to make the general and agricultural publics aware of the harm. At the same time, farmers — small or large, family or nonfamily — are property owners, a status that will make them resist initiatives to curb property prerogatives. The agricultural land reform movement should not simply be aimed at small and family farmers, nor should it ignore their economic commitments.

Public and Quasi-Public Intervention in the Rural Land Market

The United States is one of the few advanced industrial societies with little public regulation of the rural land market. Other countries, more prompt in recognizing some of the land market's undesirable tendencies, have begun significant programs to intervene in land transactions. Sweden and France, for instance, have instituted policies where local public bodies — Swedish county agricultural boards and French nonprofit companies — can disapprove land transactions, preempt them by purchasing land at the price which the original buyer offered the seller, and rent and sell lands. In Sweden the powers have been used to prevent nonfarm individuals and corporations and foreign concerns from purchasing farmland. In France the emphasis has been on consolidating fragmented farms—disapproving a sale if the land would not become part of an economic-sized unit—and on making lease arrangements to help people entering agriculture. Both countries have tried to control land speculation and inflation and so support family farming. The goals have generally been achieved (Raup, 1978b:6).

Public intervention on the scale attempted by Sweden and France is unlikely in the United States. Sweden and France had large farm populations and little nonfamily farming when land speculation began driving up land prices; thus farmers tolerated public regulation of the land market to protect their interests. But there are American possibilities for public or quasi-public intervention. One useful example is the 1976 Minnesota Farm Security Act (Laws of Minnesota, 1976, Chapter 210). The legislation, focused on a subsidized loan program, created a seven-member advisory council to screen applicants for farmland purchases. It gives preference to entering farmers and to those seeking intergenerational transfers of farm property.

A more localized intervention institution is the community land trust (CLT), discussed at length elsewhere in this volume. CLTs are generally organized as nonprofit corporations governed by boards of trustees elected from lease holders of trust-owned lands and from the community at large. CLTs basically function through the purchase of land and the retention of development and transfer rights to land. The CLT leases land to farmers and other users on a long-term, secure basis—usually a lifetime or 99-year renewable lease that can be transferred to heirs if they wish to continue use of the land. Users typically retain partial ownership rights—for instance, ownership of buildings and equity in farm improvements. But the underlying rationale is to remove land from the speculative market and introduce community concerns into the use of land. Most agricultural CLTs tend to place high priority on broadening access to land through, for example, giving leasing preference to entering farmers.

Agricultural Labor

American agriculture depends increasingly on wage labor, and the large farms that primarily use wage labor have many advantages over small and family farms—financial and technological economies of scale, disproportionate benefits from public tax and commodity policies, a favorable position in the land market. But even the most vocal academic advocates of nonfamily farming, such as Knutson et al. (1980:121), recognize that the "greatest threat to such [nonfamily] advantages could be unionization of labor employed by such integrated systems." Others have come to a similar conclusion based on quite different political and economic premises (see, for example, LeVeen, 1978). The "efficiency"—even the very persistence—of nonfamily farming depends on cheap wage labor.

There are two distinct agricultural labor markets. One is the market in migratory or temporary labor, from which large-scale industrial farms recruit most of their workers. Many migratory and temporary workers are from minority groups; they face problems because of tenuous citizenship status and because growers can use labor surpluses to depress wage rates (Thomas-Lycklama à Nijeholt, 1980). The other market is for permanent or full-time hired laborers, most of whom are nonminorities and work for larger-than-family farmers. This group has better wage rates and job security, but both groups are worse off than urban workers.

The differences between the two segments of the agricultural labor market have important implications for the land reform movement's organizing strategy in each. In the migratory minority segment, there is a high level of interaction among workers with a similar status, as well as tremendous insecurity because growers can easily replace them with workers with comparable qualifications. Labor union organizing may be the strategy by which land reformers can help this group. Full-time agricultural workers, on the other hand, are a dispersed proletariat with a small number of workers — perhaps two to five — on each farm. These full-time agricultural laborers are mostly employed on larger-than-family farms. The relative isolation of full-time workers and their closer working relationships with their employers make union organizing difficult. Thus organizing at the state level to enact minimum wage and benefit levels will tend to be more effective.

LeVeen (1978) has argued that family farmers are at a disadvantage compared to nonfamily farmers because the latter can be assured of an abundant supply of cheap agricultural wage labor. However, this advantage will be of little consequence if the agricultural labor force unionizes, if it can control the flood of labor competition through legal and illegal immigration, and if it achieves improvement in wages and working conditions (Thomas-Lycklama à Nijeholt, 1980).

If significant improvements in the position of hired agricultural laborers occur, they could undermine large-scale farming, leading to a substantial liquidation of these assets. Yet improvements in agricultural labor conditions would not necessarily result in a deconcentration of agricultural property. The equipment, buildings, and other infrastructure for a 3,000-acre Midwestern corn-soybean farm cannot readily be divided into the infrastructure for ten 300-acre family farms. Moreover, some efficiencies, especially in the use of machinery, may be lost in a widespread return to family-sized or smaller farms. There is a need to develop socially equitable and economically efficient alernatives to both the large nonfamily farm and the small family farm.

One promising alternative is large-scale group or cooperative farms that combine the scale advantages of nonfamily farms, the household or familial advantages of family farms, and other benefits — for instance, a division of labor among families unique to multifamily cooperative farming. Multifamily cooperative farms in Saskatchewan that operate under formulas for pooling of land and capital resources show better economic efficiency, especially in the use of machinery, and more enterprise diversification than do neighboring family farms. The machinery efficiencies and the ability of group farms to diversify into livestock production also appear to create conditions for improved natural resource management (Gertler et al., 1981; Gertler and Buttel, 1981). Group or cooperative farming may be attractive to family farmers who want to reduce their costs without incurring massive debts, and to larger-than-family farmers who wish to retain the economic advantages of scale without having to hire large numbers of agricultural wage laborers. The agricultural land reform movement could help increase farmers' and public knowledge of alternative organizational forms such as group farming.

CONCLUSION

Agricultural land reform is needed, and the family farm will play a part in it. Yet there are numerous political and economic constraints to the pursuit of a family farm renaissance in the United States. Efforts at agricultural land reform should not be discontinued. The small family farm should be preserved. But we need a more forward-looking set of strategies cleansed of nostalgia for imagined past utopias. We must recognize the new constraints and opportunities for agricultural development in the 1980s.

To that end, a strong case can be made for paying greater attention to tax policy and to two often-ignored land reform strategies: public regulation of the land market and improvement in the wage and working conditions of agricultural wage laborers. These strategies have been ignored in the past, probably because they only indirectly support family farming. Yet new evidence suggests that the process of rural land markets and the means of recruiting and paying hired agricultural laborers are two of the principal causes of the demise of household forms of production in agriculture. Failure to deal with these issues will render ineffective most of the present efforts of the agricultural land reform movement.

The traditional independent family farm is an attractive social institution, particularly in its democratization of access to land and in its contributions to the economic and social vitality of rural communities. But family farming, where it has been transformed and transcended, may not be a feasible direction for reform efforts. Family farming should be protected and encouraged where it is still the dominant institution of agricultural production. Yet the traditional independent family farm should not be viewed as the only — or even always the most desirable — response to the concentration of agricultural property and the demise of rural communities.

REFERENCES

Barry, P. J., and Baker, C. B. 1977. "Management of firm level financial structure." *Agricultural Finance Review* 37 (February): 50–63.
Belden, Joe, Edwards, Gibby, Guyer, Cynthia, and Webb, Lee. 1979. *New Directions in Farm, Land, and Food Policies.* Washington, DC: Conference on Alternative State and Local Policies.

Berry, R. Albert, and Cline, William R. 1979. *Agrarian Structure and Productivity in Developing Countries.* Baltimore: Johns Hopkins University Press.

Buttel, Frederick H. 1981. *American Agriculture and Rural America: Challenges for Progressive Politics.* Ithaca, NY: Cornell Rural Sociology Bulletin No. 120, March.

Cochrane, Willard W. 1979. *The Development of American Agriculture.* Minneapolis: University of Minnesota Press.

Coughenour, C. Milton, and Wimberley, Ronald C. 1982. "Small and part-time farmers." In *Rural Society: Issues for the 1980s.* Edited by D. A. Dillman and D. J. Hobbs. Boulder, CO: Westview Press.

Crouch, Luis, and de Janvry, Alain. 1979. *The Class Basis of Agricultural Growth.* Working Paper No. 70, Department of Agricultural and Resource Economics, University of California, Berkeley.

de Janvry, Alain. 1980. "Social differentiation in agriculture and the ideology of neopopulism." In *The Rural Sociology of the Advanced Societies.* Edited by F. H. Buttel and H. Newby. Montclair, NJ: Allanheld, Osmun. Pp. 155–68.

Dorner, Peter. 1972. *Land Reform and Economic Development.* Baltimore: Penguin.

ESCOP (Experiment Station Committee on Organization and Policy). 1981. *Research and the Family Farm.* Ithaca, NY: Cornell University.

Friedland, William H. 1981. "Prospects for a sociology of agriculture." Paper presented at the annual meeting of the American Sociological Association, Toronto, August.

Friedland, William H., Furnari, Mona, and Pugliese, Enrico. 1980. "The labor process and agriculture." Paper presented at the Working Conference on the Labor Process, University of California, Santa Cruz, March.

Fujimoto, Isao. 1977. "The communities of the San Joaquin Valley: the interrelations among farming, water use, and quality of life." Unpublished paper, Department of Applied Behavioral Sciences, University of California, Davis.

George, Susan. 1977. *How the Other Half Dies.* Montclair, NJ: Allanheld, Osmun.

Gertler, Michael E., and Buttel, Frederick H. 1981. "Property, community, and resource management: exploring the prospects for group farming in North America." Paper presented at the annual meeting of the Rural Sociological Society, University of Guelph, August.

Gertler, Michael E., MacKenzie, A. F., and Buttel, Frederick H. 1981. "Resource management implications of group farming in Saskatchewan." Paper presented at the annual meeting of the American Association for the Advancement of Science, Toronto, January.

Goldschmidt, Walter. 1978. *As You Sow.* Montclair, NJ: Allanheld, Osmun.

Griffin, Keith. 1974. *The Political Economy of Agrarian Change.* Cambridge, MA: Harvard University Press.

———. 1978. *International Inequality and National Poverty.* New York: Holmes & Meier.

Guither, Harold. 1980. *The Food Lobbyists.* Lexington, MA: D.C. Heath.

Heffernan, William D., and Green, Gary. 1980. "Part-time farming and the rural community." Paper presented at the annual meeting of the Rural Sociological Society, Ithaca, New York, August.

Hightower, Jim. 1973. *Hard Tomatoes, Hard Times.* Cambridge, MA: Schenkman.

———. 1975. *Eat Your Heart Out.* New York: Crown.

Hill, Frances. 1980. "Rural development and reindustrialization." Paper presented at the Farm Structure and Rural Policy Symposium, Iowa State University, October.

Holland, David. 1980. "Production efficiency and economies of size in agriculture." Part 4. In *Production Efficiency and Technology for Small Farms.* Edited by J. P. Madden et al. Washington, DC: National Rural Center. Pp. 1–39.

Hottel, Bruce, and Harrington, David H. 1979. "Tenure and equity influences on the incomes of farmers." In Economics, Statistics, and Cooperative Service, *Structure Issues of American Agriculture.* Washington, DC: U.S. Department of Agriculture. Pp. 97–107.

Knutson, Ronald D., Smith, Ed, Richardson, James W., and Shirley, Christina. 1980. "Maximizing efficiency in agriculture." In *Increasing Understanding of Public Problems and Policies—1980.* Oak Brook, IL: Farm Foundation. Pp. 115–22.

LeVeen, E. Phillip. 1978. "The prospects for small-scale farming in an industrial society: a critical appraisal of *Small Is Beautiful.*" In *Appropriate Visions.* Edited by R. C. Dorf and Y. L. Hunter. San Francisco: Boyd and Fraser. Pp. 106–25.

Madden, J. Patrick, and Partenheimer, Earl J. 1972. "Evidence of economies and diseconomies of farm size." In *Size, Structure, and Future of Farms*. Edited by A. G. Ball and E. O. Heady. Ames: Iowa State University Press. Pp. 91–107.

Madden, J. Patrick, and Baker, Heather Tischbein. 1981. *An Agenda for Small Farms Research*. Washington, DC: National Rural Center.

Miller, Thomas A. 1979. "Economies of size and other growth incentives." In Economics, Statistics, and Cooperative Service, *Structure Issues of American Agriculture*. Washington, DC: U.S. Department of Agriculture. Pp. 108–15.

Paarlberg, Don. 1980. *Farm and Food Policy*. Lincoln: University of Nebraska Press.

Pearse, Andrew. 1980. *Seeds of Plenty, Seeds of Want*. New York: Oxford University Press.

Raup, Philip, M. 1978a. "Some questions of value and scale in agriculture." *American Journal of Agricultural Economics* 60 (December): 303–8.

———. 1978b. "Recent trends in structural policies for agriculture in selected developed countries." In *Will the Family Farm Survive?* Columbia: Agricultural Experiment Station, University of Missouri. Pp. 64–71.

———. 1980. "Competition for land and the future of American agriculture." In *The Future of American Agriculture as a Strategic Resource*. Edited by S. S. Batie and R. G. Healy. Washington, DC: Conservation Foundation. Pp. 41–77.

Reimund, Donn. 1979. "Forms of business organization." In Economics, Statistics, and Cooperative Service, *Structure Issues of American Agriculture*. Washington, DC: U.S. Department of Agriculture. Pp. 128–33.

Roberts, Neal A., and Brown, H. James (eds.). 1980. *Property Tax Preferences for Agricultural Land*. Montclair, NJ: Allanheld, Osmun.

Robinson, Kenneth L. 1980. "The structure of agricultural production in North America: some alternatives for the future." Unpublished manuscript, Department of Agricultural Economics, Cornell University, Ithaca, NY.

Rodefeld, Richard D. 1978. "Trends in U.S. farm organizational structure and type." In *Change in Rural America*. Edited by R. D. Rodefeld et al. St. Louis: C. V. Mosby. Pp. 158–77.

———. 1979. "Selected farm structural type characteristics: recent trends, causes, implications, and research needs." Paper presented at the Phase II Conference of the National Rural Center Small Farm Project, University of Nebraska, Lincoln.

———. 1980. "Farm structural characteristics: recent trends, causes, implications and research needs—excerpts." Part III. In *Structure of Agriculture and Information Needs Regarding Small Farms*. Edited by Luther Tweeten et al. Washington, DC: National Rural Center. Pp. 1–80.

Rogin, Michael Paul. 1966. *The Intellectuals and McCarthy*. Cambridge, MA: MIT Press.

Sonka, Steven T. 1980. "Consequences of farm structural change." Part II. In *Structure of Agriculture and Information Needs Regarding Small Farms*. Edited by Luther Tweeten et al. Washington, DC: National Rural Center. Pp. 1–32.

Summers, Gene F. et al. 1976. *Industrial Invasion of Nonmetropolitan America*. New York: Praeger.

Thomas-Lycklama à Nijeholt, G. 1980. *On the Road for Work*. Boston: Martinus Nijhoff Publishing.

U.S. Department of Agriculture. 1976. *Fact Book of U.S. Agriculture*. Miscellaneous Publication No. 1063. Washington, DC: Office of Communication, U.S.D.A.

———. 1981. *A Time to Choose*. Washington, DC: U.S.D.A.

U.S. Department of Commerce, Bureau of the Census. 1980. *1978 Census of Agriculture — Preliminary Report*. Washington, DC: U.S. Government Printing Office.

Vogeler, Ingolf. 1981. *The Myth of the Family Farm*. Boulder, CO: Westview Press.

5

Land Reform and the Church

JOHN HART

Along rural roadways, within country communities, church steeples stand silent. Their bells no longer toll to call people to worship. Their paint peels in the sun. Their graying walls imitate the abandoned farmhouses deteriorating nearby. No longer does the sound of people singing surge through the windows or the sound of children laughing leap out open doors. The windows are shattered, the doors bang erratically on rusty hinges, the people are gone.

The scene is an all-too-familiar one for travelers in rural America. They note, perhaps with some sorrow if they have roots in the land, the result of a sixty-year exodus of farmers from the land. In 1919, 6.5 million farm families fed the nation. By 1979, only 2.7 million were left (USDA, 1979). For every six families that left, a rural business closed. Government officials congratulated themselves that far fewer people were needed now to feed a larger population, but landholdings increased in size and passed into fewer hands. Plantings from fencepost to fencepost erased soil-conserving terraces and wind shelterbelts. Toxic chemicals were dumped on the land. Consumption of energy and water resources greatly increased. Rural families joined food stamp, welfare, and unemployment lines in the cities, or else displaced urban workers onto the lines.

Such scenes have attracted the attention and aroused the concern of church leaders across the country. During the past few years a number of statements about issues of landownership and land use have emerged from mainline Christian denominations. In particular, Catholic bishops — as individuals and in regional bodies — have strongly addressed questions of land consolidation and abuse. Their pronouncements have at times put them at odds with the prevailing free-enterprise ideology, and to some extent represent a new church understanding of land questions and of the church's role as moral leader in society. At the same time, what the bishops express is an echo of progressive voices from the American ethical tradition and also a reaffirmation of the church's own moral teachings from ages past.

PERSPECTIVES ON THE LAND

The way church members — clergy and laity — have viewed the land has influenced the way they have distributed it and its fruits and the way they
have treated it. Three distinct, often contradictory, perspectives have
dominated church discussion and practices regarding land. Land has been
seen as *matter,* as *gift,* and as *trust.*[1]

To appreciate these differing views, take a walk through a city park, or
recall a walk you once took. Observe the trees that shade you from the
summer sun or shield you from the winter wind. If the park has a mature
walnut tree, reflect on it; if there is no walnut tree, imagine one stretching
upward before you. The way you look upon the tree measures the way you
look upon land as a whole. The tree is laden with nuts. The tree took some
forty years to reach its present height and fruitfulness. How do you see the
tree? How do you think others view it?

The owner of a strip mine or lumber company might see a walnut tree as
a bothersome weed on his property. For the former, it is merely overburden, something that must be removed to carve out the coal; for the latter,
it is a plant that grows too slowly for commercial profit and so must be
sprayed with herbicide or cut down to make room for faster-growing, more
profitable pine trees. For both, the tree occupies space that should have
more lucrative use.

A farmer with a stand of trees, or a carpenter, would see the walnut tree
as a resource. The farmer, especially one living on a family homestead,
might harvest the walnuts for food or harvest the mature tree for its value
as hardwood lumber, replanting so as to provide a new tree for succeeding
generations. The carpenter would see the tree as fine wood for cabinets
and furniture. In both cases, unlike the previous two, the tree helps provide a livelihood for people. It has commercial value in itself; it is not
merely an object to be removed to get at something else of value. The tree
has value both as a product and a resource. The tree is occupying space
profitably.

The owner of an orchard of nut-bearing trees or a traditional American
Indian would see the walnut tree in yet another way — as a living being, a
coinhabitant of the land, a member of the earth community. For the
orchard owner, it is valued for its nuts and wood, as was true for the
farmer and carpenter, but it is also recognized as a life form that begins as
a seed, grows, matures, and eventually dies. The orchard owner, like the
farmer cultivating crops or nursing a sick calf back to health, develops a
symbiotic relationship with each tree. He comes to know its individual
needs and responds to them with food, water, and medication. He comes
to know what its species needs to survive, and so makes new plantings. He
receives in turn nutmeats and lumber that provide a livelihood.

Similarly, the traditional American Indian sees the tree not only as a
provider of food and shelter, but also as a cocreature whose life is not to be
taken. The Indian would not cut down a living tree, but would use it for
firewood or shelter only after it died. Both the orchard owner and the

American Indian regard the walnut tree as a provider of life, as a living being to respect.

These diverse perspectives show different understandings of the earth and of people's relationship with it. For the owner of a strip mine or lumber company, land is seen primarily as *matter*. The land and whatever is on or under it is to be exploited, either by individuals seeking their personal profit or by a country pursuing its national interest. The land is an owned object serving whoever holds civil title to it. This is fundamentally an antisocial perspective, since it denies the community aspect of landownership and the social character of humanity.

For the farmer or carpenter, land is seen primarily as a *gift*. It is to be developed by the person who has received it, to benefit that individual, his or her family, and perhaps some other people. More so than the exploiter, the person who sees the land as a gift feels responsible for it and tries to conserve it for the livelihood it provides or as a potential legacy for his children. This perspective is fundamentally asocial: the social value of the land is acknowledged, but the landholder's primary concern is for the immediate human family, not the entire one.

For the orchard owner or Indian, land is understood to be primarily a *trust*. It is to be cared for, both because it has value in itself and because it is the nurturing environment for all life. Those who see the land as a trust realize that its well-being, as well as that of all whose life is sustained by it, depends on how its trustees care for it. This is a social perspective: its adherents recognize the primacy of the entire earth community, but also see themselves as part of that community.

Most people who own or use land do not fit exactly into one of these perspectives. There are some who greedily despoil the land, others who selflessly conserve it. Most people shift back and forth depending on their consciousness of the effects of their practices, and on their individual or family circumstances. Most churches have taught that the land is a gift from God, but they nonetheless have accepted as members those who exploit it. Many church members, whether exploiters or not, use the earth to benefit themselves or their families, justifying their actions by the mandate God gives to humanity in the creation story in Genesis: "have dominion over the earth."

In his well-known essay, "The Historical Roots of Our Ecologic Crisis," Lynn White, Jr., criticizes the Christian churches for accepting this interpretation of "dominion." White argues against the church's teaching of human primacy:

> man named all the animals, thus establishing his dominance over them. God planned all of this explicitly for man's benefit and rule; no item in the physical creation had any purpose save to serve man's purposes. And, although man's body is made of clay, he is not simply part of nature: he is made in God's image. . . . Christianity, in absolute contrast to ancient paganism . . . not only established a dualism of man and nature but also insisted that it is God's will that man exploit nature for his proper ends.[2]

White declares that science alone will not be able to promote ecological consciousness and practices: " . . . we shall continue to have a worsening ecologic crisis until we reject the Christian axiom that nature has no reason for existence save to serve man."[3]

Precisely as a result of the practices of those who misunderstand and misuse the teachings of Genesis and Christianity, church leaders and their members have recently begun to examine landownership and land use from the historically rooted ethical perspective that the land is God's and people are God's stewards of it. Although the teaching of stewardship has come from several Christian denominations, we shall focus on the Catholic church.

PAPAL PERSPECTIVES

Statements of the American Catholic church emerge from a global Catholic context, particularly the pronouncements and actions of the Pope. In the twentieth century, papal pronouncements on issues of social justice in general and of land justice in particular have questioned existing property relationships and proposed alternatives. The recent vocal papal concern for social justice stems from the encyclical *Rerum Novarum,* issued by Leo XIII in 1891, which focused on the wages and working conditions of industrial workers and asked whether it was just that individuals who used the land could not own it. The theme of the right of people to property was soon fused with that of the responsibility of people who had property. The church directly addressed itself to the issue of dominion over the land, proposing that its real meaning was stewardship rather than domination.

In 1937, for example, in his encyclical *Divini Redemptoris,* Pius XI declared that the rich should see themselves only as stewards of their earthly goods. Four years later Pius XII stated in a radio broadcast commemorating the fiftieth anniversary of *Rerum Novarum* that people have a natural right to make use of the material goods of the earth. The message was that the land is a gift for people to use, not an exclusive gift to the few who happen to be property owners.

John XXIII discussed land issues, particularly agriculture, in his 1961 encyclical *Mater et Magistra,* issued to commemorate the seventieth anniversary of *Rerum Novarum.* He urged farmers to form cooperatives and associations, and proposed as the ideal that families should own and manage their own farms. He condemned low wages for farmworkers. He declared that "in the right of private property there is rooted a social responsibility," because for God the Creator "the over-all supply of goods is assigned, first of all, that all may lead a decent life."[4] This statement denies that whoever holds civil title to property has the right to use it as he or she wills. Priority must go to humanity's needs.

Paul VI in 1967 issued *Populorum Progressio,* which states that everyone has "the right to find in the world what is necessary for himself." It follows that private property is not an "unconditioned right," and so one cannot keep something unnecessary "when others lack necessities." Then, in a dramatic and forceful new step for popes, Paul VI declared that the state could use expropriation to help the landless poor:

> If certain landed estates impede the general prosperity because they are extensive, unused or poorly used, or because they bring hardships to peoples or are detrimental to the interests of the country, the common good sometimes demands their expropriation.[5]

Going beyond the advocacy of individual ownership on a wide-spread basis, Paul VI suggested a practical political way to achieve it. Then, in his 1971 *Octogesima Adveniens,* Paul VI deplored the "ill-considered exploitation of nature,"[6] seeing land as a trust rather than a gift. For if the land is to be expropriated and redistributed, then it must be entrusted to a broader constituency than those who hold temporary civil title to it. Moreover, if it is not to be exploited, the responsibility of ownership is to care for it in trust.

John Paul II has addressed land issues more than any of his predecessors, frequently visiting rural areas and stressing the justice of widespread land distribution and responsible land use. To the Indians of Oaxaca, Mexico, he declared:

> There is always a social mortgage on all private property, in order that goods may serve the general purpose that God gave them. And if the common good requires it, there must be no hesitation even at expropriation carried out in the due form.[7]

John Paul added that it was unjust and unchristian when "powerful classes . . . keep unproductive lands that hide the bread that so many families lack."[8]

In Des Moines, Iowa, he stated that the land is God's gift and people's responsibility:

> The land must be conserved with care since it is intended to be fruitful for generation upon generation. . . . You are stewards of some of the most important resources God has given to the world. Therefore, conserve the land well, so that your children's children and generations after them will inherit an even richer land than was entrusted to you.[9]

In Zaire, he urged Christians to "seek more just structures in the land area" and "consider themselves managers of God's creation, which cannot be wasted or ravaged at will, for it is entrusted to men for the good of all."[10] In Recife, Brazil, he proclaimed that "the land is a gift of God, a gift that he makes to all human beings, men and women," and so it is unlawful "to use this gift in such a way that its benefits are to the advantage of only a few, while the others, the vast majority, are excluded." He advocated "the indispensable transformation of the structures of economic life" and "the environment desired for all forms of life: the life of plants, the life of animals, and above all, the life of men."[11]

John Paul sometimes shifts back and forth between the perspectives of land as gift and land as trust, but he always advocates more widespread distribution of land and careful stewardship of its resources. To some extent, then, he responds to Lynn White's criticism, for he states that the land must not be despoiled by individual property owners, since it is ultimately owned by the entire human family. Thus it must be passed on as an "even richer land."

U.S. CATHOLIC PERSPECTIVES

Catholic church pronouncements and practices that focus on issues of land justice within the United States spring from the long Christian social-ethic tradition of concern for the poor—a concern sometimes more voiced than acted. The church's contemporary involvement flows not only from papal pronouncements, but also from the biblical base of such admonitions of Jesus as "I was hungry and you gave me food, thirsty and you gave me drink, naked and you clothed me, shelterless and you took me in. . . . As often as you did this for the least of my brethren, you did it for me" (Matthew 25:31–46).

There is also the theological base provided by statements such as those of St. Thomas Aquinas, still the dominant voice in most mainline Catholic theology. For Aquinas, God gives the use of created things to humanity, for "the imperfect is always made for the perfect." However, although "man" might use things, "a man" who uses them "ought to possess external things, not as his own, but as common, so that, to wit, he is ready to communicate them to others in their need."[12]

Aquinas makes a distinction between the "natural law" implanted by God and the "positive law" devised by humanity. Because "community of goods is ascribed to the natural law," then "the division of possessions is not according to the natural law, but rather arose from human agreement which belongs to positive law."[13] Since the natural law dictates community of possessions, people are to try to alleviate others' needs. And those who are in dire need are permitted to take from another's abundance what they need for their own or their neighbor's survival:

> In cases of need all things are common property, so that there would seem to be no sin in taking another's property, for need has made it common. . . . Whatever certain people have in superabundance is due, by natural law, to the purpose of succoring the poor. It is not theft, properly speaking, to take secretly and use another's property in extreme need. . . and in a case of like need a man may also take secretly another's property in order to succor his neighbor in need.[14]

Aquinas's perspective underlies the thinking of the Catholic church worldwide as well as in the United States. The perspective both corroborates and refutes Lynn White's analysis of Christian land relations:

humanity is placed over the rest of creation, but the land is given to the whole human family, of every generation. So neither individual, corporate, or national exploitation can be permitted, since they would deplete the legacy of all people for the sake of a few. What seems to have happened, however, is that in actual practice people have either ignored the theological thrust entirely or paid attention to only that part of it which places humanity on top of a hierarchical world order.

To prevent this exploitation, members of the U.S. Catholic church have become involved in land issues. As part of a global church with a two-thousand-year heritage, they represent a long-standing moral tradition. As citizens of a nation with a two-hundred-year history, they also voice ideas about land justice that date back to the American Revolution.

The founders of the United States wanted to avoid a land tenure system in which a few large landholders would own much of the land and hence have great economic and political power. For instance, the first direct tax imposed by the new government was a graduated tax on urban land. Thomas Paine proposed a progressive tax on estates and declared that the earth in its original, natural state was "the common property of the human race."[15] Thomas Jefferson believed that the earth was given as the "common stock" for people to "labor and live on."[16] He called small landholders "the most precious part of the state," and urged that their well-being be promoted and their number increased by such means as a graduated or progressive land tax "to exempt all from taxation below a certain point and to tax the higher portions of property in geometrical progression as they rise" (letter to Rev. James Madison, 1795).[17] In later years, the ideal of a nation of small landholders was promoted by such legislation as the early nineteenth-century Pre-Emption Acts, the 1862 Homestead Act, and the 1902 Reclamation Act.

It was on such civil and religious foundations that groups such as the rural-based National Catholic Rural Life Conference and the urban-based Catholic Worker movement built their programs of land justice. In existence since 1923, the NCRLC has spoken forcefully for land justice. Its 1939 *Manifesto on Rural Life,* for example, called the earth "the heritage of all mankind," so that individual owners are "only exercising a stewardship" given by God. What must be avoided is "the extreme of individualism with its doctrine of absolute ownership and unlimited use." Additionally, "an economic system to be equitable must provide opportunity for the masses to become owners."[18]

Since its founding in 1933, the Catholic Worker has advocated land justice, but with a slightly different focus. Its program of "cult, culture, and cultivation" calls for "agronomic universities"—farming communes where Catholic laborers and scholars would work the land together and devise programs of social justice. For the Catholic Worker, the ideal is communal ownership of and communal work upon the land, as distinct from individual proprietorship. But for both organizations, the basic principle is that the land is to benefit the whole human family, not just a few property owners.

During the past ten years, the leadership of the American Catholic church has taken a different approach to land justice. The bishops of two regions have issued major statements: *The Land Is Home to Me — A Pastoral Letter on Powerlessness in Appalachia* (1975), and *Strangers and Guests: Toward Community in the Heartland* (1980).

THIS LAND IS HOME TO ME

The Appalachian bishops' statement consists of an analysis of the causes of the land problems of Appalachia, a vision of a better future, and suggestions for its attainment.[19]

The bishops state that they are responding to "the cries of powerlessness from the region called Appalachia," especially the struggles of the poor in hollows, industrial centers, and farmlands, as well as to the central, often destructive role that coal plays in the region. Coal miners and their families suffer from poor wages and dangerous working conditions. They and others also suffer when mining shuts down and they must migrate to the cities where "the people had to fight one another for the few jobs." The statement links regional exploitation with national affluence and international conflict, and calls the maximization of profit "a principle which too often converts itself into an idolatrous power." The earth's resources and human dignity are both depleted by that power: "profit and people frequently are contradictory" because, in Jesus' words, "No one can be the slave of two masters. . . . You cannot be the slave both of God and money" (Matthew 6:24). Because "a country which took such richness from Appalachia left so little for the people" and because "great fortunes were built on the exploitation of Appalachian workers and Appalachian resources," the people of Appalachia must struggle together — for example, through "a strong and broad labor movement." "Economics is made by people," and so people can change it.[20]

The bishops further state that "the goal which underlies our concern is fundamental to the justice struggle, namely, citizen control, or community control. . . . the people themselves must shape their own destiny." The bishops warn of "the presence of powerful multinational corporations" and suggest that "as a counterforce to the unaccountable power of these multinational corporations, there must arise a corresponding multinational labor movement, rooted in a vision of justice" having a global orientation. The bishops close with a challenge to the people "to be a part of the rebirth of utopias, to recover and defend the struggling dream of Appalachia itself," a dream of "simplicity and justice."[21]

The statement represented a significant departure for the American Catholic hierarchy. Rather than simply proclaiming unspecific social principles, it used examples directly pertinent to regional circumstances to promote Catholic social teachings. Its impact is still being felt in

Appalachia as its theory takes concrete form in church-supported movements for justice. The church as laity is practicing what the church as hierarchy proposed.*

STRANGERS AND GUESTS

Influenced by the Appalachian statement, a group of South Dakota farmers began a discussion among Midwestern bishops that eventually resulted in *Strangers and Guests.* It is similar to *This Land Is Home to Me,* but has a more developed theology of the land. Its title is taken from Leviticus 25:23, where God tells the Jewish people, "Land must not be sold in perpetuity, for the land belongs to me and to me you are only strangers and guests."

The document begins with a prologue expressing the bishops' concern about events in the heartland: "We are witnessing profound and disturbing changes in rural America."[22] These are the alterations in the ways in which the land is being consolidated, abused, and no longer stewarded. As the land suffers, so do those who depend on it: family farmers, farmworkers, Native Americans, and the world's hungry.

The first major section, "The Tenure of the Land," describes the ethnic, cultural, and social transformations. The land was inhabited first by indigenous nomads who "shared an attitude of respect for the earth and for all the natural world," who had "a sense of harmony with nature and a sense of gratitude to the Spirit who provided for their needs through the bounty of the earth and other living creatures." But these Native Americans were forced from the land and confined to reservations, and then "property boundaries marked off land previously regarded as belonging to all and therefore to none."[23] Family farmers and ranchers came to occupy the land—but they soon found that powerful speculators could subvert the laws. The land and people suffered as profit-oriented interests acquired and abused large holdings of land. Yet the Midwestern family farm, characterized by individual owner-operators living on the land and doing most of the labor, was able to establish itself.[24]

In recent years, however, family farmers have faced a cost-price squeeze: the prices of their land, machinery, seed, livestock, fertilizer, and other inputs—prices not set by farmers—keep rising. But the prices farmers receive for agricultural products—prices again not set by them— decline, hold steady, or rise only slightly. The result is that farmers lose ground economically and eventually are forced out of business and off the land. *Strangers and Guests* does not focus exclusively on agriculture. The bishops also deplore harmful forestry and mining practices, industrial pollution, poor wages and working conditions, and unjust treatment of American Indians.

---

*See the articles on Appalachia by John Gaventa and Bill Horton, and by David Liden elsewhere in this book.

The second part of *Strangers and Guests,* "Stewardship of the Land," proposes a theological/ethical approach to land issues. With the Bible as base, ten "Principles of Land Stewardship" are suggested:

1. *The land is God's.* This is the primary principle, the one from which all the others flow. Because "God created the earth, those living on it and the resources it provides," we who as nations or individuals temporarily control part of the earth must acknowledge that "to God's ultimate dominion all of these are subject," that "the Lord's are the earth and its fullness, the world and those who dwell in it" (Psalm 24:1).[25]

2. *People are God's stewards on the land.* God as Creator wills that people be cocreators of a world continually being created. The biblical story of Adam, placed in the Garden of Eden "to cultivate and care for it" (Genesis 2:15), symbolizes humanity's receiving responsibility for stewardship of the earth. People should be custodians, conservers of the land who exercise human dominion over particular places in particular periods and according to particular social practices and civil laws. But they remain "subordinate to God's laws and the purpose for which God created the land." They should care for their landholdings with "the best of current knowledge" so that the earth "might benefit present and future generations." In these activities they are cocreators with God, "guiding the land's productive power" and "conserving the land's natural gifts."[26]

3. *The land's benefits are for everyone.* The stewards of the land must recognize that "the land is given by God for all people, not just for those who hold civil title to it." All land has a "social mortgage" — it is mortgaged from the whole of humanity by a part of it. God gives land "for present and future generations of humanity."[27]

4. *The land should be distributed equitably.* "Land ownership should be as widely distributed as is necessary and feasible to meet the needs of the local and national communities and of the human family as a whole."[28] In some cases there might be widespread private ownership of the land, in others communal ownership of the land as described in the New Testament, where members of the early Christian community "shared all things in common" and divided everything "on the basis of each one's needs" (Acts 2:44-5). However the land is owned, it should always benefit all of the people.

5. *The land should be conserved and restored.* The land must be cared for so that it retains its regenerative power. Agricultural land must be rested periodically. Thus permanent scarring and depletion will be prevented, and the earth will retain its beauty and vitality.

6. *Land use planning must consider social and environmental impacts.* The land was shaped by nature for millions of years, by humanity for a far shorter period. But people can alter in days what nature forged in eons, harming themselves. So when changes are proposed, "land use planning must evaluate the impact that proposed courses of action would have." Local residents should have "the principal right, where possible, to decide whether or not such changes should occur."[29]

7. *Land use should be appropriate to land quality.* Decisions on whether land should be developed or left undisturbed should be based on its "best and highest" use. Because land is a limited resource that people can easily and perhaps inadvertently alter irreversibly, its use "should take into consideration the quality of the land and how it might best serve the community as a whole."[30] Prime farmland, for example, should not be paved over or stripmined. Both short- and long-term consequences of potential land uses should be evaluated.

8. *The land should provide a moderate livelihood.* Rural workers should be able to derive from their labors on the land "sufficient money to provide for their needs and the needs of their family."[31] Farmers should be able to meet their expenses and put aside some money for the future. The farm family is not to strive greedily to expand its holdings and wealth at the expense of nearby or distant neighbors. Nor is the farm family to be impoverished by policies of excessively cheap food. The farm family is to be not wealthy or poor, but moderately secure.

9. *The land's workers should be able to become the land's [civil] owners.*[32] Agricultural, mining, forestry, and factory workers are entitled to "some means of gradual entry into ownership of the land or corporation, either as individual owners or as shareholders."[33] Those who work the land should be able to earn a direct proprietary relationship with and responsibility for that land. All persons who labor on the land have a right to become the land's stewards. They should not be locked, by poor agricultural prices or low wages, into solely serving ventures of others.

10. *The land's mineral wealth should be shared.* Exploitation of the land for corporate benefit and at community expense should not continue, and "the benefit which the people in the region derive from their natural resources should outlive the availability of those resources." Profits from mineral extraction should "be shared in part by the people of the State in which mining occurs."[34]

The final part of *Strangers and Guests,* "The Future of the Land," proposes remedies. The bishops pledge themselves to "moral education" that will "effect legislative remedies if moral appeals for land stewardship do not alter the present situation." They note that "governments as public bodies have the responsibility to mediate in a just manner the conflicting claims of the governed."[35]

Among possible types of government intervention might be limiting "the rights of individual investors and of investor-owned companies to acquire land"; elimination of capital gains tax laws which favor "wealthy investors and land speculators" and harm "small and low income farm families"; enforcement of mining laws and the use of severance taxes to restore exploited areas and provide for rural community needs; encouragement of inner-city development rather than external expansion onto agricultural land; encouragement of modest-sized landholdings through a progressive land tax; stabilization of agricultural prices; renunciation of the use of food as a weapon of foreign policy; preservation of land and water resources through agricultural zoning; review of monopolistic seed patent laws; "just wages and reasonably healthy working conditions" for farmworkers, miners, and timber workers; and resolution of American Indian treaty disputes and protection of American Indian rights.[36]

THE LAND, THE CHURCH, AND THE FUTURE

Will the land become the private preserve of a few? Will land use depend primarily on selfish profit interests? The American Catholic church has begun to respond in the negative. In the face of the consolidation and despoliation of landholdings, the church proposes redistribution of and care for the land—through private initiative if possible, or through direct government mediation of competing claims if necessary. Church leaders, relying on both their American heritage and their Catholic tradition, offer a program of land reform. It reflects the attitude of the nation's founders, the intent of subsequent government legislation, and the particularity of the American context, with its emphasis on voluntary action and on government intervention only as a last resort.

Church advocacy of land reform—widespread individual ownership and stewardship—is a first step in undoing the land exploitation that has been partly condoned by church acceptance of or silence on misinterpretations of the biblical concept of "dominion" over the land. The church is rediscovering its own biblical and social-ethical roots, regaining some of the spirit of St. Francis of Assisi, who was proposed by White as a "patron saint for ecologists."[37]

Church interest in land reform is interdenominational. In recent years several churches have issued land statements, including: "Who Will Farm?", United Presbyterian Church, U.S.A.;[38] "Rural America: Life and Issues," United Church of Christ;[39] "The Human Crisis in Ecology" and "Economic Justice—Stewardship of Creation in Human Community," Lutheran Church in America;[40] "The Family Farm: Can It Be Saved?", United Methodist Church;[41] *For My Neighbor's Good*, Christian Reformed Church;[42] and an "Interfaith Statement on Public Policy and the Structure of Agriculture," signed by Jewish and Christian religious leaders.[43]

The theory and pronouncements of church officials are being put into effect by church members in Appalachia, heartland America, and other pockets of interest. As churches become involved in land issues, their landownership and tax privileges might be affected—not only because of internal church changes in consciousness and in practices on church-held land, but also because of corporate and government resentment of the new church intervention. The church's tax-exempt status stems from its social role in providing moral education. If church moral-education efforts challenge the status quo, church privileges might be jeopardized. The church will have to balance its valued privileges against the opportunity to foster its ethical values.

The U.S. church might well find itself in a position similar to that of the Third World—particularly Latin American—church. The respective churches have both doctrinal affiliation and concern, from differing national perspectives, about United States involvement in the economic and political life of Third World nations. The emergence of liberation theology, the Catholic bishops' support of the poor, and church involvement with insurgent political movements in Latin America have influenced U.S. churches.

In a broader sense, however, the churches are not so much influencing each other's course of action as causing each other to rethink, in their respective social contexts, their common traditions. Church involvement in political activity is not new, but it previously took the form of majority support for the dominant national ideology, or minority dissent from it. Broad-based church advocacy of much more alien or unpopular land causes therefore represents a new kind of church activity. If the activity continues, the church will contribute to forming the new attitude toward land so forcefully advocated by White. Church efforts to alleviate the "ecologic crisis" are ironic, considering the church's past contribution to creating it. But the efforts express the church's renewed fidelity to its own ethical teachings.

NOTES

1. For a parallel presentation, see Hart (1983). The text's discussion draws heavily from the book.
2. White in Sims and Baumann (1974), p. 23.
3. Ibid., p. 27.
4. John XXIII, in Gremillion (1976), p. 168.
5. Paul VI, in Gremillion (1976), p. 394.
6. Paul VI, in Gremillion (1976), p. 496.
7. John Paul II (1979b), p. 96.
8. Ibid., p. 97.
9. John Paul II, "Homily at Living History Farms," cited in National Catholic Rural Life Conference—Heartland Project (1980), p. 16.
10. John Paul II (1979a), p. 23.
11. John Paul II (1980), p. 1.
12. Thomas Aquinas (1947) Vol. 2, pp. 1476-77.
13. Ibid., p. 1477.
14. Ibid., pp. 1480-81.
15. Paine, "Agrarian Justice," in Foner (1974), p. 611.
16. Jefferson, "Letter to Rev. James Madison, 1787," quoted in Foner (1974), p. 605.
17. Jefferson, "Letter to Rev. James Madison, 1795," quoted in Sakolski (1957), p. 62.
18. National Catholic Rural Life Conference (1950), pp. 8-10.
19. Catholic Committee on Appalachia (1975).
20. From *This Land Is Home to Me,* in Hacala (1980), pp. 149, 153, 155-157.
21. Ibid., pp. 167, 168, and 170.
22. National Catholic Rural Life Conference—Heartland Project (1980), p. 1.
23. Ibid., pp. 4 and 5.
24. Ibid., p. 43 for a description of the characteristics of a family farm.
25. Ibid., p. 13.
26. Ibid., p. 14.

27. Ibid., pp. 14 and 15.
28. Ibid., p. 15.
29. Ibid., p. 17.
30. Ibid., p. 18.
31. Ibid., p. 18.
32. Ibid., p. 19. The word "civil," which does not appear in the original, is inserted here to eliminate an apparent contradiction between the first and ninth principles.
33. Ibid., p. 19.
34. Ibid., p. 19.
35. Ibid., p. 22.
36. Ibid., pp. 22-27.
37. White in Sims and Baumann (1974), p. 27.
38. The United Presbyterian Church in the U.S.A. (1978).
39. United Church of Christ (1979).
40. Lutheran Church in America (1972; 1980).
41. United Methodist Church (1978).
42. Christian Reformed Church (1979).
43. Interreligious Task Force on U.S. Food Policy (1980).

REFERENCES

Catholic Committee on Appalachia. 1975. *This Land Is Home to Me — A Pastoral Letter on Powerlessness in Appalachia by the Catholic Bishops of the Region.* Prestonsburg, KY: Catholic Committee on Appalachia.

Christian Reformed Church. 1979. *For My Neighbor's Good.* Grand Rapids, MI: Board of Publications of the Christian Reformed Church.

Foner, Philip (ed.). 1974. *The Life and Major Writings of Thomas Paine.* Secaucus, NJ: Citadel Press.

Gremillion, Joseph (ed.). 1976. *The Gospel of Peace and Justice — Catholic Social Teaching Since Pope John.* Maryknoll, NY: Orbis Books.

Hacala, Joseph R., S. J. (ed.). 1980. *Dream of the Mountains' Struggle — Appalachian Pastoral Five Years Later.* Lancaster, KY: Kentucky Valley Press.

Hart, John. 1983. *The Spirit of the Earth: Nature, Tradition and Social Ethics.* Ramsey, NJ: Paulist Press.

Interreligious Task Force on U.S. Food Policy. 1980. "Interfaith statement on public policy and the structure of agriculture." Washington, DC: Interreligious Task Force on U.S. Food Policy.

John Paul II. 1979a. "The church in rural Africa." *Origins 10:23.* Weekly magazine of the National Catholic Conference.

————. 1979b. *John Paul II in Mexico: His Collected Speeches.* New York: Collins.

————. 1980. "The land is God's gift for all men." *L'Observatore Romano* (August 4): 1.

Lutheran Church in America. 1980. *Economic Justice — Stewardship of Creation in Human Community.* New York: Division for Mission in North America, Lutheran Church in America.

————. 1972. *The Human Crisis in Ecology.* New York: Division for Mission in North America, Lutheran Church in America.

National Catholic Rural Life Conference. 1950. *Manifesto on Rural Life.* Third printing. Milwaukee: Bruce Publishing.

National Catholic Rural Life Conference — Heartland Project. 1980. *Strangers and Guests: Toward Community in the Heartland — A Regional Catholic Bishops' Statement on Land Issues.* Sioux Falls, SD: Heartland Project.

Sakolski, Aaron M. 1957. *Land Tenure and Land Taxation in America.* New York: Robert Schalkenbach Foundation.

Thomas Aquinas. 1947. *Summa Theologica.* Translated by Fathers of the English Dominican Province. 3 vols. New York: Benziger Brothers.

United Church of Christ. 1979. Rural America: Life and Issues. New York: United Church of Christ.

United Methodist Church. 1978. "The family farm: can it be saved?" *Engage/Social Action* (October).

The United Presbyterian Church in the U.S.A. 1978. *Who Will Farm?* New York: Church and Society Program Area, United Presbyterian Church, U.S.A.

United States Department of Agriculture. 1979. *Structure Issues of American Agriculture.* Washington, DC: U.S. Department of Agriculture.

White, Lynn, Jr. 1974. "The historical roots of our ecologic crisis." In *Human Behavior and the Environment.* Edited by John Sims and Duane Baumann. Chicago: Maaroufa Press.

6

Energy and Agriculture: Conflicts and Potentials for Structural Reform

DAVID M. HOLLAND

The late 1960s and early 1970s witnessed both the environmental movement and the back-to-the-land phenomenon. Environmentalists were concerned with issues of resource waste and pollution, while back-to-the-landers espoused life-styles of less consumption and a more reverent attitude toward nature. By the early 1970s enough such people were interested in food and farming issues to result in a genuine alternative agricultural movement (Bueshing, 1979) that promoted socially equitable and ecologically sound agriculture. The movement's spokesmen argued for small farms that would use environmentally benign production methods, perhaps even organic methods of production (Berry, 1977; Perelman, 1972). Solar energy and other forms of alternative technology would reduce the use of fuel and other energy-intensive purchased inputs. The resultant self-reliance and individual inventiveness would promote both personal well-being and a sense of shared community and culture.

The 1973 energy crisis shaped the subsequent direction of the alternative agricultural movement and its impact on mainstream agriculture. The rise in oil prices focused public attention on the role of fossil-fuel energy in the entire economic system. The energy-oriented critique of agriculture developed by various writers (Perelman, 1972; Steinhart and Steinhart, 1974) seemed to provide both a critique of the existing organization of agriculture and practical suggestions for the alternative agricultural movement.

Critiques of mainstream agriculture have experienced certain problems of their own, however. First, while debates over the proper use of energy in agriculture have led to a better understanding of the place of energy in the production and distribution of food, they have often obscured the precise relationship between energy use and structural agricultural reform. Second, the energy critique of American agriculture has been partly responsible for the inability of agricultural reform movements of recent years to build an effective political base. As a response to these problems, this paper reinterprets the implications of energy analysis for future American agricultural development.

ENERGY USE IN AGRICULTURE

The most interesting and controversial energy analysis of the food system began to appear in the early 1970s (Pimentel et al., 1973; Steinhart and Steinhart, 1974, and Perelman, 1972). This work compared the amount of food energy produced to the amount of fuel energy required to produce it. Across the entire food system (production, distribution, and preparation), an estimated ten units of fossil-fuel energy had to be consumed to produce one unit of food energy (Steinhart and Steinhhart, 1974). There was also evidence that the ratio had increased over time (Pimentel et al., 1973) — that is, the system was requiring increasing amounts of fuel energy to produce a given unit of food energy.

These early findings led some energy analysts (Perelman, 1972) to criticize the U.S. food system's dependence on massive energy expenditures that could not be sustained in the future. After 1973 the analysis took on even greater importance: perhaps we were living beyond our energy means in agriculture. Possibly the alternative agricultural movement was correct in charging that American agriculture was irrational in its use of energy. By the mid-1970s, the organization of the entire food system was under attack.

However, an effective defense was soon mounted. Led largely by agricultural economists, it proceeded on two fronts. One de-emphasized the role of energy as an input to agriculture, and thus the importance of agriculture as an energy user. It turned out that the food system did not really compare to other sectors — such as transportation — in total energy requirements. The food system (production, distribution, preparation) accounted for only 16.5 percent of the nation's total energy consumption, with agricultural production accounting for only 2.9 percent (Doering, 1977). Put another way, even if total energy use in agricultural production were cut in half, the savings would be only a little over 1 percent of the total national energy consumption.

In the production of most crops, energy accounted for roughly 10 to 20 percent of variable production costs (Energy Committee, National Rural Center, 1978). The exception was irrigated agriculture, where energy typically accounted for about 25 percent of production costs. Thus, even if energy prices were to increase by 100 percent, it would only cause about a 10 to 20 percent increase in agricultural production costs. Similarly, since only about 5 percent of total food costs goes to energy (LeVeen, 1981), little of the average annual increase in retail food prices of 9.5 percent between 1972 and 1980 could be attributed to increases in energy cost. The average annual price rise of energy over this period was 13 percent. Even assuming no input substitution in place of energy-intense inputs, this increase would cause food prices to rise at only 0.7 percent per year.

The other defensive front questioned the usefulness of analyses based purely on energy ratios (Ruttan, 1975; Pasour and Bullock, 1977). It argued that the energy input/output ratio, an apparently pure measure of energy efficiency, was not really very meaningful: from society's point of view, a calorie of energy in the form of petroleum was not the equivalent of a calorie of energy in the form of food. What was necessary was to look at both inputs and output in terms of their social usefulness, which could be measured simply by the prices of the commodities. When viewed in the context of relative input prices, the rationale for the seemingly excessive energy requirements of U.S. agriculture became clear. The price of farmland and labor during most of the post-1945 period increased much faster than the price of energy; thus energy was substituted for more costly inputs. Between 1960 and 1970, for example, the price of labor went up 74 percent, while the price of fertilizer, an energy-intense input, declined by 3 percent (Energy Committee, National Rural Center, 1978).

ASSESSMENT OF THE DEFENSE

Those who mounted the energy defense were quick to realize that implicit in the early energy analysis was a critique of the rationality of capitalism itself. The opposed energy analysis implied that the rationality of the agricultural system should be evaluated on the basis of a set of weights based on energy content of inputs and output rather than market-determined prices. In the language of economics, the energy-based system would be considered an energy theory of values. Its weakness is that it does not recognize that energy as embodied in commodities will vary in usefulness, depending upon its form. In other words, a measure that equates a calorie of oil with a calorie of food is of little help in assessing agricultural performance from a social point of view.

However, the argument that a proper set of weights will rely on prices is also incorrect. In theory, a market economy's prices will be determined mainly by the cost of producing goods and the tastes and preferences of those with sufficient money to purchase them. Demand will indicate mainly the distribution of income, not the needs of people. The observer need not be happy with market-determined prices unless also satisfied with the distribution of income. Furthermore, there are practical reasons — government and corporate monopoly, for instance, or environmental externalities — why existing and past energy prices do not even indicate either relative production costs or relative preferences. But in a capitalist society, commodity prices rather than embodied energy intensity will determine economic behavior. Thus energy prices are of special importance.

The issue of relative price weights versus relative energy weights diverts attention away from the issue of structural agricultural change. The post-1945 agricultural use of relatively cheap energy has not simply substituted relatively cheap inputs for relatively expensive ones, but has involved fundamental changes in farm structure and landholding. These structural changes have taken advantage of cheap energy but are not merely an input substitution of it. Changes in farming practices spring from the need to maximize profits. The 1970s' energy analysis is controversial not because it shows the low energy productivity of U.S. agriculture or because it raises doubts about agriculture's future. It is controversial because it suggests that higher energy productivity in agriculture may require large-scale structural change in agriculture and the entire food system.

Fossil fuel is a nonrenewable resource that is in relatively short supply. Unless activities with huge environmental or military costs are undertaken, it is likely to remain so for the foreseeable future. For agriculture, the question then becomes: should adjustment to these circumstances occur without changes in the size and organization of farms? Some energy analysts, as well as members of the alternative agriculture movement, believe that small farms are more efficient than large ones in their use of energy. Thus increased emphasis on small-scale agriculture would increase the energy productivity of agriculture. The next section reviews the data for this claim, which turn out to be mixed.

ENERGY USE AND FARM SIZE

One approach to measuring the energy intensity of agricultural production has been to calculate on a per-unit-of-land basis — for example, to estimate the energy per acre for corn production. A drawback is that a given agricultural production system may require considerable energy input per unit of land but then be able to produce high levels of output. When viewed in terms of energy per acre, the system appears energy-intensive — that is, to have low energy productivity. When viewed in terms of energy per unit of output, however, the system may turn out to be highly efficient. Because these distinctions have not always been clear, potentially misleading conclusions have been drawn about energy productivity. Although it is only a partial measure of energy productivity, some sort of calculation per energy input or per cost of energy input still tends to be the most revealing measure of agricultural energy efficiency. But since previous studies often used energy per acre as a measure of energy intensity, we will also pay attention to this measure.

There are several reasons, discussed by Buttel and Larson (1979), for believing that energy productivity would be lower for larger farms. For one thing, increasing farm size historically has been accompanied by increasing mechanization, and many large farms cannot be operated profitably without mechanization. Because mechanization displaces human and animal power, the fuel requirements for mechanized farms should be larger than for unmechanized ones. Yet farms of all sizes in the U.S. are more or less mechanized. The real question is: what size of farm is best suited to obtaining maximum energy efficiency from present and future machine technology? Large machines on large farms may be more efficient per unit of output than small machines on small farms.

The second main reason for expecting energy productivity to be lower for large farms is that larger farms depend more upon energy-intensive manufactured inputs. Small farmers, for instance, can control weeds by hand, while large ones must use energy-intensive herbicides. In addition, large farms usually have a comparatively homogeneous mixture of crops, and these monoculture conditions tend to encourage population explosions of harmful pests, which then require more pesticides. Finally, the large monoculture farm is less likely to build soil by rotating crops and so requires more manufactured fertilizer.

In the study by Buttel and Larson, correlations between various measures of energy use in agricultural production and farm size indicators were calculated using the state as the statistical unit (see table 6.1). For crops, all the farm size indicators were positively correlated with energy intensity measures, but the relationship did not hold for livestock. Measures of energy per acre were not more highly correlated with farm size than were measures of energy per unit of output—a finding perhaps implying that production techniques requiring large amounts of energy per acre may still yield low energy productivity. The overall results support the idea that small farms are more energy-efficient than large ones.

In the data summarized in table 6.2, a somewhat different approach is taken. The table uses farm size categories—that is, agricultural sales per farm as defined by the 1974 Census of Agriculture—and crosses them with indicators of energy efficiency. These data do not depend on Buttel and Larson's state averages, which may conceal large variations within states. The more direct examination of the farm size data should give a clearer picture.

Table 6.2 indicates that small farms have lower energy productivity ($ Output/$ Energy Input) than large farms. On the other hand, the large farms are shown to apply energy inputs on a per-acre basis at a much higher rate than small farms. The table implies that while large farms apply large amounts of energy per unit of land, they also produce high levels of output per unit of land. The energy productivity of large farms is therefore greater than that of small farms.

Table 6.2 also shows that large farms do not spend as large a proportion of their production costs on energy-intense inputs as do small farms. Perhaps energy price increases raise total production costs more for small farms than for large ones. Small farms may be more vulnerable to increases in energy prices.

Both sets of findings, although somewhat different from those of the Buttel-Larson work, are supported by a study that attempted to replicate the Buttel-Larson study by using counties as the observation unit rather

TABLE 6.1. FARM SIZE AND ENERGY INTENSITY
(CORRELATIONS BY PRODUCT AND ACROSS STATES, 1974)

Energy Intensity	Average Farm Size, All Farms	Average Farm Size, Farms with Sales >$1,000	Proportion of Sales, Farms with Sales >$100,000
BTU/1,000 acres, all crops	.333	.340	.642
BTU/1,000 acres, winter wheat	.574	.589	.490
BTU/1,000 acres, corn	.650	.659	.417
BTU/$1,000 production, all crops*	.428	.427	.206
BTU/1,000 bu., winter wheat*	.324	.336	.450
BTU/1,000 bu., corn*	.808	.820	.464
BTU/$ production, total livestock	.126	.124	−.027
BTU/acre, irrigation**	.455	.454	.521

Source: Buttel, Frederick H., and Larson, Oscar W. 1979. "Farm size, structure, and energy intensity: an ecological analysis of U.S. agriculture." *Rural Sociology* 44(3):471–88.
*Billions of BTU
**Per acre irrigated

than states (Heaton and Brown, 1982). My preliminary analysis of data from the 1978 Census of Agriculture also supports these findings.

There are three important qualifications to the findings in table 6.2. First, the data include livestock production, so that large feedlots may distort the information for the categories of largest farm size. Second, the data indicate sales of agricultural commodities, not actual production of them. Small farms typically produce more for household consumption, a category not recorded in the sales data. Third, large farms may be getting quantity discounts in the prices they pay for items such as fertilizer or diesel fuel—meaning that the expenditure data would underreport actual energy use on large farms. But none of these qualifications overrides the basic finding of greater energy efficiency on large farms.

The main question the energy issue raises for future agricultural development is whether adjustment to a relative shortage of fossil-fuel energy should occur within the existing agricultural structure. The tables are only

TABLE 6.2.   U.S. FARM SIZE AND ENERGY USE

Farm Size: 1974 Sales, Average Size/Acres	Number & Percent of Farms	Total Prod. Costs (Mil.)	Millions & Percent of All Agr. Energy Exp.	Energy Input Costs*		
				Percent of Production Costs	$Energy per Sales	$Energy per Acre
$2500–4999 184 acres	289,983 17.1%	$1283	$240 2.5%	18.7%	$.25	$4.50
$5000–9999 222 acres	296,273 17.5%	$1723	$387 4.0%	22.5%	$.18	$5.89
$10000–19999 330 acres	310,011 18.3%	$3178	$723 7.4%	22.8%	$.16	$7.06
$20000–39999 499 acres	321,771 19.0%	$6190	$1363 14.0%	22.0%	$.15	$8.48
$40000–99999 761 acres	324,310 19.1%	$13438	$2799 28.7%	20.8%	$.14	$11.35
$100,000– 199,999 1299 acres	101,153 6.0%	$9585	$1778 18.3%	18.6%	$.13	$13.53
$200,000– 499,999 2287 acres	40,034 2.4%	$8544	$1338 13.7%	15.6%	$.12	$14.62
$500,000 or more 4718 acres	11,412 0.7%	$15915	$1097 11.3%	6.9%	$.06	$20.39
Total, all farms 534 acres	1695047 100%	$598556	$9725 100%	16.2% 100%	$.12	$10.74

Source: 1974 Census of Agriculture
*Energy inputs include gasoline and other petroleum fuel for farm business, commercial fertilizer, herbicides, and pesticides

partly instructive; they provide some information on how farms of different sizes have used energy in the past. They say little about how farms of different sizes can adjust to energy shortages in the future. It is possible that large farms not only are currently more energy-efficient, but that they will also be more able to adjust to future scarcity. On the other hand, the alternative agriculture movement may be correct that medium-size and small farms will be more flexible in adjusting.

There are three important qualifications to the findings in table 6.2. First, the data include livestock production, so that large feedlots may distort the information for the categories of largest farm size. Second, the data indicate sales of agricultural commodities, not actual production of them. Small farms typically produce more for household consumption, a category not recorded in the sales data. Third, large farms may be getting quantity discounts in the prices they pay for items such as fertilizer or diesel fuel — meaning that the expenditure data would underreport actual energy use on large farms. But none of these qualifications overrides the basic finding of greater energy efficiency on large farms.

The main question the energy issue raises for future agricultural development is whether adjustment to a relative shortage of fossil-fuel energy should occur within the existing agricultural structure. The tables are only partly instructive; they provide some information on how farms of different sizes have used energy in the past. They say little about how farms of different sizes can adjust to energy shortages in the future. It is possible that large farms not only are currently more energy-efficient, but that they will also be more able to adjust to future scarcity. On the other hand, the alternative agriculture movement may be correct that medium-size and small farms will be more flexible in adjusting.

Farm size and organizational type should be explicitly treated as issues in decisions about the direction and emphasis of future agricultural development — a difficult task (Holland, 1980). Attempts to mitigate the impact of agricultural energy price increases by means of technological change and government policy are affected by economic interest. Research and policy institutions are now dominated by large-farm interests, and the directions emerging from them will favor these interests. Energy price rises will then squeeze medium-sized and small farms, which will not be aided by the private sector or government. The result will intensify and confirm the dominance of large farms.

ENERGY AND THE POLITICS OF AGRICULTURAL CHANGE

If existing agriculture cannot easily be adapted to the alternative agriculture ideal, how can the necessary transition best be achieved? To answer this question, we must first clear away some conceptual roadblocks.

There has been a tendency to misunderstand the implications of the energy shortage. It has often been argued that the shortage would force agriculture to change in directions desired by the alternative movement. As energy became more expensive, the economic rationality of the existing agricultural system would be undermined. Large-scale farming, industrial-style mechanization, and long-distance transportation of food would become unprofitable. A new food system would emerge, one based on small-scale farming mainly for local consumption.

The argument failed to understand that adjustment options threatening the existing structure were uninteresting to those influencing agricultural policy making and technological change. Energy prices were important, but the existing structure responded to them selectively. Consider a simple example. Increasing energy prices have raised transportation costs to the point where fresh vegetable processors on the Pacific Coast now may lose some Eastern and Midwestern markets. The processors have reacted not by shifting to more local markets, but by becoming interested in penetrating Japanese and other Pacific Rim markets. The increases in energy prices may result in West Coast food being shipped farther.

As this example suggests, the problem with the alternative agriculture movement is that it has not distinguished between useful on-the-job farming experience and the building of a political base necessary to achieve structural change. As a result, the movement has not matured into an effective force for change. Thousands of individuals have become involved in small-scale farming and experimented with alternative technology. Farming on a small scale, often using untested production techniques, is a great adventure that has left little capacity or economic surplus for anything else. Moreover, the movement's political base, such as it is, tends to be populist — in particular, interested in restoring the economic viability of the small farm. But since nearly all politically acceptable agricultural policies that are good for small farms are even better for large farms, populist policy cannot change the main direction of U.S. agricultural development.

For instance, to populists an important reason for the financial squeeze on agriculture is the high cost of credit, possibly including unscrupulous lending practices by bankers. A solution might be government regulation of credit and lending practices, perhaps even a government bank. But large farmers would be overwhelmingly likely to take better advantage of such new mechanisms than small farmers. Similarly, low farm prices threaten the family farm. If government should respond by trying to raise prices, the results are likely to improve the competitive position of large farms in relation to small ones. The main prescription of the alternative movement — that is, small-scale farming — would have the effect of preventing the creation of a political force able to challenge the trends toward agricultural centralization and concentration.

Left to itself, the existing food system will achieve increasing energy productivity, but this increase will also harm small and family farms. The natural workings of the economic system will not automatically ensure the emergence of either a socially equitable or an ecologically sound agriculture, because acceptable directions for public policy and technological change are influenced by existing concentrations of economic power.

Moreover, the superior potential of small-scale agriculture for achieving maximum energy efficiency is empirically debatable and politically questionable. The practice of small-scale farming weakens the movement by geographically separating its most avid proponents. It also generates no surplus to support reform efforts and tends towards a populist political posture not likely to generate fundamental structural reform. To achieve its goals, the alternative agricultural movement must give more attention to the politics of shaping agricultural development and less attention to the actual practice of small-scale farming.

The alternative movement must recognize that large farms can be highly energy-efficient. If it continues to stress small-scale farming, the movement will become increasingly isolated and marginal. The question it should emphasize is: how should large farms be controlled? We should probably be concentrating on achieving more efficient use of energy in agriculture not so much through alternative technology and small farms but rather through large-scale farming that also embodies energy productivity and economic democracy.

The obvious place to focus such a strategy is in California and much of the rest of the West, where large public irrigation projects provide a lever for increased public control. Many of the farms in these areas are already large, and will be compelled to become more efficient in their use of both energy and water in the future. Rather than calling for enforcement of the 160-acre law — which the Reagan administration is now overturning anyway — land reform groups and agriculture labor should be arguing for large-scale production cooperatives and/or government-owned farms. By stressing economic democracy, such units could provide a political base for progressive agricultural policy at the same time that they achieve maximum energy productivity for irrigated agriculture.

REFERENCES

Berry, Wendell. 1977. *The Unsettling of America: Culture & Agriculture.* San Francisco: Sierra Club Books.

Buesching, D. 1979. "The alternative agriculture movement: origin, development, and current composition." *Agricultural World* (November/December): 1–8.

Buttel, Frederick H., and Larson, Oscar W. 1979. "Farm size, structure, and energy intensity: an ecological analysis of U.S. agriculture." *Rural Sociology* 44(3): 471–88.

Energy Committee, National Rural Center. 1978. *Energy and Small Farms: A Review of Existing Literature and Suggestions for Further Research.* Washington, DC: Project on a Research Agenda for Small Farms, National Rural Center.

Heaton, Tim B., and Brown, David W. 1982. "Farm structure and energy intensity: another look." *Rural Sociology* 47(1): 17–31.

Holland, David. 1980. "Energy and the structure of agriculture: a political economic analysis." *American Journal of Agricultural Economics* 62(5): 972–75.

LeVeen, E. Phillip. 1981. "Toward a new food policy." *Cry California* (Summer).

Pasour, E. C., and Bullock, J. B. 1977. "Energy and agriculture: some economic issues." In *Agriculture and Energy.* Edited by William Lockertz. New York: Academic Press. Pp. 683–94.

Perelman, Michael. 1976. "Efficiency in agriculture: the economics of energy." In *Radical Agriculture.* Edited by R. Merrill. New York: Harper Colophon. Pp. 64–86.

Pimentel, David, et al. 1973. "Food production and the energy crisis." *Science* 182 (2 November): 443–49.

Ruttan, Vernon W. 1975. "Food production and the energy crisis: a comment." *Science* 184 (14 February): 560–61.

Steinhart, John S., and Steinhart, Carol E. 1974. "Energy use in the U.S. food system." *Science* 184 (19 April): 307–15.

PART THREE

Land Reform and Natural Resources

7

Pulling the Pillars: Energy Development and Land Reform in Appalachia

DAVID LIDEN

We know that the edge of the American plate was thrust upward to produce the Appalachian Mountains . . . the roots of the very mountains we see today. They are thus one of the oldest landscape features of the United States . . . they are the majestic harbingers of our land; they served their major purpose long before man existed, then lingered on as noble relics to provide man with an agreeable home when he did arrive.

James Michener, *Centennial* (1974:34–35)

Somewhere way back we lost ourselves. I think it was when the companies bought up the land.

A West Virginia farmer[1]

"Pulling the pillars"—removing the residual coal that supports a mine roof and overhead surface land to get every last bit of profit—is a vivid reflection of the priorities that have prevailed in the Appalachians for generations. Now, because of both international pressures and domestic policy, these priorities are becoming even more exaggerated not only in Appalachia, but throughout the mineral-rich portions of rural America.

The so-called energy crisis, the tenuousness of American mineral supply lines from the Third World, new technologies for extraction, and the massive aggregation of capital by energy conglomerates have drastically accelerated domestic mineral speculation and exploration. At the same time, they have strengthened energy and mineral companies' control of the land. Because of its long-standing mineral reserves (coal, oil, and natural gas) and the discovery of a host of new minerals (such as olivine, gypsite,

monosite, lead, silver, oil shale, possibly uranium), Appalachia has become the object of intense corporate activity. Its relatively dispersed population and its geography — suitable for underground storage, dams, pump
storage, and other large water projects — have reinforced the attraction.

This new wave of energy development can be characterized by the unprecedented scope of land acquisition, the pyramiding of control by interests increasingly located at a distance from the region, and the huge scale
of projects based on advanced technology and vast capital. Synthetic fuel
plants, gas wells ten thousand feet deep, enhanced oil recovery techniques,
strip mine drag lines, slurry lines, long-wall deep mining, coke plants,
765-kilovolt power lines, pump storage dams, and large highway and
water transportation links demand a seemingly endless amount of Appalachian surface and mineral land. They have also stimulated local interest
in land reform.

The Appalachian experience is important for two reasons. First, other
rural communities can look to Appalachia for evidence of what decades of
energy development can mean for a region. Much of the intermountain
West, areas of the South, and even portions of New England, Ohio, and
New York are facing the kind of development pressures that came to
Appalachia at the turn of the century. Second, Appalachia is evolving a
grass-roots resistance to the wholesale removal of its natural resources and
to the power configurations the removal requires.

SEVERED WEALTH: EXTENT AND IMPACT

Columbia Gas (Wilmington, Del.)	342,236 acres
N & W Railroad (Roanoke, Va.)	201,950 acres
Continental Oil (Stamford, Conn.)	193,061 acres
Pittston Corporation (New York)	185,254 acres
Occidental Petroleum (Los Angeles)	144,741 acres

Appalachian Land Ownership Task Force (1980, I:47)

The real problem started when they separated the mineral from the surface.
That's the first step toward anything about the land making sense again.
Resident of Lincoln County, West Virginia

Appalachian Land Ownership Task Force (1980, VII:84)

The new wave of energy development overlays what many have labeled a
colonial legacy.[2] The mineral holdings originally put together decades ago
have been greatly expanded in recent years. The combination of market
incentives, price decontrol, tax incentives, regulatory relaxation, huge oil
company profits, and Third World assertiveness has encouraged the aggregation of millions of acres of surface and minerals.

The mineral industry argues that the nation has to compensate for
"years of shortsightedness" which has left the United States too dependent
on foreign suppliers (Coates, 1981). Secretary of the Interior James Watt
has focused on minerals as "the problem of the '80s" (Coates, 1981). At the
local level, county record rooms are swarming with company landmen try-

ing to track down remaining available acreage. Both companies and independent speculators are negotiating leases sight-unseen, based on the mere possibility that minerals might exist. The economics are such that, even if subsequent exploration indicates no minerals are present, a few years of royalty payments are worthwhile in order to lock out competitors.

The federal government has stewardship over millions of increasingly valuable Appalachian acres. One lease from the federal government can capture years of reserves. During congressional testimony on military preparedness, General Alton Slay, former chief of the Air Force Systems Command, warned that laws enacted to protect federally owned lands from development are endangering national security by creating unnecessary mineral and metal shortages (Coates, 1981). The laws under attack are the Forest Service Act, the Wilderness Act, the Wild and Scenic Rivers Act, the National Wildlife Refuge Act, and the Endangered Species Act. Appalachian state governments have endorsed dams, power plants, and mining projects that would displace farmers and destroy scenic lands. In West Virginia, for example, Governor Rockefeller has appealed to the citizens to rise to patriotic heights to help meet the country's rising energy needs. The implied logic — that the state should make itself a "national sacrifice area" — has not been lost on local people.[3]

A recently conducted study by the Appalachian Land Ownership Task Force (A.L.O.T.F.) for the Appalachian Regional Commission vividly indicates the extent and impact of such outside and corporate acquisition and control (A.L.O.T.F., 1980:I). This unprecedented survey of 80 counties in six states found that corporations, government agencies, and large individual owners — representing only 1 percent of the local population — owned over twenty million acres, or 50 percent of the surface land and 30 percent of the mineral land.[4] Forty percent of these twenty million acres was owned by 50 private owners and ten government agencies. The top 25 percent in the sample of the landowners owned 85 percent of the surface land and 90 percent of the mineral land; the bottom 25 percent owned only 12 percent of the surface land and 0.7 percent of the mineral land. Mineral ownership is most concentrated in West Virginia; in the fifteen-county state sample, large individual, corporate, and government interests owned 75 percent of the mineral land (3,273,242 acres) and 50 percent of the surface land (2,315,419 acres).[5]

Landownership patterns are power patterns. In Appalachia the economic results has been single-commodity economies, land-starved communities, and speculation-fueled land prices rising beyond the reach of local residents. The environmental results have been a countryside pocked with wells, eroded hillsides, creeks reddened with mine runoff, watersheds choked by gob and siltation. Social services have been stifled by years of gross underassessment of some of the most valuable natural resources in the nation. The Appalachian Land Ownership Study simply confirms in a systematic way what local people have known for generations.[6]

Naturally, oil and chemical conglomerates and foreign capital have undertaken massive acquisition of coal lands. According to *Business Week,* "Thanks to a careful acquisition strategy that began fifteen years ago, eleven oil companies now own 25 percent of all coal in the country, and the oil industry has the future of coal in its grip" (*Business Week,* 1980:104). Oil-owned companies may capture 50 percent of American coal production by 1985 (*Business Week,* 1980:104).

The trend is clear in Appalachia. Diamond Shamrock recently acquired Amherst Coal, West Virginia's last large family-owned coal operation; Sun Oil absorbed Elk River Resources; Ashland Oil bought out Kentucky Highland River Coal; Standard Oil of Ohio has acquired the coal interests of U.S. Steel and has become a major shareholder in AMAX; Occidental Petroleum has purchased Island Creek Coal; Continental Oil owns Consolidation Coal; Quaker State Oil owns Valley Camp Coal; and Exxon owns Monterey Coal. In the fifteen West Virginia counties examined by the Appalachian Land Ownership Study, seven major oil conglomerates hold more than 400,000 acres of mineral and surface land. An estimated 75 percent of the state's natural gas reserves are owned by oil companies.[7]

Increased foreign ownership and control of the region's energy is becoming a political issue, even an international one. The largest landowner in the study's sample is Bowaters Corporation of London, England; Royal Dutch Shell is now part owner of coal formerly owned by Allied Chemical; Ashland Oil has sold a 12 percent interest in its coal to the German government; the Flick family of West Germany is now the largest stockholder in the W.R. Grace mineral empire; and AMAX is owned in part by the Japanese Mitsui Corporation.

The rate of acquisition, though, is even more disturbing than the acreage involved. Locally owned mineral companies are being bought out by larger interests, large holdings are being aggregated further, and speculative leasing on the Eastern Overthrust Belt and oil shale lands is sending both multinationals and "cowboy" independents into virgin areas of the region. Oil and gas interests are leasing at a rate of more than a half-million acres per year in West Virginia. The state tax department estimates that eleven million of the state's fourteen million acres are now rented through such leases.[8] In many cases the lessee is also an absentee corporate interest.

The corporate impacts of the acquisitions are enormous in terms of social services, economic development, employment, housing, community stability, and overall quality of life. The study indicates, for instance, that as the concentration of corporate/absentee ownership increases in recreation and tourism counties, unemployment and cyclical employment also increase, wages stagnate or decline, and the level of job skills decreases (A.L.O.T.F., 1980, I:114–121). In coal counties, manufacturing establishments, job opportunities, local capital in banks, and the amount of value-added production all decline as ownership becomes more concentrated (A.L.O.T.F., 1980, I:102–113). Water and sewer infrastructure, the strength of agriculture, and population stability also are affected by the concentration of land-ownership. The counties with most concentrated ownership have in general suffered the greatest population out-migration and the greatest decline in agricultural land and production (A.L.O.T.F., 1980, I:132).

The connection between corporate scale, concentrated ownership, and underassessment of land largely explains the grave deficiencies in Appalachian social services. The top 1 percent of owners hold 22 percent of the land and pay only 4.7 percent of the property tax — often fractions of a cent per acre of immensely valuable land (A.L.O.T.F., 1980, I:93). The counties with the richest resources have the greatest corporate and absentee ownership and the oldest and most crowded housing, the poorest education and medical facilities, nonexistent public recreation, and the greatest dependence on outside (usually federal) subsidies (A.L.O.T.F., 1980, I:92).

The connection between corporate scale, concentrated ownership, and underassessment of land largely explains the grave deficiencies in Appalachian social services. The top 1 percent of owners hold 22 percent of the land and pay only 4.7 percent of the property tax — often tractions of a cent per acre of immensely valuable land (A.L.O.T.F., 1980, I:93). The counties with the richest resources have the greated coporate and absentee ownership and the oldest and most crowded housing, the poorest education and medical facilities, nonexistent public recreation, and the greatest dependence on outside (usually federal) subsidies (A.L.O.T.F., 1980, I:92).

Private- and public-sector policymakers are compromising long-term needs for short-term gains. Strip mines are permitted because companies promise to maintain buffering stations to offset acid runoff into stream headwaters. Reclamation experts promote strip-mine sites as dumps for urban sludge waste full of PCBs and other, less documented, toxic materials. Planners anticipate surface subsidence as a predictable contingency. Administrators ignore the connections between polluted aquifers and force-injection oil and gas projects. Local influentials act as go-betweens, leasing oil shale land for outside corporations without informing property owners that it will be stripped. Strip mining accelerates at contours above communities with a history of dangerous floods. Corporations and government agencies continue to tout mountaintop-removal housing projects while ignoring the real costs and the record of failure. County commissioners go on record in support of uranium mining without examining the social, economic, and human consequences.

Appalachia has been fully integrated into the national energy economy, but at tremendous cost to Appalachians. As exploration for natural gas begins in Vermont, as strip mining for coal spreads in the West, as on-site lignite-fed power plants are proposed in Texas, and as boom-and-bust towns spring up in the mineral-rich Colorado Rockies, concerned residents can learn from both the experience of mineral development in

Appalachia and the growing opposition to the "pulling-the-pillars" mentality.

RESISTANCE, REFORM, AND REDISTRIBUTION

> You tell us what you need to know and we'll tell you how to get along without it.
>
> AMAX's response to a community in
> West Virginia (A.L.O.T.F., 1980, VII:242)

> West Virginia is used to being exploited by outsiders, whether they come from Philadelphia or Japan. . . . We are in sad need of land reform. We have haciendas; we just don't call them that.
>
> A Randolph County, West Virginia,
> resident (A.L.O.T.F., 1980, VII:271)

The growing resistance to decades of absentee control and abuse of Appalachia's mineral wealth has taken varied forms. Groups first sprang up on an intermittent and local basis after strip-mining violations, job layoffs, mine accidents, housing shortages, water-pollution incidents, and shortfalls in public services (especially education). After the devastating floods in the strip-mine region of Kentucky, Virginia, and West Virginia in spring 1977, several groups came together as the Appalachian Alliance, a coalition based on a common recognition that many regional and local problems sprang from the control by absentee/commercial interests of Appalachia's land and natural resources.

The Appalachian Alliance tried to convince policymakers that decisions about where people could and could not live, the quality and security of available housing, where and whether people would work, the availability of educational opportunities, and the very lives of the people themselves were being determined by outside interests with little or no regional or local accountability. The alliance recognized that local control of knowledge about the region's land was as weak as local control of the land itself. It recognized, too, that landownership conferred political power. The alliance formed a Land Task Force charged with undertaking a thorough examination of Appalachian landownership patterns and their impacts.

The Appalachian Land Ownership Study that resulted represents more than two years of research by local people. Grass-roots groups created the research design, bargained with the Appalachian Regional Commission for funding, hired staff people and recruited volunteers, did the actual courthouse research and interviewing, and helped in the editing of seven volumes of findings.[9] The process confirmed the validity of community-based research and mobilized people around a common theme. The grass-roots groups now have strong documentation of who owns the land, how each holding is valued and taxed, and where the owner lives. They have compiled socioeconomic and statistical descriptions of how each county is affected by landownership patterns and transcribed a powerful oral history of how local people feel landownership relates to their lives.

The Appalachian Land Ownership Study is now being disseminated and popularized for further community education and organization. To some Appalachians, the findings merely document what their daily experience has taught them. Others can use this material to work out for themselves the detailed effects of highly concentrated landownership on land prices, job opportunities, population stability, agricultural strength, environmental quality, and housing availability, as well as the web of connections between corporate landowners and local political power brokers. Appalachian people now can prove that the disadvantages so long characteristic of the region are not simply, as they have been led to believe, a result of its topography or its people. Instead, they are largely a consequence of the pattern of landownership and control. The study goes a long way toward explaining the ancient paradox of desperate need amid natural wealth.

The findings, as well as the process of the study itself, emphasize both the importance of a region-wide perspective and the efficacy of coalition building. Much of the original inspiration and ongoing determination behind the study is captured in words which became the study's motto:

> What is research? Research is digging facts. Digging facts is as hard a job as mining coal. It means blowing them out from underground, cutting them, picking them, shoveling them, loading them, pushing them to the surface, weighing them, and then turning them over to the public for fuel—for light and heat. Facts make a fire which cannot be put out. (John Brophy, 1921)[10]

Using the facts it mined, the study suggested three strategies to begin to restore local control of land resources to Appalachia—saving the land not yet lost, mitigating the impact of large-scale ownership, and redistributing land.

SAVING THE LAND NOT YET LOST

> The most unfortunate thing about Appalachia is that so much of the land was lost so long ago.
> Editorial in *Charleston* (West Virginia) *Gazette* (1981)

Lincoln County, West Virginia, is the only county in the country where strip mining is prohibited. The prohibition resulted from wide and deep local opposition, months of organizing, and a now locally famous public hearing. Some five hundred people presented such an overwhelming front that the director of the West Virginian Department of Natural Resources ruled against the county's first strip-mine permit application on the grounds that approval would "disrupt the social fabric of the county." A subsequent attempt by American Electric Power to overturn the ruling had no success.

The Lincoln County story has encouraged Appalachians in places not yet stripped. In areas with especially vulnerable ecologies, local people have put together petitions to have their areas legally deleted from strip-mine activity under provisions of the 1977 federal Surface Mine and Reclamation Law. In West Virginia the Tug Valley Recovery Center has attempted, so far unsuccessfully, to have the entire Tug Fork Valley watershed in West Virginia and Kentucky deleted because of the possibility of flooding. The Highlands Conservancy in West Virginia is attempting to do the same for parts of the Monongahela National Forest. Lincoln County Citizens for Reform has submitted a petition that, if successful, would put the federal government's weight behind the position taken by the state Department of Natural Resources.[11]

Because of the lack of any real regulation and the false impression that oil and gas drilling is a benign form of mineral development, increased oil and gas activity in the region is even more insidious than strip mining. The attempt to convey the implications of Appalachian oil and gas development has been primarily a public education campaign. Material prepared by the Appalachian Alliance, the Kentucky Rivers Coalition, the Southern West Virginia Land Reform Project, and the Charlottesville (Virginia) Sierra Club analyzes the environmental and legal hazards of development to mineral and surface owners. The information is based on first-hand accounts of destruction of water and topsoil. It gives examples of lease arrangements lacking adequate guarantees and royalty provisions for owners. The guides on what to expect and resist are particularly useful in areas not yet fully affected by mineral extraction.

A surface owners' movement, spawned by the Oil and Gas Reform Coalition (West Virginia) and the Concerned Land and Natural Resource Owners (West Virginia), is attempting to protect water and surface land in the face of irresponsible oil and gas drilling. The movement argues that owners have the right to be notified before any mineral development begins on their property and that owners can object to the well location and reclamation plans if they threaten water sources or continued use of topsoil. The movement has been sparked by numerous accounts of erosion and water pollution, and by the destruction of roads and arable ground across the West Virginia oil and gas fields.[12]

The Appalachian Land Bank Project could also become a mechanism for preserving land. It would pool funds and then move quickly to save land and minerals on the market for commercial and absentee acquisition. A report on such a project's feasibility has recently been completed by the HEAD Corporation, a nonprofit group in Kentucky (HEAD Corporation, 1979). Various small Appalachian land trusts use this concept.

While the demand for mineral land is the most visible consequence of the current energy program in Appalachia, the development needs water. The area's topography and hydrology are suitable for synthetic fuel, pump storage, and enhanced oil recovery projects. Synthetic fuel plants consume so much water that the proposed plant in Morgantown, West Virginia, would have radically decreased the flow of the Monongahela River. The project's proponents denied any relation between its need for water and the plans for the huge Stonewall Jackson Dam upriver, but the connection was not lost on critics of both projects. The Mountain Community Union, the Monongahela Alliance for Community Protection, Stop the Stonewall Jackson Dam, and the West Virginia Rivers Coalition have helped focus opposition to the synfuel plant and its financial and environmental risks.[13] The original financial package, calling for 95 percent financing by the federal government, Japan, and West Germany—and only 5 percent private capital (Gulf Oil)—has been withdrawn and the project shelved.

Opponents of the Stonewall Jackson Dam, which is to be built by the Army Corps of Engineers, sold hundreds of separate square yards of property in the dam's path to hundreds of people to require condemnation proceedings against each new landowner. Dam critics hope that they may have bought enough time to disprove what they believe is the Corps's ill-conceived cost-benefit calculation for the project, which would displace hundreds of people and flood some of the state's finest farmland. They have been able to obtain a congressional investigation of the data and procedures used by the Corps. There have also been a number of victories and/or stalemates in other water-related Appalachian projects: residents of Summers County (West Virginia) and Brumley Gap (Virginia) have been able to hold up pump storage projects that would have consumed prime agricultural land; Save Our Cumberland Mountains (Tennessee) has been successful in Roane County in preventing another river-diverting synfuel plant.

MITIGATING THE IMPACT OF LARGE-SCALE OWNERSHIP

> The interests which own 50 percent of the surface land and 75 percent of the minerals pay only 16 percent of the property tax. (A.L.O.T.F., 1980, VII:47)

The clearest link between massive corporate landownership and the quality of community life in Appalachia is the property tax. One cannot ask "Who owns property?" without also asking "Who pays taxes on it?" After generations of near-resignation (except for the hard-won gains of the United Mine Workers in the coalfields), resentment and even hatred of absentee control have produced a property tax reform movement.

This movement represents a conventional, easily replicable, and in most cases highly successful campaign aimed at increasing the fairness of a mechanism that, for the most part, is already in place and specifically intended to compel those who control the wealth to take a role in supporting the community. Groups like West Virginians for Fair Assessment of Taxes, Save Our Cumberland Mountains (Tennessee), the Kentucky Fair Tax Coalition, Lincoln County Citizens for Tax Reform (West Virginia), the Concerned Citizens of Buchanan County (Virginia), and the Tug Valley Recovery Center (West Virginia) have done research, now reinforced by the Land Ownership Study, to support the arguments and organization necessary to change the property tax system.

The Land Ownership Study demonstrates the gross underassessment of Appalachian natural resources, especially minerals. In McDowell County, West Virginia, large individual and corporate interests own 84 percent of the surface and 122 percent of the minerals (combined coal, oil, and gas, compared to the surface) in the heart of the state's coalfields. Yet local residential and commercial interests who own only 16 percent of the surface and essentially no minerals pay 41 percent of the property tax. This is a county where some of the poorest housing in the state sits atop enormous mineral wealth. In Mingo County, West Virginia, land for sale at $4,500 an acre was assessed at a value of $163 per acre. Kentucky has essentially no minerals tax; the average tax on an acre of coal is only a tenth of a cent. In Martin County the Pocahontas Land Company, a subsidiary of N & W Railroad, owns 81,000 acres of minerals but in 1978 paid only $76 in property taxes (A.L.O.T.F., 1980, VII:216 and I:81).

The taxation of other natural resources — oil and gas, other minerals, and timber — is even more inequitable. The Southern West Virginia Land Reform Project has found that commercial oil and gas estates are simply going untaxed in a number of counties, while others are assessed at a value of a dollar or less per acre. Some minerals and timber are not assessed at all for tax purposes.[14]

The mineral companies' resistance to taxation has been predictably intense. In response to West Virginia citizen initiatives, corporations prepared extensive legal arguments against the idea of one property owner having the right to challenge another's taxes.[15] In opposition to the Kentucky Fair Tax Coalition campaign, the Oil and Gas Reform Coalition in West Virginia, and arguments for increasing severance taxes across the region, companies maintain that increased taxation would discourage development.

When West Virginia began condemnation proceedings against Cotiga Development Corporation on the grounds that the people in Mingo County needed land for housing above the floodplain, the company was caught in an embarrassing contradiction. A citizens' group tried to have the taxes raised, and the company argued that the land had only limited value; when the state tried to establish an acquisition price, the company claimed the land was worth over $4,000 an acre. Other companies have ridiculed West Virginia's new appraised values for coal land, yet none has actually been willing to test them in court. Corporate resistance to equitable tax responsibility is epitomized by a Georgia Pacific lawyer caught in his own word tricks: "the services [we] get for the taxes [we] pay are zero." (A.L.O.T.F., 1980, VII:211).

By using existing laws in some cases and changing laws in others, citizen complaints and suits have focused public attention on the underassessment and begun forcing reluctant county officials to raise taxes. In one case the West Virginia Supreme Court affirmed any taxpayer's right to challenge the tax paid by another and instructed the assessors in the two counties involved to put realistic values on company-owned minerals. In Lincoln County, the ruling raised an additional half-million dollars, 70 percent of which will go to the school system.[16] Also as a result of public pressure, the West Virginia Tax Department began a program to reappraise coal lands in the 1970s and recently hired staff to examine the value of oil and gas lands. Although the coal program is proceeding very slowly and new values are being levied on only the least valuable of multiple seams, the program encourages citizen groups in other coal states.[17]

Commercial property, especially expensive mining machinery, has been an elusive source of tax revenue. Because the machinery is often mobile and, in the cases of underground use hard to find, assessors willingly overlooked millions of dollars in potential tax base. Save Our Cumberland Mountains (Tennessee) has doggedly pursued such property; after years of effort, it is obtaining court rulings that force assessors to locate and accurately appraise it.

These citizen efforts have produced millions of dollars of new revenue to rejuvenate decrepit school systems. They have led to effective coalitions between parent-teacher organizations, reform organizations, and church-supported social and economic programs. At the same time, Appalachian citizens recognize that more remains to be done. All county property books need to be carefully scrutinized to ensure that holdings are accurately reported and valued. More systematic comparison and equalization are necessary between the appraised values of local and residential property as against absentee and commercial property.

Some citizens argue that land should be taxed according to its use. Others advocate an excess-acreage tax, arguing that the value of property increases geometrically as land is aggregated. The hope is that both kinds of taxes would either help discourage vast, dormant holdings or establish more equitable rates. Large corporate mineral owners can also be required to compensate communities for the strain they put on roads, water sources, and the general ecology of the area. Effective severance and production taxes are needed on all natural resources, especially nonrenewable ones, to ensure long-term community stability after the minerals are gone.

In West Virginia the Oil and Gas Reform Coalition, the Committee of Concerned Land and Natural Resource Owners, and the Southern West Virginia Land Reform Project are also arguing for a thorough reworking and renegotiating of old leases that do not adequately compensate small mineral landowners or protect the interests of surface landowners and their heirs. Old flat-rate royalties, for example, are fixed at a specified amount per acre, ignoring the huge increase in the market value of minerals in recent years. Other states now have the model of a 1982 West Virginia law which stipulates that archaic flat-rate royalties are "unfair, oppressive, work an unjust hardship on the owner . . . and unreasonably deprive the economy of the state of the just benefit of the natural wealth of the state" (West Virginia House, 1982). The West Virginia Supreme Court has further restricted the latitude allowed in lease or contract agreements negotiated years ago, ruling that right-of-way agreements negotiated prior to the advent of herbicide spraying could not be interpreted now as permission to apply that technology. Such "unnecessary damage on the land" could not have been "within the specific contemplation of the parties" at the time (West Virginia Supreme Court, 1982). These two pieces of law add important constraints to lease arrangements.

REDISTRIBUTING LAND

> You know what happened in other countries when they got to where we're headed? They redistributed the land. We've got to do that.
> A West Virginia farmer (A.L.O.T.F., 1980, VII:127)

Appalachian people are beginning to envision the redistribution of control over the land itself. This redistribution is a natural next step when one considers the historical origin of existing landownership patterns and the present local reactions against them.

Until recently, the phenomenon of severed minerals was accepted as a way of life in Appalachia. Following the discovery of coal and, later, oil and gas, East Coast entrepreneurs combed the mountains, acquiring the minerals that underlay the region. According to the oral history of the area, in some cases baffled mountaineers sold an invisible and incomprehensible commodity for pennies. The old timber companies often sold the interests under their denuded and worthless surface. At least one imaginative traveling entrepreneur traded sewing machines for land. In all too many cases, company agents used questionable historical charters or patents, or quitclaim deeds signed by local opportunists who in fact never owned the land in the first place. In some cases, courthouses were burned to cloud people's title to their land. Typically, when confronted with this form of "documented" title, local people were cajoled or compelled into a compromise: the company would allow them to stay on the land if they acknowledged the company's claim to the minerals.

The development of Appalachian severed minerals inherently threatens the surface land and water over and near them. Moreover, energy that comes cheaply from under local farms and communities is returned to them at rates fast becoming prohibitive. And concentrated landownership patterns often allow one or two property owners, whose corporate headquarters may be hundreds of miles away, to determine when and if local people will work and where they will live. Citizen concerns spring from a growing resentment toward the very idea of severance and skepticism over the validity of company titles themselves. Such concerns animate the work of groups like the Southern West Virginia Land Reform Project, Knott County Citizens for Economic and Social Justice (Kentucky), Lincoln Citizens for Reform (West Virginia), the Virginia Land Alliance, and members of the Council of Southern Mountains.

For example, the delinquent tax sale mechanism can be modified so that when mineral land comes up for sale because of nonpayment of taxes, the surface owner can have the first option to buy back the mineral rights for the amount of back taxes before any auction occurs. Alternatively, severed mineral rights might be extinguished if, after a specified period of time, there have been no taxes paid on them or no development of them. This concept was recently upheld by the U.S. Supreme Court (U.S. Supreme Court, 1982).

In addition, there are leases negotiated many years ago that have been nullified or forefeited by the lessee: thus, unbeknownst to the current heirs or surface owners, the minerals now belong to them. Other leases are arguably unconscionable because of a lack of protection or just compensation for local people. Various surface owners' rights proposals use the concept of explicit prior consent from the surface owner before mineral development can begin. There is a precedent in West Virginia, where a surface owner's permission is required before both strip mining and the drilling of wells over 6,000 feet deep. Such proposals assume that the original mineral owner could not have anticipated the destructive impact of today's extraction technology in the period—often distant—when the severance occurred. The proposals would result in de facto control of the minerals under a surface owner's land.

Participants in the Land Ownership Study hope that it can arouse an Appalachian consciousness that will react against decades of land loss. Some local people emphasize buying the land back through land banks and trusts. Others argue that buying the land back is impractical in a region where local capital is scarce, and that it is not the way to deal with land illegitimately acquired in the first place. In any case, a number of families are initiating heirship claims to land they believe was stolen or swindled from their ancestors. In some cases, the families have brought lawsuits; in others they have simply retaken the land—either by occupying the surface or by mining the coal—to force the company to prove ownership in court.

CONCLUSION

The "energy problem" will never be solved until the national energy agenda is reconciled with the requisites of community well-being in the mineral-rich Appalachian region. (A.L.O.T.F., 1980, VII:61)

The new wave of Appalachian mineral development is supposed to be different. The new middle-class miner may soon make over $20,000 a year.[18] New mining and coal-conversion techniques will create unprecedented jobs and income. Oil and gas development will create a demand for pipe, drilling apparatus, trucking, and other ancillary enterprises. Increased strip mining will produce millions of tons of lucrative coal and other minerals. The electric power generated in Appalachia will expand enormously. Yet if these predictions come true, Appalachians will be virtually landless. Where will people be housed? What will happen to the family farm? Where will the acid runoff go? What will the remaining land cost and who will be able to buy it? Where will the schools and public facilities be built?

There is little or no public planning to prepare for the new develop-ment. While some agencies of the government — particularly at the federal level — offer technical assistance, tax write-offs, price deregulation, and regulatory exemptions as incentives to corporate energy interests, there is no corresponding or countervailing assistance to local communities. Most federal and state planning projects continue to ignore the relationship between landownership distribution and mineral development, on the one hand, and local life, on the other. The work done by federal programs such as the President's Coal Commission, the Energy Impacted Area Assistance Program,[19] the Appalachian Regional Commission development districts, and state development offices assumes the continuation of existing tax-revenue and landownership patterns. County and local governing bodies do not have the money, knowledge, or (frequently) the inclination to do any sustained land-use planning or impact analysis.

To fill this gap, a host of community and regional groups have begun grappling with the stresses produced in Appalachia by the national and international energy agenda. The varied struggles throughout the region represent a fundamental challenge to the economic and political power that has for generations been free to pull the pillars out from under the Appalachian communities. Local groups are attacking and restraining tra-ditional concepts of private property. They are arguing that private own-ership also implies responsibility for public stewardship. The Appalachian land reform movement has begun to explore the ways in which the right to private property can be balanced against the right of local communities to safe and plentiful housing, to protection from flood-ing and pollution, and to a future that they themselves determine.

NOTES

1. Appalachian Land Ownership Task Force (A.L.O.T.F.), 1980, VII:84.

2. See, for example, the readings in Lewis (1978).

3. *National Sacrifice Area* is a publication by the Appalachian Alliance, 1979, Williamson, West Virginia. Following the discovery of coal, oil, and gas in Appalachia at the turn of the century, eager entrepreneurs devised tactics to acquire mineral rights from local people while allowing them to retain surface land. Over the years legal judgments supported the concept of unrestricted access to these minerals, declaring that these were the "primary" estates and the surface was "secondary." These severed estates have been bought, sold, and developed virtu-ally independently of the surface land.

4. This does not include land controlled through leases, discussed later.

5. Minerals can be layered by type and coded separately for the same surface. Corporate interests in some counties own more than 100 percent of the minerals compared to the surface.

6. For an elaboration of this point, see the article by John Gaventa and Bill Horton in this volume.

7. Based on research done by West Virginia Congressman Bob Wise in 1981 (personal communication).

8. Personal communication with Don Hebb, West Virginia State Tax Department, Office of Local Government Relations.

9. The methodology was designed to be easily repeated. See Horton, Liden, and Weiss (1983).

10. John Brophy, introducing his plan for public ownership of resources at the 1921 Convention of the United Mine Workers.

11. For an example of such a petition, see Tug Valley Recovery Center (1979) for an especially good analysis of the relationship between strip mining and flooding.

12. For a call for a national surface owners' rights movement, see Appalachian Alliance (n.d.). The handbook may be obtained by writing the Alliance at P.O. Box 66, New Market, TN 37820.

13. For a discussion of the relationship between synfuel plants and strip mining, see Hoover and Doyle (1980).

14. This information was prepared by the author as testimony in a landmark case dealing with taxes and school funding, West Virginia Circuit Court, May 1982, and appeared in similar form in a two-part series in the *Charleston Gazette* (1982) by the author.

15. West Virginia Supreme Court, *Tug Valley Recovery Center, Inc.* v. *Mingo County Commission,* 1979.

16. The Lincoln County suit was joined with that of Mingo County under the title of *Tug Valley Recovery Center, Inc.* v. *Mingo County Commission,* 1979.

17. In counties where there are multiple seams of coal, a value is often established for each seam on the basis of seam width and the quality of the coal. Unfortunately for assessment purposes, only the least valuable seam is used.

18. This characterization comes from the President's Coal Commission (1980).

19. This program is run through the Farmers Home Administration under the Power Plant and Industrial Fuel Use Act of 1978.

REFERENCES

Appalachian Alliance. 1979. *National Sacrifice Area.* Williamson, WV: Appalachian Alliance.
————. n.d. *Residents' Handbook on Oil and Gas Development and Leasing.* New Market, TN: Appalachian Alliance.
Appalachian Land Ownership Task Force. 1980. *Appalachian Land Ownership Study.* Vol. I: Land Ownership Patterns and Their Impact on Appalachian Communities: A Survey of Eighty Counties. Vol. II: West Virginia Study. Boone, NC: Appalachian Land Ownership Task Force (November).
Brophy, John. 1921. Speech at Convention of the United Mine Workers on plan for public ownership of resources.
Business Week. 1979. "The oil majors bet on coal." (September 24): 104.
Charleston (West Virginia) *Gazette.* 1981. "End the exploitation." Editorial, May 26.
Coates, James. 1981. "Minerals war reaches the parks." *Chicago Tribune* reprint in the *Kingston* (Tennessee) *Times-News* (July 5).
HEAD Corporation. 1979. *The Feasibility and Design of a Central Appalachian Land Bank.* Berea, KY: HEAD Corporation (November).
Hoover, Jeff, and Doyle, Jack. 1980. *Synfuel vs. Agriculture.* Washington, DC: Environmental Policy Institute (August).
Horton, Bill, Liden, David, and Weiss, Tracy. forthcoming. *How to Find the Facts: A Handbook on Land Ownership Research.* New Market, TN: Land Ownership Task Force of the Appalachian Alliance.
Kanawha County Circuit Court (West Virginia). 1982. *Pauley* v. *Bailey,* May 24, 1982, Case No. CA–75–1268.
Lewis, Helen. 1978. *Colonialism in Modern America: The Appalachian Case.* Boone, NC: Appalachian Consortium Press.
Liden, David. 1982. "Taxing companies properly could net state $150 million." July 9, part one. "Updating resource taxes to aid schools." July 10, part two. *Charleston* (West Virginia) *Gazette.*
Michener, James. 1974. *Centennial.* New York: Random House.
The President's Coal Commission. 1980. *The American Coal Miner.* John D. Rockefeller IV, Chairman of the Commission. Washington, DC: The President's Coal Commission.

Tug Valley Recovery Center. 1979. *A Clear and Imminent Danger: The Case for Designating the Tug Fork Valley Watershed Unsuitable for Stripmining.* Williamson, WV: Tug Valley Recovery Center.

United States Supreme Court. 1982. *Texaco Inc.* v. *Short.* 450 U.S. 993.

West Virginia House. 1982. "Flat rate royalty bill." Bill 1254. 1982 West Virginia Legislative Session.

West Virginia Supreme Court. 1979. *Tug Valley Recovery Center, Inc.* v. *Mingo County Commission,* December 13, 1979, Case Nos. 14455 and 14456, Vol. 261, SE IId, 165.

———. 1982. *Kells* v. *Appalachian Power Co., Inc.,* March 22, 1982, Case No. 15067, Vol. 289, SE II, 450.

8

The Ambiguous End of the Sagebrush Rebellion

FRANK J. POPPER

Eastward I go only by force; but westward I go free. . . . The future lies that way to me, and the earth seems more unexhausted and richer on that side.

Henry David Thoreau (1862)

Primarily through the Interior Department's Bureau of Land Management (BLM), the federal government owns 86 percent of Nevada (Wolf, 1981:445). The state has long resented the federal landlord, particularly the environmental and natural-resource regulation it imposes. In 1979 the state filed a lawsuit claiming the BLM land, and the Sagebrush Rebellion was born. Arizona, New Mexico, Utah, Washington, and Wyoming, all with large federal ownerships and state grievances, made similar claims through legislation. The legislature of Alaska, then the state with the highest federal ownership (96 percent), endorsed "the efforts of the Western states to gain control of their lands" (Stegner, 1981:30). The rebels sought to put large parts of the federal holdings—the public lands of the West—in the hands of states, localities, individuals, corporations. It was a land reform promoted by conservatives against their ancient enemy, the federal government.

Asked about the rebellion in 1980 while compaigning in Salt Lake City, Ronald Reagan said, "Count me in" (Lamm and McCarthy, 1982:317–18). He won every Western state but Hawaii. He appointed James Watt, a prominent rebel, Interior Secretary. The new administration moved quickly and effectively to achieve the rebellion's goals—but mainly by loosening federal regulation rather than transferring federal land. The rebellion disappeared, the landholdings and the landlord remained. This story of mingled federal acquiescence and betrayal is as old as the settlement of any region of the United States. It also reveals the master predicament of American land history.

THE WEST AS A FEDERAL FIEF

It is still possible to surprise an Eastern or West Coast listener with the fact that the federal government owns a third of the nation's land (Wolf, 1981:442–46). The vast bulk is in the intermountain West (from the Sierra-Cascades to the Rockies) and Alaska, and it is all but uninhabited. You could hike 1,800 miles, from central Oregon southeast to southern Nevada, northeast to the midpoint of the Utah-Colorado border, southeast again to southeast New Mexico on the Mexican border. Except for minor jumps — mostly across other public land — you would never leave BLM property.[1] It comprises 44 percent of the land in states west of the Rockies.[2]

You could take another 1,800-mile BLM hike from southeast California on the Mexican border to northeast Montana on the Canadian border. The California-Montana hike fittingly intersects the Oregon-New Mexico one in southern Utah, one of America's most forbidding places. You could take a 2,300-mile BLM hike around Alaska, from the southern Yukon Territory border northwest to near Barrow (the northernmost town in the United States), southwest to the Yukon River Delta and then to the middle of the Alaska Peninsula on the Bering Sea (*National Geographic Magazine,* 1982:map). The BLM hikes — call them branches of the James Watt Trail — would cross deserts, mountains, forests, plains, rivers, tundra, ice. You would rarely encounter a settlement or even step on the property of the Agriculture Department's Forest Service, the second largest federal land agency (16 percent of the land in states west of the Rockies), or that of the Interior Department's Fish and Wildlife Service (8 percent) and National Park Service (6 percent).[3]

The public lands contain a prodigious share of America's resources. Forest Service land, mainly in Oregon, Washington, and northern California, produces 40 percent of the nation's salable timber and 60 percent of its softwood sawtimber — wood for building houses (Wolf, 1981:447). Fourteen percent of American livestock — primarily cattle and sheep — graze on BLM and other public land (Wolf, 1981:454). Public lands, particularly the Powder River Basin in northeast Wyoming and southeast Montana, contain a third of the nation's known coal reserve (Nelson, 1982:20). A third of its uranium reserve is on public land in the Wyoming Basin and Colorado Plateau (Nothdurft, 1981:20). Eighty percent of its oil shale lies on public land in the Green River formation under Colorado, Utah, and Wyoming (Nothdurft, 1981:20). Almost all large Western ski resorts use Forest Service land. Public lands supply most of the nation's copper, silver, asbestos, lead, geothermal energy, brown and grizzly bears, caribou, bighorn sheep, moose, mule deer, and antelope; much of its oil, natural gas, antimony, beryllium, molybdenum, phosphate, and potash; and all its natural parks, monuments, and wildernesses (Nelson, 1982:18–26; Harvey, forthcoming).

These national storehouses are often state and local headaches. The governments of Alaska, Idaho, Nevada, Oregon, and Utah have no formal jurisdiction over more than half their territory. Arizona, California, Colorado, New Mexico, and Wyoming lack jurisdiction over more than a third of theirs (Wolf, 1981:445). The average citizen of a Western state cannot live, work, or even vacation on much of the federal land, let alone buy, sell, or develop it. Land-use regulations and policies made in Washington, or in the regional offices of federal agencies, are often the main influence on state and local patterns of grazing, forestry, energy and other mineral development, tourism, recreation, and water development — the last especially vital in the vast arid stretches of the West that get less than twenty inches of rain a year.

The effects of decisions on federal lands reverberate onto the remaining (often surrounded or interspersed) nonfederal ones. Some state and many local governments are little more than land-use dependencies of the federal one. Thus the politics of the Sagebrush Rebellion as land reform involve a struggle against the federal landlord not only by Western individuals and corporations, but also by Western state and local governments.

For instance, almost every city and town in the intermountain West and Alaska amounts to an urban island in a sea of public land. Federal landholdings around cities such as Albuquerque, Anchorage, Las Vegas, and Phoenix have the direct or indirect effect of constraining urban growth, raising land and housing prices, and forcing construction into environmentally risky areas. The federal holdings sometimes determined where the cities were in the first place. Western real-estate agents are always amused when transplanted Easterners try to buy seemingly cheap, abundant rural land — the wide open spaces — and find that none is available. Energy boomtowns — such as Rock Springs, Wyoming, or Colstrip, Montana — are overcrowded, slumlike, and expensive partly because they cannot expand to surrounding public land or build housing on it.[4]

Federal land policies have enormous effects on Western economies, public treasuries, and the public-service demands on them. Small changes in federal logging contracts, mineral leases, grazing permits, recreation fees, irrigation allowances, and the procedures for deciding on them, can have boom-or-bust, live-or-die consequences for Western localities, particularly small ones. Some Western towns exist essentially at the sufferance of federal agencies.

There are compensations. The federal government has rarely charged Western industries high prices for the use of the public lands, and the charges have often amounted to subsidies.[5] Federal agencies pay states and localities large sums as replacements for lost property taxes and as royalties for the resources extracted from the public lands. The federal agencies also pay for what would otherwise be state and local public services. In places such as Boise, Denver, and Salt Lake City, the national parks and forests are practically local playgrounds. Grand Canyon, Yosemite, Yellowstone, and other national parks anchor local economies based on tourism and recreation. Yet the federal landlord — an apparently remote but intrusive force that is locally uncontrollable — is resented anyway.

The public lands pit state and local interests against federal and national ones. When federal administrations are liberal, Democratic, environmentalist, federally oriented, urban, or simply Eastern — as they mostly have been — the conservative, Republican, development-minded, localist, rural West objects to their public-land policies and to the federal government's role as a super zoning board, development agency, and sugar daddy to the West. Resistance movements such as the Sagebrush Rebellion emerge. They raise three good questions. Why does the federal government own so much land? Why is nearly all of it in the West? Should the federal presence be reduced?

THE SURVIVAL OF THE FIEF

The federal government owns a third of the country because in the past it owned four-fifths. As one of the compromises leading to the signing of the Articles of Confederation, the 1781 predecessor to the Constitution, New York, Massachusetts, Connecticut, Virginia, North Carolina, South Carolina, and Georgia agreed to cede their trans-Appalachian land claims — amounting to all or almost all of what is now Illinois, Indiana, Michigan, Ohio, Wisconsin, Alabama, Mississippi, and Tennessee — to the federal government (Gates, 1968:49–57). As the United States expanded across the continent, most of its land acquisitions entered the nation as public land that became part of territories and then states. The main Western exceptions, Texas and Hawaii, previously had been independent nations that had little public land on entry and have little now — 2 and 10 percent, respectively (Wolf, 1981:445).

Behind slavery, the public lands were nineteenth-century America's dominant domestic issue. The 1803 Louisiana Purchase from France doubled the nation's size, added its present midsection, and more than tripled its stock of public land. Further acquisitions followed which were nearly all public land — for instance, the 1846 Oregon Compromise (Oregon, Idaho, Washington, parts of Wyoming and Montana) from Britain; the 1848 Mexican Cession (California, Nevada, Utah, most of Arizona, parts of Colorado, New Mexico, Wyoming); and the 1867 Alaska Purchase from Russia. The acquisitions had to be defended — against not only the Indians, but also the French, Spanish, Mexicans, British, and Russians. The nation, desperately poor, needed what we now call economic development. Its Eastern cities were full of immigrants with rural backgrounds, its Eastern farms full of farmers who wanted better land. The territory from the Appalachians to the Pacific spelled personal and national opportunity. Nineteenth-century America called it Manifest Destiny.

Thus was born the largest regional development project in American history, the white settlement of the West — a huge real-estate conveyance, aimed at getting the public lands out of federal hands. The federal government happily cooperated in a long series of successful Sagebrush Rebellions. Between 1818 and 1833 Alabama, Illinois, Indiana, Louisiana, and Missouri asked Congress to cede them the states' public lands (Mollison,

1981:4), and soon enough all the Midwestern and Southern states, their residents, and corporations got nearly everything they wanted. Later California, Oregon, and Washington got much of their public lands west of the Sierra-Cascades.

Throughout the nineteenth century and well into the twentieth, there were sales and grants to states (including the land-grant colleges), localities, railroads, road and canal companies, farm and ranch companies, veterans, squatters, homesteaders, other concerned citizens. There were special giveaways of swamps, deserts, and mining and timber land (Wolf, 1981:36–37). In 1811 the federal government received 7 percent of its income from the sale of public land; in 1836 it received 36 percent (Gates, forthcoming). Thereafter its terms became increasingly liberal. Over time claimants had to put up less money, could get more land and easier credit, had to do less with the land, were more likely to avoid paying for it, and were less restrained — today we would say regulated — by the federal government. The federal government wanted the land settled and was separated from it by nineteenth-century transportation and communications conditions. It was a time of spectacular land fraud.

The Manifest Destiny land rush was greedy, gory, grim — what the eminent critic Vernon Parrington, one of the founders of American studies, called the Great Barbecue (Watkins and Watson, 1975:10, 45–71). Except for one trip around the Great Lakes to central Minnesota just before he died, Thoreau — maker of some of the most effective, authentic wilderness-West rhetoric in American literature — never traveled west of Philadelphia, never saw the frontier in full cry, as a quietist would have been repelled by it.[6] In the real-life nineteenth-century West, it was frequently unfulfilling to be an overworked cowboy, an uprooted Indian, a Chinese coolie laying railroad track, a Scotch-Irish miner, one of the majority of ethnically various homesteaders who couldn't make a go of it, a boomer in the majority of towns that didn't boom, or their womenfolk. But by the turn of the twentieth century, their sacrifices — their exploitation — meant that the West was being won. The giant land transfer was working.

It was also subsiding. Because of what we would now term the environmental excesses of the land rush — the abundant herds of Western buffalo, for example, were extinguished in a few decades, as were millions of passenger pigeons and the Upper Midwest pineries (Nelson, 1982:29) — the federal government began to set aside land (often over Western objections) for national parks in the 1870s, forests in the 1890s, fish and wildlife refuges in the 1900s, wildernesses in the 1920s. A great deal more land — most of the desert core that University of Texas historian Walter Prescott Webb in the late 1950s called "the low-intensity fire that has been burning for a million years in the West," also much of the Great Plains, Webb's "burnt right flank of the desert"[7] — proved nearly uninhabitable, except occasionally for scattered, physically difficult, economically chancy mining and ranching. The deepest desert in general had few takers, and they rarely lasted. Homesteading, the most symbolic and widespread act of settling the West, peaked in 1910, but the bulk of the successful claims were not in the intermountain West or the Great Plains, but in areas with more rain — the Pacific Slope, the Midwest, and the South, where farms of the allowed 160 acres could work. The amounts were later increased to 320 and 640 acres, but these were still not enough for successful Western farming.[8]

Most intermountain and plains homesteading was wiped out by the small size of the farms, and a train of droughts and rural depressions, and then the Great Depression. The 1934 Taylor Grazing Act largely abolished homesteading and ended the federal conveyancing; established what later became the BLM; and created the boundaries and legal form of most present public lands. The federal government owns large parts of the West mainly because no one wanted the BLM lands, and to a lesser extent because it preserved the national Forest, Fish and Wildlife, Park Service, and wilderness lands. The vast bulk of the Western federal holdings have been public land for as long as they have been part of the United States. They are the leftovers of the Great Barbecue.

THE REBELLION RAMPANT

The late-1970s' rise of the Sagebrush Rebellion was predictable. The basic outlines of the public lands and their management had not changed in forty-five years or more. Prices for the commodities they produced — especially energy and timber — had risen dramatically. The West was growing fast, becoming the wealthiest and by some measures the most urban part of the nation, no longer a poor-relative region that needed special federal tutelage. Conservatism was resurgent, environmentalism losing its bloom, federal regulation increasingly seen as onerous, particularly in the rural, rugged-individualist West that was often still poor. The federal lands — their size, their state and local consequences, and the restrictions on their use — appeared an anomaly, a throwback.

Some elements in the West — notably the ranching and mining industries and their allies in state government — had always been reluctant to see the Great Barbecue end. Wyoming, Idaho, and Colorado attempted a small Sagebrush Rebellion in the 1890s, and most of the Western states took part in a larger, again unsuccessful one in the 1910s (Lamm and McCarthy, 1982:307, 308). In 1930, even as federal conveyancing and homesteading were in steep decline, a presidential commission with many Western business executives recommended to Herbert Hoover that federal lands be divested to the states and the private sector (Lamm and McCarthy, 1982:309). In the late 1940s and early 1950s, cattle and sheep ranchers sought in effect to repeal the Taylor Act by selling public grazing lands — whether held by BLM, the Forest Service, or other federal agencies — to the stockmen and the states at about ten cents an acre (Stegner, 1981:33). In 1970 the Public Land Law Review Commission, an important federal advisory group, recommended against the concept of future large-scale federal disposals, but Arizona and Nevada petitioned the commission for land anyway (Mollison, 1981:4).

The Sagebrush Rebellion could count on some tacit support outside the West. Those parts of the rural East with heavy federal holdings—the most Western parts of the East—have traditionally had complaints much like those of the rebels. In the late 1970s, Northeast Minnesota fought a long battle against Forest Service wilderness designations in the million-acre Boundary Waters Canoe Area (Gorton, 1977). A 1981 Appalachian Regional Commission report quoted a resident of Swain County, North Carolina (80 percent federally owned), as saying that the Great Smoky Mountains National Park "is the most visited national park in the U.S., but that doesn't help our economy any" (Appalachian Land Ownership Task Force, 1981:84). County residents have set fire to land in the Great Smokies as a way of harassing the Park Service (Appalachian Land Ownership Task Force, 1981:91). Residents and vacation-home owners on North Carolina's Outer Banks object to restrictions on their driving 4.5 miles through Virginia's Back Bay National Wildlife Refuge on their way to Virginia Beach or Norfolk when the alternative route off public land is up to two hours longer (Nunes, 1982:C1). More generally, Eastern sentiment against land-use regulation, environmental laws, the federal government, and its landlord role is often as strong as Western.

The federal government was a provably—self-admittedly—mediocre manager of its Western holdings. In 1975 the BLM estimated that 83 percent of its rangeland was in environmentally "unsatisfactory" or worse condition because of overgrazing (Culhane, 1981:13). The Forest Service's figures showed that its timberland yields were less than 40 percent of what the same land could produce were it managed by private corporations—that might still allow considerable recreational use (Wolf, 1981:458). Many national parks were decrepit and overextended, some national wildernesses—for instance, Rahwah in the Colorado Rockies (Lamm and McCarthy, 1982:305)—overused by seekers of solitude. Large parts of public lands produced neither the commodities nor the amenities they should. In a practical economic sense they were ownerless, passively operated. The Sagebrush Rebellion appealed to its supporters because it suggested the lands could have large numbers of active owner-operators. It outraged its opponents for the same reason.

By 1979 conservative Republican congressmen from the West were introducing far-reaching Sagebrush Rebellion bills. Utah's Senator Orrin Hatch proposed a Western Lands Distribution and Regional Equalization Act that would have transferred to the states 544 million acres—almost all the federal Western holdings (Lamm and McCarthy, 1982:277–78). Nevada's Representative Jim Santini offered a similar bill that excluded the national forests (Lamm and McCarthy, 1982:278). New Mexico's Senator Harrison Schmitt suggested that the states be allowed to select federal public lands in exchange for state lands in federal military holdings; since the state lands were effectively under federal control, the result would be a something-for-nothing trade in favor of the states (Gregg, 1982:11).

Thus the Sagebrush Rebellion seemed historically justifiable, economically sensible, regionally equitable, politically powerful. It appeared to be (even if it was not) a new wrinkle in the settlement of the West — a right-wing land reform. Yet in September 1981 James Watt told the Western Governors Conference, meeting in Jackson, Wyoming, that the rebellion was over: "I'm a rebel without a cause. You hardly hear about the rebellion in Washington anymore." The governors cheered (Prochnau, 1981:A9). The rebellion was suddenly past history, an abortive episode. What had gone wrong? Why did the rebellion end?

THE REBELLION REDIRECTED

The Sagebrush Rebellion did not fail — it ended. It got a great deal of what it sought. At the same time, some of its objectives on examination proved impractical, alienated possible supporters, were abandoned by the Rebels. The Western governors, for instance, were quick to notice that if they acquired responsibility for the public lands, they would also acquire new costs and duties, and would eventually lose the federal replacement payments and public services — which were generous subsidies, not easily duplicated from state treasuries (Nelson, 1982:62–65). The governors realized that they were having a hard enough time managing existing, often extensive, state lands — they did not need large amounts of new ones, especially considering the scandals the state lands had caused in nearly every Western state.[9] State agencies might be no better managers than federal ones.

The rebels — macho masters of rural West blowhard speechifying, capable of invoking the Boston Tea Party as a precedent for resisting small increases in small BLM grazing fees for large, rich ranchers (Stegner, 1981:30) — had antagonized Western (and Eastern) liberals and city dwellers. These groups might conceivably have supported a large-scale land transfer as a decentralizing measure, a way to promote locally sensitive regulation, environmentally balanced economic growth, or equality between the regions. Instead they opposed it as a giveaway to large mineral, timber, and cattle companies, an invitation to environmental damage and land fraud on the scale of the Great Barbecue, a device to offer national parks, forests, wildernesses, and monuments to national predators.

Rural conservative Republican Westerners — the natural supporters of the Rebellion, the people who knew the land at issue best — also had second thoughts. Federal disposal would still leave most of the land arid, isolated, rocky, difficult to cultivate, far from utility lines, desert, mountainous, or arctic. It was unclear how the disposals would occur, what prices (if any) would be charged for the newly available land, whether neighbors harmed by the disposals would be compensated.[10] Most rural land and housing markets were already down; more land on the private market would depress them further. If much of the land ended up in the hands of states and localities, they were still the hated public sector. When it was politically convenient, rural Westerners might espouse states' or local rights in preference to federal ones, but they were not interested in replacing the federal landlord with a state or municipal one. If the land ended up with corporations, they were often huge, destructive, aloof, out-of-state, even based in the East, on the West Coast, or abroad — anathema to the rural populist West. The corporations were even more likely than the federal government to lock up the land, to keep the public from using it. Perhaps the federal holdings were not so bad after all.

With the election of Ronald Reagan, the holdings got better fast. Massive land transfers became unnecessary to much of the rural West — it could get what it wanted in other ways. The federal land agencies began to regulate less stringently and pay more attention to state and local complaints. Oil, gas, coal, and timber leasing was accelerated, more land opened to it, parkland and wildlife refuge acquisitions frozen, wilderness designations slowed down, private conservation efforts encouraged as an alternative to public ones. Hard, short-term economic considerations were overriding soft, long-term environmental ones.

The Reagan administration found clever, politically appealing ways to start to transfer some public lands — serious amounts, but nothing on a genuinely West-wide scale — without having to ask Congress for new legislation. Watt's Interior Department undertook a good-neighbor policy that allowed state and local governments to request the department's "surplus" public lands. The initiative was soon broadened to an Asset Management Program whereby all federal agencies could sell their excess land, in the West and elsewhere; the eventual sale of 35 million acres — an area the size of Iowa — was anticipated. Separately, the Forest Service began moves to sell up to fourteen to seventeen million acres of small tracts that would probably be mostly Western. The federal land-management agencies speeded up the transfers to Alaska's state government and natives which had been authorized by the 1958 Statehood Act, the 1971 Native Claims Settlement Act, and the 1980 National Interest Lands Conservation Act. The BLM revived homesteading in the Kuskokwim Mountains in central Alaska. Numerous federal-Western state land exchanges were in exploratory stages, and seemed most advanced in Utah.

Defused, coopted by Ronald Reagan and James Watt, the Sagebrush Rebellion wound down. Nevada's lawsuit that began the rebellion was rejected by a federal district court in Reno in 1981. The state has appealed the decision to the circuit court level, but with little hope (Balz, 1982:A2). To Western state and local officials, the politics of the rebellion had always been uncertain, for in truth it was hard to tell what the Western public thought. Washington's voters rejected the state's Sagebrush Rebellion legislation in a 1980 referendum when approval would have helped the movement. Arizona's and Alaska's voters supported their legislation in 1982 referenda that came too late to make a difference. Western polls showed that the only state that consistently and heavily supported the rebellion was Nevada,[11] but in 1982 Reno's Republicans refused to endorse a Sagebrush Rebellion plank (Balz, 1982:A2). It was political wisdom not to resist the rebellion's end.

THE FATE OF THE FIEFDOM

The West will probably see more land transfers in the next few decades, and the Sagebrush Rebellion will have made them possible by making them thinkable. A number of plausible alternatives have surfaced in the wake of the rebellion. Dean Rhoads, the Nevada state legislator and rancher often considered the father of the rebellion, now supports allowing cattle and sheep raisers to buy surface rights to public land, keeping the mineral rights in federal hands, and letting the states take over day-to-day management and regulation (Balz, 1982:A2). The 1982 report of the President's Commission on Housing advocates "townsteading" on public land (President's Commission on Housing, 1982:103). Others have suggested the creation of public-private development corporations; direct transfers to private interests ("privatization"); long-term leasing to private interests for terms as long as 100 years; procedures to allow private interests, environmentalists, and state and local governments to challenge bids for public land; expansions of the Alaskan homesteading initiative; or — most sensibly — a series of experimental programs on relatively small parcels to test differing concepts of land management.[12] The BLM grazing system created by the 1934 Taylor Act originated with such an experiment in the Mizpah-Pumpkin Creek area in southeast Montana in the late 1920s (Culhane, 1981:83).

We are almost certainly entering a new phase of America's growth into its gigantic physical setting. There will be changes — reforms — in public land policy. From the Articles of Confederation to the Taylor Grazing Act, federal policy essentially was to acquire and dispose of public land. From the Taylor Act to the advent of James Watt, it was to retain it. The Sagebrush Rebellion marks the transition back to what will probably be a long period of disposal. For nearly fifty years, disposal has been interrupted; new land demands, new extraction and construction technologies have built up and now seek consummation. The environmental movement, its laws, and its protection technologies are here to stay. Many public lands — nearly all national parks, monuments, and wildernesses, some national forests, other high-grade recreation areas — are politically sacred places that disposal cannot touch because they are acknowledged as physically sacred places it should not touch. But disposal — mainly of the more numerous, less distinctive BLM lands, especially those near big cities — could take place gradually so as not to invite fraud, disrupt local land markets, or overburden states and localities. A key problem will be gradually weaning Western governments and resource-based industries from their dependence on federal subsidies. Disposal will not necessarily lead to environmental, economic, or intergovernmental debacle. Under hardline antifederal administrations, it could. But it need not.

There is a hitch, however, in the idea of massive disposals. The true architect of the West — the ultimate landlord — has never been governmental or even human; it has been the desert, its immense expansions and contractions, its pitiless resistance to cultivation. Most of Alaska, too, except for the coastal strip south of the Alaska Range, gets less than twenty inches of rain a year. The state, the sixth of America that bulks so large in Western development plans, is a cold desert, as Arizona is a hot one. Throughout the West, water supplies have been under severe, mounting strain for the last decade. If large-scale disposals of public land are to be feasible in coming ones, we will need technical and institutional breakthroughs in conserving water and probably in pumping, transporting, storing, and sharing it. An administration that really thought in terms of building the West, of transforming the face of America, would need to look no further for enterprises to support. Western land reform means Western water reform.

It is extraordinary that after more than 180 years of often feverish pioneering, large parts of the West remain nearly untouched. Seventeen percent of the country — 383 million acres of Western public land — has never even been surveyed, and more than 50 million additional acres were surveyed inadequately over a century ago (USDI, 1980:129-30). According to the 1980 census, over a quarter of the United States — all in the West, almost all in or near public land — falls in counties with an average of two people or less per square mile (Popper, 1983). This was the standard the 1890 census used to define the frontier (Toole, 1976:210). We are no longer a frontier nation, but we are a nation with a frontier. It is a gift of history, a part of our endowment — one of the reasons we are a lucky country. The frontier survives. We have nearly forgotten we have it. So we have no clear national idea what to do with it. We have no notion of what it will mean to subject it to land reform.

NOTES

1. *National Geographic Magazine* (1982), a map. Also available separately.
2. Computed from Nelson in Portney (1982), pp. 16-17.
3. Computed from Nelson in Portney (1982), pp. 16-17.
4. On Rock Springs, see Toole (1976), pp. 108-10.
5. See, for example, Nelson in Portney (1982), pp. 56-57.
6. For a map of Thoreau's travels, see Howarth (1981), p. 358.
7. Webb (1957) and (1958), both quoted in Toole (1976), pp. 31-32.
8. On homesteading generally, see Culhane (1981), pp. 76-84. For the 1910 date, see Libecap (1981), pp. 16 and 38.
9. Personal communication, Marion Clawson, Senior Fellow Emeritus, Resources for the Future, Washington, D.C., January 27, 1983.
10. See, for example, U.S. General Accounting Office (1981).
11. For an example, see Stegner (1981), p. 30.
12. See, for instance, the suggestions in Brubaker (forthcoming).

REFERENCES

Appalachian Land Ownership Task Force. 1981. *Appalachian Land Ownership Study.* Vol. IV: North Carolina. Washington, DC: Appalachian Regional Commission.

Balz, Dan. 1982. "Once riding high, sagebrush rebels turn in midstream." *Washington Post* (April 10).

Brubaker, Sterling (ed.). Forthcoming. *Rethinking the Federal Lands.* Baltimore and Washington: Johns Hopkins University Press and Resources for the Future.

Culhane, Paul. 1981. *Public Lands Politics: Interest Group Influence on the Forest Service and the Bureau of Land Management.* Baltimore and Washington: Johns Hopkins University Press and Resources for the Future.

Gates, Paul. Forthcoming. "Federal lands: why we retained them." In *Rethinking the Federal Lands.* Edited by Sterling Brubaker. Baltimore and Washington: Johns Hopkins University Press and Resources for the Future.

———. 1968. *History of Public Land Law Development.* Washington, DC: U.S. Government Printing Office.

Gorton, Tom. 1977. "What shall be the fate of the boundary waters?" *Planning* (September).

Gregg, Frank. 1982. *Federal Land Transfers: The Case for a Westwide Program Based on the Federal Land Policy and Management Act.* Washington, DC: Conservation Foundation.

Harvey, D. Michael. Forthcoming. "The federal lands today: uses and limits: who cares and how should the current law work?" In *Rethinking the Federal Lands.* Edited by Sterling Brubaker. Baltimore and Washington: Johns Hopkins University Press and Resources for the Future.

Howarth, William. 1981. "Thoreau, a different man." *National Geographic Magazine* (March).

Lamm, Richard, and McCarthy, Michael. 1982. *The Angry West: A Vulnerable Land and Its Future.* Boston: Houghton-Mifflin.

Libecap, Gary. 1981. *Locking Up the Range: Federal Land Controls and Grazing.* San Francisco and Cambridge: Pacific Institute for Public Policy Research and Ballinger.

Mollison, Richard. 1981. "The sagebrush rebellion: its causes and effects." *Environmental Comment* (June).

National Geographic Magazine. 1982. America's Federal Lands. A map. (September). Also available separately.

Nelson, Robert. 1982. "The public lands." In *Current Issues in Natural Resource Policy.* Edited by Paul Portney. Baltimore and Washington: Johns Hopkins University Press and Resources for the Future. Pp. 16–17.

Nothdurft, William. 1981. "The lands nobody wanted." *The Living Wilderness* (Summer).

Nunes, Don. 1983. "Tug-of-war." *Washington Post* (September 26).

Popper, Frank. 1983. "The surviving American frontier." *American Land Forum Magazine* (Summer).

President's Commission on Housing. 1982. *Report of the President's Commission on Housing.* Washington, DC: President's Commission on Housing.

Prochnau, Bill. 1981. "Sagebrush rebellion is over, interior secretary says." *Washington Post* (September 12).

Stegner, Wallace. 1981. "If the sagebrush rebels win, everyone loses." *The Living Wilderness* (Summer).

Thoreau, Henry David. 1950. "Walking." In *Walden and Other Writings of Henry David Thoreau.* Edited by Brooks Atkinson. New York: Random House.

Toole, K. Ross. 1976. *The Rape of the Great Plains: Northwest America, Cattle and Coal.* Boston: Atlantic-Little, Brown.

United States Department of the Interior, Bureau of Land Management. 1980. *Public Land Statistics 1980.* Washington, DC: U.S. Government Printing Office.

United States General Accounting Office. 1981. *Numerous Issues Involved in Large-Scale Disposals and Sales of Federal Real Property.* Washington, DC: U.S. General Accounting Office (December).

Watkins, T. H., and Watson, Charles, Jr. 1975. *The Lands No One Knows: America and the Public Domain.* San Francisco: Sierra Club Books.

Webb, Walter Prescott. 1958. "The west and the desert." *Montana: The Magazine of Western History* (Winter).

———. 1957. "The American west: perpetual mirage." *Harper's* (September).

Wolf, Peter. 1981. *Land in America: Its Value, Use and Control.* New York: Pantheon.

9

Partnership in the Pinelands

KEVIN J. RIELLEY, WENDY U. LARSEN, AND
CLIFFORD L. WEAVER

The New Jersey Pinelands—an expanse of forest covering one million acres, fifty-two municipalities, and one-quarter of a state in the midst of the country's most densely populated region—has long been recognized as an environmental treasure. The area harbors many endangered plant and animal species, in combinations found nowhere else. The comprehensive management plan adopted by the Pinelands Commission on 21 November 1980 represents the culmination of extensive efforts to preserve the Pinelands (Pinelands Commission, 1980).

For at least three hundred years, the Pinelands have supported lumbering, bog-iron production, and sand and gravel extraction. Settlements have appeared and disappeared as new resources were found and exhausted. The Pinelands ecosystem historically has retained its ability to maintain itself, and some uses—particularly cranberry cultivation—have actually helped preserve the ecosystem.

Activities in recent years, however, have proved less compatible. Development pressures have grown throughout the Pinelands, threatening the ecosystem and resulting in numerous protection efforts over the last fifteen years. Several Pinelands municipalities have attempted to control development impacts by improving their local land-use regulations. In addition, there has been an increasing awareness that the Pinelands form a total ecosystem whose preservation requires a regional approach.

The earliest regional effort was carried out by the former Pinelands Regional Planning Board, which in 1965 published four growth scenarios for the region, including the famous "Jetport in the Pines" proposal. Later, a major study by Jack McCormick, prepared for the Philadelphia Acad-

The authors appreciate the help the New Jersey Pinelands Commission staff provided for this article.

emy of Sciences and published by the New Jersey State Museum, detailed the plant and animal species of the Pinelands and asserted that their ecological setting was interdependent and easily disturbed (McCormick, 1967 and 1970). John McPhee's popular book, *The Pine Barrens,* promoted a wider understanding of the region (McPhee, 1968).

In 1968 the National Park Service developed alternative plans for the Pinelands. In 1972 the state legislature established the Pinelands Environmental Council; in 1975 the council produced its report, *A Plan for the Pinelands.* Other groups that have studied and made recommendations regarding the future of the area are the federal Bureau of Outdoor Recreation (B.O.R., 1975); Rutgers University's Center for Coastal and Environmental Studies (C.C.E.S., 1978); and the Governor's Pinelands Review Committee (The Governor's Pinelands Review Committee, 1979). The last study recommended creating a fifteen-member body to forge a plan for the Pinelands, dividing the region into an inner preservation area and an outer protection area, and also recommended the use of development controls during the planning period. These recommendations became the basis of the current Pinelands protection strategy.

EXISTING LEGISLATIVE AUTHORITY

The current federal legislative mandate to protect the Pinelands appears in Section 502 of the National Parks and Recreation Act of 1978.[1] This legislation established the Pinelands National Reserve, containing parts of seven southern New Jersey counties and all or part of 56 municipalities. It also authorized a planning entity to prepare a comprehensive management plan for the reserve which was to be submitted to the Secretary of the Interior within eighteen months of the receipt of federal funds appropriated to carry out the act.

To comply with the federal law, Governor Brendan T. Byrne issued Executive Order 71 on 8 February 1979, creating the Pinelands Planning Commission and making most Pinelands development subject to commission approval during the planning period. The order incorporated many of the recommendations previously offered by the Governor's Pinelands Review Committee. The deadline for adoption of a comprehensive management plan was 8 August 1980, eighteen months after the executive order went into effect.

In June 1979 the New Jersey legislature passed the Pinelands Protection Act.[2] This legislation endorsed the planning effort; formally designated the Pinelands Commission, headquartered in New Lisbon, as the regional planning entity called for in the federal legislation; and continued the interim restrictions on development. The fifteen-member commission consists of one member appointed from each of the governing bodies of the seven Pinelands counties, seven appointed by the Governor of New Jersey, and one designated by the U.S. Secretary of the Interior. The commission is attached to the New Jersey Department of Environmental Protection.

The state legislation specifies, however, that the commission is independent of any supervision or control by the department and has the authority to exercise all powers and duties necessary to carry out the state and federal legislation.

The Pinelands Protection Act defines the "Pinelands area," consisting of a 368,000-acre, semiwilderness preservation area and a 566,000-acre, somewhat more developed, protection area. The Pinelands area is slightly smaller than the federal Pinelands National Reserve and takes in all or part of fifty-two municipalities (see map, figure 9.1).

The state and federal enabling legislation triggered a year-long series of studies, conducted by independent experts in many areas of the natural and social sciences, under the oversight of the Pinelands Commission and its staff. These studies culminated in the adoption, after a series of public hearings throughout the Pinelands region, of a comprehensive management plan for the Pinelands on 21 November 1980.

EVOLUTION OF THE ROLE OF
THE PINELANDS COMMISSION

Every land-use program has two basic elements: substantive regulations and an organizational and procedural framework. These elements are inversely related — that is, the more one is able to define clear and specific substantive regulations, the less one need worry about organizational and procedural devices. Conversely, where constraints of time and budget, lack of data, or the complexity of the problem prevent the development of clear, specific, self-executing substantive regulations, the need for a sophisticated, smooth-running, and equitable organizational and procedural framework increases dramatically.

The Pinelands Commission faced unusual problems. Seldom, if ever, has a regional management agency been asked to address such complex issues in so short a time. Enormous amounts of data were generated. Yet the complexity of the political, social, and ecological environment which the commission was charged with regulating tended to overwhelm the available data. Thus the commission chose to focus its attention on devising an organizational and procedural framework that could accommodate the substantive regulations the commission was able to develop immediately from the available social and scientific data. The framework also needed to allow a gradual shift from a procedural program to a more substantive one as available data expanded over the years.

The central question that faced the commission was how it should discharge its responsibility to oversee the implementation of a comprehensive management plan. A partial answer was found in the Pinelands Protection Act itself. Once the comprehensive management plan was prepared and adopted, Pinelands counties and municipalities were to submit, for commission review and approval, revised local master plans and land-use regulations to implement the plans. If a county or municipality failed to

FIGURE 9.1. MAP OF NEW JERSEY PINELANDS

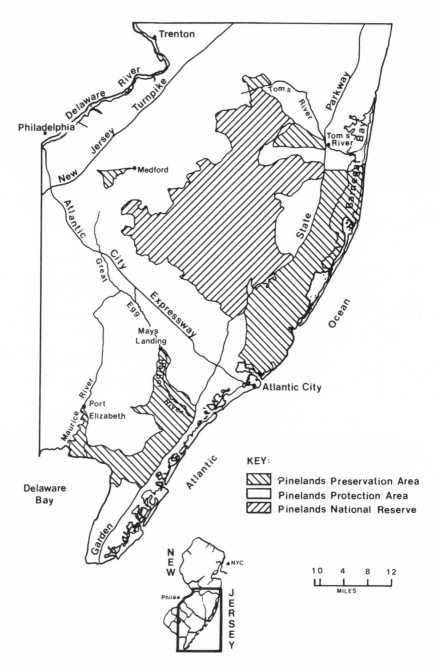

KEY:

▨ Pinelands Preservation Area
☐ Pinelands Protection Area
▥ Pinelands National Reserve

adopt or enforce a commission-certified master plan and implementing regulations, the commission was required to "adopt and enforce" rules and regulations necessary to implement the comprehensive plan. The Pinelands act, however, did not limit the commission's oversight role to this plan review function. Several other methods were available to the commission.

Regional management agencies vary considerably in jurisdiction and responsibilities. Some agencies depend for implementation of regional policies on advisory review-and-comment authority over individual local decisions. Achievement of regional goals depends on the persuasiveness of the regional agency's comments. Other regional authorities possess direct regulatory authority over proposed developments. Between these two approaches lies a variety of management roles that a regional authority like the Pinelands Commission could employ. The commission's preliminary analysis suggested that the options could be organized and evaluated by focusing on a small number of building blocks that seemed to appear in most regional programs the commission examined. These alternatives and their advantages and disadvantages are discussed below.

THE BALANCE BETWEEN MAJOR PROGRAM ELEMENTS

The commission first needed to decide on the most effective balance between the two functions of nearly all regional land-use programs: planning and regulation. Numerous possible balances were available. Regional agencies such as the Oregon Land Conservation and Development Commission[3] and the Twin Cities Metropolitan Council[4] devote most of their effort to planning. The Wisconsin Shoreland and Floodplain Protection Program[5] and the Tahoe Regional Planning Program[6] place greater emphasis on regulation. Other regional agencies, such as the Adirondack Park Agency,[7] attempt to give the functions equal weight.

The planning function seems to predominate in regional agencies having jurisdiction over large geographic areas with dramatically different development needs but not complex or fragile environments. Such regional agencies need not undertake the nearly impossible burden of adopting and enforcing development regulations applicable to the entire geographic area. Instead they often prescribe general planning goals for the region without fear that minor deviation from these goals will harm it.

On the other hand, where a regional program is designed to protect the complex and fragile environment of areas facing substantially similar impacts from development, a strong regulatory program is necessary. The regional agency will not be able to accomplish its goals through general planning guidelines because even minor deviation from such guidelines may harm the environment irreparably. The agency therefore must become involved in specific regulatory programs.

The Pinelands Commission faced the most troublesome aspects of both situations—a fragile and diverse ecosystem spread over a large area with diverse social, political, and developmental pressures. Thus it had to balance planning and regulation. The commission first sought to identify Pinelands subareas that were subject to similar pressures; it then adopted specific performance standards for regulating development in them.

ROLE OF PARTICIPATING AGENCIES

The commission had to decide which of several government agencies should exercise planning and regulatory functions. The primary agency was the commission itself, but it could have assumed a variety of roles, depending on the amount of authority it chose to retain. However, the commission recognized early that it could not do everything to implement the comprehensive plan, so it chose to find ways to delegate responsibility, authority, and workload to other agencies.

One option it considered was simply to create subcommittees of the commission and give them some autonomy. The Development Board of the Hackensack Meadowlands Commission used this technique for the granting of permits.[8] Similarly, the Twin Cities Metropolitan Council has used a "task force" approach for parts of its planning and has also created some agencies whose planning and budgets it controls.[9]

Another possible device was to give the commission staff a significant role in the permit process. Examples of this technique would include de facto recognition that staff recommendations are to be accepted unless an extraordinary case to the contrary is presented; delegation of hearing-examiner functions to the staff; and delegation of final decision-making authority (with some right of appeal to the commission) in a variety of minor matters.

Some regional programs establish new subregional agencies between the regional agency and local governments. For example, under the California Coastal Zone Management Program, six regional commissions have played a significant role under the Coastal Commission and have had both planning and permitting functions.[10] Under Vermont's Act 250, nine district commissions were created under the State Environmental Board; the district commissions have no planning function but play a significant role in the granting of permits.[11] The Wisconsin Shoreland and Floodplain Protection Program employs an existing governmental unit, the county, as a subregional authority between the Department of Natural Resources and local municipalities.

In addition, some role in the permit process could have been delegated to the Pinelands municipal governments. Most regional land-use programs accord some role to local government. The Pinelands Act, of course, anticipated a continuing role for local governments in the region, but did not specify it. Recognizing the diversity of the more than fifty Pinelands municipalities and hoping to avoid unwieldy bureaucratic layers or broad delegations of policy-making power to the staff, the commission gave each local government an opportunity to exercise as much control over development within its jurisdiction as it chose. The local government had only to demonstrate to the commission that it would exercise its authority in accord with the comprehensive management plan and the Pinelands Act.

ALLOCATION OF THE PLANNING FUNCTION

The Pinelands Commission also had to assign responsibility for planning. Four options were available. First, the commission could have adopted a program similar to the Wisconsin Shoreland and Floodplain Program, which has no regional planning component. That regional agency serves primarily as a provider of data and expertise to local governments. The commission recognized that the generation of data used by local governments would be critical in the Pinelands program, but chose to go well beyond this limited role.

A second option considered by the commission was represented by many of the major facility-siting acts and critical-area programs. Under these programs, the regional planning function applies only to a specified type of facility or area. The Pinelands Commission largely rejected this option, recognizing the need for a comprehensive planning program for the entire Pinelands. But some elements of these programs are evident in the Pinelands comprehensive management plan, which gives local governments more leeway for planning in developed or developing areas than in pristine or environmentally sensitive ones.

A third approach would have limited the commission's role to developing broad policies and guidelines for local governments, which would bear the primary responsibility for planning. The California Coastal Zone Program, the Twin Cities Metro Council, and the Oregon Land Conservation and Development Commission provide examples of such programs.

The final option considered by the commission was the development of a comprehensive end-state land-use plan. Programs in the Adirondack Park, Lake Tahoe, and the Hackensack Meadowlands take this approach. Vermont's Act 250 represents a variation on this theme. Vermont's experience convinced the commission not to commit itself to a formal comprehensive land-use plan, however. In Vermont, the first stage of the plan — a general policy document — was adopted with little difficulty. The second plan, a more specific set of policies, was adopted only after extensive revision by the legislature. The final land-use plan required by Vermont Act 250, however, has not been adopted by the state legislature in the more than nine years since its submission. No such plan is expected to be adopted.

The Pinelands Commission chose a program that combined aspects of the third and fourth options. The Pinelands Protection Act required all Pinelands counties and municipalities to adopt local master plans and land-use regulations that were consistent with the Pinelands comprehensive management plan within one year of the plan's adoption.[12] To facilitate this local planning and regulatory process, the commission included in the plan general policy guidelines and performance standards to protect the Pinelands area from harmful development.[13] These guidelines and standards must be supplemented by local land-use planning and regulation, but each local government can adopt a plan and land-use regulations different from those in the comprehensive management plan so long as the commission certifies them as consistent with the Pinelands Protection Act and the comprehensive plan. The certification process is provided for in the plan.[14]

The broad policies and general performance standards of the comprehensive plan, when combined with the development review authority of the commission, guarantee preservation of the Pinelands even where local cooperation cannot be obtained. If the local governments refuse to obtain commission approval of these plans and regulations, permit-granting authority for all significant development remains with the commission. Thus a planning program consisting of broad policies and guidelines for local governments that want to retain a great deal of control over planning and development becomes the equivalent of a comprehensive land-use plan if local cooperation is not forthcoming. The plan provides for local autonomy while guaranteeing that it will not result in the degradation of the Pinelands.

AGENCY ROLES IN GRANTING OF PERMITS

The commission had to decide what role each existing agency should play in the granting of permits. If, for instance, the commission were to have final authority for all permits in critical environmental areas, it would still be necessary to decide whether the commission should have original jurisdiction or, instead, appellate jurisdiction after a preliminary local decision. There were several options.

One possibility would be a program that allocated final authority to the local jurisdiction and provided for no regional role whatsoever. Such programs, generally involving critical areas or developments with regional impacts, involve the exercise of significant regional controls over specific projects falling within the programs' jurisdiction, but the regional agency exercises no authority beyond these narrow jurisdictional definitions. Such an approach in the Pinelands might have given the commission no planning or regulatory control within specified developed areas, or control only over specified minor developments.

Another possibility would allow the local jurisdiction to make the initial regulatory decision, but then give the regional agency the right of review. The right might be exercised in all cases, or only in cases appealed by one of the parties, or in cases "called up" by the regional agency. For example, upon petition of any county, city, special district government body, state agency, individual, or group whose interests are substantially affected, the Oregon Land Conservation and Development Commission may review any comprehensive plan, implementation ordinance, or conservation or development action taken by a local governing body to determine whether the action violates the commission's statewide planning goals. Such regional appellate jurisdiction over local decisions is common to many regional programs.

A third option was to retain final authority to issue or deny permits, but to require that the commission take account of local views. Statutes siting energy facilities frequently have such provisions. The extent to which the siting agency must consider local views varies. In some cases the local government's role is only that of a witness who can offer testimony. At the other extreme, the regional agency may not grant any permit that would violate a local ordinance unless there is some extraordinary, overriding state interest. Vermont's Act 250 provides that the district commissions may not grant a permit unless it is in accord with all duly adopted local plans.

Some statutes totally preempt any local role. A few regional programs—for instance, those involving the siting of hazardous waste facilities or nuclear power plants—supplant the localities' regulatory authority by providing that the regional permit is enough to allow developments to proceed. In such cases, there is usually informal political consultation with the localities.

The most common option requires both local and regional permits for development, as in the Adirondack Park Agency Act. That legislation encourages local governments to develop plans and ordinances consistent with the regional program (and gives them some permit-granting authority if they do), but does not require them to do so. The local government can totally ignore the regional agency. Yet a local permit does a developer no good unless he also obtains a permit from the regional agency. Similarly, obtaining a permit from the Adirondack Park Agency will get the developer nowhere unless he also obtains one from the local government. Thus the standards of both government bodies are upheld.

The Pinelands Commission chose an approach that would maximize local involvement while minimizing the possibility of harmful development. Once a local master plan and land-use regulation have been approved by the commission, the locality can review permit applications for conformity with the regulations. But if commission certification has not been obtained, no development can be undertaken without a commission permit. Development in an area *not* subject to a commission-certified plan and regulations can go forth once approved by the commission, even if the local government has refused to issue a permit.

Allocation of the Permitting Function

The commission had to decide how to allocate the final authority for granting permits. Two basic alternatives, each with variations and combinations, were considered. The first system would allocate authority to grant permits on the basis of preordained rules and definitions. The second would allow more ad hoc decision making.

If the commission chose a program of preordained rules and definitions, it would also choose among several bases for them. The most prominent device allocates responsibility on the basis of the type or scale of the development, as in programs involving energy-facility siting and developments of regional impact. Other programs, such as that in the Adirondack park, divide responsibility on the basis of a definition of "significance." For each land-use area designated by the Adirondack Park Plan, the plan defines "Class A" projects (those that are large or presumed to have significant environmental impact) and "Class B" projects (those that are smaller or of presumed lesser impact), with local authorities being given greater control over the less significant Class B developments. Other devices that allocate permit-granting authority are contained in the New Jersey Coastal Area Facility Review Act's definition of "facility"[15] and in the definitions of "development" and "subdivision" contained in Vermont's Act 250.

Another method for allocating permit-granting authority is to utilize preordained rules based on the environmental location of the proposed development. The classic example is the American Law Institute Code's "critical areas" concept. Other examples are programs which allocate permit authority depending on whether a proposed development is located within a specified number of feet of a streambank or shoreline; in a wetland or a fire hazard area; or in some other area of special environmental or cultural significance.

Another device allocates permit-granting authority on the basis of the man-made character of the area in question. The Adirondack Park Agency plan employs this technique by creating six separate land-use areas based in part upon the amount of existing development. The division of permit-granting responsibility between the regional agency and local governments varies across the land-use classifications. In other programs, developments near a specified man-made feature such as a travel corridor are given special treatment.

Some programs allocate the permitting function along jurisdictional lines. For example, land under the jurisdiction of the Hackensack Meadowlands Development Commission is specifically excluded from the wetlands permitting authority of New Jersey's Department of Environmental Protection.

A final device allocates authority depending whether or not a local government has satisfied specified conditions — usually involving the adoption of local plans or regulations that conform to regional policies or programs. This allocation device has the advantage of providing local governments with an incentive to bring local regulations in line with regional plans.

As noted, the Pinelands Commission could also have chosen to allocate final authority for granting permits on an ad hoc basis. Two variations were considered. The Massachusetts "Anti-Snob" Zoning Act is one example of what might be termed "party-initiated" allocation devices; low- and moderate-income housing developments are subject to the usual local permit requirements, but a developer may request a state agency to take over responsibility for reviewing and permitting the project. The other type of ad hoc allocation is the "agency-initiated." Under this type of program, the regional agency monitors the activity of local agencies and has the right to "call up" any application for review.

The Pinelands Commission chose to divide permitting authority based on both ad hoc decision making and preordained rules. Once a local government has had its master plan and land-use regulations certified by the Pinelands Commission, it is free to issue and deny permits for development on the basis of the regulations. But no application for development approval can be filed with a local government unless a copy is first filed with the Pinelands Commission, a requirement that gives the commission a chance to review development proposals at the earliest possible stage. Regional concerns can be voiced by the commission before substantial amounts of developer and local agency time and money have been expended for local review of a regionally unacceptable development.

Each local government also is required to give notice of any preliminary or final development approval to the Pinelands Commission. The commission may then "call up" the local approval for commission review. If the commission finds that the local approval is inconsistent with the policies of the comprehensive plan, the local government must modify its approval to conform to the commission's concerns or revoke the approval.

Allocation by preordained rules appears in the requirement that all local governments obtain commission certification of local master plans and land-use regulations before they can exercise any meaningful permit function. If a local government does not obtain certification, development in its jurisdiction may not be carried out without approval by the commission. The comprehensive plan also provides that commission approval will supersede any local decision within the jurisdiction. No development can take place without commission approval, and the commission can approve development denied local approval.

Thus the commission has allowed local governments to retain as much local autonomy as they choose. The only restriction is that local master plans and land-use regulations be consistent with the comprehensive plan. The commission has relieved itself of the responsibility of reviewing all development and can devote its time and resources to reviewing those developments of truly regional importance. Moreover, by retaining jurisdiction in areas where conforming local plans have not been adopted and by selective review jurisdiction in others, the commission has assured that it can protect the Pinelands.

Permit Coordination

The Pinelands Commission considered several options for coordinating permits between levels of government. Every development in the

Pinelands might require at least two permits—one from the commission and one from the relevant local government. Many developments would require permits from other state, regional, and local agencies. Many state and regional land-use programs employ a permit coordinating procedure; some, like the Washington Environmental Coordination Procedures Act, involve just that and nothing more.

Three basic approaches to the multiple permitting problem were available. One was simply to ignore the problem. The Pinelands would not have been the first area in which a developer was required to go from agency to agency to agency in quest of a multiplicity of permits. Legitimate policy arguments could be made that the commission should not expend its limited time, staff, and resources to rationalize a complex permit system it had not created. The commission recognized, however, that the political and legal success of the Pinelands program might depend on efforts to build speed, ease, and fairness into the review process.

A second approach was to attempt to establish a coordinated permitting process for all developments under the commission's jurisdiction, along the lines of the American Law Institute's Model Land Development Code. The commission could maintain a permit register listing all permits required by governmental agencies. Developers needing more than one permit could institute a joint hearing procedure. A hearing panel, consisting of representatives from the relevant permitting agencies, would come to a decision containing proposed findings of fact and conclusions of law. Within a specified period of time after the hearing panel's decision, each permitting agency would be required to issue or deny its permit. The individual agencies would not be bound by the panel's decision, but the panel's findings and conclusions would be part of the decision of each agency unless the agency specified otherwise. Vermont's Act 250 and California's Coastal Zone Management Program both contain such permit-coordinating procedures.

The final option was one-stop permitting, whereby a single agency is given authority to issue one permit that takes the place of all permits otherwise required. One-stop permitting is not common aside from major power-plant siting statutes. The extent to which the permitting agency must consider the standards of other agencies varies. Under some statutes, the permitting agency must apply all pertinent regulations and standards of all superseded agencies. Under others, the agency must consider the standards of superseded agencies but can modify or overrule them. Under a few state siting acts (Maryland, Minnesota, and North Dakota), a permit from the state siting agency totally preempts approvals and standards of local governments.

The Pinelands Commission adopted a permit coordinating mechanism that combined aspects of all these procedures. Where master plans and land-use regulations do not conform to the comprehensive plan and are not certified by the commission, the commission ignores the issue of multiple permits. No developer can seek a local permit without first having applied to the Pinelands Commission, but no attempt is made to coordinate the commission approval process with any local ones. The developer must seek permits from the commission and from any local agencies with jurisdiction over the development. The requirement creates pressure for local agencies to bring their regulations into conformity with the comprehensive plan in order to qualify for more streamlined procedures. The arrangement also protects the comprehensive plan and its goals when a local agency ignores them.

In areas that have local master plans and land-use regulations certified by the commission, a developer must submit a copy of any application for a local permit to the commission before filing it locally. The commission and its staff can review the application as early as possible to assess the role it should play in the local permitting process. The commission's role often may be limited to voicing commission concerns in person or through written comments, at local hearings. In such cases, a formal commission review may prove unnecessary.

The comprehensive plan also provides that the commission may call up any preliminary or final local approval for a second hearing and formal review by the commission. This review will generally be necessary only when a developer or local permitting agency does not take commission comments into account during the course of the local permitting process, or when the local permitting agency misinterprets the comprehensive plan.

When permits must be obtained from both the commission and other state agencies, a developer must file an application with the commission prior to filing with the relevant state agency. The commission must then decide whether its review of the development proposal should occur before, during, or after other state proceedings. The commission and the state agencies can refer specific matters to each other, minimizing the possibility of duplicative reviews. The procedure also reduces the likelihood that a developer will obtain one permit only to discover that another is unobtainable.

Developments in the Pinelands undertaken by state and local agencies present a sensitive political problem for the commission. Ultimately, the commission decided that no public agency should carry out any development in the Pinelands without its approval. But the commission may enter into agreements with other agencies to authorize them to carry out specified development activities without securing individual approvals from the commission. This procedure should minimize the frequency with which public agencies must submit to formal hearing.

PROMOTION OF LOCAL COMPLIANCE

Many of the alternatives selected by the commission were designed to enable each local government to retain as much control over development within its jurisdiction as possible. This approach was chosen not only to maximize local autonomy, but also to minimize the burdens on the commission. Several methods remained available to the commission to achieve maximum local cooperation and consistency.

The first option was one of primary regional responsibility for local conformity; under this option, the commission would simply develop and promulgate local plans or regulations to be enforced by the local governments. The Lake Tahoe program provides one illustration. The Tahoe Regional Planning Agency not only adopted a regional plan, but also adopted all the ordinances necessary to enforce the plan's policies, including the "Tahoe Regional Planning Agency Land Use Ordinance," essentially a regional zoning ordinance. The local governments in the region are required to enforce it.

The commission also considered the concept of regional fallback, wherein the regional agency would mandate local adoption of consistent plans and ordinances. It would enforce that mandate by threatening that, if a local government did not adopt the necessary ordinances, the regional agency would impose its own ordinances.

The third option considered by the commission involved the transfer of permit-granting authority. The commission would encourage local compliance with the comprehensive plan by offering to surrender some or all of its review and permitting powers to the local government as a reward for its achieving local compliance.

Consistency can also be encouraged by providing technical assistance and data. Under the Wisconsin Shoreland Program, the state has successfully produced a series of model ordinances which local governments can adopt to meet state requirements. The state also has developed much of the technical information necessary in order to implement the program, and every county in the state has brought its regulations into compliance with it.

The final method of encouraging consistency is one which, in light of its success at the federal level, has been used surprisingly infrequently in regional land-use programs — the provision of financial incentives for local consistency. If a regional agency can control the flow of funds to the local government, it has a powerful tool for obtaining quick compliance with its policies. The Twin Cities Metropolitan Council has used this method effectively to encourage suburban communities to provide low- and moderate-income housing.

The Pinelands Commission chose to employ all these options. Where a local plan has not been certified by the commission, no development can be undertaken within that jurisdiction without commission approval. Nor can the local government prevent such development once it has been approved by the commission. But once a local government has brought its local master plan and land-use regulations into conformity with the comprehensive plan, initial permitting authority reverts to the local government. The commission exercises only a discretionary right of comment and review.

In addition, the substantive regulations of the comprehensive plan can, with minor modifications, be adopted by local governments as self-contained land-use regulations. The social and technical data accumulated by the commission during the preparation of the comprehensive plan is available to all local governments. Planning funds have been appropriated by the state legislature and made available by the commission to municipalities for financing the necessary revisions in local master plans and zoning ordinances.

It is difficult to assess the commission's success. All local plans were to have been brought into conformance by 14 January 1982, but this one-year deadline was probably unrealistic. Only three of the 52 Pinelands municipalities had their plans certified by the commission within that legally mandated one-year period. But by January 1983, 31 municipalities and three counties had obtained commission certification. All but a handful of the rest are working with the commission. Most Pinelands governments are staffed by volunteer and part-time employees and officials and meet only irregularly. Serious local resistance to the comprehensive plan is not widespread.

Regional Direction

The commission needed to decide its role in guiding the regional program. Again several alternatives were available. The commission had to consider the possibility that for some developments and areas, no regional guidelines were necessary. The commission faced an undeniably heavy administrative burden. It needed to consider how it wished to focus its time and resources toward the most critical areas, and whether it would be willing to play a more limited (or nonexistent) role in other areas.

Another option available to the commission was the adoption of general regional policies. The Oregon Land Conservation and Development Commission and the California Coastal Zone Management Program are two examples where the regional agency makes no attempt to go beyond broad policy statements. They are so broad as to invite differing interpretations and conflicts between different policies of the same program. The commission noted that both of these programs rely on case-by-case review procedures to determine consistency with regional goals.

Other programs analyzed by the commission, like the Adirondack Park Agency program, attempt to go beyond broad general policy statements without adopting specific development regulations. Under the Adirondack plan, six land-use areas are identified, and allowable uses and overall density requirements are specified for each one. But if a developer can demonstrate to the agency that a proposed use is compatible with the character of the land-use area, the regional agency can issue the permit. Similarly, there are overall guidelines for density but no specific lot size and bulk regulations.

The third option considered was specific development regulations similar to those in traditional local zoning. The Adirondack plan establishes such regulations for shoreland areas. The Tahoe Regional Planning Agency Land Use Ordinance establishes standard zoning districts, allowable uses, land coverage and other similar regulations, and gives local permitting authorities a significant role in the permitting process. The regional agency reviews only those permit applications that require an administrative permit or a variance permit.

The commission recognized that more specificity in regional regulation would increase its reliance on agency-generated data. In many regional programs the requirement that the developer prepare and submit an environmental impact statement is merely a device to shift the burden of data generation to the developer. Any move toward a more specific regulatory program would increase the initial time and cost necessary to establish the program. The practical and political difficulties of creating a program of specific land-use regulations are significant, especially in an area as diverse as the Pinelands. It was by no means clear that a specific regulatory program would be more successful at protecting a complex environment or more equitable in permitting development.

The commission recognized the difficulty of devising rules and regulations that would accurately identify which developments could be environmentally accommodated and which could not be. The rules could be drawn too conservatively and impose unnecessary burdens upon property owners and developers; or they could be drawn too liberally and bring damage to the environment. The more a system can assess proposals on a case-by-case basis, the more it can be fine-tuned and the more likely it is that all legitimate interests will be treated optimally.

But there are many drawbacks in a system that relies upon general policies and case-by-case review. Perhaps the most troublesome is that such systems create uncertainty for development and environmental groups. No hard and fast rules govern. The entire program depends upon the attitude of the decision maker. The potential for inconsistent application of the commission's policies would be great. Such flexible programs generally mean that the regional agency is under constant attack, and the credibility of the commission could suffer. The time and cost burdens for the developer, the agency, and interested parties could become unduly large. The commission decided that it should combine aspects of all of these programs. The exact way in which they are combined is discussed below.

HIGHLIGHTS OF SUBSTANTIVE PROGRAMS ADOPTED

The Pinelands comprehensive management plan consists of a series of policies and programs that are the product of studies of natural resources, historic and archaeological resources, sociocultural factors, and physical resources. Additional studies analyzed current and anticipated growth pressures. A financial study examined the cost of implementing the plan. An extensive land management component examined numerous options employed in the United States and abroad.

Environmental Programs

The environmental programs treat surface and groundwater resources, vegetation and wildlife, wetlands, fire management, forestry, air quality, and waste management. Each program sets forth specific objectives and techniques designed to achieve the preservation of the Pinelands' fragile ecosystem.

The Pinelands have low, dense forests of pine and oak, cedar and hardwood swamps, pitch-pine lowlands, and bogs and marshes. This vegetation contains a rich diversity of species, including some threatened and endangered ones. In addition, the cranberry and blueberry industries depend on the lowland soils and existing water quality.

Thus the comprehensive plan is intended to protect the habitats of Pinelands vegetation and animal species. A prime factor is the preservation of larger contiguous parcels of undisturbed or minimally disturbed land. Leapfrog, scattered, or fragmented development isolates species and makes it more difficult to maintain their diversity. The plan tries to maintain a continuous corridor connecting ecologically sensitive areas in the south of the region to the preservation area in the north. It attempts to encourage development near existing communities and away from more sensitive, pristine areas. It permits only development designed to avoid irreversible harm to the populations of plants and animals that are threatened or endangered. Limitations on the removal of vegetation and on permitted landscaping are intended to preserve existing native vegetation and minimize nonnative competition.

The plan includes detailed regulations for development in and near wetland areas so as to protect species dependent on them. Berry agriculture and horticulture are permitted, as is foresting, but only in conformance with federal, state, and local regulations. Low-intensity recreational uses are permitted, but only if they do not alter the character of the wetlands. Other miscellaneous low-intensity uses may be permitted on a site-by-site basis, depending on factors such as public need and the availability of alternative sites. A buffer area of 300 feet is created around wetlands to minimize the impact of upland development. Development is permitted in buffer areas only if it will not harm the wetlands.

The plan contains a fire management program that encourages both controlled burning and development that takes into account the continued danger of fire. An area's fire hazard rating determines the standards for development and for vegetation removal. The plan's forestry program sets standards designed to discourage forestry in wetland areas, minimize adverse impacts on water quality, minimize erosion, and promote reforestation to ensure regeneration, particularly of Atlantic white cedar. Forestry is a permitted use throughout the Pinelands, but commercial forestry operations must be carried out in accordance with a management plan reviewed by the New Jersey Bureau of Forest Management.

One of the principal features of the Pinelands area is an extensive groundwater reservoir containing water that is unpolluted and characterized by low nutrients, hardness, and alkalinity. The Pinelands depends on maintaining existing water quantity and quality, and so the plan sets water-quality standards. The plan's land-use program is intended to protect regional water quality and directs development so as to preserve it. There are standards for wastewater treatment facilities as well as a prohibition on nondomestic discharges, the use of septic tank cleansers, and on other toxic chemicals and materials. The densities established for residential development are designed to minimize the water-quality hazards of on-site wastewater disposal. Where landowners can develop at higher densities, approved alternative technologies to the standard septic tank must be utilized. New landfills are severely limited. New facilities that would export surface- or groundwater from the Pinelands are prohibited. Water-saving technology is required. The commission recognized, however, that further study is needed to determine the environmentally safe level of groundwater withdrawal.

Agriculture

The comprehensive plan for the Pinelands has an agricultural program that delineates agricultural production areas. These include not only existing farming areas, but also adjacent Pinelands tracts with prime agricultural soils or soils of statewide importance. Landowners not included in these areas may petition local municipalities for inclusion. The ultimate decision is subject to commission review during the course of local plan certification. Within the preservation area, only special agricultural production areas can be created. Concentrations of cranberry and blueberry production and lands used for horticulture of native plant species are eligible for such designation. Additional encouragement for indigenous agricultural activities is found in the plan's requirement that, in order to obtain commission certification of its local master plan, each municipality must adopt a "right-to-farm" ordinance that minimizes the potential conflicts between agricultural activities and adjacent developing areas. Agricultural activities also are exempt from many of the other requirements, such as land-clearing standards, that are imposed on other forms of development. Other management techniques are recommended to minimize agricultural degradation of surface- and groundwater resources.

Culture

The comprehensive plan recommends that, during the local plan certification process, municipalities develop a historic and archeological preservation program similar to those already in place in some Pinelands municipalities. A scenic program is also in the plan. Special setbacks and height limitations for specified scenic corridors are required. Municipalities in the preservation area are required to adopt regulations on many aspects of sign construction. Guidelines are provided for municipalities in the protection area.

One of the more unusual attempts at preserving the cultural resources of the Pinelands is what has been known as the "Piney exception." This exception permits individuals who are able to establish a "cultural, social, or economic link to the essential character of the Pinelands" to build a primary residence on lots considerably smaller than those otherwise permitted in the central part of the Pinelands. The applicant must satisfy these tests:

> (i) the parcel of land for the proposed dwelling must have been owned by the applicant or a member of his immediate family on 7 February 1979; and either
>
> (ii) the applicant must be a member of a two-generation extended family that has resided in the Pinelands for at least twenty years, or
>
> (iii) the primary source of the applicant's household income is employment or participation in a Pinelands resource-related activity.

This provision has been challenged by some municipalities and by the "Coalition to Save Agriculture" as being unconstitutionally discriminatory.[16] The suit, however, was voluntarily withdrawn.

Pinelands Development Credits

Another important element of the comprehensive management plan is the Pinelands Development Credit (PDC) program. The PDCs are transferable development rights allocated to properties proposed for the plan's most restrictive regulations. The receiving areas are those designated by the plan for urban or suburban uses. Both the scale of the PDC program and the fact that PDCs may be transferred from property in the jurisdiction of one local government to property in that of another distinguish this program from other similar ones.

The basic purpose is to redirect development away from sensitive areas and toward areas designated by the plan for more intense development. Thus PDCs were allocated to privately held property in the preservation area district (upland — 1 PDC for each 39 acres; wetland — 0.2 PDCs for each 39 acres) and in agricultural production areas (upland — 2 PDCs for each 39 acres; wetland — 0.2 PDCs for each 39 acres; actively farmed wetland — 2 PDCs for each 39 acres). PDCs may be used only for residential development at a rate of four residential units for each PDC in the regional growth districts and two residential units for each PDC in the rural development areas. No PDCs were allocated to lands developed for uses permitted under the plan.

An owner wishing to make use of a PDC need only record its severance on the title to the property. The PDC may be utilized by its original owner or transferred in any way desired by its owner. The commission has no involvement in severance, transfer, or use. No discretionary approval is necessary. The increased densities represented by the PDC may be obtained by its owner as a matter of right.[17]

CONCLUSION

It is still too early to assess the success or failure of the Pinelands effort as an instance of regional land-use planning reform. That the commission was able to adopt a plan that is truly comprehensive in the short period of time allotted by the enabling legislation is remarkable. Equally remarkable is that the commission has encountered little resistance from local governments. The absence of significant legal challenges to the plan by property owners and the relative efficiency with which its permitting programs have been implemented thus far can be viewed as a positive sign. The plan seems to have generated less serious opposition and fewer significant problems in the early stages than have similar regional land-use programs.

NOTES

1. 16 U.S.C. § 4711 (1980).
2. N.J.S.A. § 13:18A-1 to 29.
3. Ore. Rev. Stat. ch. 197.
4. Minn. Stat. ch. 473.
5. Wis. Stat. Ann. § 144.26.
6. P.L. 91-148, 83 Stat. 360 (Dec. 16, 1969).
7. N.Y. Exec. Law §§ 800, *et seq.* (McKinney Supp. 1978).
8. N.J.S.P. § 13: 17-1 *et seq.*
9. Minn. Stat. ch. 473.
10. Cal. Pub. Res. Code § 30302.
11. 10 U.S.A. § 6026(b) (1979).
12. N.J.S.A. § 13:18A-11.
13. Management Plan Act. 5 & 6.
14. §§3-201 *et seq.;* §§ 3-401 *et seq.*
15. N.J.S.A. § 13: 19-1 *et seq.*
16. *Township of Folsom et al.* v. *State of New Jersey and the N.J. Pinelands Commission.* (Superior Ct. 1981).
17. For further discussion of the PDC program, see Randle (1982). For a more general treatment of the Pinelands, see Goldstein (1981).

REFERENCES

Center for Coastal and Environmental Studies. 1978. *A Plan for a Pinelands National Preserve.* New Brunswick, NJ: Center for Coastal and Environmental Studies, Rutgers University.
Federal Bureau of Outdoor Recreation. 1975. *Pine Barrens of New Jersey: Study Report.* Washington, DC: U.S. Government Printing Office.
Goldstein, Joan. 1981. *Environmental Decision Making in Rural Locales: The Pine Barrens.* New York: Praeger.
The Governor's Pinelands Review Committee. 1979. *Planning and Management of the New Jersey Pinelands.* Trenton, NJ: State Archives.
McCormick, Jack. 1967 and 1970. *A Study of the Significance of the Pine Barrens of New Jersey.* Trenton, NJ: New Jersey State Museum. Revised edition 1970.
McPhee, John. 1968. *The Pine Barrens.* New York: Farrar Strauss and Giroux.
Pinelands Commission. 1980. *New Jersey Pinelands Commission Management Plan.* November 21, 1980. New Lisbon, NJ: Pinelands Commission.
Pinelands Environmental Council. 1975. *A Plan for the Pinelands.* Trenton, NJ: State Archives.
Randle, Ellen. 1982. "The national reserve system and transferable development rights: is the New Jersey Pinelands plan an unconstitutional 'taking'?" *Boston College Environmental Affairs Law Review* 10 (1).

PART FOUR

Land Reform and Minorities

10

Land Reform and Indian Survival in the United States

ROXANNE DUNBAR ORTIZ

Will American Indians survive as a people into the twenty-first century? Though they once flourished over a whole continent, though many of them were the finest cultivators known to history, American Indians approach the turn of a new century in doubt about their continued existence. The reason for their doubt lies — as it has for the past century — in land. To say that land reform is necessary understates the situation of American Indians today. But the land reform perspective is a useful way to view the central resource for Indian survival — the land base.

The story of Indian lands is not a pretty one. The expropriation of Indian territories was an important factor in assuring rapid accumulation of capital for developing the United States' economy. The expropriation of Indian lands and resources was accomplished by brutal annihilation and dispersal of Indian populations through direct military attacks, settler attacks, and refugee conditions with their related diseases and demoralization. As a result, American Indians have suffered from genocidal policies, colonial conditions, racism, discrimination, the most extreme kinds of economic and social deprivation (including malnutrition and disease), astronomical unemployment, and the gross exploitation of their labor when employed. These everyday realities of Indian life exist and are perpetuated because of Anglo-American cultural and economic superiority that in turn supports governmental expropriation of Indian territories and special rights.

In all regions of the United States, indigenous Americans have been and still are being deprived of their lands and resources. They have been left with reduced territories inadequate to their needs. Their lands have been divided into parcels that often split up their communities. They have been deprived of the most fertile lands and, in many cases, have lost nearly their entire guaranteed land base. The extraction of water and other resources from their lands threatens their lives and their future. The United States' courts and legal system have not done justice to the claims of American Indians.

In order to consolidate its political and economic control, the United States, through major transnational corporations, has recently accelerated domestic projects to exploit remaining Indian lands and resources. Government-recognized Indian lands hold approximately 3 percent of the total U.S. reserves of oil and natural gas, amounting to 4.2 billion barrels of oil and 17.5 trillion cubic feet of gas. Estimates of coal reserves range up to 200 billion tons of identified reserves on 33 Indian reservations in eleven states — that is, 15 percent of the total identifiable reserves of coal in the United States. Indian uranium reserves amount to 55 percent of U.S. reserves and 11 percent of the world total, making Indian reservations potentially the fourth leading producer of uranium in the world. The U.S. government has made unfair agreements on behalf of Indian peoples and cooperates closely with large corporations in identifying strategic resources and land areas (American Indian Policy Review Commission, 1978; Nafziger, 1980).

Consequently, there is a serious shortage of nonrenewable Indian water supplies: water is used in the Western reservations as a primary energy source in coal transportation, industrial development, and hydroelectric projects. The desertification of Indian lands has become a major new phase of the genocide for which the United States is responsible.

Given these circumstances, land reform becomes a highly complex social question. Imre Sutton, an expert on Indian land tenure, puts it this way:

> The unique status of Indian land necessitates its separate treatment in any classification of tenures. . . . Born of colonial experiences and fashioned as settlers moved westward, land reservations for indigenous Americans became accepted policy more than a century ago. Applied first of all to Indians as part of broad treaty powers with nations, the reservation practice comprehended "Indian country" and later smaller, often non-contiguous reserves scattered throughout the West. (Sutton, 1970:8, 18)

In the two centuries of U.S. policy development toward American Indians, a variety of distortions and destruction of the Indian land base has occurred. In many areas, the U.S. government acquired land by treaty making, a policy which prevailed until 1871. In these treaties Indian nations defined their territorial boundaries and in all cases ceded portions of their national territories to the United States — nearly always because they were under threat of military annihilation or swamped by hostile, acquisitive settlers.

In exchange for such concessions, Indian peoples received the ambivalent right to U.S. government trusteeship — protection of their property and provision of basic services and technical assistance in perpetuity. The

U.S. government holds title to Indian lands as trustee but it may not dispose or manage these lands, for possession rests with Indians. "This means that while the United States Government has the appearance of title as the nominal owner of Indian trust lands, it is actually holding title entirely for the benefit and use of the Indian owners" (American Indian Policy Review Commission, 1978:Vol. 1:126). Trusteeship is fundamental. But the land question for many Indian communities and nations is a question of treaty guarantees to special rights and services and to self-government. Even though the rights have been made general for all Indians, they have also been eroded and the land base diminished to a small fraction of treaty or other agreed territorial bounds.

The removal of the Cherokee, Choctaw, Chickasaw, Creek, and Seminole peoples from the Southeast through forced treaties and legislation, under the threat of genocide, guaranteed a permanent territory in Oklahoma, which was to remain an "Indian Territory." However, with the discovery of oil in Oklahoma in the 1880s, the territory was "opened" for homesteading, and Indian lands were allotted into family-owned parcels. A number of other Indian lands throughout the West also were divided by allotment through the Dawes General Allotment Act of 1887. Areas acquired by the United States were designated as territories for administrative purposes that had little to do with the Indian lands within their boundaries. Settlers moved in, organized politically, and petitioned for statehood. By 1916, all Indian lands existed within states. In Oklahoma, the former "Indian Territory" where nearly three hundred Indian groups were placed as they were defeated in war, the Indian land base today is practically nonexistent, and only one reservation — Osage — exists under trust.

Other Indian territories in the United States have been diminished to a minimum or entirely eradicated. The process continues today, mainly through legislation and policy regulations (those of the Department of the Interior principally, within which the Bureau of Indian Affairs is located). The land question for Indian peoples east of the Mississippi and in parts of the West, notably California, revolves around the establishment or expansion of land bases that have trust status. In addition, Indian issues in Alaska involve protection and preservation of the fragile Arctic tundra that has nurtured self-sufficient fishing and hunting economies for native people. Alaska has been a focus of boom development by major energy corporations. Many of the village economies and societies have already been wrecked, and it is possible that there will be no native communities in the next generation.

All Indian lands are threatened by reckless exploitation that brings high social and environmental costs and few benefits for the local population. Mining, industrial, and agricultural interests are intensifying their efforts to separate Indian peoples from their land base and to block the restoration of lost lands. Working out of Denver prior to his appointment as the Reagan administration's secretary of the interior (a position carrying veto power over all Indian decisions), James Watt's law firm brought court cases against Indian claims. The United States government, in a surprising admission of powerlessness in the face of giant corporate interests, often claims that it cannot play its role as trustee for Indian lands, resources, and interests.

In areas where there are majority Indian populations, the attacks on Indians are particularly brutal and intense, nothing less than terrorism. Using racism and the "will of the majority" as their slogans, vigilante groups appear in increasing numbers, backed by wealthy right-wing political cliques such as the Committee for Equal Rights and Responsibilities, which is active in the Dakotas and the Northwest and closely associated with the John Birch Society. The Reagan administration's policy of opening all federal lands and shores to industrial development and mining accelerated the process. Further, much of the "federal" land is Indian land that the government took illegally in the first place, often by abrogating treaties with Indians.

Economic development policies, in the form of industrialization and mining activities, constitute the principal land initiative pressed on the reservations by the federal government. However, Indian communities are — on the whole — opposed to development on reservations. Few reservations have undertaken projects for infrastructure development or land reclamation to mitigate overgrazing and mining. Practically none have plans to expand traditional economic bases — such as fishing, intensive garden farming, sheep and cattle raising — into vertically integrated operations. None has been given federal support for either community food sufficiency or the development of market commodities. The federally promoted strategy for industrial economic development claims to have the potential to produce income from capital-intensive projects that will then allow investment in infrastructure and other local development. This claim is itself shaky, and Indian people do not want to participate in an industrial, materialistic, capitalist-oriented economy, though they do seek culturally, socially, politically, and economically integrated — that is, nonharmful — development. This view is supported not just by elderly, traditional people who recall earlier times, but by practically the entire younger generation of Indians. Indian people are also fully aware that commercial development and the income generated from it would become a pretext for the withdrawal of U.S. trusteeship. Ambivalent and unreliable as the trusteeship is, it is also the main force preventing the annihilation of the Indian land base and perhaps of Indian peoples.

THE HISTORICAL BACKGROUND OF THE RESERVATIONS

The geopolitical entity of the United States exists by virtue of the taking of land, usually by official military force, from the American Indian homeland. The taking of Indian lands was necessary to distribute land to settlers, communities, railroads, schools, and universities, and to form states. The Northwest Ordinance of 1787, although guaranteeing Indian occupancy and title "as long as the grass shall grow and the rivers flow," in fact amounted to a plan for the colonization of Indian lands. The lands were first to be militarily occupied, then to become territories under civil authority, and finally to be granted statehood. Statehood was typically not granted until a territory's settlers outnumbered its indigenous population (Ortiz, 1980b).

Once the United States was formed as a nation, it created what was an innovative land system for a colonial power: land sales in the early days of the United States were an important means of accumulating capital and building the national treasury. Up until the Civil War, some of the principal agents for expansion were the Southern capitalist planters who required an ever-expanding land base for increased production of nonfood cash crops, mainly cotton. Within this complex agenda, the Indian reservation was formed as an afterthought and without great attention or planning. Indian reservations were probably never intended to be an integral or permanent part of the U.S. political system. They were simply a result of the negotiated settlements that took place when Indians, in weak but never totally defeated positions, resisted land thefts.

American Indian reservations today comprise some 50 million acres (78,000 square miles) of noncontiguous lands across the continental United States. In 1873, however, when Indian armed resistance was nearly subdued and practically all Indians were required to live in reservations, the landholdings were three times larger. This stunning loss of treaty-guaranteed land was caused by legislation which divided many reservations into small family allotments, and which then declared the land in excess of the individual allotments to be public domain and therefore marketable. The residual 50 million acres constitute 2 percent of U.S. territory—the size, were it contiguous, of South Dakota. The largest Indian reservation, only a small part of which was allotted (land was actually added to it), is the Navajo reservation, with twelve million acres—approximately the size of West Virginia. But this is only about half the land needed to support the Navajo pastoral economy (American Indian Policy Review Commission, 1978).

Nearly all federal Indian trust lands are in the West. At one time, this "Great American Desert," as it was designated on official maps, was considered uninhabitable by the European colonialists and later U.S. authorities. The early U.S. conquest of the region was intended to connect the valued coasts of the continent by railroad and to extract gold and hides. But soon, large-scale ranching, grain production, commercial timbering in the mountains, and mining and oil production took hold. These remain among the primary economic pursuits of the region and demand vast land and particularly water supplies, primarily for corporations. As a result, Indian reservation water supplies have been polluted and destroyed, losses that currently pose the greatest threat to the majority of Indian communities in the region. The water rights of Indian peoples directly conflict with the preemptive water rights of states, although many judicial decisions have found Indian water rights to be "implied reservations," property rights that cannot be taken from federal lands and federal trust lands, no matter how the lands were acquired. But the water is taken and used, the Indians are powerless to prevent the theft, and the U.S. government has refused to carry out its trusteeship responsibilities. Indian water has been principally diverted from reservations by hydroelectric projects — fully funded, planned, and built by the Indian's trustee, the United States government (Hundley, 1979).

The land question of American Indian peoples is fundamentally an economic issue of production and livelihood. But it is also a social issue of basic human rights, even of genocide. Indian ceremonial practices, religious beliefs, and cultural integrity are deeply rooted in their homelands, even when the present homeland is not the original or traditional one. Indian culture is inseparable from the land, because Indian culture is not primarily material. Historical memory, which in the Indian oral tradition is much longer and more powerful than it is for most U.S. citizens, tells Indians that their ancestors, often their grandparents, died by the millions fighting for their homeland and for liberty and self-determination.

The reservations parallel, but are not an integral part of, the U.S. system of land tenure. Most North Americans apparently conceive of the reservations as marketable real estate. They do not compare it to nonmarketable federal land such as game reserves, national parks, or military bases. They do not see it as the home of human societies. In particular, the idea that Indians have power over non-Indians on the reservation seems offensive or curious to them. Yet reservations are not like municipalities, federal districts, or public lands; they are the remaining enclaves of the free American Indian nation.

Indian reservations have no legal connection to states, which in many cases were created after the reservations, but reservations are subject to both federal and state powers. Moreover, beyond the reservation there is "Indian country" — the larger Indian area around reservations, containing many isolated hamlets, as in Oklahoma and the Northwest where the contiguous reservations were broken up by allotment. Yet these communities remain within the old treaty boundaries as well as within the boundaries never ceded by treaty or other means. Indian country communities maintain historical and legal rights in land, water, and wildlife, even when these areas are heavily occupied by non-Indians. U.S. courts have found that Indians have hunting, fishing, and water rights in Indian country beyond reservation boundaries when these rights derive from long customary use (Sutton, 1975).

Lacking clearly defined relationships with other U.S. government bodies, Indian communities are often caught in conflicts between various bureaucracies. There are conflicts between the Bureau of Indian Affairs (BIA) and the rest of the Interior Department, between Interior and other federal agencies, and between federal agencies and states where reservations are located. Whatever legislation favors Indian self-determination is usually contradicted by other legislation that gives powers to the states, such as Public Law 280 — passed in 1953 and still in effect — which gives power to many states over Indian communities within reservation boundaries. This state jurisdictional power extends state police power to the reservation and its population.

Since the New Deal, Indians have been organized into "tribal governments" that hold certain limited powers. The decisions of these governments are subject to veto by the secretary of the interior. These governments have allowed the U.S. government to carry out its trust responsibility at a minimal level. They place Indian trust funds in the hands of a portion of the Indian population the Interior Department can control. Moreover, these minigovernments have promoted factionalism within Indian communities, established privileged elites, and eroded unified Indian nationalism.

Many non-Indians live within Indian reservations, particularly those reservations that were allotted. In some reservations, non-Indians far outnumber Indian residents. The Dawes General Allotment Act of 1887 and the Curtis Act of 1887 allotted nearly half the reservation lands before the acts were rescinded by the Indian Reorganization Act of 1934, which established the tribal governments. Most of the land allotted was on the Great Plains, particularly in Oklahoma, where all reservations but one were allotted, and in the Dakotas, where a slightly smaller number were allotted. Some of the allotted parcels were taken out of trust protection, and these were often sold by Indians who had no other means to function in a cash economy. Many of the allotments that remained in trust were leased by the Interior Department to non-Indian occupants or corporations, often with 99-year leases. A number of cities, towns, and resorts — including, ironically, the extremely affluent Palm Springs, California — sit on 99-year leases that will begin expiring in the late twentieth century.

"Open" reservations, as the allotted ones are called, are under the jurisdiction of surrounding state and county governments, which has consistently been devastating to Indian communities. Federal trust protection, however weak or irresponsible, is often the only way to prevent exploitation of Indians, their lands, and their resources by local elites and absentee corporations. Indians have long fought for the maintenance of federal responsibility, which is mandated by Article 3 of the U.S. Constitution: "The Congress shall have Power. . . . to regulate commerce with foreign Nations and among the several states, and with the Indian Tribes." American Indians now hold that this provision obligates the United States government to uphold not only Indian trusteeship, but also Indian self-determination.

CONTEMPORARY INDIAN LAND REFORM DEMANDS

After decades of petitioning Congress, filing court cases, and attempting to work with federal programs, Indians have begun to focus on self-determination as the central strategy for reform. The prime mode of ac-

tion, which began in the mid-1960s and continues in the 1980s, is the occupation of land. These occupations create militant encampment
communities that sometimes become permanent — for instance, Akwesasne
in New York State and DQ University near Davis, California.

In 1968, the Mohawks in upper New York State confronted Canadian
officials about their requirement that Indians pay tolls to use the Cornwall
International Bridge that links the United States and Canada but also divides the Mohawk communities. The Mohawks invoked the Jay treaty of
1794 between the United States and Great Britain, an agreement that gave
the Mohawks rights to cross the border freely. The Mohawks eventually
blockaded the bridge and were arrested. In the highly publicized trial that
followed, they won a partial victory. Soon after, they seized territory in
New York State near the border, called it "Akwesasne," and with American, Canadian, and international support from many organizations, they
prevailed in keeping it. Akwesasne continues as a land base and activist
center.

Of the hundreds of occupations during the 1970s, several emerged as
particularly significant. The watershed was the November 1968 seizure of
Alcatraz, which persisted for eighteen months. Every Indian in the United
States was aware of the Alcatraz occupation and thousands visited it. Indians from all parts of the United States, from varying situations and different cultures and divided sharply by federal programs and funding, found a
point of unity in Alcatraz — particularly in the call for Indian self-
determination, treaty guarantees, and a secure land base. When it became
certain, after President Nixon came to office, that U.S. Marines would be
used to oust the Indians, most of them evacuated the site because maintenance of the island was not the goal being sought (though the demand for
an Indian museum on the island seemed manageable enough). Alcatraz
was merely a symbol; many Americans thought it strange and unjust that,
after everything Indians had suffered from the United States, the simple
demand to make an unused island an Indian cultural center was rejected
by the federal authorities.

Some of the leadership then led a seizure of abandoned federal property
near Davis, California, in order to establish a free Indian-Chicano university, DQ University. After months of struggle, publicity, and threats of
police intervention, the federal government negotiated a 33-year lease settlement on the property, which continues as a center of Indian activism. In
1980, Dennis Banks, one of the founders of the American Indian Movement (AIM), became chancellor of the university. He had been given a
home there in 1976, when Governor Brown refused a South Dakota extradition warrant for his arrest. However, in 1982 Banks had to flee to the
Onondaga reservation in upstate New York, when the newly elected Republican governor of California assured South Dakota authorities he
would honor their extradition request. DQ University itself was threatened with closure by the Reagan administration.

The pressure brought by these Indian actions and many others led to the proclamation of Indian "self-determination" by Nixon. Just before the 1972 election the Indian activists whose numbers had surged in the four years since Alcatraz, responded to Nixon's hypocrisy with the "Trail of Broken Treaties" caravan from Minnesota to Washington, D.C., arriving in the capital on November 1. While a large number of Indian demonstrators inside the Bureau of Indian Affairs building were awaiting promised talks with government officials, an order came from some source to lock the doors from the outside. Due to this mysterious, still-unexplained action, the Indian group took control of the building from November 2 through November 8, renaming it the "Native American Embassy." The document the group had presented the government, the "20-Point Position Paper," remains the chief statement of the activist Indian movement. Several of the points deal with treaties: resubmission of unratified treaties to the U.S. Senate; restoration of treaty making between Indians and the U.S. government; creation of a treaty commission; creation of a commission to review U.S. violations; and recognition of Indians' rights to interpret their own treaties.

The struggle soon intensified, with the siege of Wounded Knee from 27 February through 8 May 1973. In commemoration of the 1890 massacre of unarmed Indian refugees by the U.S. army, a ceremony was held at the site of that massacre, the town of Wounded Knee, South Dakota. Those who came did not leave. This was not, strictly speaking, an "occupation," since the Indians were completely within their own, officially recognized reservation territory, the Pine Ridge Sioux reservation. However, both the official tribal chairman, Dick Wilson, and the Nixon administration called the event an "occupation." The federal government responded as if it were a war, with troops, tanks, and planes. It also sealed in the demonstrators in the hope of starving them out.

Wounded Knee catapulted the American Indian Movement (AIM) into both public attention and the leadership of a mass Indian nationalist movement concerned primarily with the land. At Wounded Knee, international observers gathered in hopes of preventing a massacre; airlifts were organized to drop food and supplies. AIM, founded in Minneapolis in 1968 as a "Red Power" self-defense and civil rights organization, had played a role in the "Trail of Broken Treaties," but until Wounded Knee it had been primarily a local urban group much like the Chicano Brown Berets and the Black Panthers. The local Pine Ridge Sioux's Oglala Civil Rights Organization had invited AIM, known for its militancy, to come to Wounded Knee to demonstrate for the ouster of tribal chairman Wilson. The meeting of urban nationalist Indian youth and traditional reservation groups at Wounded Knee galvanized Indians from all over the United States. The alliance of elders—the militants of the 1930s and the 1940s who had refused to recognize the authority of the U.S. government or the tribal governments—with the nationalist urban youth became the pattern of the Indian struggle. Indians, traditional and urban, old and young, traveled to Wounded Knee and then returned home to organize support for those under siege. AIM chapters, as well as Wounded Knee solidarity groups, sprang up everywhere.

The siege ended with a negotiated settlement, the U.S. government promising to investigate AIM and Oglala allegations. The two key local leaders of the Oglala Civil Rights Organization were killed by troops during the siege. Afterwards a reign of terror was waged against the Pine Ridge reservation and nationwide against all those who had participated in or supported the action. By some counts, more than 300 Indians were to die within a year at the hands of police and federal agents. The culmination was the death of two FBI agents at Pine Ridge, for which AIM leader Leonard Peltier was sentenced to two life terms; his attorneys insisted that he was innocent and the trial rigged. The reservation was an occupied zone for several years after Wounded Knee. FBI provocateurs and counter-insurgency elements infiltrated local AIM chapters and the national staff. The organization was named "number one terrorist organization in the USA" by the FBI in 1976. Local leaders and organizers were framed and assassinated. There were intense covert efforts to discredit and destroy the organization. Some activists "disappeared," later to be found dead.

AIM formed an international organization in June 1974. Thousands of Indian activists met at the Standing Rock Sioux reservation in South Dakota and formed the International Indian Treaty Council (IITC). Its founding document, "The Declaration of Continuing Independence," directed the council to work at the United Nations and to "approach all international forces necessary to obtain the recognition of our treaties." The declaration expresses its identification with national liberation movements in Africa, Asia, and Latin America, and specifically with the "colonized Puerto Rican People in their struggle for Independence from the same United States of America" (Ortiz, 1977: Appendix).

In December 1974 AIM attempted to have the hundreds of Wounded Knee criminal charges dismissed for lack of federal jurisdiction in accordance with the Sioux Treaty of 1868. However, the federal judge upheld the federal jurisdiction over the reservation:

> . . . relations with American Indians are rooted in international relations . . . including the laws of conquest and of treaties developed over centuries, not by courts, but by executive heads of nations through negotiations. . . . The defendants, then, are addressing the wrong forum for gaining relief in their sovereignty grievances. (Ortiz, 1977:198)

Other occupations followed Wounded Knee. They occurred both inside and outside reservations, and at factories, an oil refinery, and ancient burial sites.

TWO CASE STUDIES

Two land struggles, those of the Big Mountain on the Navajo reservation and the Yellow Thunder camp in the Sioux Treaty land in the Black Hills of South Dakota, have involved long-term occupations. Both have broad support from all sectors of the Indian population and significant support from national and international organizations. Navajos and Sioux together comprise more than half the entire American Indian population. Both carried on a prolonged armed resistance to U.S. colonization between 1850 and 1868, when each negotiated practically identical "Peace and Friendship" treaties that established their reservations. These reservations have been primary centers of struggle in Indian country. Each reservation is under intense pressure from transnational energy corporations for development of mineral resources — uranium, coal, and petroleum. Unemployment and poverty rates on the reservations force many to migrate to urban areas, where Navajos and Sioux make up the majority of most large urban Indian populations. Thus these land struggles have implications far beyond the occupied sites or the reservations.

Yellow Thunder Camp

On 29 December 1890, following forty years of armed resistance, the last remaining group of Sioux refugees who refused to submit to U.S. authority — an unarmed, freezing, starving group of several hundred mothers, children, and grandparents — were surrounded and massacred in the Sioux district called Wounded Knee. Regular U.S. army troops, under orders, carried out the bloody massacre. It quieted effective Indian resistance for a generation. Wounded Knee was only one of thousands of such Indian massacres, but Wounded Knee 1890 has a very special meaning. It is an undeniable proof of official genocide, a sad turning point in Indian-U.S. relations, and a testimony to Indian survival and resistance. So December 29 is a day of mourning for Indian people.

On 27 February 1973, the descendants of the Wounded Knee martyrs gathered there with other Indians and proclaimed their liberation from the United States. They were surrounded by U.S. troops and by BIA police. The Indians at Wounded Knee were prepared to die if need be and believed they would be required to do so. Although the U.S. government averted outright massacre, many participating Indians were killed or imprisoned afterwards.

The historical background is deep. The first relationship between the Sioux nation and the U.S. government was an 1805 treaty of peace and friendship. Other treaties followed in 1815 and 1825 which obligated the United States to protect the Sioux against any other power. The Fort Laramie Treaty of 1851 between the Sioux and the United States further defined their mutual relationship but was immediately followed by a decade of war between the two nations, ending with the Peace Treaty of Fort Laramie in 1868 (Institute for the Development of Indian Law, 1973). Both of the Fort Laramie treaties, though not reducing Sioux independence, ceded large parts of Sioux hunting territory and granted trade concessions to the United States. During the nineteenth century, the Sioux were gradually enveloped in the fur trade (particularly for bison hides) and became dependent on European manufactured guns, ammunition, and other commodities. The Sioux abandoned agricultural production and turned entirely to bison hunting for their own subsistence and for hides to trade for manufactured goods.

Dependency on the buffalo and on trade was replaced with dependency on the U.S. government rations and commodities guaranteed in the 1868 treaty, to which the United States added the stipulation that the Indians receiving them must be living in the reservation and reporting to the U.S. Indian agent. Then the Appropriations Act of 3 March 1871, which allocated money for the food supplies, notified the Sioux and other Indian peoples that colonization was complete:

> For insurance and transportation of goods for the Yanktons [Sioux], $1,500: Provided that, hereafter no Indian nation or tribe within the territory of the United States shall be acknowledged or recognized as an independent nation, tribe, or power with whom the United States may contract by treaty. (25 USC 71)

Colonization meant disregard for Sioux rights under the 1868 treaty, which had stipulated that

> no treaty for the cession of any portion or part of the reservation herein described which may be held in common shall be of any validation or force against the said Indians, unless executed and signed by at least ¾ of all the adult male Indians. (15 USC 635)

The U.S. military took the Black Hills, a large resource-rich (in gold and timber at the time; now in uranium, oil, and timber) part of the guaranteed Sioux territory, and also a mountainous religious sanctuary, the center of the Great Sioux Nation. A few years later, the federal government completed the carving of the faces of American presidents on the sacred mountain (Forty-fourth Congress (1872), p. 393; Forty-fifth Congress (1873), p. 413).

In 1883, the first Mohonk Conferences were held at Lake Mohonk, New York, by a group of influential and wealthy advocates of the "manifest destiny" policy. This group called itself "Friends of the Indians," and it developed recommendations that were formulated into the act written by a member of the group, Senator Henry Dawes. This was the General Allotment Act of 1887, which allowed the division of reservation land. The rationale expressed in the Mohonk recommendations persists today:

> The defect of the [reservation] system was apparent. It is Henry George's system, and under that there is no enterprise to make your home any better than that of your neighbors. There is no selfishness, which is at the bottom of civilization. Till this people [the Cherokees in this case] will consent to give up their lands, and divide among their citizens so that each can own the land he cultivates, they will not make much more progress. (Prucha, 1978:53)

Though allotment did not create the desired selfishness among Indians, it did reduce the Indian land base by half so that whites could homestead it — which many observers assert was the real goal of allotment. And it further impoverished the Sioux, among many other Indians.

The policy of creating enclaves of contiguous territories broke up the Great Sioux Nation into six small reservations that were then allotted again. American settlement was allowed in the middle of the Sioux territory. The policy also allowed for tighter control by the Bureau of Indian Affairs, whose boarding schools removed young Indian children by force from their homes. For their entire childhood and youth, they were put with children of different language groups, and English was forced upon them as a common language. The Sun Dance, the annual ceremony which bound the Sioux communities of the Great Sioux Nation, was banned by law.

The Sioux began developing a modest collective cattle production to replace the former bison-hunting economy. But in 1903 the U.S. Supreme Court ruled in *Lone Wolf* v. *Hitchcock* that the 1871 act was constitutional and also that Congress had "plenary" power to manage Indian property. This ruling legally permitted the Interior Department to dispose of Indian lands regardless of the terms of previous treaty provisions. Further legislation opened reservations to settlement through leasing and even sale of allotments taken out of trust. Non-Indian cattlemen grabbed nearly all prime grazing lands and water rights by the 1920s. Trust funds accruing from these activities were handled by the Bureau of Indian Affairs and managed essentially for the benefit of corporations (Miner, 1976).

By the time of the New Deal, non-Indians outnumbered Indians on Sioux reservations by three to one. However, the drought and Depression drove most Anglo-American ranchers off Sioux land. The "tribal governments" were introduced on most of the Sioux reservations (Philip, 1977). Matthew King, an elder from the Pine Ridge Sioux reservation and AIM activist, has commented:

> The Bureau of Indian Affairs drew up the constitution and by-laws of this organization with the Indian Reorganization Act of 1934. This was the introduction of home rule. . . . The traditional people still hang on to their Treaty, for we are a sovereign nation. We have our own government. (Ortiz, 1977:156)

Home rule or "neocolonialism," (see Jorgensen, 1972:89–146) was interrupted in the early 1950s, when the United States developed a policy of gradually terminating every Indian reservation by withdrawing trust protection. Several reservations were terminated with immediately catastrophic results; the best-known case was that of the Menominee in Wisconsin, who went from total self-sufficiency to poverty in a short time. The Menominees led a fight for restoration of trusteeship, which they won in the early 1970s; however, the economy of commercial forestry and milling which they had built has not been reconstructed. The process of termination was halted during the Kennedy administration.

In 1955, the income on Sioux reservations stood at $355 per capita per year, compared with $2,500 for nearby South Dakota non-Indian communities. In this setting of poverty, the Bureau of Indian Affairs attempted to carry out the termination policy by reducing services and relocating Indians in urban industrial centers. Nearly half the Sioux population was removed during twelve years of relocation, which proceeded even after trust termination stopped.

Matthew King has noted that the U.S. government historically alternates between a "peace" policy and a "war" policy toward Indians. These policies, he explains, are based on the strength or weakness of Indian resistance. When Indian resistance is strong, a peace policy of preserving reservations predominants. But when Indian resistance is weak, a war policy of extermination appears (Ortiz, 1977:155).

But following Wounded Knee, concurrent war and peace policies were employed by the U.S. government—that is, both repression and bribery. Indian activists were arrested or assassinated, while enormous financial grants were made to the tribal governments. A reform tribal government was elected at Pine Ridge, with an advisory council of traditional elders receiving salaries. But poverty went on unabated. Elders and activist youth tried to work with the tribal government but eventually gave up. Indian activists did community organizing, concentrating on developing collective community services, including independent "survival schools."

On 4 April 1981, a date chosen to honor Dr. Martin Luther King on the anniversary of his assassination, members of the Dakota (Sioux) American Indian Movement nonviolently began the process required by U.S. law to reclaim 800 acres of uninhabited land controlled by the U.S. Forest Service. The land is located in the sacred Paha Sapa (Black Hills) of the Sioux, which had been guaranteed by the 1868 treaty, but which was later illegally seized by the U.S. Army. The community was intended to develop self-reliant technologies, such as solar energy and wind power, and to pursue the Indian way of life. The community was named "Yellow Thunder" after Raymond Yellow Thunder, a Sioux man who was brutually murdered in 1972 by a non-Indian in front of numerous witnesses. The murderer was charged with second-degree manslaughter.

The Yellow Thunder Camp was established under existing U.S. laws. The members of the camp cited Article 6 of the U.S. Constitution, which states that treaties are the supreme law of the land; the 1868 Fort Laramie Sioux Treaty with the United States, which guarantees the Black Hills as a part of the Sioux territory and requires a plebiscite among the Sioux for any alteration of the terms; the American Indian Religious Freedom Act of 1978; and the 1897 federal statute (16 USC 479) relating to sites for schools and churches on National Forest lands. The Sioux occupants of the community reported that they had tried to obtain a "special use permit" from the U.S. Department of Agriculture which would have allowed them to begin building schools, houses, cooperative gardens, and religious structures. The permit was denied by the Department of Agriculture with the explanation that it was "not in the public's interest." There is no indication that any person has been displaced to establish the community, and local non-Indian residents wrote letters of support for the community. Objections came only from federal authorities.

The federal motivation is clear. Various large corporations want to exploit the vast natural resources in the immediate area, and the Reagan administration has opened the door for them. The other reason for refusal was undoubtedly that the United States would be recognizing the continuing validity of the 1868 Sioux Treaty claim to the Black Hills. The Indian Claims Court has already made an award of millions of dollars to compensate the Indians for the illegal taking by the United States, but the Sioux people have consistently refused to accept the money because, they feel, it would legitimate the theft.

The occupants of Yellow Thunder received letters of support from thirty-eight U.S. Congressmen as well as locally and nationally prominent individuals, churches, and other groups. The International Indian Treaty Council complained to the United Nations Human Rights Commission. Yet the occupants were notified by the U.S. government that federal forces would attempt to evict the community by force on 8 September 1981. The occupants vowed at a United Nations special session on human rights in Geneva:

> In the spirit of Crazyhorse, and the liberation of Wounded Knee in 1973, the men, women, and children residents of the Yellow Thunder Camp will resist eviction by any means necessary in the interest of their human right to self-determination. (UN Commission on Human Rights, 1981)

The IITC informed the UN body that Indians have faced genocide, assassination, and massacres too many times in the past four hundred years to be intimidated any longer. They asserted that

> a people's right to self-defense in resisting oppression is well accepted, and that, if it comes to armed attack by the U.S. government, the right of the community to resist will also be accepted. . . . The Lakota people might very well be killed for upholding the Constitution of the USA. (UN Commission on Human Rights, 1981)

Instead of evicting the occupants on 8 September, the federal government brought trespass charges against their leaders, throwing the case into court. The occupation continued through 1983 with no sign of ending. Buildings were constructed and living quarters established. National support by Indians and non-Indians included airlifts of food and winter clothing.

Big Mountain Navajo

In November 1980, representatives of the Navajo Big Mountain community traveled to Rotterdam, Holland, to present their complaint against the U.S. government to the Fourth Russell Tribunal on Violations of Human Rights and Genocide, whose subject was Indians. The Navajo representatives described their urgent situation. Approximately 8,500 Navajos in the western Arizona part of the Navajo reservation, living by means of a sheep subsistence economy, are facing forced removal from their traditional grazing lands within the reservation. They are to be relocated in towns outside the Navajo territory, more than 100 miles away from their community. Most of these people do not speak English and have spent all their lives raising sheep. The meat provides their basic food staple, and the wool is handspun, dyed, and made into rugs and blankets, both for Navajo use and for sale at nearby trading posts. The land, semiarid and mile-high, had long been designated by the U.S. government as the "joint use area" of the Navajos and Hopis.

The joint use area was established on 6 December 1882, when President Arthur set aside 4,000 square miles in the Arizona Territory for Hopi Indians and "other" Indians and gave governmental authority over the land to the secretary of the interior. Though Navajos were not named specifically in the order, they were already living on this land which was their ancestral territory. No one had ever questioned that "other" Indians meant the Navajos. For many years, there was no real problem in the JUA between the Navajos and the Hopis, since the Hopis are farmers who lived then, as now, in ancient villages built on the mesas in the southern part of the JUA. Hopi farming is intensive, dry farming on the terraced slopes below the villages. The Navajos always have relied on sheep grazing. The two economies had long complemented one another. The tribes exchanged meat and vegetables, intermarried, and shared use of certain areas for ceremonies.

However, in 1934 the Navajos decisively rejected the tribal government scheme of the Indian Reorganization Act. An election was also held among the Hopi, who had had virtually no contact with the North Americans who claimed political authority over them. Most of them ignored the election, assuming that — in accordance with their own practices — the proposal would require participation and unanimity. But there were votes from approximately 650 Hopis who were Christian and Mormon converts, or "progressives." Thus was born the unpopular Hopi "Tribal Council" and the "Hopi-Navajo land dispute."

The progressives, who were allied with the nearby American Mormons, had taken up commercial cattle raising. Cattlemen who were members of the Hopi Tribal Council pressured the Bureau of Indian Affairs to set aside a portion of the reservation for their exclusive use as a grazing district. Subsequent pressure by the Hopi elite, probably with a great deal of advice and pressure from the wealthy and powerful Mormon financial interests to the north, resulted in federal legislation in 1958 creating a special three-judge federal court to handle disputes over the rest of the JUA. The progressives immediately filed a lawsuit claiming all the land within the JUA. The special court ruled in 1963 that the Hopi grazing district belonged exclusively to the Hopi and that the rest of the reservation was to be divided evenly between the Hopi and the Navajo. Approximately ten thousand Navajos and only one hundred Hopis used the transferred area. Despite a long struggle by the Navajos and despite their refusal to leave the area — an action supported by the majority of the Hopi people — the U.S. Supreme Court in 1974 confirmed the 1963 decision.

A relocation plan was then drawn up by the Bureau of Indian Affairs. The Navajo Tribal Council, with its newly elected reform government of Peter MacDonald, officially condemned it. Legally required reviews by experts on the effects and feasibility of relocation of the Navajos, and on the general views of Hopi villagers, clearly indicated that the relocation scheme, while not even desired by the Hopis, would be devastating to the thousands of uprooted Navajos. Relocation would destroy the already beleaguered traditional pastoral economy of the Navajos. Nevertheless, the relocation plan was undertaken. From 1975 to 1981, more than a thousand Navajos were relocated to border towns. Studies of their postrelocation experience revealed the barbarity of the action. Though they were given a cash payment for the purchase of a home, inexperience with managing business affairs, lack of knowledge of the English language, inadequate income to maintain property and pay taxes, and general alienation all led to severe depression and loneliness. Most of the relocatees were elderly, and the move separated them from the complex extended blood and clan families that reach outside the particular community to bind together the entire Navajo nation.

From the early 1970s on, many Navajos and Hopis cooperated to publicize the issue and pressure the government. The American Indian Movement assisted the Navajos designated for relocation and helped them form a permanent resistant community called "Big Mountain." Eviction notices were posted, and the federal government attempted to fence the eviction area in 1975. But the fences were torn down every night. Another eviction attempt was made in 1980. This time elder Navajo women — a powerful force in Navajo society because they actually own the sheep herds — did the fence cutting. They were arrested and later acquitted.

The resistant community has gained considerable support; the International Indian Treaty Council and many other groups have taken the case to international and national forums. Petitions and resolutions abound condemning the relocation plan, including a petition from a long list of anthropologists. Clearly, the only option for the federal government is to move the army or BIA police in to force evictions. The resistant community has vowed to die fighting before they will leave. The resistant Navajos know that the real motive behind the relocation scheme is to extend the vast coal strip mining that is taking place on the Navajo reservation.

The events surrounding Big Mountain reflect the larger pattern of colonization, exploitation of Navajo land and resources, and oppression of the Navajo people that followed U.S. military conquest in the 1860s. The Navajo population is now approximately 150,000 with about 30,000 living away from the reservation primarily in towns bordering the reservation and in California. The entire Navajo territory is located in the Four Corners region of Arizona, New Mexico, Utah, and Colorado, with reservation land in all but Colorado. The reservation was part of the territory taken by the United States from the Republic of Mexico in 1846. The Navajos had never been conquered and colonized by the Spanish or the Mexicans, though there were many attempts. And the Navajos successfully resisted U.S. military might for seventeen years after the United States took the region. However, the military launched expeditions of regular and irregular units under the command of Kit Carson (a merchant resident of Taos, New Mexico), whose mission was to carry out a scorched-earth policy. Every Navajo corn field and orchard was burned, every community pillaged, every sheep slaughtered until there was nothing; the starving Navajos surrendered in 1863–64. The 8,000 Navajos who were rounded up were put in a military camp at Bosque Redondo in the desert of southeastern New Mexico. "The Long Walk" is the name the Navajos use to describe the forced march to imprisonment. In the four years of incarceration, 2,000 Navajos — 25 percent — died of starvation and exposure. Based on congressional objections to the *cost* (no mention made of the inhumanity) of the concentration camp, a trusteeship treaty was negotiated with the surviving Navajos in 1868. It confirmed their traditional homeland, and they returned home.

From 1868 to 1922, when oil was discovered in Navajo territory, the Navajos were virtually ignored by the federal government. The land itself had been assessed as worthless for homesteading or cattle grazing. However, the oil brought intensive U.S. intervention, beginning with a massive stock reduction policy. Government agents slaughtered tens of thousands of sheep and left the carcasses to rot under the rationale that overgrazing was a problem. Certainly, sheep production had intensified as Navajos were brought into the exchange economy through the national and international marketing of Navajo rugs. Overgrazing had also occurred, though it probably did not require such a drastic solution. Government agents did not have the Navajo land and welfare in mind at all in the stock reduction program. Instead, they wanted to eliminate the subsistence base of the Navajo economy so as to remove Navajos from the land (Lamphere, 1979:78–90). Though Navajos rejected the federally promoted tribal governments in 1934 — largely because of the stock reductions — the Interior Department established a Navajo business council in 1937. The council was made up of seventy-four elected Navajos. The present Navajo government originated with the council and has somewhat more popular acceptance than most tribal governments established by the 1934 legislation.

According to 1975 economic estimates, only 50,000 acres of the 17 million acres in Navajo territory are under cultivation, though the Navajos possess water rights sufficient to irrigate 5 million acres. Most of the land is used for grazing 500,000 sheep, 50,000 cattle, and 30,000 goats. Much of the agricultural production is food grains for these animals. Stock production clearly could become the major factor in the Navajo economy, a point grasped by both the traditional subsistence Navajos and many economic experts (Reno, 1981). However, a pastoral economy is rejected by some "progressive" Navajos who wish to accede to intense pressure from the U.S. government and large energy corporations to allow more extractive industries in the territory. A great deal of Navajo land was leased to corporations by the Bureau of Indian Affairs in the 1920s and 1930s without Navajo consent. There are over 400,000 acres of commercial forest which yield from one to three million dollars in annual stumpage payments to the Navajos. The territory is rich in subsurface and surface mines: 100 million barrels of oil, 25 billion cubic feet of natural gas, 2.5 to 5 billion tons of easily accessible surface coal, and 80 million pounds of uranium are the known reserves (Ruffing, 1979:93).

Beginning in the 1920s, mineral exploitation steadily increased, followed in the 1950s by a growth in manufacturing. The reform governments of Peter MacDonald, who was first elected in the early 1970s, continue to be reelected on this commitment to limit industrialization and mining and to renegotiate past unfair leases. However, by the time MacDonald retired from the chairmanship in 1982, mining had increased, 500,000 acres had been leased to Exxon for uranium strip-mining, and no leases had been renegotiated. The growing influence of the Big Mountain community posed real questions for the Navajo people to consider, especially at a time of disillusionment with the promises of wealth from resource exploitation; the unemployment rate is 60 percent in the reservation. The decisions taken by the Navajos on economic policy and the Big Mountain community are expected to affect not only Navajos, but all Indian people in the United States.

CONCLUSION

What measures of land policy could help indigenous Americans? What possible mode of land reform would be applicable to such a complex situation? What could undo the conflicts of interest on the part of the federal government, the Indians' trustee? There are a number of possibilities that could be workable. Let us look at what would be required in the United States to create a minimum five-year land reform program for Indians:

1. An immediate halt to all commercial energy, mineral, forestry, and agribusiness activities by outside corporations in and near Indian land areas.

2. A thorough inventory of all resources and all tenure on Indian land.

3. U.S. governmental financing of both the inventories and the replacement of income lost to ousted business interests.

4. The development of overall socioeconomic plans by Indian communities, without federal interference and with disinterested technical assistance from the United Nations or the Organization of American States.

5. An inventory and analysis of water rights and their distribution within reservations.

6. Creation of equitable, contiguous land bases for each Indian group, including those who have lost their land, and the restructuring of original reservation territories for those whose lands were allotted. Private lands for these purposes would be acquired by creating life estates for the present

owners and then paying heirs. The majority of the land added, however, would be from territory that is under federal jurisdiction — Bureau of Land Management, Forest Service, and National Parks Service lands.

7. U.S. financial support for reservation infrastructure development, planned by the local Indians with international technical assistance.

8. Reconstruction of Indian economies on their modified traditional basis (sheep production — Navajo; cattle production — Sioux, Plains; garden farming — Pueblos and Hopis; fisheries — Northwest and Northeast, etc.), including a system of coordinated regional exchanges among Indian communities and internal vertical integration of processing and marketing.

The short-term cost of the above five-year crash program, a "Marshall Plan" for American Indians, would be offset by long-term savings in social costs and future transfer payments from the federal government.

Perhaps such a program is visionary. But Indians are and should continue pushing for something like it, for not much is likely to be achieved except in a context of overall national social transformation. If Indians have learned any certain lesson from their relationship with the United States, it is that the present political economy based on limitless expansion and corporate profits will never allow for Indian survival, much less land reform. But time is running out, and survival is the essential question. Many Indians have come to think that Yellow Thunder and Big Mountain represent the best strategies for land reform.

REFERENCES

American Indian Policy Review Commission. 1978. *Final Report.* Submitted to Congress 17 May 1977. Washington, DC: U.S. Government Printing Office.

Hundley, Norris C., Jr. 1979. "The dark and bloody ground of Indian water rights." In *Economic Development in American Indian Reservations.* Edited by Roxanne Dunbar Ortiz. Albuquerque: Native American Studies Department, University of New Mexico.

Institute for the Development of Indian Law. 1973. *Treaties and Agreements of the Sioux Nation.* Washington, DC: IDIL.

Jorgensen, Joseph. 1972. *The Sun Dance Religion.* Chicago: University of Chicago Press.

Lamphere, Louise. 1979. "Traditional pastoral economy in the Navajo nation." In *Economic Development in American Indian Reservations.* Edited by Roxanne Dunbar Ortiz. Albuquerque: Native American Studies Department, University of New Mexico.

Miner, H. Craig. 1976. *The Corporation and the Indian.* Columbia: University of Missouri Press.

Nafziger, Richard. 1980. "Transnational corporations and American Indian development." In *American Indian Energy Resources and Development.* Edited by Roxanne Dunbar Ortiz. Albuquerque: Institute for Native American Development, Native American Studies Department, University of New Mexico.

Ortiz, Roxanne Dunbar. 1977. *The Great Sioux Nation.* Berkeley: Moon Books.

——— (ed.). 1979. *Economic Development in American Indian Reservations.* Albuquerque: Native American Studies Department, University of New Mexico.

———. 1980a. "Wounded Knee 1890 to Wounded Knee 1973: a study in U.S. colonialism." *Journal of Ethnic Studies* 8 (Summer).

———. 1980b. *Roots of Resistance: History of Land Tenure in New Mexico.* Los Angeles: American Indian Research Center and Chicano Research Center, UCLA.

————— (ed.). 1980c. *American Indian Energy Resources and Development*. Albuquerque: Institute for Native American Development, Native American Studies Department, University of New Mexico.

Philp, Kenneth R. 1977. *John Collier's Crusade for Indian Reform, 1920–54*. Tucson: University of Arizona Press.

Prucha, Francis Paul (ed.). 1978. *Americanizing the American Indian: Writings by the 'Friends of the Indian,' 1880–1900*. Lincoln: University of Nebraska Press.

Reno, Phillip. 1981. *Mother Earth, Father Sky and Navajo Resources*. Albuquerque: University of New Mexico Press, with the Institute for Native American Development.

Ruffing, Lorraine. 1979. "Dependence and underdevelopment." In *Economic Development in American Indian Reservations*. Edited by Roxanne Dunbar Ortiz. Albuquerque: Native American Studies Department, University of New Mexico.

Sutton, Imre. 1970. "Land tenure in the West: continuity and change." *Journal of the West 9* (January): 1–23.

—————. 1975. *Indian Land Tenure*. New York: Clearwater Publishers.

United Nations Commission on Human Rights. 1981. "Oral intervention by International Indian Treaty Council." Subcommission on the Prevention of Discrimination and Protection of Minorities: Thirty-seventh Session, Geneva, August 31.

United States House of Representatives. 1872. House Executive Document 1, Part 5, p. 393. Forty-fourth Congress, Second Session.

—————. 1873. House Executive Document, Part 5, p. 413. Forty-fifth Congress, Second Session.

United States Supreme Court. 1868. The Treaty of 1868 between the U.S. and the Sioux Indians. 15 USC 635.

—————. 1871. Appropriations Act of March 3, 1871. 25 USC 71.

—————. 1887. General Allotment Act. 24 USC 388.

—————. 1903. *Lone Wolf* v. *Hitchcock*. 187 USC 553.

11

Land Reform and the Struggle for Black Liberation: From Reconstruction to Remote Claims

HAROLD A. McDOUGALL

Black people's desire for land is deep-seated and acute. Black people want land for many reasons, among them: status; a physical framework for the consolidation of African culture (predominantly agrarian at its roots); a family resting place; a communal home for the living, dead, and unborn;[1] a source of wealth; and a political power base. A variety of organizations and movements in the history of the Black community have appealed to this desire. Five examples will sketch the history, and suggest a thematic unity in the struggles of African people in the United States for land. These are, "40 acres and a mule," the dictum that was to be imposed on a vanquished Confederacy; the self-help efforts of ex-slaves and their children to acquire land during the era of Booker T. Washington; the Back-to-Africa movement of Marcus Garvey; the struggle of the Southern Tenant Farmers' Union during the Depression and the resultant redistributive concessions made by the federal government; and, finally, the multifaceted, multiclass Black movement for land that grew up after World War II and which continues to this day.

BLACK LAND REFORM I: "FORTY ACRES AND A MULE"

The U.S. Civil War made millionaires out of men like J. Pierpont Morgan, John D. Rockefeller, Andrew Carnegie, James Mellon, Philip Armour, and Jay Gould. These men were premier members of the rising industrial class of the North that fought the slave-owning aristocracy of the South for control of the national government and for the land west of the Mississippi, then being ripped away from the Indians. Between these two great contending forces stood the masses of small farmers and agricultural workers who saw the West as a chance for free land.

Another, less numerous group of agrarian people also expected land as a result of the Civil War — the newly freed African slaves. The alternative of repatriation to Africa, though considered early on by President Lincoln, was not seriously considered as an alternative by the Black leaders, mustered-out Black soldiers, Radical Republicans, and abolitionists who, after the war, pushed for the confiscation of Southern plantations and redistribution of plantation lands in forty-acre plots to freedmen. Black people, who had put so much energy into the development of the United States, particularly the South, were ready in 1865 to believe they would receive "40 acres and a mule" from the U.S. Government to make up for their expatriation from Africa and their enslavement in the United States (McPherson, 1964:254; Abbott, 1967:8). Two truths eluded the Blacks of the time. First, the land they had worked more than two centuries was the rightful homeland of Indians who had been driven West or exterminated. Second, the political and economic forces reigning after the Civil War precluded any large-scale land reform programs — the vigorous and aggressive Northern capitalists, in full control of the economy and national and state governments, were much more likely to benefit from land redistribution. Only a handful of Blacks saw the latter truth, among them Osborne Anderson, a free Black and graduate of Ohio's Oberlin College, who was one of the seventeen Blacks who joined John Brown in the abortive raid on Harper's Ferry. Anderson believed that the example of such guerrilla actions, combined with the arsenal secured at Harper's Ferry, would inspire a general slave uprising that would overturn the Southern power structure and create the conditions for land reform.

Thaddeus Stevens, a Radical Republican congressman from Pennsylvania, was the first white to advocate comprehensive land reform in the rebel states, even before the Civil War was over. In 1861, Congress passed the Confiscation Act, over Lincoln's opposition, which enabled the Northern army to acquire large tracts of abandoned plantations. Under the authority of the act, General William Sherman issued Special Field Order 15 in 1865, which provided "40 acres and a mule" for over 40,000 freedmen on the Sea Islands of South Carolina and Georgia. This experiment was a success, but it was an exception. Most freedmen occupied land under leases, if at all, and had only vain hopes of acquiring full ownership (McFeely, 1968:192, 230).

The Bureau of Refugees, Freedmen, and Abandoned Lands — The Freedmen's Bureau — was established in 1864 to manage abandoned lands, oversee relations between freedmen and their employers, and provide shelter to newly freed slaves. The bureau could lease forty acres of land to each loyal freedman and white refugee for a term of three years. It could temporarily settle emancipated slaves on confiscated or abandoned plantations. But at war's end, Lincoln's successor, Andrew Johnson, pardoned many Southern rebels and restored them to the land Blacks occupied.

The Bureau believed that it was protecting freedmen by establishing a system of contract labor between ex-slaves and their former masters on the restored plantations. The Bureau also helped establish wage and hour pay scales—ten dollars per month and ten hours per day. The contract labor system and the return of the former slave masters kept the Black man subservient and resulted in the system we know today as sharecropping. Sharecropping was much like slavery; Black people were bound again to land owned by non-Blacks.

When the Bureau closed in 1872, it had reestablished and solidified the oppressive land tenure patterns which existed in the antebellum South. The slogan, "40 acres and a mule," which fired the collective imagination of the Black "nation" in the South, and still echoes in the ideology and culture of Black Americans, has ironically come to be associated with the Freedmen's Bureau. A much better contemporary example was the successful struggle of the Sea Island Blacks, the only recipients of the fabled 40 acres, who not only refused to give up the land granted them by General Sherman, but engaged in armed resistance to retain it.

BLACK LAND REFORM II: "CAST DOWN YOUR BUCKETS WHERE YOU ARE"

There were three alternatives facing freedmen after the Civil War—full citizenship with no reparations, reparations in the form of 40-acre plots in the South, or repatriation to Africa. Only the first was offered in any tangible sense. Return to Africa would have respected the rights of Indians, but the necessary financial and logistical support was simply not forthcoming. Some free Blacks had been repatriated to Africa early in the 1800s, and had founded the colony of Liberia in 1822, but this opportunity was never realistic for most Blacks, and was foreclosed completely when Henry Clay's Colonization Society closed its doors in 1840 (Stange, 1967). "Forty acres and a mule," as noted, did not materialize, and the Homestead Act of 1862 fulfilled little of its promise to non-Blacks, let alone Blacks. The chief beneficiaries of the act, and of what parceling-out of rebel plantations actually took place, were the victorious Northern capitalists, particularly in timber, mining, and agriculture. Those in railroads were also eligible to acquire vast territories, particularly in the West and South, through a special right of eminent domain granted by Congress.

The Northern capitalists finally reunited the country with the "Compromise of 1877," which amounted to a massive sellout in which even the citizenship rights of the freedmen, let alone their promised lands, were sacrificed. President-elect Rutherford Hayes withdrew federal troops from the South, in exchange for the Southern electoral votes needed to wrest the presidency from the winner of the popular vote, Samuel Tilden. With the withdrawal of the troops, Reconstruction came to a close. The Supreme Court sanctioned the subsequent denial of the fundamental freedoms associated with citizenship in a series of infamous court decisions culminating with *Plessy* v. *Ferguson.*

With national unity achieved, the Gilded Age began. The 1880s saw the Rockefellers and their like carve huge corporate empires out of public money and public land. They took great interest in the emerging Black petite bourgeoisie of the South, which made its living providing services to the segregated Black community. Rockefeller and others provided the funds to establish and maintain Black colleges and universities such as Tuskegee Institute, base of operations for Booker T. Washington.

Accepting the denial of citizenship rights and renouncing dreams of African repatriation, Washington urged Blacks to "cast down your buckets where you are" and help themselves by buying land and becoming merchants, farmers, and artisans. The self-help philosophy inspired many Blacks not to wait for the state to help them.[2] These Blacks bought nearly 15 million acres of land by World War I and established a number of autonomous Black agrarian communities. In 1889, for example, in Oakland, Texas, Blacks banded together, established Oakland as an all-Black town, and formed a cooperative where they bought and sold supplies and crops so as to avoid being thrust into debt by sharecropping (Taylor, 1976:88).

The majority of Blacks could not follow Oakland's lead. Significant numbers acquired the land they worked, but it remained a fragile shelter in an extremely hostile environment. The Gilded Age was extremely volatile, experiencing chaotic fits and starts as the new financial and industrial giants battled on Wall Street. The Depression of 1893 left men like Rockefeller, Morgan, and Carnegie in control of the American economy. From 1898 to World War I, control became more and more concentrated, with a large number of trusts being formed. Agriculture felt the shock; roughly half of all farms were mortgaged by 1890. Yet through sheer determination, 25 percent of Blacks living on farms during the era of Booker T. Washington actually owned them by the end of the nineteenth century. In 1890, 120,738 Blacks owned farm homes, of which only 12,252 were encumbered by debt. By 1900, 148,000 Blacks owned farms.

Yet the position of those exceptional former slaves who raised themselves to the level of a peasant class was still unstable. Due to a lack of capital and agricultural training, many Blacks who were independent farmers in prosperous times became tenant farmers and sharecroppers in hard ones. To protect themselves and their gains, Black peasants banded together into the Colored Farmers' Alliance, which focused primarily on cooperative marketing and purchasing.

The Populist movement expressed the political aspirations of the American peasant class, regardless of race. Various farmers' alliances opposed big banks and large corporations. The Populists aimed primarily at ending the exploitation of farmers by banking and railroad interests, but soon broadened their perspective to include nationalization of the banks and progressive redistribution of the land. The farmers' and labor movements briefly joined forces, presenting a serious challenge to American capitalism, but eventually the farmers' movement—such organizations as the Grange, the Greenbackers, and the various farmers' alliances—became deeply divided along racial lines.

At the dawn of the twentieth century the great industrialists solidified the country around a platform of imperialism and racism under the aegis of Presidents McKinley and Roosevelt. While monopoly capital prospered, the lot of the small farmer, especially the Black small farmer, rapidly deteriorated. By 1910, when Black landownership reached its peak of 22 million acres, mortgaged farms numbered 54,017—a nearly five-fold increase since 1890. During the first decade of the twentieth century, often referred to as the golden age of American agriculture, Black farmers were already squeezed by increasingly concentrated competitors; by 1920, farming became a business in which a few small farmers, mostly white, struggled for the profits left by the big farms that had come to dominate the industry. The Black land base, larger in 1910 than at any time before or since, was beginning to dwindle because of the increasing tendency toward concentration and monopoly in agriculture (Haywood, 1948:58).

BLACK LAND REFORM III: "BACK TO AFRICA"

Blacks began to leave the rural South for the urban North. World War I and the advent of assembly-line production created an urgent need for labor in Northern cities. The war reduced the flood of European immigrants that filled that need. American industry, forced to search for an alternative source of labor, found it in the Black farmers and sharecroppers of the South who had already begun to leave the South in droves. From 1900 to 1910, Blacks left the South at a rate seven times greater than their non-Black counterparts. Between 1910 and 1930, 26.3 percent of the South's Black population migrated north, forming a Black urban proletariat—a class base separate from and in addition to the rural Black peasantry of the South.

This new proletariat had somewhat hostile relations with the existing white working class. Blacks were immediately placed in separate urban ghettoes. The simultaneous urbanization and segregation of Blacks accelerated, particularly when veterans of both races came home after World War I. Interracial hostility was seriously inflamed by the competition for jobs, especially during the great recessions of 1920 and 1921. Despite bloody riots in many cities, the migration of Blacks to the North continued and increased.

Marcus Garvey, an expatriate Jamaican and follower of Booker T. Washington, expounded a philosophy of "cast down your buckets where you *were*." To a recently urbanized Black proletariat, fleeing the South and confronted by Northern racism, terrorism, and economic exploitation, the idea of returning to the African homeland was particularly compelling. In 1917 Garvey, a printer and editor by trade, founded the first American chapter of the Universal Negro Improvement Association (UNIA), a nationalist and Pan-Africanist organization begun by him in Jamaica in 1914. Garvey's principal support was among the Black working class and lower middle class of the North, though he also enjoyed considerable popularity among Southern Blacks. At its peak in the 1920s, the UNIA claimed more than four million members (Weisbord, 1968:36).

Garvey aroused the pride of the masses of Black people, increased their knowledge of their African heritage, and exposed and attacked the racist oppression endured by American Blacks. He opposed differential wage scales for workers on the basis of race, Black exclusion from unions, the taxing of politically disenfranchised Blacks, the drafting of Black men into the military, and the outrages of Jim Crow and lynching. Garvey also praised the Soviet Union's 1917 revolution, and promoted the theory of self-determination for all peoples. Garvey thus was one of the first to comprehensively analyze the material conditions of American Blacks and to connect their struggle to those already under way in Africa, the Caribbean, and the Third World.

Garvey believed that the Black struggle was inherently an African one. It could not be waged successfully except in Africa, where Blacks were a majority. Garvey's attempt to build a trans-Atlantic shipping line able to transport Black people back to Africa (the "Black Star Line") was destroyed by infiltrators and petite bourgeois Black opportunists. Garvey had solicited contributions to the Black Star Line through the mails. When the line failed, Garvey was charged with mail fraud, imprisoned, and later deported as an undesirable alien. He eventually died in exile.

Garvey made a profound impression not only on the masses of American Blacks but also on the American Communist Party (CPUSA), which had failed dismally in its efforts to recruit Blacks. The result was the adoption by the Third Communist International of two resolutions on the "Negro National Question" in the United States, one in 1928 and the other in 1930. They exposed a viewpoint that was in some sense an answer to the nationalist aspirations aroused by Garvey. The resolutions focused not on Africa, but rather on the "Black Belt" of the South, so named because of the rich black earth of the area. In 1928, 80 percent of the Black population lived in Southern states, and approximately 74 percent lived in rural districts. Thirty-five percent of the Black population lived in the counties of the Black Belt, where they constituted a clear majority of the population. The Third International considered Black agricultural workers and tenant farmers a revolutionary vanguard, and directed the CPUSA to begin organizing among these classes. They were to use as the principal organizing theme the right of Black people to national self-determination in the Black Belt. A basic demand, articulated in the 1930 resolution, was to be "confiscation of the landed property of the White landowners and Capitalists for the benefit of the Negro farmers."[3]

Between 1928 and 1935, this was one of the principal slogans of the CPUSA. Extensive organizing was carried out along these lines. Though the National Sharecroppers' Union (primarily Black), a forerunner of the Southern Tenant Farmers' Union, was developed by the CPUSA in the rural South, the ideology of self-determination in the Black Belt did not extend much beyond the CPUSA cadre during this era.

BLACK LAND REFORM IV: SHARECROPPERS AND TENANTS UNITE

For farmers, the Great Depression began long before the 1929 stock-market crash. Farm commodity prices had collapsed as early as 1920. The McNary-Haughton Act of 1924, introducing government price supports to compensate "for the disadvantaged position of the commercial farmer in his relation with the overall economy," totally ignored the needs of small farmers, sharecroppers, tenant farmers, and agricultural workers. During 1930, 25 percent of the nation's farmers each sold less than $600 worth of farm products. Many farmers abandoned their farms, and Black land-ownership dropped from 22 million acres in 1919 to 18.3 million by 1930. Black sharecroppers and agricultural workers were squeezed tight by land-lords and merchants.

The CPUSA began sending organizers to the rural South to help start locals of the National Sharecroppers' Union (NSCU) which could demand better living and working conditions from landlords, merchants, and local government. The struggle to win these demands, the CPUSA cadre believed, would increase the level of unity and discipline among Black peasants, and prepare them to struggle for self-determination in the Black Belt. But in most cases, rural Blacks could not see past the immediate struggle to survive and hold onto land that they owned. Further, efforts at organizing NSCU locals were almost always met by violence from both established law-enforcement agencies and vigilante groups. Despite some modest successes, the severe repression inflicted on the NSCU undermined the organization's effectiveness. More and more, the NSCU locals turned to the federal government for protection and relief. By 1935, the NSCU was in effect an intermediary between Black peasants and the New Deal. By 1938, NSCU tenants and sharecroppers had affiliated with the Southern Tenant Farmers' Union (STFU).

The STFU was concerned less with "self-determination" in the Black Belt than with classic farmers' problems such as credit and marketing. The STFU also focused heavily on inequities in the administration of New Deal agricultural programs. Franklin Roosevelt had come into office in 1933 promising to fight for equality between agriculture and the rest of the economy, to strengthen the established machinery of the Department of Agriculture, and to promote a more rational and efficient use of the land; to give farmers fair prices for their products and to reduce taxation and mortgage indebtedness (Baldwin, 1968). In May of 1933 the Agricultural Adjustment Act was passed. Like preceding legislation, the AAA worked principally to the advantage of large farmers. For example, the acreage reduction plan — a plan for rental and parity payments to those who voluntarily reduced their acreage from the cotton crop already planted — proved beneficial for non-Black owners of larger farms, but forced many Black tenant farmers off the land (Fishel, 1964–65:115). Government cotton contracts provided that benefits were to be paid to landowners, and distribution was to be made to tenants through the landowner, according to the tenants' interest in the land. This financial control by the landowners set the stage for numerous incidents of fraud and deception. When landowners received a tenant's money, it was often used to pay the tenant's unpaid debts or was applied to the tenant's future supplies.

Protests from tenants and sharecroppers of both races against AAA policies and practices and against landlord fraud provided the setting for the founding of the STFU. Many organizers and members of the STFU were harassed and threatened by landlords and public officials. Many persons, particularly Northern liberals and intellectuals, gave financial and political support to the STFU, and focused attention on violence against the group. Pressure built in Washington and various states for programs to address the demands of the STFU and the needs of small farmers and tenants generally.

The National Industrial Recovery Act of 1933 had created in the Department of Agriculture a Division of Subsistence Homesteads, designed to relocate destitute families onto small farms and to train them to raise food for their own survival. The regulations of the subsistence-homesteads program, drafted in 1933, emphasized "a maximum of local initiative and control." The initial plan was to transfer administration of homestead communities to tenant corporations, but in 1934 the plan was abandoned, and each project remained under the control of federal authorities. In early 1935, the program met local resistance and was allowed to expire. But in April 1935, in response to the pressure built by the STFU movement, President Roosevelt issued an executive order reviving the program. The order established a "Resettlement Administration" to carry forward the work of the defunct Division of Subsistence Homesteads. The Resettlement Administration was charged by the order to make loans to needy farmers and "to administer projects involving resettlement of destitute or low-income families from rural and urban areas." Although under Roosevelt, the number of Resettlement Administration personnel grew to twice the number of homesteaders and many needy applicants were turned down, it surpassed other New Deal reforms in putting Blacks securely on the land.[4]

This potential "land reform" initiative thus focused primarily on successful farmers, and even these were not dealt with competently. Homesteaders lived under the constant scrutiny of officials, social scientists, news reporters, and the public. The settlers were physically cut off from the world — they had no cars, no radios — and were psychologically isolated as well. The Resettlement managers who oversaw the day-to-day operations of the projects gained reputations for being overbearing and officious. Many homesteaders complained that they were treated like serfs. At Cumberland Homesteads, Tennessee, a band of dissatisfied homesteaders threatened the life of their Resettlement manager, whom they accused of siding with Washington against them. These settlers, like others who bucked the system, were quickly evicted from their projects by a termination-at-will clause in their contracts and were replaced by more docile people.

The results were perverse. The Administration achieved the opposite of its own stated objectives of building community and self-reliance. Instead, "obedient" settlers — responding primarily to commands from the Resettlement managers — withdrew almost entirely from decision making and responsible involvement. The agency then hired a group of experts to foster a sense of community among the homesteaders! Soon, most of the projects fell apart, despite infusions of additional funds and supervisory personnel. The agency itself was kept alive only until January 1937, when Congress abolished the Resettlement Administration and transferred its functions to the Farm Security Administration.

The legislation which accomplished this transfer was the Bankhead-Jones Farm Tenant Act of 1937, which provided for loans to assist tenants, sharecroppers, and farm laborers to become owner-operators; established a rural rehabilitation loan program; and set up a program for submarginal land retirement and development. The act also created the Farm Security Administration (FSA), a new Agriculture Department agency, to administer the new programs. But the FSA, like its predecessor the Resettlement Agency, deferred to local autonomy and local attitudes; hence racial discrimination ran rampant through its programs. Blacks were often disqualified for assistance as the families least likely to succeed. On 14 August 1946 the Farmers Home Administration (FmHA) was given jurisdiction over FSA programs, with instructions to liquidate most of them.

The Resettlement Agency and the FSA proved only a temporary palliative — certainly not true land reform. In fact, many New Deal techniques only accelerated the trend toward monopoly capitalism in agriculture, a trend which was to increase dramatically after World War II. Racism, of course, remained a formidable obstacle. The STFU was organized essentially to protect tenants from oppression by large farm landlords; it did not specifically address the political future of the Black "nation" in the South. The goal of land redistribution was never central to the STFU. The initiative for land redistribution came from the federal government, as it had during and immediately after the Civil War. The FSA, like the Freedmen's Bureau before it, proved illusory.

BLACK LAND REFORM V: MULTIDIMENSIONAL EFFORTS IN THE POST-WORLD WAR II ERA

The displacement of Southern Black farmers, including tenants and sharecroppers, continued after World War II. In 1910, at the height of Black landownership, 15 million acres were fully or partially owned by

Black Americans. This figure has declined steadily—to 12 million in 1950, to just 6 million in 1970, to less than 4 million today.[5]

In 1968, Calvin Beale, the USDA's chief population specialist, stated that the most dramatic rural exodus in the nation had been that of Blacks. It had left only 5 percent of an estimated 22.3 million Blacks on farms as of July 1968 (Beale, 1969). This figure is all the more striking when we compare it to the analogous figure for 1910, when nearly twice as many Blacks were owners or operators of farms—890,000 out of a population of 9.8 million (Payne, 1981). Yet the "new" industrialized South is still rural, and relentlessly concentrated agriculture continues to influence rural economies. More than 69 percent of the farms operated by nonwhites in the South were valued at less than $10,000 in 1964, and 75 percent of nonwhite operators of commercial farms sold less than $5,000 of farm products. The number of Black farm operators in the South decreased 68 percent in the 1960s, and of the 84,000 Black farms remaining today, nearly 95 percent are small operations with sales under $10,000 (U.S. Census Bureau, 1970 and 1980). Their chances of success are slim.

Present government policies for agriculture and rural development do not help. Federal tax policies encourage land speculation, tax-loss farming for the high-income individual or corporation, and the invasion of rural areas by large absentee owners. The exemption of agriculture from minimum-wage and collective-bargaining legislation, as well as incentives for the immigration of temporary workers from outside the United States, enable large farms to thrive at the expense of impoverished agricultural workers and small family farmers. The traditional underlying flaw of all agricultural subsidy programs is that they subsidize ownership of land rather than labor upon it.

The small Black farmer in the South is critically affected by the substitution of capital for labor in agriculture, a substitution encouraged and exacerbated by more than a generation of government policies. The Black farmer's inability to acquire capital means that he cannot obtain the machinery necessary to keep pace with changes in agricultural technology. Without such machinery, he must shift to crops not yet fully affected by mechanization or else leave farming altogether. Lack of credit hinders the Black farmer from making his land productive. Many efforts at saving Black-owned land focus on this lack of credit. Most rural Southern banks are conservative lenders, refusing to extend credit without highly valuable collateral or substantial profit margins, thus eliminating credit for most small farmers, especially Black ones. The Farmers Home Administration (FmHA), and the instrumentalities which make up the Farm Credit System (FCS) are the only resources to which farmers rejected by commercial financing can turn. FmHA is chartered not only to provide direct financial assistance, but also management consultation and technical assistance, in order to help low- and moderate-income borrowers take full advantage of the program.

Yet FmHA loan and technical assistance programs are not being provided for Blacks on an equal basis with non-Blacks, in clear violation of federal guidelines, and so have come under attack in recent years (Payne, 1981). The FmHA is unwilling to accept as collateral land encumbered by any ownership rights — even those which have little possibility of maturing. The interests of common heirs to property who are physically and legally far removed from the land are good examples of such encumbrances, often known as "remote claims." Because of the general failure of elderly rural Black landowners to write wills, their property often passes to the next generation through intestate succession, creating a far-flung group of common heirs with varying rights of ownership. Such "heirs' property" is virtually impossible to develop, as no bank or even the FmHA will accept it as collateral.

A 1980 study commissioned by FmHA to develop techniques for freeing property from remote claims — through eminent domain, open-market purchase, adverse possession, land trusts, and the like — focused on the rights to land of the three minority groups represented in this book: Native American, Black, and Chicano. Only in the case of the Blacks would the elimination of remote claims have a positive effect. While there is some problem of extensive cotenancy in Indian trust lands, the principal "remote claim" problem is the *Indian* claim to lands which are now owned by non-Indians and which were purchased directly from Indians by private individuals in violation of the Indian Non-Intercourse Act. Techniques developed to free Black-owned land from the remote claims of distant cousins could also be used to free white-owned land from the "remote claims" of Native Americans or of Chicanos who claim much of the Southwest by virtue of original Spanish land-grant titles. Black farmers as a class may be extinct in twenty years. Yet the efforts of the federal government to help remove "remote claims" that cloud Black titles should be examined closely to make sure that Blacks do not inadvertently become instruments in a program which might ultimately harm their Indian and Chicano brothers and sisters.

Farmers' Cooperatives, Self-Help, and Technical Assistance Groups

The Emergency Land Fund, started in 1971 specifically to counter Black land loss, has focused less on extending the land base than on stabilizing present landownership patterns. ELF provides legal, financial, and technical assistance to Southern Black landowners who want to retain and develop their land. ELF has prevented the loss of over 250,000 Black-owned acres in a variety of contexts: adverse possession, tax foreclosure, mortgage foreclosure, eminent domain, and partition sale. These are all ways in which Blacks can lose land in the South, often to unscrupulous whites conspiring to steal it.

One of the most famous ELF cases is the ongoing struggle of Black farmers from Harris Neck, Georgia, to regain their land. On 26 July 1942, one hundred Black farmers were forcibly removed from 2,681 acres of prime land on Georgia's south coast by the federal government, ostensibly to make way for the construction of an Army air base (*Atlanta Constitution*, 1979:1). The bulk of the land apparently first came into Black hands as a result of Sherman's Special Field Order 15; adjoining parcels were later purchased by Black families, and the Harris Neck site took shape. Local whites, including the county sheriff, tried to take the land away from the Black owners long before condemnation. The owners were forced to vacate under the threat that their homes would be torn down and burned. They were paid only ten dollars an acre in compensation. The land was never developed for an air base. It was eventually turned over to the county as surplus federal property, subject to restrictions generally designed to preserve the property. The county did not abide by these restrictions; local officials cut nearly all the timber off the property and grazed their livestock on it. Fifteen years of misconduct by county officials followed, including the pirating of building fixtures by county officials—some houses were even transported whole to the land of the local sheriff. The federal government finally took the property back and turned it over to the Interior Department's Fish and Wildlife Service on 25 May 1962. The former residents of Harris Neck, despairing of any relief, forcibly occupied the land in early 1979 and were evicted. With ELF help, they brought suit in federal court on 12 June 1979 for damages and for return of their land. A compromise is now in the offing, by which the Interior Department would grant the former residents a 99-year lease on 900 acres, for residential purposes. The Reagan administration apparently sees such a concession as a way to regain lost political mileage with Black Americans. Whether the former residents will accept the compromise remains to be seen.

ELF and other organizations have also helped Black landowners struggling to organize themselves into cooperative and trade associations. The Southern Cooperative Development Fund (SCDF), the Federation of Southern Cooperatives (FSC), and the Southeast Alabama Self-Help Association (SEASHA) have focused on the development of various forms of agricultural cooperatives. In June 1976, ELF and the Alabama Center for Higher Education organized a meeting of more than 150 Black landowners at Tuskegee Institute to develop strategies and programs to halt the decline of Black landownership, primarily by putting idle land into use. Idle land is clearly the most vulnerable to loss. The focus of the meeting was the development of a Black landowners' association. The new organization should provide educational and legal information and management guidance, assist in obtaining loans and other financial resources, and aid in land development. In February 1977, over 400 Black landowners met at the first national convention in Atlanta, where they formed the National Association of Landowners (NAL). This is probably the most promising attempt since the 1930s to organize Black landowners and farmers on a national basis. The NAL's rapidly growing membership is focusing on developmental rather than political activities at the present time, however.

In the face of economic oppression, Black farmers, tenants, and agricultural laborers, like their counterparts in other races, have typically organized to get help from the federal government, especially marketing and agricultural expertise and credit. NAL and SEASHA are in this tradition. ELF, FSC, and SCDF represent a new type of technical assistance group organized to help Black farmers help themselves.

The "Five States" Program

In the early 1960s, Malcolm X, on behalf of Elijah Muhammad and the Nation of Islam, called for the United States government to give Blacks five states in the South as a reparation for slavery. The proposal was somewhat reminiscent of the "nation within a nation" agenda of the Third International and the Depression era CPUSA.

An interesting historical footnote: W. D. Fard, the founder of the Nation of Islam, began organizing among Blacks in Detroit in 1930, teaching of the duplicity of the white man and the cultural superiority of the Black man. Malcolm X, Chief Lieutenant of Elijah Muhammad (himself Fard's successor), was in the 1960s to strongly press the idea of land in the Black Belt as reparations for the 400-year enslavement and exploitation of the Black man. The extent to which Garvey or the CPUSA influenced Fard or Muhammad is not clear. A large number of Garveyites joined the Nation of Islam after Garvey's downfall, however, and Malcolm's father was a Garveyite. When the U.S. government ignored the proposal, the Muslims set out to acquire a land base on their own. By the mid-1960s, the Muslims had developed a sophisticated strategy to purchase land in Mississippi, Florida, Texas, North Carolina, and South Carolina. The goal was to accumulate enough productive agricultural land to feed the Black "captive nation," which had abandoned agriculture and rural life-styles and become totally dependent upon the agricultural economy of the majority white population. As their plans bore fruit, the Muslims produced wheat, vegetables, soybeans, corn, and peanuts. They developed slaughterhouses, dairy farms, and a complete processing, distribution, and marketing system.

In July 1969 the Muslims, using a front corporation called the Progressive Land Development Corporation, purchased 376 acres of land in St. Clair County, Alabama, for $115,000. The Alabama farm was modeled after the highly successful Muslim farm in Dawson, Georgia, which had been started in the early 1930s. Unlike the Georgia farm, however, the farm in Alabama met with determined resistance from the local white community. The *New York Times* reported on 23 November 1969 that 2,200 whites from St. Clair County had publicly vowed to keep the Muslims from occupying the land they had purchased. The Muslims eventually sought relief from the courts, and on 29 January 1970 a three-judge court was called to determine, among other things, whether the Muslims were a "dangerous foreign nation" that could legally be prevented from purchasing land in the state of Alabama. On 11 June the court ruled in favor of the Muslims. Thus the Muslims were able to establish their democratic right to own property and make it productive.

By the early 1970s the Muslims, in a report to the Congress of African People, documented the existence of a thriving agricultural economic development program in three Southern states — Georgia, Alabama, and Mississippi. The Nation of Islam brought trucks and planes to move produce and entered into lucrative contracts with supermarkets. It had also made contact with several wealthy Arab countries, and was soon to receive a $3-million, interest-free loan from Libya. But when Elijah Muhammad died, the Muslim organization and economic base began to crumble. Eventually the Muslims had to sell all the farms but the one in Dawson. Their farms in Greene and Marengo Counties in Alabama were sold to Mennonites, for example. These two farms alone comprised 4,000 acres. Much of the deterioration of the Muslim land and business empire has been attributed to the anticommercial posture of Elijah's son and successor, Wallace Muhammad. Now leader of the American Muslim Mission, Wallace is apparently having second thoughts on his original position, and has indicated his readiness to revive his father's agenda for land.

Any attempt by Blacks to acquire or retain land in the South, however, must not only survive the onslaught of monopoly capitalism in agriculture nationwide, but must also challenge the entrenched political and economic power structure of the region. The Republic of New Africa, for example, which bought land in Mississippi in 1971 as a first step toward the establishment of a Black republic in the South, had its purchases nullified outright by the state of Mississippi. The RNA residence in Jackson was raided by state police and FBI agents allegedly seeking a fugitive. The ensuing gun battle left one FBI agent dead and led to the imprisonment of eleven RNA members, five for life.

The RNA had been founded in Detroit in 1967. The purpose of the organization was to establish an independent Black nation in five Southern states: Louisiana, Mississippi, Alabama, Georgia, and South Carolina. Negotiations between the United States and the RNA began in May 1969 with delivery of a diplomatic note to Secretary of State Dean Rusk by Brother Imari Obadele, Minister of Information for the RNA and a Yale Law School graduate. In addition to five states, demands included $200 billion in reparations for the enslavement and exploitation of Africans in the United States.

The RNA rested its claim to land in America on the basis of long-standing Black labor on, and occupancy and development of, the land. It called for a plebiscite in the Black Belt to determine whether Blacks would choose a separate nation rather than U.S. citizenship. The RNA claimed the U.S. had the power to offer the freedmen the choice, but not to force them to accept the latter alternative. The Malcolmites, the military wing of the RNA, were to arm the Black community generally, North and South, to protect RNA organizers, who would as a first step mobilize Southern Black voters to vote all non-Blacks out of office in the five states in question. The Mississippi state attorney general, upon hearing of the RNA plan to set up shop in Mississippi, wired the U.S. attorney general, interpreting the RNA presence as an armed invasion. Soon after, local police and the FBI raided RNA headquarters. The current status of the RNA is uncertain.

The call for a nation within a nation in the South draws Blacks into a conflict reminiscent of the Civil War, which was itself fought to prevent the secession of the five states claimed by the RNA as well as several more. Land reform, in the sense of a separate community for Americans of African descent, cannot take place under current American economic, political, or racial conditions.

CONCLUSION

If racist and capitalist exploitation face the rural Black as surely as they did during the era of Booker T. Washington, then the alternatives of separation — to Africa or to five states in the South — remain as alive in the Black American lexicon as they were when Marcus Garvey seared the concept of Black nationalism into the consciousness of the masses of Black workers and farmers in the 1920s. Thus, the Black land base of 1980, less than four million acres in size, not only constitutes an important economic force but also a powerful political symbol, comprising as it does the five old plantation states of the South (South Carolina, Georgia, Alabama, Mississippi, and Louisiana) and their heavily Black populations. The "Black Belt" has fired nationalist sentiment among Blacks for generations. Black leaders as diverse as Harry Haywood, a Black former member of the Communist Party, and Elijah Muhammad, the leader of the Black Nation of Islam, have embraced the theory of a "Black Nation" in the Deep South states.

Long after the CPUSA had abandoned the "nation within a nation" thesis, Haywood insisted that the land-based struggle of Blacks, from slavery through World War II, was a struggle against capitalism, particularly against large landowning whites who exploited Black farm laborers and tenants in a new kind of slavery. Haywood dreamed of linking the land struggle of Southern agricultural laborers and tenants with a revolutionary struggle against capital by the working class as a whole. The coalition would incorporate a program of agrarian reform into the social transformation that would follow the defeat of capitalism. Black landowners, tenants, and agricultural workers cannot isolate themselves from related classes and their struggles against monopoly capitalism: the white small farmers, tenants, and agricultural workers (who, with their Black comrades, formed the base of the Populist movement, the NCSU, and the STFU); the Black working class; and the other land reform movements represented in this book. In particular, we Blacks cannot isolate ourselves from the struggle of Indians to regain their land, which raises the most original and basic question of land distribution in the United States, and which none of us who demand justice can ignore.

NOTES

1. Joseph Brooks, president of the Emergency Land Fund, estimates on the basis of a recently completed study that as many as one in every twenty-five Black Americans may have a fractional interest in land. Author's interview with Brooks, 1 March 1983.

2. Of the 18,874 Black farm owners in South Carolina in 1900, only about 4,000 had acquired their land through government programs (Taylor, 1976:71).

3. Quoted in Young (1975).

4. See Salamon's (1976) favorable evaluation of the Security Administration's efforts to relocate landless people on the land, including Blacks.

5. Recent estimates by the Emergency Land Fund indicate that this figure, contrary to 1980 census data, may be much greater—ten to eleven million acres—because the U.S. Census Bureau has traditionally not counted idle land as "farm land." Nonetheless, because such undercounting has probably existed since the earliest census, these figures probably represent the *rate* of decline in Black landownership accurately.

REFERENCES

Abbott, Martin. 1967. *The Freedmen's Bureau in South Carolina 1865–1872.* Chapel Hill: University of North Carolina Press.

Atlanta Constitution. 1979. (May 11): 1.

Baldwin, Sidney. 1968. *Poverty and Politics: The Rise and Decline of the Farm Security Administration.* Chapel Hill: University of North Carolina Press.

Beale, Calvin H. 1969. "The Negro in American agriculture." In *The American Negro Reference Book.* Edited by John P. Davis. Yonkers, NY: Educational Heritage, Inc.

Costello, Paul. 1981. "Racism and Black oppression in the United States: a beginning analysis." *Theoretical Review* 24 (September/October).

Eddie, Scott M. 1971. *The Simple Economics of Land Reform: The Expropriation-Compensation Process and Income Distribution.* LTC, No. 75 (February). The Land Tenure Center, University of Wisconsin, Madison.

Farmers Home Administration, United States Department of Agriculture. 1980. *Remote Claims Impact Study.* Washington, DC: Farmers Home Administration.

Fishel, Leslie H., Jr. 1964–65. "The Negro in the New Deal era." *Wisconsin Magazine of History* 48 (Winter): 111–26.

Haywood, Harry. 1948. *Negro Liberation.* New York: International Publishers.

McFeely, William S. 1968. *Yankee Stepfather: General O. O. Howard and the Freedmen.* New Haven and London: Yale University Press.

McPherson, James M. 1964. *The Struggle for Equality: Abolitionists and the Negro in the Civil War and Reconstruction.* Princeton, NJ: Princeton University Press.

Payne, Velma. 1981. "Major causes and effects of the decline of Black-owned land in five southeastern states." Unpublished degree paper for the Master of Public Administration, Atlanta University, Atlanta, Georgia.

Rosengarten, Theodore. 1974. *All God's Dangers: The Life of Nate Shaw.* New York: Avon.

Salamon, Lester M. 1976. *Land and Minority Enterprise: The Crisis and the Opportunity.* Washington, DC: U.S. Government Printing Office.

Stange, Douglas C. 1967. "Lutherans and the American Colonization Society." *Mid-America* 49 (April): 140–51.

Taylor, Arnold H. 1976. *Travail and Triumph: Black Life and Culture since the Civil War.* Westport, CT: Greenwood Press.

United States Bureau of the Census. 1970 and 1980. *Census of Agriculture.* Washington, DC: U.S. Bureau of the Census, Agriculture Division.

Wasserman, Harvey. 1972. *History of the United States.* New York: Harper's.

Weisbord, Robert G. 1968. "The back-to-Africa idea." *History Today* 18 (January): 30–37.

Young, Lowell (ed.). 1975. *The 1928 and 1930 Comintern Resolutions on the Black National Question in the U.S.* Washington, DC: Revolutionary Review Press.

12

Ancient Aspirations: A Mexican-American View of Land Reform

GUILLERMO LUX

Much of what is now the Southwest — all of California, Nevada, and Utah, and large parts of Arizona, Colorado, New Mexico, and Wyoming — was conquered by the United States in its war with Mexico. The most volatile issue for the Southwestern Mexican-American community has always been and continues to be the land-grant violations of the Treaty of Guadalupe Hidalgo that ended the war. Today, more than 135 years later, these systematic violations continue to produce more anger and frustration among Mexican-Americans than any other ethnic issue. They are sometimes sufficient to impel Mexican-Americans to last-ditch, desperate acts of political insurgency.

The 1848 treaty promised the Mexican people "the enjoyment of all the rights of the United States according to the principles of the Constitution . . . [and that they would be] protected in the free enjoyment of their liberty and property." Secretary of State James Buchanan wrote at the time that under the United States Constitution and the laws of the United States "the Mexican inhabitants and all others [are promised] protection in free enjoyment of their liberty, property and . . . religion" (Hammond, 1949:23). But nineteenth-century economic and political relations between Mexicans and Anglos led to repeated land struggles, from Texas to California. They consistently resulted in Mexican losses despite promises of political freedom and protection of private property. Within this historical context, the story of the 1980s' Southwestern land-reform struggle is one of an impossible war, waged against great odds by an infuriated and economically damaged people, to recover belatedly the lands illegally taken from them.

THE HISTORICAL BACKGROUND BEFORE 1891

In 1837, a year after Texas asserted its independence as a nation from Mexico, the most important bill before its new legislature was a land bill. The great Western historian Hubert Howe Bancroft wrote:

> To distinguish legitimate claims and guard against fraud was a most diffi-
> cult matter; and to frame a bill that would defeat the ingenuity of land-
> stealers without violating the rights of citizens of Texas, justly acquired
> under the legislation of Mexico, of Coahuila and Texas, was almost an
> impossibility. (Bancroft, 1889:307).

To secure their claims to their lands, the original settlers and the soldiers who had fought for independence were given a six-month headstart over newcomers and speculators. "Early in 1838 a large number of claims were presented and decided upon, old Spanish grants being generally sustained; . . . [the legislature] set aside only grants on the ground of non-performance of conditions." (Bancroft, 1889:309)

The new nation's uncertain state of independence forged a common bond among the original settlers, both Anglo and Mexican. And together the settlers, the soldiers of the independence movement, and the newcomers looked covetously to the lands of the Indians:

> The lands occupied for many years by the Cherokees became . . . subject
> to . . . invasion. Their title had never been disputed. They had been recog-
> nized by the Mexican authorities, had never intruded on the whites, and in a
> great measure had become an agricultural tribe. But their territory in point
> of richness of soil, and the beauty of situation, water, and productions would
> vie with the best portions of Texas. . . . it was determined to remove the
> tribe. . . . Negotiations for the peaceable removal of the tribe to Arkansas
> whence they had migrated, having failed, on July 15th [1893] [General]
> Douglas advanced against the Indian camp. . . . Thus were the Cherokees
> driven from their homes and cultivated fields. . . . (Bancroft, 1889:324)

Referring to the subsequent operations of 1840 against the Comanches, Bancroft wrote that "President Lamar's system of extermination was well carried out. Men, women, and children alike were put to death" (Bancroft, 1889:326).

After annexation and the war between the United States and Mexico, Texas's land policy became curiously schizophrenic: while some Indians were displaced, others received help to colonize their land. In the latter cases game had diminished to the point where Indians were impoverished:

> As a remedy for this evil, a system of colonization was applied, means fur-
> nished by the United States Government to aid and instruct Indian settlers
> in the cultivation of land. (Bancroft, 1889:406)

Two reservations were established, at Brazos and Clear Fork, with Anadahkos, Caddoes, Tahwaccorroes, Wacoes, Tonkahwas, and Comanches as settlers:

> Within three years these settlements attained a high degree of prosperity, especially that of the Brazos agency. The Indians tilled their land, tended and garnered their crops, and possessed stocks of cattle, horses, and hogs. They erected comfortable dwellings, had school-houses, and were steadily progressing in civilization, peaceably pursuing their agricultural occupations. . . . But they were doomed to be driven from the homes they had made for themselves, deprived of the lands they had put under cultivation, and removed, in almost a destitute condition, beyond the borders of Texas. The aggressive nature of Anglo-American settlers would not let them rest in peaceful possession of their small domains. (Bancroft, 1889:408–09)

It was the bitterness of the Mexican War and its aftermath that created problems between the Anglos and the Mexicans. Many soldiers and other Anglos shifted their hatred of Mexicans — precipitated by cruel acts such as Santa Ana's execution of prisoners — to the Mexican colonists of Texas, who found the acts equally despicable. "Juan N. Seguin, for example, had fought with the rebels and had been elected mayor of San Antonio. Yet, by 1844, just eight years after the Battle of San Jacinto, mob action drove him to exile" (Rosenbaum, 1981:35). The eminent Texas historian Walter Prescott Webb wrote that "the old landholding families found their titles in jeopardy and if they did not lose in the courts they lost to their American lawyers" (Webb, 1935:175).

> Adverse court rulings and lawyers' fees paid in land were two ways that Anglo American law separated the new citizens from their property. Law enforcement, or its absence, was another. A ranchero's cattle would be killed or stolen. If economic ruin did not convince him to sell, then he would be charged with and convicted of rustling, which usually convinced his widow. (Rosenbaum, 1981:41)

Then there were the land speculators. *Los agraciados* (the Mexican upper class) and those who worked for them did not compete well with the outsiders attracted by land speculation possibilities. "Capitalized land companies . . . purchased the riverside tracts, improved them, and broke up large tracts into smaller lots" (Rubel, 1966:35). One Anglo writer noted, "In many cases when Americans sought to buy these lands, the Mexican owners were more than delighted to receive even a small sum for their rights" (Graf, 1942:256). Another noted that

> [a favorite] technique by which to acquire land was the sheriff's sale, an occasion when lands appropriated by a county sheriff to cover back taxes were sold at auction. Land thus sold was bought for so ridiculously low a sum that contemporary Mexican-Americans of the lower valley contend that

their ancestors were swindled of their holdings. The contention is nursed as a sore grievance, and contributes greatly to present-day tensions between the groups. (Rubel, 1966:35)

In Texas, as in other areas of the Southwest, Mexicans were treated as a conquered people. Despite treaty guarantees, their property was subject to confiscation almost as a spoil of war.

In 1891, Frank Blackmar, one of the earliest historians to be concerned with the Mexican loss of land, wrote of California:

> The fifteen or twenty ranchos said to be granted [at the end of the Spanish] period were held provisionally by their occupants. This may be true, but it was owing to some informality of the law; for the grantors gave and the grantees accepted the grant in good faith, and never considered it otherwise than genuine, unless so specified. The carelessness in making records and in the final execution of the law, rendered the grants technically, and perhaps legally, defective. The greater number of grants was made during Mexican rule, particularly between 1833 and 1846. At the latter date, the total number of grants was nearly eight hundred, the most of which varied from one league to five leagues in extent. As each league contained something over 4,428 acres, it is easily seen to what an extent the fertile valleys of the coast of California were occupied. (Blackmar, 1891:322–23)

To settle questionable land claims in California and New Mexico in 1849, when *Californios* (Mexican settlers of California) alone still owned more than fourteen million acres, a bill was introduced in Congress to create the Office of Surveyor General. Missouri Senator Thomas Hart Benton spoke against it, helping to secure its defeat:

> Each claimant throughout the entire country is to come in with his title and make it good before a board to be composed of foreigners, whose language they cannot speak. Terror and consternation will pervade the land when a helpless people, ignorant in our language, find the very titles to their property subjected, not even to the law under which they have lived, but to the pleasure of the agent of their conquerors. How is this to act, Sir? At the first summons to appear before such a board, I say—and I say it with a knowledge of what took place under similar boards in Louisiana—terror and consternation will pervade the land. (Quoted in Sunseri, 1979:113)

Perhaps because gold had just been discovered in California, Congress later disregarded Benton's wise counsel and submitted to political pressure from the state:

> In 1851, the 31st Congress of the United States passed an act "to ascertain and settle the private land claims in the state of California." This act provided for a commission of three persons, appointed for the purpose of hearing testimony and settling all claims to lands granted prior to the accession

of California to the United States. This commission was empowered to investigate all claims of grants by the Mexican Spanish authorities. They were empowered to sit at different places and listen to claims, hear testimony, and give decisions.

The Commission was furnished with a secretary well versed in the Spanish language. Each person holding a title under the Mexican or Spanish laws was obliged to file his claim within two years, with such evidence as he was able to summon. . . . The dearth of reliable witnesses, the incompleteness of records, imperfect surveys, and contentious lawyers working in somebody's interest, all combined to render the proper adjustment of affairs very difficult. (Blackmar, 1891:324)

The Board of Land Commissioners proceeded to review all California land grants made when California was part of Spain and Mexico. Instead of resolving questionable land title problems, the commission brought into question the validity of all land titles. Such titles became vulnerable to expropriation by squatters who viewed the land as vacant, thereby creating legal problems for the *Californios*. The commissioners, as well as the lawyers who presented claims before them, were not fluent in Spanish or versed in Mexican law. Other difficulties were posed by the "obsolete legalisms which were almost impossible to translate well. Each case had its own peculiarities and necessitated long and costly archival translations" (Pitt, 1971:92). Often documentation was lost, or the owners could not prove that a house had been constructed within a year of the grant, as required by law. Many grants were turned down by the commission because of vague boundaries.

Probably the most difficult problem for the *Californios* was that the lawyers who posed as their friends and won their confidence abused it to profit from their adversity. According to Leonard Pitt, a social historian,

since most *Californios* scarcely understood English, much less the technical language of the courts, they had to depend greatly on their attorneys, whom they usually paid in land itself and only rarely in cash. Sad to say, of the fifty or so attorneys who specialized in claim law in the 1850s, most were shysters who lacked not only honesty but also knowledge and experience. (Pitt, 1971:91)

Some lawyers disappeared with irreplaceable documents.[1] It is estimated that perhaps a quarter of the *Californio* land was taken by lawyers or disallowed by the courts.

Californios also lost their land through sheriffs' auctions for nonpayment of taxes and through mortgage default. Pitt provides the following two examples, the first being Julio Verdugo, who mortgaged his ranch in 1861:

He signed for a $3,445.37 loan at 3 percent monthly interest, which by 1879 had ballooned into a debt of $58,750 and ended in foreclosure, sheriff's sale and ruination. . . . One claimant who needed cash for taxes and lawyer's fees was so hemmed in by squatters in 1853 that he could no longer raise and sell cattle and had to take a $10,000 mortgage payable at 10 percent monthly; *weekly* interest of 12 percent on loans and of 3 percent on mortgages was common in the 1850s. (Pitt, 1971:100, 252; Pitt's italics)

The mission lands—those that had escaped the Liberals' secularization during Mexican rule—should have become the property of the Indians who had developed them. But Blackmar explained why this did not occur:

There were, with two exceptions, no legal titles given. . . . This merely followed the Mexican and Spanish law, and was no injustice to anybody except to the credulous neophytes, who had been allowed to live so many years under the fiction that they had a right to the lands upon which they dwelt. (Blackmar, 1891:325–26)

In his history of the *Californios,* Pitt summarized their plight:

In the north of California, then, the basis of land ownership had changed drastically by 1865. Through armed struggle, legislation, litigation, financial manipulation, outright purchase, and innumerable other tactics, Yankees had obtained a good deal of interest in the land. (Pitt, 1971:103)

In Southern California, *ranchos* were lost to creditors in the 1870s through mortgage defaults resulting from financial difficulties after a severe drought. The *Californios* bitterly blamed both the Mexican government that had sold them out in 1848 and the *gringo* buyers.

The ranchero never understood, much less accepted, the gringo's concept of land tenure. The Land Law, pre-emption and occupancy rights, and the "jungle-thickets" of land litigation made him not only violently angry but also mystified him. Even if he did comprehend the basic logic of owning land for speculative purposes or for family farming, the seeming heartlessness of the speculators and yeomen repelled him . . . .

Even when they realized that the Yankee demanded solid, "gold-plated" documentary proof of ownership, which they had either never possessed or had misplaced or lost, the *Californios* nevertheless still banked on "common knowledge." Had most of them earned their property through hard labor as soldiers and colonists? . . . Were not herds and homes sound enough proofs of tenure? Was it justice that a man lose his patrimony because he lacked some papers? (Pitt, 1971:88, 90)

In New Mexico, the pattern of blatant, systematic violations of treaty property rights recurred. No action was taken until late 1854, when a single surveyor general was given the same responsibility that a commission had received in 1851 in California. "When William Pelham arrived in New Mexico as the territory's first Surveyor General . . . he immediately set out to familiarize himself with Spanish and Mexican law, the decisions of the Supreme Court of the United States and to collect the archive documents relating to land grants" (New Mexico State Planning Office, 1971:29). He reported that "he found in the archives 1,715 'grants of conveyances of land and other documents referring to claims of land,' some of which were on 'scraps of paper which can never be bound in any convenient form' " (McCarty, 1969). Some thirty-five years later, the historian Blackmar noted the archival disarray that made Pelham's task of documenting and validating legitimate claims close to impossible:

> there was great carelessness in regard to titles and surveys. The subdividing and re-granting of ranchos had added to the confusion, and the public archives were very imperfect in their information. (Blackmar, 1891:326)

As in other areas, New Mexicans were put on the defensive by being required to file documents and prove their ownership.

> [Pelham] issued notice to the people of New Mexico that he was prepared to entertain claims to lands, but "many of the owners of grants were adverse to responding to this notice and declined to file any papers." One reason for this was a "fear of losing the evidence of their titles, inspired as is supposed, by designing individuals." Another was the cost involved in prosecuting a claim to confirmation. (Twitchell, 1963:210)[2]

New Mexicans were at a further disadvantage because some officials in the bureaucracy conspired to take their land:

> As an example of their activities, one C. P. Clever wrote John V. Watts, who was in Washington, and requested information on any land bills being considered. . . . He promised that Watts would be well compensated for this information. Congress, however, passed no bill dealing with New Mexican land and neither of them realized a profit. This correspondence suggests that there were men in the territory who were aware of the potential profit in land speculation. Again in 1857 Watts attempted to make a profit when he wrote the Surveyor General William Pelham a confidential letter asking that some land warrants be held for him and transferred at a later date. He also requested Pelham to purchase any available land claims for later speculation. By the end of 1857 Watts was up to his neck in land dealings. (Sunseri, 1979:114)

Such conduct typified a pattern:

> Of the nine men to hold the office of surveyor general before the Court of Private Land Claims was established, three were land grant speculators: Dr. T. Rush Spencer, 1869–1872, owned a 1/5 interest in the Mora Grant with Thomas B. Catron and Stephen B. Elkins in 1870 and at the same time served as an official of the Maxwell Land Grant and Railroad Company along with Governor William A. Pile. James K. Proudfit, 1872–1876, was one of the incorporators of New Mexico's first cattle corporation with Catron and Elkins among others. At the same time he was openly propagandizing

for the cattle industry in his official capacity and striving to secure increased appropriations to accommodate its need for surveys. He was finally asked to resign. Henry M. Atkinson, 1876–1884, continued to survey large areas of land usable only as cattle range, contrary to the homestead and preemption laws which required that surveyed land be agricultural and that it actually be cultivated. He was an incorporator of four cattle companies with a combined capitalization of $5,000,000, along with Catron and Deputy Surveyor William H. McBroom. The most notorious example of corruption in the Surveyor General's office was the survey of the Maxwell Grant under Atkinson by John T. Elkins and R. T. Marmon. John Elkins was the brother of Stephen who was not only a bondsman for the surveyors, but also was promoter for the grant. (Westphall, 1965:21–32)[3]

Blackmar, summarizing the record in 1886, wrote that the

> number of land claims filed in the Surveyor-general's office . . . was two hundred and five. These were exclusive of the Pueblo Indian claims which were approved at an earlier date. Of the claims referred to, thirteen were rejected and one hundred and forty-one approved. Of those approved, Congress had confirmed forty-six leaving ninety-five still in controversy. (Blackmar, 1891:326–27)

Part of the responsibility for the fact that so few grants were confirmed rests with Congress, which hastily confirmed some early grants that turned out to be invalid. Thereafter Congress became very reluctant to act. No claims at all were confirmed after 1879, even though the 1854 legislation was not repealed until 1891 (New Mexico State Planning Office, 1971). This was the pattern for forty-three years. "Thus does justice," wrote Blackmar, "drag its slow length along in this age of steam and electricity" (Blackmar, 1891:328).

The people of New Mexico were confronted with the same problem that had plagued the *Californios* — their attorneys. Since they did not always have cash to pay the attorneys, they usually paid them with land. Some attorneys saw the situation as an opportunity to speculate in land. "The 'dominant element' with whom the Surveyors General were aligned was commonly know as the Santa Fe Ring, a group of ambitious, unscrupulous Anglo lawyers who regarded the confused legal status of land grants as an ideal opportunity for adding money and land to their personal assets" (New Mexico State Planning Office, 1971:31). The individual that exemplified this questionable land speculation was Thomas B. Catron, who may have held interests in as many as 75 different Spanish and Mexican land grants.

Not all Anglo politicians condoned the land grant abuses. In 1885 Edmund G. Ross was appointed territorial governor and George W. Julian surveyor general. Both opposed the powerful Santa Fe Ring. Julian wrote a scathing article, "Land Stealing in New Mexico," that was widely circulated (Julian, 1887:28). He described the land speculators as a "pestilence" that "to a fearful extent . . . have dominated governors, judges, district attorneys, legislatures, surveyors general, and the controlling business interests" (New Mexico State Planning Office, 1971: 33). In response to the actions of men like Ross and Julian, Congress in 1891 created the Court of Private Land Claims.

The court was organized in Denver, but soon moved to Santa Fe to adjust the remaining land claims for Arizona, Colorado, and New Mexico. It was to work for the next thirteen years on the 231 New Mexico claims submitted to it. Twelve other claims were transferred to Tucson, Arizona, where the court was also held. "When the Court of Private Land Claims finished its work . . . it had confirmed only 2,051,526 acres of the 35,491,020 acres claimed in 301 cases" (Tucker and Fitzpatrick, 1972: 281). Over 33 million acres were lost — mostly by Mexican-Americans.

THE HISTORICAL BACKGROUND AFTER 1891

Congress after 1891 was no better prepared to deal with the land-grant question than it had been before. Congressional activity continued to be inconsistent, often illogical. In some instances it confirmed the *ejido* lands (usually grazing lands held in common); in others it disallowed them, arguing that they were part of the public domain. Congress confirmed the Maxwell Grant, which included *ejido* lands, for a total of about 1.75 million acres — well beyond the maximum allowed by Mexican law (Espinosa, 1962). In other claims — the Sandoval case, for example — only the village lands were confirmed. Such discrepancies may have been partly attributable to a misunderstanding of the *ejido* concept, but they were also due to the sordidness of territorial politics. Some land grants were not confirmed because the Spanish or Mexican official did not follow the proper procedure in making the grant — matters that would have been remedied had the original government still been in power. Some were disallowed because the wrong official made the grant, mistakes easily made given the remoteness of the frontier and the period of flux between 1821 and 1846, when New Mexico's status went from province to territory to department and the authority of Mexican officials changed accordingly. Again, these were errors that could have been easily rectified if the original government were still in authority.

Historian Victor Westphall points out other problems that prevented Mexicans from securing title to their New Mexico lands. Congress in effect applied criteria different from those that were necessary to secure title under Mexican law:

> The land was invariably in narrow strips. . . . This was not compatible with the rectangular pattern that was the mode of the United States surveys. Then, too, it was the custom of these people to live around a plaza where they could rally in case of Indian attack. In contrast, national land laws required actual residence on the land. (Westphall, 1965:18–19)

Blackmar at the end of the nineteenth century aptly summarized the quandary in which New Mexicans, the last Mexican-Americans in the Southwest to lose their land, found themselves:

> The original holders of lands have lost most of their holdings either through the misjudgments of the courts and commissions, or else by the wily intrigues of the Anglo-Americans, especially the latter. The Mexican has been no match for the invader in business thrift and property cunning. (Blackmar, 1891:327–28)

Accustomed to the *ejido* system of equal access for all to both water and grazing land, *Neomexicanos* (New Mexicans of Mexican descent) slowly were crowded out by a coalition of Texas ranchers and Eastern-owned cattle companies. Access to the public domain and water was controlled by Anglos in the federal government's General Land Office. In less than a generation, the sheepmen, usually Mexican-Americans, lost another fundamental land struggle.

Historically, part of the problem has been the lack of understanding of the *ejido* concept. The King of Spain and the Mexican government granted a perpetual right to use the *ejido* lands on condition that the users maintain the land. While the grantees did not hold the *ejido* in fee simple, they did possess the right to use it (Rock, 1976). The actions of the Supreme Court of New Mexico have modified this notion of property considerably, generally denying Mexican-Americans their *ejido* property rights. For example, in viewing the Tierra Amarilla Grant as a grant to Francisco Martinez, the court denied the other residents of the grant any right to the *ejido*. However, the court did increase the property rights of Francisco Martinez. In another case, the residents of the Atrisco Grant incorporated it as the Town of Atrisco, and in 1905 the town received a patent to its lands. One of the residents questioned the Supreme Court concerning his individual rights in relation to the common lands. The court ruled that the residents were stockholders, without individual property rights, in a corporation where control was vested in the corporation directors.

In a 1903 case involving the common lands of the San Cristobal Grant, the court decided that the original grantees held the common lands in fee simple as cotenants (Rock, 1976), which greatly expanded their property rights. In the 1930 case of the Tecolote Land Grant, the court declared that the residents had a very vague, undefined right to their common lands (Rock, 1976) — the closest the court has come to affirming the usufruct rights granted by the King of Spain and the Mexican government. Nevertheless, the property rights of Mexican-Americans have been and continue to be denied.

Considerable Mexican-American property has been lost to state governments because of taxation policies. In California and Texas, the state governments first confiscated the property of Mexican-Americans for nonpayment of taxes. It was not until the 1870s that taxes were levied directly upon real estate in New Mexico, so losses there occurred later.

But by the twentieth century, much New Mexico land had been and was being taken by local government for nonpayment of taxes. The 35,000-acre Elena Gallegos Grant, for example, was taken by Bernalillo County in 1910 for $14.10 owed in taxes. By 1930, the Belen Land Grant owed about $30,000 in delinquent property taxes to New Mexico; a loan was obtained from some Eastern industrialists, who later bought the grant at thirty-five cents an acre (Center for Environmental Research and Development, 1975). The La Joya Grant several miles to the south suffered the same fate. These taxes owed were usually on the extensive *ejido* lands.

After 1906, Interior and Agriculture Departments' irrigation and flood control projects in south-central New Mexico displaced Mexican farmers.

> [Thousands were driven] from their lands through their inability to pay the financial charges imposed upon their small farms. . . . One authority estimates that the Spanish Americans conservatively lost between 1854 and 1930 a minimum of over 2,000,000 acres of privately owned lands, 1,700,000 acres of communal or 'ejido' lands, and 1,800,000 acres of land taken by the Federal Government without remuneration. (Inter-Agency Committee on Mexican-American Affairs, 1968:233–34)

By 1970, 33.88 percent of the total land area of New Mexico had become federally owned (Bureau of Land Management, 1970).

> Of the nearly 9 million acres of national forest land . . . [in New Mexico] 626,644.23 acres is on grant lands which were confirmed by the Congress in courts. These lands, in 18 different grants, were obtained by direct purchase or trade over the past 31 years. Some of the lands were purchases from banks which had foreclosed on mortgages. Many of the grant lands were lost to heirs who were unable to pay taxes on the property, especially the common lands. (McCarty, 1969)

Another problem of Mexican-Americans in their land struggle has been the sheer size, anonymity, and unresponsiveness of the federal government. Consider, for example, the Santa Fe National Forest, which contains more than 1.5 million acres—an area larger than Delaware. Like other national forests, it is operated like a business with foresters as business managers. They prepare land-use documents, do computer-assisted planning, draft environmental impact statements, and are expected to produce a sustained yield. Washington supervises. Mexican-Americans trying to secure an audience to discuss the forest's violations of the Treaty of Guadalupe Hidalgo have been unable to secure a forum. Several incidents of low-level violence in the middle 1960s were unsuccessful attempts to force the land-grant question, the basic issue, into court. But the claimants were tried for trespassing and destruction of government property, and were threatened with kidnapping charges.

THE INSURGENCY

The loss of land in the Southwest naturally precipitated a reaction. By the last decades of the nineteenth century, the reaction had become a revolution, questioning the evolving land-tenure patterns and their social justice. Exasperated to the point of frustrated anger, some Mexicans sought recourse in political insurgency.

As early as 1852, "the *Californios* had to engage in relentless backyard guerrilla warfare with settlers bent on outright confiscation . . . with each passing week in 1852 the . . . field of battle grew wider" (Pitt, 1971:95). Guerrilla warfare gave way to what some have called social banditry. "For many Spanish-American youths, California represented a place that had robbed them of their birth-right, but had meanwhile provided innumerable opportunities to steal back parts of it. In any event, many of the disaffected still turned badmen" (Pitt, 1971:256).

Mexican-Americans struggled against the unjust manner in which the land was taken and the uneven overall application of *gringo* justice. The social bandit Tiburcio Vasquez, a famous *Californio,* when asked at his trial why he had lived his life of crime, explained that he intended to avenge *gringo* injustice (May, 1947). Thus:

> the *Californios* perceived themselves not merely as the victims of annexation, but of deliberate betrayal and bone-crushing repression. . . . a few of them had managed to retain enough of their birthright to hand it on to their heirs; but few had held property as confidently as the conqueror had promised. Of the forty-five *Californios* representing the twenty-five families whom Thomas Oliver Larkin had enumerated in 1846 as "principal men" of the regime, the vast majority went to their graves embittered. (Pitt, 1971:278)

Social banditry in Texas was directly attributable to the loss of land. In 1859, the former owner of the Espíritu Santo Land Grant, Juan Nepomuceno Cortina, who had lost much acreage to Anglos because of unfavorable court decisions, rebelled, proclaiming, "our personal enemies shall not possess our lands."[4] In a seven-month war, he fought the Texas Rangers and the United States Army.

In New Mexico the battle over the land began late but continues to the present day in Colfax County, in the northeastern part of the Territory. *Neomexicanos* (New Mexicans of Mexican descent) fought the Maxwell Land Grant Company in the late 1880s. With the support of some territorial politicians, the company had staked out an excessively large claim which was confirmed by Congress. In 1887 the United States Supreme Court ended legal challenges by ruling in the company's favor. Thus began a survival fight by small Anglo and *Neomexicano* homesteader farmers and ranchers, many of whom had better titles than the questionable Maxwell Land Grant title. It was the *Neomexicanos* who held out to the last:

At the beginning of the 1890's the company faced bands of angry *Mexicanos* fed up with company demands and determined to retain their holdings. They were angry but not organized: neighbors gathered around local leaders and struck against immediate threats with little, if any, communication or planning between the different groups. (Rosenbaum, 1981:88)

By 1900 the northeast of New Mexico was calmed. A posse, working its way valley by valley, forced leases for the land on *Neomexicanos,* or served and enforced ejectment writs. Land ploys were often subtle as well as clever:

The device of mimicking a patron by taking a percentage of crops for rent proved the deciding blow; in effect, it manipulated *Mexicano* traditions in order to obtain precedents recognized in Anglo courts; once done, the company could eliminate *Mexicanos,* who did not understand the rules of the game, one by one. (Rosenbaum, 1981:90)

In San Miguel County, New Mexico, the land struggle centered about a court battle in 1887 over the Las Vegas Land Grant, a community grant made to a group of families at the beginning of the nineteenth century. On 20 August 1887 in *Millhiser* v. *Padilla,* the two cultures came into direct conflict over the *ejido* lands. Anglo investors who had purchased *Neomexicano* lands from some of the original grantees argued that they were also entitled to a fractional portion of the *ejidos* — in the form of private property. *Neomexicanos* argued that a division of the common lands required agreement of a majority of the grantees. The case was unusual since the plaintiffs, Millhiser et al., did not challenge the validity of the grant, but supported it because they had acquired an interest in it.

Neomexicanos were convinced that they could not win direct confrontations with Anglo institutions. Consequently, when the wheels of justice turned too slowly in *Millhiser* v. *Padilla,* a second frontal attack was made by the *Gorras Blancas* (the White Caps), *Neomexicano* night riders who pulled down fences; burned railroad ties, bridges, and electric light poles; and otherwise conducted guerrilla warfare against symbols of Anglo dominance. They explained that

the land grabbers fenced up our public domains where they chose, without the shadow of a title. Or if they purchased a tract of land with a title, they would fence in ten times as much as they bought.[5]

Suspected fence cutters were arrested, but would not be convicted by sympathetic local juries. Action was demanded of Governor Prince, who traveled to Las Vegas, New Mexico, to personally attempt — unsuccessfully — to resolve the problem.

Judge Elisha V. Long and Colonel R. W. Johnson, who had been appointed to take testimony in the *Millhiser* case, agreed with the Padilla *Neomexicano* position but could not accept the ethnic overtones or the tactics of violence of the *Gorras Blancas.* Nevertheless, after a two-year delay,

Judge Long wrote an opinion stating that the Millhiser investors could not take possession of any *ejido* land.

The case was the first and only time in New Mexico or the rest of the Southwest that Mexican-Americans were successful in blocking the efforts of those who used the confused status of land titles for speculation. In part, that success was due to outside help from the Knights of Labor, a national organization. (The local people called themselves the *Caballeros de Labor*, the Knights of Labor in Spanish, rather than the *Gorras Blancas*, but much of their memberships were identical.) The success may also be attributed to the tactics of using fear and violence in a remote and isolated area like northeastern New Mexico.

In the twentieth century, the adversary was no longer an individual or groups of individuals, but the federal government — difficult for a disorganized community to oppose. After World War II, the Mexican-American community began to organize itself but still found it difficult to oppose the government. In the 1960s decisive action was finally taken. In October 1966, the *Alianza Federal de Pueblos Libres* took over the Echo Amphitheater, in Río Arriba County, New Mexico, proclaiming the Republic of San Joaquin de Río de Chama. In June 1967, the Río Arriba Courthouse was raided. The following January, a Río Arriba jailer was found murdered, allegedly by *Aliancistas*. In New Mexico, the *Alianza* remains the most militant group within the Mexican-American community seeking to regain the *ejido* lands, and threatening action.

THE FUTURE

What course of action will Mexican-Americans choose in the 1980s? Some Mexican-Americans look to the courts. On 20 February 1982, a Taos attorney stated before members of the National Lawyers Guild meeting in Albuquerque that the land grant issue "remains very hot in Northern New Mexico. . . . It is not one that is going to cool off and the people are behind it" (Frei, 1982).

Other, more alienated, Mexican-Americans seek to apply the revolutionary demands for land reform that emerged at the end of the nineteenth century in Mexico. There the agrarians formed an integral part of the 1910 revolution that undertook — often violently — to restore the land to the people. The parallel with northern New Mexico is strikingly close.

Still other Mexican-Americans are demanding a separate state — the ultimate rejection of the United States' justice. Such demands appeared in early California; in San Miguel County, New Mexico, in 1890; in San Diego, Texas, in 1915; and in Río Arriba County, New Mexico, in 1968. In the Plan of San Diego, Mexican-Americans proclaimed "the independence and segregation of . . . Texas, New Mexico, Arizona, Colorado, and Upper California." Apaches and other Indians were sought as allies. Mexican-Americans agreed to fight for the return of Indian lands in exchange for Indian help. The plan was to form a coalition led by a "liberating army of races and peoples" — a familiar concept in what we now call the Third World. In 1969 the *Alianza* petitioned President Nixon for permission to establish an independent nation in northern New Mexico, the Republic of San Joaquin.

An Hispanic Land Claims Commission (like the Indian Claims Commission) has been proposed repeatedly, but to no avail. The first request for a new federal court of private land claims to complete the task begun by the earlier court was made by Texas Congressman Henry B. Gonzalez. In 1973 and again in 1974, the New Mexico State House of Representatives asked Congress to establish a Spanish and Mexican land grant claims commission. In 1979 it again petitioned Congress for adjudication, this time only of the land titles in the San Joaquin and Gallinas region "so that justice might be done for the *vecinos* [residents] . . . as set out in . . . the Organic Act, the Treaty of Guadalupe Hidalgo, and the United States Constitution" (New Mexico House of Representatives Joint Resolution 15, 1979).

Any prospects for the future must involve a return of the land, certainly a recognition of property rights, and revised federal policies concerning the use and taxation of the land. In particular, present federal policies must be replaced with sound policies encouraging land reform. For instance, tax exemption could be granted to cooperatives pooling their limited resources and to communities that still retain their *ejido* lands. In studying northern New Mexico in 1940, scholar George I. Sánchez recognized that the area's poverty was attributable to the loss of land, the economic base for New Mexicans. He noted that along with returning the lands, it would be necessary "to safeguard them from confiscation through taxation" (Sánchez, 1967:89). Thirty years after Sánchez's work, the *Alianza* reaffirmed the necessity of returning the land as the basis of socioeconomic reform in neighboring Río Arriba County.

Finally, there is the noncompliance with the Treaty of Guadalupe Hidalgo. Mexican officials must work with officials on this side of the border to resolve the problem. William W. Morrow, Judge of the United States Circuit Court of Appeals for California in 1923, concluded that

> the fault has not been entirely with the United States or its courts. The fundamental error was with the Mexican territorial authorities who failed to give to their grantees proper evidence of the titles to the lands granted. It was an error that prevailed in a majority of the cases, both in California and in New Mexico, and entered into all of the proceedings relating to the land claims and delayed their progress. Delay in such cases was unavoidable in the effort of the court to do justice to the claimants.
>
> Another serious fault on the part of the Mexican authorities was their neglect and lack of system in preserving and recording the evidence of titles in their archives. When the original grant had been lost or destroyed (which was frequently the case), the next best evidence was the archives and when these failed to furnish any satisfactory evidence of the title, the complainant

was compelled to resort to the evidence of long, open and continued possession and occupation of the granted land under a claim of title. (Morrow, 1923:26–27)

The *Asociación de Reclamantes* (Association of Claimants) in Texas goes one step further. Since 1932, it and similar groups have been working to secure Mexican assistance. More recently, they have been attempting to secure damages as well from Mexico. Hispanic lawyers from Colorado, New Mexico, and Texas representing the *Alianza Federal de Pueblos Libres* and the Texas *Asociación de Reclamantes* (the latter with a purported membership of three to four thousand) traveled to Mexico in 1976 to persuade Mexico to "pay money believed due under the Treaty of Guadalupe Hidalgo." There was no response from Mexico until 1978, when Mexican President Jose López Portillo said that Mexico had no intention of "paying millions of dollars sought from Mexico by Americans of Mexican descent" (Roybal, 1978).

In September of 1981, one of the founders of the *Asociación* filed a class action suit on behalf of the Texas heirs against the government of Mexico in U.S. District Court in Washington, D.C. *Asociación* attorneys argued that Mexico was obligated to pay approximately a billion dollars because of a 1941 United States–Mexico treaty which was to have resolved the land claims filed with an earlier 1923 commission. In a January 1983 decision, the U.S. district judge agreed. He said the plaintiffs were owed compensation, but questioned whether the court had jurisdiction "to order the Mexican Government to pay the claims."

Clearly, provisions of the Treaty of Guadalupe Hidalgo have been slighted and ignored — a fact that is properly a matter of international concern for Mexico on behalf of the descendants of former Mexican citizens. How have Mexican-Americans reacted to Mexico's role in the violations of the treaty?

> Whom did they blame? Doubtless each victim had his own answer, but it is noteworthy that many of them spoke of the land settlement as a massive betrayal. They charged the Mexican government with having sold them in 1848 as a "shepherd turns over his flock to a purchaser," and the gringo buyer with having led them to slaughter. (Pitt, 1971:103)

In the 1980s Mexican-Americans will increasingly assert their long-dormant claims for a local, self-sufficient land base — an entirely reasonable proposition for a society long committed to the Jeffersonian ideal.

NOTES

1. See, for example, Pitt (1971), p. 102.
2. As cited in New Mexico State Planning Office (1971), p. 29.
3. As quoted in Ebright (1980), p. 3.
4. Proclamation signed Juan Nepomuceno Cortina, Rancho del Carmen, September 30, 1859, cited in Rosenbaum (1981), p. 44.
5. Frank C. Ogden, et al. to Terence V. Powderly, National Grand Master Workman,

dated August 8, 1890, taken from Governor L. Bradford Prince Papers, New Mexico State Archives and Records Center, Santa Fe, New Mexico.

REFERENCES

Bancroft, Hubert Howe. 1889. *The History of the North Mexican States and Texas*. San Francisco: McGraw-Hill. Volume II.

Blackmar, Frank W. 1891. *Spanish Institutions of the Southwest*. Baltimore: Johns Hopkins University Press.

Bureau of Land Management. 1970. *Public Land Statistics*. Washington, DC: U.S. Government Printing Office.

Center for Environmental Research and Development. 1975. *Manual on Land-Use for Rural New Mexico*. Albuquerque: Center for Environmental Research and Development.

Ebright, Malcolm. 1980. *The Tierra Amarilla Grant: A History of Chicanery*. Santa Fe: Center for Land Grant Studies.

Espinosa, Gilberto. 1962. "New Mexico land grants." *State Bar of New Mexico Journal* (January).

Frei, Mary. 1982. "New Mexico land grants called 'hot issue.' " *Albuquerque Journal* (February 2).

Graf, Leroy P. 1942. "The economic history of the lower Rio Grande Valley, 1820–1875." Ph.D. dissertation, Harvard University.

Hammond, George P. (ed.). 1949. *The Treaty of Guadalupe Hidalgo, February Second, 1848*. Berkeley: University of California Press.

Inter-Agency Committee on Mexican-American Affairs. 1968. *The Mexican American: A Focus on Opportunity*. Testimony presented at the Cabinet Committee Hearings on Mexican-American Affairs, El Paso, Texas, October 26–28, 1967. Washington, DC: U.S. Government Printing Office.

Julian, George W. 1887. "Land stealing in New Mexico." *North American Review* 145 (July).

May, Ernest. 1947. "Tiburcio Vasquez." *Historical Society of Southern California Quarterly* XXIX (January): 123–34.

McCarty, Frankie. 1969. "Land grant problems in New Mexico." *Albuquerque Journal* (September 28).

Morrow, William W. 1923. *Spanish and Mexican Private Land Grants*. San Francisco and Los Angeles: Bancroft-Whitney.

New Mexico House of Representatives. 1979. *Joint Resolution 15*. Santa Fe: New Mexico House of Representatives.

New Mexico State Planning Office. 1971. *Land Title Study*. Santa Fe: State Planning Office.

Pitt, Leonard. 1971. *The Decline of the Californios: A Social History of the Spanish-Speaking Californios, 1846–1890*. Berkeley: University of California Press.

Prince, Governor L. Bradford. 1890. Papers from the New Mexico State Archives and Records Center, Santa Fe, NM.

Rock, Michael J. 1976. "The change in tenure New Mexico Supreme Court decisions have effected upon the common lands of community land grants in New Mexico." *The Social Science Journal* XIII (October).

Rosenbaum, Robert J. 1981. *Mexican Resistance in the Southwest: The Sacred Right of Self-Preservation*. Austin, TX, and London: University of Texas Press.

Roybal, David. 1978. "Decision goes against Tijerina." *Santa Fe New Mexican* (February 24).

Rubel, Arthur J. 1966. *Across the Tracks: Mexican-Americans in a Texas City*. Austin, TX, and London: University of Texas Press.

Sánchez, George I. 1967. *Forgotten People: A Study of New Mexicans*. Albuquerque: Calvin Horn.

Sunseri, Alvin R. 1979. *Seeds of Discord: New Mexico in the Aftermath of the American Conquest, 1846–1861*. Chicago: Nelson-Hall.

Tucker, Edwin A., and Fitzpatrick, George. 1972. *Men Who Matched the Mountains*. Washington, DC: U.S. Government Printing Office.

Twitchell, Ralph E. 1963. *Leading Facts of New Mexico History.* Albuquerque: Horn and Wallace. Volume II.

Webb, Walter Prescott. 1935. *The Texas Rangers: A Century of Frontier Defense.* Cambridge: Houghton Mifflin.

Westphall, Victor. 1965. *The Public Domain in New Mexico, 1854–1891.* Albuquerque: University of New Mexico Press.

PART FIVE

Land Reform and Rural Communities

13

Reallocating Equity: A Land Trust Model of Land Reform

JOHN EMMEUS DAVIS

Land reform is commonly equated with land redistribution. Some people own more land than they need (or deserve). Others need more land than they own. So the deck is reshuffled at the command of the state and dealt out differently than before. Large estates are broken up and placed in the hands of landless peasants, agricultural laborers, or small farmers. However, redistributing the ownership of land is only one "tradition" of land reform,[1] and transferring title to small producers but one "model" by which this tradition has been made a reality. There are other traditions and other models. Particularly within the United States, a more politically acceptable approach has been to leave untouched the distribution of land and to focus instead on restricting the use to which the land is put. This is the only tradition of land reform to which most Americans have been willing to submit. Nonetheless, a third tradition of land reform is alive and well in this country — though it is often obscured by the rhetoric and reality of the more familiar approaches of redistributing ownership and restricting use. This third tradition may be conveniently called "reallocating equity."

Equity refers to the value inherent in land and buildings: that portion of a property's market value that is unencumbered by a mortgage or lien; the value that exists free and clear once any liability on a parcel of property has been paid off or subtracted.[2] Part of this value is created by the dollars and labor of the property's owner, poured into the property over a period of time to purchase, build, maintain, and improve it. Another part of the property's value, however, is less a product of the owner's investment than a gratuitous windfall, bestowed by changes in the larger society. Changes in the level of private investment in surrounding parcels, changes in the level of public investment in the surrounding neighborhood, changes in the population of the region or in the price of oil throughout the world—any of these may add considerable value to an individual parcel of real property. To the value created by the capital and labor of the property's owner, there is thus added a "social increment" created by the investment and development of society. Equity is a mix of both kinds of value, one earned and the other unearned by the investment of the property owner, yet *both* are claimed by the individual owner as a proprietary right, guaranteed by custom and law. In the United States, equity is usually synonymous with the "owner's interest."

The third tradition of land reform confronts this custom head-on by reallocating the equity embedded in real property between the individual owner and the larger community. To the individual goes the fruits of individual labor; to the community goes the social increment. There are several ways to accomplish such a result. This paper will focus on a model of reallocation that is being used increasingly in urban and rural communities across the United States, particularly by grass-roots groups which are struggling against land speculation, absentee ownership, and residential displacement. This model is the community land trust.

The community land trust (CLT) is a mixed-ownership arrangement. Title to land is held by a nonprofit corporation—the CLT—based in and accountable to the local community. Title to buildings and other improvements on the land is held by an individual owner—a person, a family, a business, or another nonprofit organization. Though never sold by the CLT, lands are leased to individuals under long-term, renewable, inheritable leases. By holding the land beneath the buildings and controlling the price at which these buildings may be resold, the CLT is able to achieve a just and lasting reallocation of equity between individual leaseholders and the local community. It is able to reverse the worst effects of land speculation. It has the potential of altering, quite fundamentally, the ways in which local lands are held, used, and developed. In short, the CLT is a community-based model of land reform, effective both in its own right and as a complement to other land reform measures.

THREE TRADITIONS OF LAND REFORM

Land reform is a term with innumerable meanings and connotations. It is like a suitcase that is seldom packed the same way twice. Any discussion of land reform should therefore begin with a mutual understanding of how the term is to be used. Our "suitcase" will be filled with three elements. First, land reform is a purposeful response to a land-related problem that is deemed socially harmful; it is undertaken to correct a tenure system that is considered defective from the point of view of the broader public interest. Second, land reform restructures the institutional framework of landownership and use. It is, to paraphrase Peter Dorner (1972:17–18), a significant change in the rules and procedures governing the rights, duties, and liberties of individuals and groups as to the control and use of real property. Finally, land reform transfers power, property, and status from one group to another (Galbraith, 1951:695). To the extent that this transfer occurs across class lines, land reform represents a revolutionary step. Although other elements are commonly included in definitions of land reform,[3] these three should suffice to provide both a shared sense of the term and a general standard with which to compare the various traditions of land reform reviewed below.[4]

Redistributing Ownership

Outside the United States, land reform has usually meant redistributing the ownership of landed resources from one social class to another in order to achieve a more equitable allocation of wealth, income, and political power. The state condemns or confiscates land from the largest owners and either parcels it out among numerous small holders (distributionist reform) or transfers undivided estates to cooperatives, collectives, or state-run farms (collectivist reform).[5] The land-to-the-tiller programs of Taiwan and Japan are effective examples of distributionist reform. The most striking examples of collectivist reform are the state farms of Eastern Europe and the Soviet Union.

A less drastic means of redistribution is found in the attempt of some countries to *buy* lands from large landowners, without the imminent threat of seizure, for the purpose of making these lands available (and affordable) for small farmers, small businesses, and low-income housing. The land reform programs of Venezuela and Iran (Dorner, 1972:47), the land bank programs of Canada and Western Europe (McClaughry, 1975; Strong, 1979), and the New Deal community programs of the Resettlement Administration and the Farm Security Administration in the United States (Conkin, 1959) have all had ingredients of distributionist reform.[6]

Redistributing ownership is often accompanied by a fundamental change in the institutional framework within which land is held and used. There is, however, no necessary link between the two. It is possible to alter the pattern of ownership through the intervention of the state without changing the rules, procedures, or prerogatives of the tenure system itself. Distributionist reform is especially problematic in this regard. Parceling out large estates, while leaving intact a private, market-based system of land tenure, leaves open the possibility that what is owned today by a multitude of small, low-income producers may be owned tomorrow — because of sale, foreclosure, or unpaid taxes — by an exclusive coterie of wealthy individuals and corporations. Collectivist reform, on the other hand, may significantly alter the tenure system but do nothing to alter the concentrated pattern of ownership that was regarded as undesirable in the first place. Furthermore, as the history of eminent domain in the United States shows, lands that are taken by the state for a public purpose often benefit only a narrow range of private interests — and often end up in the hands of private corporations (see Scheiber, 1975).

At any rate, the United States has shied away from dissolving *or* collectivizing the holdings of its largest landowners.[7] American policy has periodically disbursed public lands and provided public funds to make land and housing more affordable for persons of modest means, but this has been more a matter of passing out subsidies to would-be buyers than of redistributing lands held and hoarded by a privileged few. The simple fact is that redistributing the ownership of land has had scant acceptance in the past and is likely to prove politically unacceptable for the foreseeable future. Land reform in the United States, such as it is, has customarily followed a different course.

Restricting Use

Americans have embraced, however reluctantly, a tradition of land reform that places public restrictions on the use of private property. The ends here have less to do with how the ownership of property might be made more widely available than with how the use of property might be made more safe, healthy, efficient, secure, or environmentally sound for the public at large. The means of this tradition are different, too. While the redistribution of ownership relies primarily upon the power of the state to seize private property, restrictions on use rely primarily upon the power of the state to police the behavior of property owners — regulating the ways in which they manage, develop, or dispose of their property.[8] Zoning laws and health and building codes, are long-established representatives of this tradition. More recent additions include environmental regulations, prohibitions designed to preserve historic structures, and various ordinances intended to retard or prevent tenant displacement due to condominium or cooperative conversions.

Restricting use alters the tenure system by diminishing the rights that owners have traditionally held when holding title to real property. Private rights of ownership are subordinated to the public purpose of relieving society of a prospective or actual harm believed to be associated with the unrestricted use and development of land. This "harm" — whether defined as "urban sprawl," "congestion," "pollution," "displacement," or something else — is eliminated in the public interest, either by preventing certain kinds of use and channeling development in more socially desirable directions, or by forcing private developers to bear the cost of certain "externalities" previously inflicted on society as a whole.

Although this tradition does not produce a redistribution of property *titles* among social classes, it does engender a redistribution of property *rights* (Geisler, 1980a:497). The results have been rather mixed. Restricting use has, on the one hand, preserved the status quo in the distribution of land, transferred power to large developers, and in many cases enhanced the value of private property held by the few (Walker and Heiman, 1981). Yet restricting use has also tended to transfer substantial power from landowners to local units of government and, increasingly, from local government to higher units of government (Popper, 1981). The exercise of this power, to the extent that private owners are forced to internalize costs previously borne by the public, tends to shift wealth away from individual property owners toward the larger society (Hite, 1979:37).

Restricting use allows the community to avoid costs that it did *not* create. The third tradition of land reform — reallocating equity — takes a different tack. It enables the community to reclaim value that it *did* create.

Reallocating Equity

Each tradition of land reform tends to stress a different land-related problem. Redistributing ownership confronts the problem of concentration — the accumulation of property and power by a landed elite. Restricting use is a response to the private abuse of landed resources and the private landowner's imposition of costly externalities on the general public. The problem that motivates the third tradition of land reform is speculation and the land monopolization and absenteeism which accompany it.

Under the fee-simple concept of private property, Americans have considered the "right to speculate" a basic prerogative of landownership.[9] Landowners claim most, if not all, of the increases in value which accrue to their property. Since appreciation will often occur even if the landowner does nothing to improve or develop the property, land has long been seen as a low-risk investment.[10] It has, from America's earliest days, attracted persons with less interest in *using* the land to meet their own productive, residential, or aesthetic needs than in holding it and later selling it for profits they did little to earn.

This is the heart of the problem: speculation so inflates the commodity value of land that socially desirable uses of land are often thwarted. For the local community, there are a number of negative consequences. Speculation makes access to land and housing more and more difficult for those of modest means: small farmers, small businesses, and low-and moderate-income residents. As the price of land is bid ever higher, only a few investors — many of them from outside the local community — can afford to acquire and hold the land. Concentration increases, as does absentee ownership and control. Agricultural producers are unable to compete with nonfarm investors for farmland that is soaring in price (USDA, 1981:77). Urban land for commercial and residential development is priced so high that one-fourth of all privately held land is left vacant in America's largest cities (U.S. House Subcommittee on the City, 1980). Speculation in land is also one of the factors that has helped to push the cost of new homes beyond the reach of three-quarters of the nation's families.[11] In urban neighborhoods, speculation in land and housing by brokers, developers, and affluent professionals has spurred gentrification and helped to displace the poor, the elderly, and the working class (see LeGates and Hartman, 1981); and in residential communities throughout the country, petty speculation by those selling a home and claiming the unearned increment as their rightful due has helped to nudge the price of housing beyond the means of a growing number of households.

Speculation also prevents a community from using its land as an equity base for its own development. A community's land is the original "commonwealth"; on that land and from that land is produced much of the community's wealth. If most of the land is held by investors who reside outside the community, much of this wealth will be drained away. Furthermore, if most of the value that accrues to land is captured by a privileged few, wherever they reside, much of the "commonwealth" will be unavailable to promote the development and prosperity of the community as a whole.

Finally, speculation makes it more and more difficult for the community to guide the pace and direction of its own development. Restless buying and selling of real estate tends to undermine whatever legacy of careful planning and thoughtful preservation the community would leave to future generations. Speculation is a threat to nearly every use of land that cannot be measured in the highest monetary terms. Aesthetic uses are the most vulnerable of all, for the single-minded pursuit of unearned profits in land has little regard for ornate structures of yesteryear, urban belts of green, or amber waves of grain.

The third tradition of land reform seeks to reverse the ravages of speculation by removing the *incentive* to speculate. Individual landowners are no longer permitted to exercise an undivided claim over the equity that accrues to real property. Local communities are empowered to recover the value which society had a hand in creating. There are two principal means by which this may be done: one model employs the public power to tax; the other mixes public and private elements of ownership. Both models attempt to reallocate equity between individual property owners and the larger community.

The proposition that the state can and should discourage speculation by taxing away increases in land value that are not the result of the owner's investment was popularized in the United States by Henry George (1839–1897).[12] He believed that individual landowners have no right to the equity created by others, private or public. Owners do, however, have an absolute right to the fruits of their own labor. To allow individual landowners to profit from appreciation caused by others is to handsomely reward those who monopolize and idle land instead of those who put the land to productive use.[13] George therefore proposed a "single tax" which would confiscate the socially created value of land and generate enough public revenue, so he claimed, to eliminate the need for all other levies on owner-made improvements.

Whatever the merit of George's single-tax proposal, his provocative idea that equity buildup contains a "social increment" has surfaced again and again since the turn of the century, inspiring many taxation schemes. There are Georgist elements, for instance, in the "betterment recapture" provisions of the 1967 British Land Commission Act and in the "unearned increment" taxes of Australia, New Zealand, and Alberta, Canada (Glickfeld and Hagman, 1978). There are echoes of Georgist ideas in the American planning system proposed by Donald Hagman which would tax away "windfalls" bestowed on lucky landowners by governmental activity, in order to compensate unlucky landowners for "wipeouts" in property value caused by other governmental activity (Hagman, 1974; Hagman and Misczynski, 1979). There is also a certain Georgist logic in Vermont's special capital gains tax on land sales, enacted in 1973 to discourage the rapid turnover of land by out-of-state speculators. Land that is purchased and quickly resold, presumably to reap speculative gains, is taxed at a higher rate than land that is held for many years (Glickfeld and Hagman, 1978). Implicitly acknowledged is the community's need to stop speculation and its right to share in the short-term surges in property value that the community, not the individual owner, happens to create.

Mixed-ownership models of equity reallocation attempt to accomplish similar ends by other than Georgist means. These models give the community a direct ownership interest in lands that are used and developed by private individuals. Outside the United States, mixed ownership has usually entailed *public* ownership of land, either by the state or by a quasi-public association. This has been accompanied by *private* ownership of the structural improvements upon these lands, with private owners leasing the land beneath their buildings. The Ujamma program of Tanzania, the *ejidos* of Mexico, and the settlements founded upon the lands of the Jewish National Fund in Israel are representative examples (Dorner, 1972; Tai, 1974; Orni, 1972). Public acquisition and permanent municipal ownership of lands, dispersed into private hands by means of long-term leases, is also a mainstay of England's Garden Cities.[14] All of these programs permanently remove land from the speculative market, while making it available for private use. Equity buildup is allocated between the leaseholder, who receives a just return on any investment of capital or labor, and the larger community, which retains the unearned increment.

The mixed-ownership model need not depend, however, upon public subsidies and public ownership. In India, the Bhoodan and Gramdan movements—part of Gandhi's political legacy—have placed nearly 4½ million acres of privately donated land into "village republics," private associations that combine local self-government with the common ownership and private use of local lands. Gandhi hoped that such independent village republics would form the basis for a decentralized structure of economic and political development for all of India (Linton, 1970).

Private associations figure prominently, as well, in the mixed-ownership model that is quietly taking root among urban and rural communities of the United States. This American model is the community land trust, a distinctive approach to land reform which interweaves many strands of thought and practice found within the larger tradition of reallocating equity. From Henry George, the CLT draws its focused opposition to speculation. George's influence is also apparent in the CLT's preoccupation with the origins and allocation of property value. From Gandhi, the CLT draws its emphasis on decentralization—political and economic development that proceeds from the bottom up, controlled by community-based associations. From the mixed-ownership models of Israel and England, the CLT draws the practical details of leasing land and guiding local development. In addition, the CLT implements a conception of land that is, at once, both Gandhian and Native American in regarding land as a common trust rather than a commodity, a common heritage that may be individually used but not individually owned. The community land trust combines these disparate strands within itself to form a community-based model of land reform—a grass-roots approach to the reallocation of equity.[15]

THE COMMUNITY LAND TRUST

Land trusts are neither new nor uncommon. For years, environmentalist and preservationist groups have been using local nonprofit corporations to protect endangered lands and buildings. The Nature Conservancy has established hundreds of local organizations to preserve unusual natural areas for posterity. The National Trust for Historic Preservation has helped local chapters to protect hundreds of historic landmarks from destruction and decay. The Trust for Public Land has helped to establish many local land trusts to defend open space against needless development. Organizations of this sort are painfully aware of the threat that is posed by speculation. All act decisively to remove property from the speculative market by acquiring selected parcels and holding them in perpetual trust.

Land trusts, then, are nothing new. Reallocating equity via a community land trust, however, is very new indeed. It is the question of equity that sets the CLT apart: how is property value created; how does the present allocation of value generate or aggravate the land-related problems that bedevil a local community; how might the reallocation of value begin to alleviate these troublesome problems? Like the more familiar trusts of the environmentalists and preservationists, the CLT removes property from the speculative market. Unlike these trusts, the CLT returns property to individual use, attempting to balance the legitimate interests of the individual user and those of the surrounding community through a just allocation of equity.

The CLT Model

The CLT is legally established as a nonprofit organization, with a membership that is open to any resident of the surrounding community. Out of this membership is elected a board of trustees that is empowered to acquire land, housing, and other real property by purchase or gift. Land is held by the CLT with the intent of retaining title forever. It is never resold, though it *is* made available for individual use. Appropriate uses are determined for the land by a committee of the CLT. Then the land is leased to individuals, families, businesses, or another nonprofit organization. The lease is a long-term use agreement, typically guaranteeing lifetime occupancy and specifying the uses to which the land may be put. This agreement may be transferred to a leaseholder's heirs, should they wish to continue using the land. Leaseholders pay a nonrefundable annual lease fee to the CLT, based on the current "use value" of the land, not its "exchange value."

Improvements on the land are treated differently. Any buildings acquired by the CLT are sold off to whoever leases the land beneath them. Any buildings constructed on lands that are leased from the CLT are owned by whoever had them built. The CLT retains title to the land; the leaseholder obtains title to buildings and other improvements.

If leaseholders later wish to leave the land, they may sell their improvements. They cannot sell them, however, for whatever the market will bear. Were the land to be removed from the speculative market, but not the house that is on the land, any social increment that would have accrued to the land would merely be transferred to the house. To prevent this, the CLT removes one "stick" from the bundle of rights held by the home owner — the right to an undivided claim on the appreciating equity in the house which the leaseholder owns. Utilizing a resale formula that is incorporated both into the home owner's lease and into a first-option agreement which the CLT retains on all improvements, the CLT limits the owner's equity in any improvements on CLT land.[16] The leaseholder/home owner is guaranteed a fair return on any personal investment in structural improvements, but is not allowed to profit from increases in the improvements' market value.

Applications of the CLT Model

CLTs have recently appeared in Cincinnati, Trenton, and Dallas to oppose gentrification and secure a base of decent, affordable housing for the neighborhood's present population.[17] A CLT was founded in an Appalachian community of east Tennessee to promote access to lands long monopolized by absentee land and mineral companies. In a middle-class neighborhood of Minneapolis and in one of the poorest counties of rural Maine, CLTs have been established to complement ongoing programs of community-based economic development. Variations on the basic CLT model have sprung up in Marin County, California, to deal with the loss of farmland; in Vermont to preserve open space and promote low-density development; and in New Hampshire to improve the management of forest lands. Their numbers are few — less than fifty in the United States — and their holdings not yet large, but CLTs are attracting serious attention and winning steady acceptance among a remarkably diverse population. By mixing various features of private and "public" ownership, the CLT is able to secure — and to balance — the legitimate interests in real property of both private individuals *and* the larger community.[18] These interests, which the CLT is designed to meet, are mirrored in the scattered struggles of numerous local groups to defend or develop their own communities. Among such groups, the CLT is finding a natural constituency.

The political acceptability of this model has much to do with its "conservative" promise of fulfilling the most fundamental expectations that Americans have traditionally held regarding the ownership of real property. Three of these are paramount: *security* against unfair eviction, unexpected increases in shelter costs, and unwarranted invasions of privacy; *equity* for one's personal investment; and a *legacy* for one's children. Because the CLT is able to meet the security, equity, and legacy needs of individual leaseholders, it is possible to persuade a diverse cross-section of the community that this alternative institution — this new approach to land reform — is worth supporting. Security of tenure is assured by means of a long-term lease for the land and a clear title to the land's structural improvements, both of which are placed in the leaseholder's possession. The CLT guarantees the leaseholder a fair equity in the resale of these improvements. Furthermore, the leaseholder may bequeath these improvements to designated heirs, along with the use rights in any lands that are currently leased from the CLT.

At the same time, the community has its own set of legitimate interests. A unique advantage of the CLT is that individual needs for security, equity, and a legacy may be met even as the CLT is serving the more general interests of the community at large. The first of these community interests is *access,* extending the privileges and prerogatives of property to those who would be denied them otherwise. CLTs have used their tax-exempt status[19] as a vehicle for low-cost acquisition by coaxing donations and bargain sales from local governments, charitable institutions, and wealthy individuals. As for raising funds, CLTs have been able to attract low-interest loans from a growing number of institutions and individuals seeking socially responsible ways to invest their money. Then, too, since they are mixed-ownership organizations, CLTs provide greater access to land and housing: leaseholders do not need a large downpayment to gain long-term use of land, and prospective CLT homeowners do not need to purchase the land that is under a house — a cost which now makes up 25 percent of the purchase price of most new homes (Cigler and Vasu, 1982:91).

As useful as the CLT may be in making property available now, its greater effectiveness lies in assuring that whatever is made affordable today will remain so tomorrow. By removing land from the speculative market and limiting the equity which leaseholders may claim as their own, the CLT should make it possible for future leaseholders to purchase homes at a price below the inflated market rate. In effect, this feature reallocates equity not only between the present leaseholder and the broader community, but between the present generation of home owners and those of the future.

The second interest of the broader community is *development,* exercising enough control over local land and housing to promote local economic development. The CLT attempts to place an increasing proportion of local lands under its stewardship. As absentee ownership is gradually reduced, the drain on the community's financial resources diminishes; rents and mortgage payments are no longer siphoned off to other neighborhoods or regions. These local resources may be augmented by using the CLT's lands as collateral in leveraging new funds into the community.[20] Equally important, over the long run, is the prospect that lease fees will eventually reach a volume sufficient to fund community services and other community development efforts.

There is the additional prospect that CLTs will either generate jobs themselves or support the development efforts of other community-based organizations. New Communities, a CLT in Georgia, has created new jobs in agriculture. The Community Land Association in Tennessee is engaged in housing construction; the Community Land Cooperative of Cincinnati and the Mill Hill II CLT in Trenton, New Jersey, are engaged in housing rehabilitation. These are labor-intensive activities, employing skilled and semiskilled people from the surrounding area. In other communities — where cooperatives, community development corporations, and the like have already begun tackling problems of unemployment and underdevelopment — CLTs may serve a more passive role, holding lands that other organizations utilize and develop. This is the nature of the relationship that currently exists, for instance, between the H.O.M.E. Co-op and the Covenant CLT in Hancock County, Maine.

The community also receives a developmental bonus in that increases in property value (unrelated to the leaseholder's personal investment) are retained by the CLT. They are neither removed by absentee landowners nor captured by individual home owners. Consequently, any general improvement in community well-being — whether due to public investment from outside or indigenous self-help — will benefit the community's present population. Many low-income communities, and an increasing number of middle-class ones, face the dilemma that creating parks, rehabilitating houses, or strengthening the local economy tends to fuel market forces that accelerate speculation, increase property values, raise taxes and rents, and ultimately — perversely — drive many residents out of the area. By capturing the social increment in land and housing, the CLT can control these market forces, while securing the community's present residential base and locking in the benefits of outside subsidies and internal improvement for long-time community residents.

Finally, every community has an interest in leaving a long-term *legacy* of thoughtful planning and preservation for its future members. This legacy is secured by the CLT's perpetual ownership of local lands. In the end, no method of land-use control can be as effective as outright ownership — the method employed by the CLT. The use and development of CLT lands are guided by plans drafted by a committee of the CLT and enforced by means of the lease agreement negotiated between the CLT and individual leaseholders. Some lands are leased for residential use. Some are reserved for present and future productive, commercial, or industrial activity. Some, requiring a more conservationist approach, may be managed directly by the CLT as forests, farmland, urban parks, or protected wilderness. Urban CLTs in Trenton and Boston have proceeded in conjunction with ongoing community garden programs. New Communities, Inc., directly manages all of its arable land as a cooperative farm. The Monadnock CLT has joined with other landowners in southern New Hampshire in developing a cooperative forest-management program for the owners and leaseholders of small woodlots.

Of equal importance to local planning is the social legacy. Here, the diverse interests of individuals and communities coincide. Since the time of Jefferson, Americans have professed a policy goal of giving as many citizens as possible an ownership interest in real property. Not only has this been seen as a matter of simple justice, but also as a way of promoting good citizenship and stable communities. As fewer households come to have the security, equity, and legacy that ownership affords — and as those that have them are threatened with their loss — the character and stability of many communities are jeopardized, along with whatever private investment and political participation that these ownership interests encourage. One of the finest legacies which a community may bequeath to the next generation, therefore, is the opportunity for most of its members to acquire these interests for themselves, their families, and their heirs. The CLT — by promoting access, limiting owner equity, and guiding community development — becomes the locally accountable steward of this social legacy.

These are the kinds of community interests that speculation does the most to thwart. Moreover, these are the kinds of individual interests that the private market in real estate is less and less able to secure — *even for families of the middle class.* This impasse occurs at a time when the other traditions of land reform appear to have reached, perhaps temporarily, the limits of their own political acceptability. Out of this situation, among grass-roots groups struggling to realize these *same* community and individual interests, there has arisen a growing willingness to experiment with the CLT model, adapting it to meet particular circumstances and needs.

THE LAND TRUST AS LAND REFORM

The strengths and weaknesses of the CLT as an actual method of land reform can now be explored in some detail. The three definitional elements of land reform, discussed earlier, serve as something of a general yardstick against which to measure the model's effectiveness. What, then, is the CLT's potential — and its limitations — in (1) solving the land-related problems caused by speculation, (2) changing the tenure system, and (3) transferring property, power, and status from one social class to another?

Land Reform Potential of the CLT

The effectiveness of the CLT in treating the *symptoms* of speculation has already been examined. The CLT is capable of ameliorating the most harmful social, economic, and environmental consequences of valuing land primarily as a profitable commodity. It is able to secure precisely those community interests that are made so precarious by speculation and its twin offspring, absenteeism and land monopolization. But the CLT goes further than this, for it treats the *causes* of speculation as well. The underlying system of land tenure that permits and promotes speculation is fundamentally changed within the CLT's domain.

Reallocating equity, by whatever means, removes the speculative incentive from land. The imbalance produced by the private market in real estate, where a property's use value becomes subordinate to its exchange value, is reversed. The exchange value is taxed or taken away. Land, for the most part, ceases to be a commodity. The CLT, in particular, accomplishes this feat by permanently removing land from the marketplace. Once land is acquired, it is never again resold. Future transactions occur by lease, not by sale.

The lease itself represents a significant tenure reform, a marked departure from the way that land is usually rented in the United States. The lease is long term, typically extending for many years. It is automatically renewable, upon the leaseholder's request. It is inheritable, with the leaseholder able to bequeath use rights to specified heirs. Furthermore, it contains provisions which protect both the quality of life for the leaseholder (privacy, quiet enjoyment of property, freedom of association and belief, flexibility of land use and development within negotiated parameters, etc.) and the environmental quality of the leasehold itself.[21]

The tenure system is further transformed by limiting the equity that homeowners receive from the property they own. The CLT goes one step beyond the reallocation prescribed by Henry George. It claims not only the socially created value embedded in land, but the socially created value that becomes attached to structural improvements as well. Achieved by means of the lease agreement and a first option (held by the CLT) on any improvements, a ceiling is placed on the owner's equity. Housing and other improvements are made less a commodity than ever before.

The third element of land reform is, in many respects, the most important. Unless a model can redistribute property, power, and status among social classes, transferring control over land-based resources from those who have to those who have not, the land reform potential of that model must be considered rather small. This will usually be true even if the model is quite effective otherwise in solving various land-related problems or in actually changing the established system of land tenure.

The CLT distributes the privileges of property more widely than before. Access to land and housing is increased for the community's current residents and preserved for the low- and moderate-income residents of future generations. There is, moreover, an implicit transfer of landed wealth in the CLT's enforcement of equity limitation. Value embedded in real property, customarily reserved for the home owner alone, is now shared with members of the larger community — present and future.

As a complement to equity transfers of this type, the CLT may also be effective in *preventing* the transfer of land and housing *away* from low- and moderate-income families. This is, in fact, precisely the hope of those who have organized CLTs in the rapidly changing inner-city neighborhoods of Cincinnati and Trenton. Their expectation is that the CLT may be able to acquire enough of the neighborhood's real property, in advance of the invasion of affluent investors, to reserve a portion of the locality's land and housing for less affluent families who already live there.

The transfer of power and status may be less apparent than the transfer of property, but still may be very real. Propertylessness and powerlessness tend to go together. As more property is brought under the control of the CLT and gradually removed from the grasp of absentee owners or indigenous landlords, the power to plan and develop the local community is returned to local hands and distributed among the many, not just the privileged few. The CLT provides the institutional vehicle by which such power may be both wielded and shared.

The contribution of the CLT to local empowerment, however, may go beyond granting local people greater control over the use and development of lands within its domain. Inherent in the base of community support on which the CLT is founded is a potential *political* base from which may be mounted local demands for further transfers of property, power, and status. The CLT is a membership organization, with a community-wide constituency. This constituency includes not only the CLT's leaseholders, but anyone who wishes to support the CLT's attempt to solve the many land-related problems that plague most local communities. In striking a unique balance between individual and community interests in land, the CLT has a special ability to pull together diverse groups of people — even across ideological and class lines. The CLT either puts together its own grass-roots organization or works to strengthen community-based organizations which already exist. Organizations of this sort will often perform an advocacy role on behalf of powerless groups within the community or in defense of the community itself, often exacting significant transfers of wealth and power from economic and political elites.

Finally, it should be noted that empowerment also has a personal dimension. The CLT provides a modicum of residential and (perhaps) economic security for persons who are normally reluctant to participate in political action because of the precariousness of their own circumstances. Political activism and personal security may be closely linked. Persons without security of tenure, in residence or job, are often slow to press for improved conditions or to confront powers-that-be for redress of grievance; conversely, the same persons, when granted more security, will frequently display a greater willingness to act politically in the interests of themselves and their neighbors (see Salamon, 1974; Cox, 1982). The com-

munity land trust may underwrite the expanded political involvement—
and empowerment—of persons of modest means.

Land Reform Limitations of the CLT

There are, however, several limitations in the land trust model of land reform. The model makes no frontal assault on the large concentrations of
property and power which already abound in the United States. Only
within its own domain does the CLT effect an actual transfer of property;
only within the confines of its own beachhead does the CLT change the inequitable tenure system. The pattern of landownership and the institutional framework of land tenure in the rest of the country remain intact.
Although there may eventually be enough CLTs with enough property to
constitute an alternative to the status quo, the current reality is that CLTs
are still few in number and most are fairly small. Established one community at a time, CLTs would seem a painfully slow, expensive, and piecemeal approach to land reform.

As a community-by-community affair, CLTs may also contribute to the
"balkanization" of a city or region. The public interest of the individual
community, organized around a CLT, may not be consistent with the
public interest of society as a whole—or the interests of other communities
in the same city or region. A region dotted with CLTs, each with a political base in its local community, may degenerate into a struggle of each
against all, each community competing with every other for land, subsidies, loans, and political support.[22]

There may even exist serious legal limitations that will render the CLT
model ineffective. Land and housing in the United States are legally
treated as commodities, freely traded at the highest price agreeable to both
buyers and sellers. The value inherent in a parcel of property (minus outstanding liens and liabilities) belongs to the person who holds the deed.
But the CLT operates on the assumption that land and housing should *not*
be commodities and that equity buildup does *not* necessarily or entirely belong to the individual property owner. Because the CLT acts to limit the
equity of its leaseholders, it risks someday running afoul of the legal prohibition against "unreasonable restraint" on the buying and selling of
property. This is not idle conjecture. As CLTs begin to amass larger holdings, the likelihood grows of legal challenges from local real estate interests, threatened by the CLT's expanding store of property and power, or
from a disgruntled leaseholder, rebelling against the CLT's attempt to
impose a ceiling on the profitability of his home.

There are reasons, however, for believing that these limitations will
prove less of a problem than they might at first appear. It is true that CLTs
will not soon have a major impact on national, regional, or city-wide patterns of landownership and land use. Even so, at the community level,
CLTs can—and do—make a difference now. CLTs can reduce the absentee ownership of land and housing and spread the benefits of ownership

more widely. They can retard speculation and give communities a new way of resisting displacement and guiding their own development. They also perform an important pedagogical function: teaching people to understand and accept new tenure arrangements, while encouraging them to develop innovative arrangements of their own. The community land trust is perhaps at a stage of development and acceptance today comparable to the stage that zoning had reached in the early 1920s. The CLT stands on the brink of wider adoption, legal sanction, and years of experimentation and fine-tuning. There is ample reason to proceed.

This does not, of course, completely address the problem of expense. Land and housing are costly acquisitions. Unless public powers and public funds are eventually offered in support of land trust expansion, it is difficult to see how CLTs can ever control enough property to have an appreciable effect on speculation, absenteeism, and long-term community development. But even without state support, CLTs have made significant progress. The Community Land Cooperative of Cincinnati (CLCC), to take a single example, started out in 1980 with no assets whatsoever. In the next two years, by combining gifts and bargain sales of property with grants and low-interest loans from individuals, churches, and religious orders, CLCC managed to acquire ten buildings — over twenty units of housing — valued at more than $250,000. More acquisitions are underway. Admittedly, this barely begins to meet the land and housing needs of this inner-city community. Yet twenty families that would have faced displacement from the next wave of gentrification have found secure housing through the CLT. Land is being gradually acquired; housing is being provided; people are being helped. However difficult, a start has been made.

Meanwhile, community land trusts have already begun confronting the problem of balkanization. Most CLTs reserve at least a third of the seats on their boards for public-interest representatives — persons who are not necessarily members of the CLT or even members of the immediate community. CLTs are also urged to include at least one representative from *outside* the community — preferably someone from another CLT.[23] This strategy offers a possible long-term solution to the problem of intercommunity rivalry: municipal or regional federations of CLTs, linking one community with another.

The prospect of legal challenge will probably loom over CLTs for many years to come. Yet the notion that equity buildup contains a social increment that society may claim as its own — an idea at the heart of the CLT — has recently won unexpected endorsement from an influential corner of the legal community, the New York Court of Appeals. In the case of *Penn Central Transportation Company* v. *New York City*,[24] the court had to decide whether the plaintiff was unconstitutionally deprived of a "reasonable return" from its investment in Grand Central Terminal when the city's Landmarks Preservation Commission refused to allow construction of an office tower above the terminal. Deciding against the plaintiff, the court noted that "society as an organized entity . . . has created much of the value of the terminal property."[25] A private owner has the right to a reasonable return only on that portion of a property's value created by his own investment:

> It is that privately created and privately managed ingredient which is the property on which the reasonable return is to be based. All else is society's contribution by the sweat of its brow and the expenditure of its funds. To that extent society is also entitled to its due.[26]

Appealed to the U.S. Supreme Court in 1978, the ruling of the New York court was upheld, but on different grounds.[27] Nationally, the question of socially created value was put aside for another day, even though "the social increment theory should still be considered good law in New York" (Scott, 1978:317). The case suggests that a new idea of property value is clearly in the air—one that seems remarkably consistent with the reallocation of equity pursued by the CLT.[28]

> What seems to be emerging is a concept of property value more relevant to the reality of the contemporary, highly interdependent system of urban land use. The concept would not seek to deny an individual the fruits of his labors but would examine increments in property value to ascertain what proportion might have been directly the result of collective action. . . . (Conrad and Merriam, 1978:24–25)

Whatever the present limitations in the land trust model of land reform, there is reason to believe that they will neither undermine nor unduly restrict the model's effectiveness. Considered by itself, the CLT holds great potential. Yet the CLT will seldom function *by itself;* in the short run and in the long, CLTs will coexist with other land reform measures. There is much advantage in this, for there are many ways in which the CLT may complement these other models and programs, representing other traditions of land reform. Such complementarities enhance the effectiveness of the CLT while reducing the most common flaws in these other approaches to land reform.

COMPLEMENTS AND CONCLUSIONS

Redistributing ownership is not completely alien to the United States. There seems little chance of the state soon moving to dissolve the huge holdings of our latter-day land barons, but sporadic redistribution does occur and is likely to increase. In the 1970s, for instance, West Virginia's governor used the power of eminent domain to seize lands of an absentee-owned land company in order to provide housing for victims of a devastating flood. In the nation's largest cities, where housing shortages are beginning to reach crisis proportions, pressure is mounting on municipal officials to move more quickly against the owners of tax-delinquent, substandard, and abandoned properties and to turn them over to tenants' unions and other community-based organizations. Such a strategy avoids a common problem of public ownership—the tendency for condemned property either to deteriorate while awaiting a public use or to slip back into a private use that benefits only a privileged few. CLTs provide an excellent vehicle for receiving such property, developing or rehabilitating it for residential (or other) use, and keeping it available and affordable for community residents, one generation after another. A Boston CLT has already been offered a multi-unit apartment building taken in receivership by the local housing court. The Cedar-Riverside CLT in Minneapolis may eventually acquire nearly 300 housing units that the city's community development agency was left holding upon the collapse of a large federal project.

Should the federal government eventually return to a distributionist policy of subsidizing home ownership for families of limited means, CLTs would also be effective guardians of these public funds. When a public subsidy goes into a property to improve its condition or increase its affordability for low- and moderate-income families, the subsidy should remain with the property. Otherwise, the subsidy must be repeated again and again—at increasing amounts—each time the property is sold. This has been the flaw in many housing and community development programs of the past. The CLT, on the other hand, is able to lock in public subsidies, assuring that public monies continue to provide public benefits—not unearned profits for a small handful of lucky homeowners.

Within the tradition of *restricting use,* land-use planning and environmental protection can both be strengthened by a CLT. The Ottauquechee Regional Land Trust in Vermont, for example, was founded in 1977 to retain open space and preserve agricultural land in ways that public restrictions could not. The situation demanded a private nonprofit entity that could acquire threatened lands and channel them into the hands of individuals willing to put them to environmentally benign uses. The Ottauquechee Trust deviates somewhat from the basic CLT model, but its success in working with local planners to guide development in socially desirable directions has been repeated by CLTs of every kind. The willingness of CLTs to participate actively in land-use planning and environmental stewardship was clearly revealed in a 1980 survey of American CLTs. Over half of the thirty-one respondents included "environmental preservation" among their founding rationales (Geisler, 1980b).[29]

Community land trusts may even complement models of land reform that *reallocate equity* through taxation. As John Costonis (1977:417) has remarked, the innovative reasoning in the Grand Central Terminal case lends "implicit support for public measures that seek partial recapture of private property's social increment of value to finance community amenities." Such measures may take the form of a tax on property sales (as is done in Vermont's land gains tax) or an annual assessment on the appreciating value of property, but the problem will remain of ensuring that recaptured value is productively and equitably reinvested in the local community—a problem which the CLT may help to solve.

Tax increment financing is a case in point. Tax increment financing implicitly accepts the Georgist notion, mirrored in the Grand Central Terminal opinion, that the community has a right to share in increases in property value brought about by community development. (Contrary to Georgist theory, however, the community shares in the appreciating value of buildings, as well as land.) In a typical project making use of this financing tool, a municipality designates certain neighborhoods as "tax increment districts" and records the current volume of property taxes being collected from these districts. Then, in ensuing years, any increments collected over this base volume are returned directly to each district and used to capitalize local redevelopment projects. Variations of this scheme are used in fourteen states, most extensively in California and Minnesota (Davidson, 1979).

Minneapolis provides an instructive example of both the use and abuse of such social increment financing. Specified districts in Minneapolis receive millions of dollars in tax increment funds to promote community development. However, local residents contend that only in the Cedar-Riverside neighborhood have these funds been used to benefit the entire community. The difference in Cedar-Riverside has been the presence of a strong tenants' union, a community-controlled development corporation, and a community-wide technical assistance and advocacy group. A community land trust was added to this ensemble in 1981. A local activist had this to say:

> If (tax increment financing) is not abused, it's a really good tool for the city to use to get neighborhoods developed. Unfortunately, in Minneapolis this is the only project that is not a prime example of abuse of tax increment funds. What it has turned out to be is just a free pot for big developers. And I think without the strong neighborhood involvement in this project, that's exactly what it would be here, too.[30]

Recapturing the social increment in property is not enough. Just as public subsidies for housing and community development often wind up in private pockets, socially created value may be returned to private developers and do little to promote wider access to land and housing, encourage local development, or preserve the community's legacy for its future members. Community land trusts, like the one in Cedar-Riverside, can serve as community-based complements to state and municipal programs that reallocate equity through taxation, ensuring that these public funds are put to more equitable, productive, and permanent use.

The CLT, therefore, may enhance the effectiveness of a wide assortment of public measures designed to correct various defects in the present system of land tenure. Complementing these public programs, drawn from all three traditions of land reform, the CLT may itself be made more effective. There is another complementarity, however, that is *not* dependent upon public policies or programs. The CLT may support — and be, in turn, supported by — "private" indigenous efforts to defend or develop the local community. As in Cedar-Riverside, the CLT can complement existing organizations and ongoing movements of insurgency, improvement, or reform. Land is a thread running through many community-based endeavors. Issues intersect. Constituencies overlap. The CLT may become advantageously entwined in an ever-widening web of local affiliation and mutual aid.

Within such a web, land reform and community reform are drawn together, meeting and mixing in the CLT. The CLT expands the focus of traditional community development practice, interjecting issues of land-ownership and land use into the midst of other efforts to empower and rehabilitate the local community. At the same time, the CLT's involvement in such grass-roots endeavors expands the focus of its own tradition of land reform. Reallocating equity becomes a means not only of stopping the reign of speculation, but of startgapoeso ommunity redevelopment; a means not only of removing socially created value from private hands, but of returning the power to plan and develop to local hands. Land reform and community reform tend to become two sides of the same movement — the warp and woof of a changing pattern of property and power, given form by the CLT.

By itself, therefore, the CLT may begin to address many of the land-related problems that plague urban and rural communities throughout the United States. The CLT is an effective instrument of land reform. Its effectiveness, however, does not depend upon itself alone. The community land trust is a remarkably gregarious model, teaming well with other measures of tenurial, political, and economic reform. It is in conjunction with these other measures that the CLT will have its greatest effect and fulfill its highest potential, now and in the foreseeable future.

NOTES

The critical comments of Charles Geisler and Chuck Matthei at various stages of this manuscript's preparation are gratefully acknowledged.

1. "Tradition" is used in preference to terms like "strategy" or "technique" because I wish to suggest a more general and long-standing pattern of perception and practice — a distinctive way of seeing and doing land reform that has been handed down by example, writing, and word of mouth. There is, as well, an older meaning that makes the term especially appropriate here. In Roman, civil, and Scottish law, tradition has meant "the transfer or acquisition of property by mere delivery with intent of both parties to transfer the title . . ." (*Webster's Third International Dictionary*). A "tradition" of land reform therefore has the connotation of one party surrendering property to another.

2. Excepting the question of ownership — i.e., to whom the equity belongs — this definition is consistent with the conception of equity generally held by those who deal in real estate. See, for instance, the definition of "equity" proposed by Wiedemer (1980:346).

3. Two definitional criteria of land reform that are frequently mentioned — but rejected here — are land reform as a rapid, drastic process (see Tai, 1974) and land reform as a product of compulsory state power.

4. There are three clarifications that should be noted at the outset. First, while the focus here will be on land, the discussion will frequently extend to housing and to other forms of real property. Second, despite the habit of many writers of using "land reform" and "agrarian reform" interchangeably, the present discussion will consider land reform as both a rural and urban phenomenon. Finally, examples of land reform in other countries will be presented only in passing; the focus will be on land reform in the United States.

5. This distinction between "distributionist reform" and "collectivist reform" is suggested by Lipton (1974).

6. The Resettlement and the Farm Security Administrations contained certain collectivist ingredients as well. Even though the establishment of viable family farms and subsistence homesteads remained the primary objectives of these New Deal agencies, both supported the development of model communities and large-scale agricultural cooperatives. Such "collectivist" elements later made the FSA quite vulnerable to red-baiting attacks from the Right.

7. During the final years of the Civil War, Northern military authorities distributed a number of confiscated and abandoned plantations to over 40,000 former slaves, who successfully worked the land as small farmers until President Johnson returned these estates to their original white owners (Moore, 1966:145). Such cases of redistribution are rare in U.S. history. Redistributing the ownership of land has not been a topic of serious discussion among policymakers since the Great Depression, when the need for agrarian land reform was a subject of intense national debate, with those who favored distributionist reform pitted against those who favored a more collectivist approach. For an excellent review of this debate, see Gilbert and Brown (1981).

8. Though the police power is the principal means of carrying out this tradition, the importance of tax incentives and disincentives in restricting and guiding the use of land should not be ignored, nor should the utilization of private restrictions on land, such as covenants and easements.

9. "The dubious tradition of land speculation is so strongly embedded in the American character that it is probably only realistic to take it as a given. Many Americans who are not land speculators at least aspire to be. As a result, the public at large seems unwilling to constrain the freedom to speculate. Indeed, such constraints, when proposed, are attacked as outright un-American." (Hite, 1979:65).

10. As of 1979, land prices had declined in only nine years of the twentieth century. Eight of these years were during the Great Depression. (Hite, 1979:62).

11. "According to a recent study by the Harvard-MIT Joint Center for Urban Studies, less than one-quarter of U.S. households can now afford to buy a home, compared to two-thirds in the 1930s." (Atlas and Dreier, 1980:14)

12. An introduction to the thought of Henry George can be found in George (1955), Andelson (1979), and Ross (1982).

13. In Georgist thought, there is a decided bias in favor of pushing all land to its "highest and best" use. Land which is "idle" is regarded as one of the worst symptoms of land speculation. This bias has been a source of much antagonism between Georgists and conservationists. Even more antagonistic have been the relations between Georgists and social reformers of the Marxian Left, who have accused George of being so concerned with the monopolization of land that he ignored the monopolization of capital—and the exploitation of labor.

14. Under the New Towns Act of 1946, twenty new towns were founded in Great Britain, essentially conforming to the "garden city" model proposed by Ebenezer Howard in 1898 (see Howard, 1965). Howard proposed the permanent municipal ownership of land as a means whereby equity buildup could be used to promote the public good rather than to enrich a privileged few.

15. The credit for this synthesis belongs, in large measure, to Robert Swann and the late Ralph Borsodi, the intellectual fathers of the CLT model. For the original formulation of this model, see Swann's book, *The Community Land Trust: A Guide to a New Model for Land Tenure in America* (International Independence Institute, 1972).

16. This limited-equity formula varies from one CLT to another. Each CLT must decide for itself the precise balance that it wishes to strike between fairness to the present leaseholder and fairness to future ones. Some CLTs, wishing to make housing as affordable as possible for future generations, will allow present leaseholders only a dollar-for-dollar return on anything invested in acquisition and capital improvement. Other CLTs, wishing to be more generous to present leaseholders, will factor in adjustments for inflation and the time value of money. For an excellent discussion of the kinds of choices and trade-offs that confront a CLT in deciding upon a limited-equity formula, see Kirkpatrick (1981). Even though his subject is equity limitation in housing cooperatives, Kirkpatrick's remarks are relevant to CLTs as well.

17. Specific CLTs will be mentioned only to illustrate specific points in the text, not to hold these few cases up as ideal applications for the CLT model. The fact remains that the CLT is a fairly recent innovation. Few CLTs are old enough or large enough to serve as full-blown examples of what a CLT can do.

18. This discussion of community and individual "interests" draws upon material in chapters 1 and 2, Institute for Community Economics (1982:1–35). An earlier version of some of the same ideas appeared in Matthei (1981).

19. While all CLTs are chartered as nonprofit corporations, not all are exempt from federal and state income taxes. Those that have obtained tax-exempt status under 501(c)(3) of the IRS Code tend to work primarily on low-income housing or environmental protection. None have sought exemption from local property taxes. CLTs do not remove land and housing from local tax rolls.

20. But many CLTs will not use lands held in trust as collateral, fearing that these lands might be lost through foreclosure.

21. See "Model Lease Agreement" for CLTs, available from the Institute for Community Economics, 151 Montague City Road, Greenfield, MA 01301.

22. A more general political critique — one leveled against the entire neighborhood movement and the institutions arising out of it — is that organizing around place instead of class will inevitably diffuse the power of low-income, minority, and working-class populations. According to this view, territorial consciousness and class consciousness are incompatible. Yet the CLT is merely a means to an end, not an end in itself. Incumbent upon the organizers of a CLT is the responsibility for determining the uses and ends to which this instrument will be put.

23. See "Model CLT By-laws," available from the Institute for Community Economics, 151 Montague City Road, Greenfield, MA 01301.

24. 366 N.E. 2d 1271 (1977).

25. Ibid., at 1275.

26. Ibid., at 1273.

27. 438 U.S. at 121 n. 23 (1978).

28. New ideas of property *rights* are in the air as well — and these, too, are conducive to CLT development. John Cribbet (1978:677), for instance, has predicted that in the near future: "The non-freehold estate will come into its own. . . . The diminishing fee will be further eroded as the lease becomes more like 'true' ownership and, at times, it will be difficult to say who has the greater bundle of sticks, the landlord or the tenant. Even today, the long-term leasehold is a major form of land holding with great advantages in terms of financing, land use control, and investment opportunities."

29. Land-use planning and environmental protection, placed in the hands of CLTs, would also seem to satisfy those critics of traditional restrictions on use who decry the confiscatory nature of zoning and other police-power regulations, and who fear the centralization of land-use planning in higher and higher units of government. See, for example, McClaughry (1976:528–29, in particular).

30. Dorothy Jacobs, quoted on pp. 112–13 of Institute for Community Economics (1982).

REFERENCES

Andelson, Robert V. (ed.). 1979. *Critics of Henry George.* Cranbury, NJ: Associated University Presses.

Atlas, John, and Dreier, Peter. 1980. "The housing crisis and the tenants' revolt." *Social Policy* 10 (January/February).

Cigler, Beverly, and Vasu, Michael. 1982. "Housing and public policy in America." *Public Administration Review* 42 (January/February).

Conkin, Paul K. 1959. *Tomorrow a New World: The New Deal Community Program.* Ithaca, NY: Cornell University Press.

Conrad, Jon M., and Merriam, Dwight H. 1978. "Compensation in TDR programs: Grand Central Station and the search for the Holy Grail." *University of Detroit Journal of Urban Law* 56 (Fall).

Costonis, John J. 1977. "The disparity issue: a context for the Grand Central Terminal decision." *Harvard Law Review* 91 (December).

Cox, Kevin R. 1982. "Housing tenure and neighborhood activism." *Urban Affairs Quarterly* 18 (September).

Cribbet, John E. 1978. "Property in the twenty-first century." *Ohio State Law Journal* 39.

Davidson, Jonathan. 1979. "Tax increment financing as a tool for community redevelopment." *Journal of Urban Law* 56.

Dorner, Peter. 1972. *Land Reform and Economic Development.* Baltimore: Penguin Books.

Galbraith, John Kenneth. 1951. "Conditions for economic change in under-developed countries." *Journal of Farm Economics* 33.

Geisler, Charles C. 1980a. "The quiet revolution in land use control revisited." In *The Rural Sociology of the Advanced Societies.* Edited by F. H. Buttel and H. Newby. Montclair, NJ: Allanheld, Osmun.

———. 1980b. "In land we trust." *Cornell Journal of Social Relations* 15 (Fall).

George, Henry. 1975. *Progress and Poverty.* New York: Robert Schalkenbach Foundation.

Gilbert, Jess, and Brown, Steve. 1981. "Alternative land reform proposals in the 1930s: the Nashville Agrarians and the Southern Tenant Farmers' Union." *Agricultural History* 55 (October): 351-69.

Glickfeld, Madelyn, and Hagman, Donald G. 1978. "Special capital and real estate windfalls taxes." In *Windfalls for Wipeouts: Land Value Capture and Compensation.* Edited by D. G. Hagman and D. F. Misczynski. Chicago: American Society of Planning Officials.

Hagman, Donald G. 1974. "Windfalls for wipeouts." In *The Good Earth of America: Planning Our Land Use.* Edited by C. L. Harriss. Englewood Cliffs, NJ: Prentice-Hall.

———, and Misczynski, Dean F. 1978. *Windfalls for Wipeouts: Land Value Capture and Compensation.* Chicago: American Society of Planning Officials.

Hite, James C. 1979. *Room and Situation: The Political Economy of Land-Use Policy.* Chicago: Nelson-Hall.

Howard, Ebenezer. 1965. *Garden Cities of Tomorrow.* Cambridge, MA: M.I.T. Press.

Institute for Community Economics. 1982. *The Community Land Trust Handbook.* Emmaus, PA: Rodale Press.

Kirkpatrick, David H. 1981. "Limiting the equity in housing cooperatives: choices and tradeoffs." In *Legal Issues in the Development of Housing Cooperatives.* Report XI. Berkeley: Economic Development and Law Center.

LeGates, Richard, and Hartman, Chester. 1981. "Displacement." *Clearinghouse Review* (National Clearinghouse for Legal Services) 15 (July).

Linton, Erica. 1970. *Gramdan — Revolution by Persuasion.* London: Headley Brothers.

Lipton, Michael. 1974. "Towards a theory of land reform." In *Peasants, Landlords, and Governments: Agrarian Reform in the Third World.* Edited by D. Lehman. New York: Holmes & Meier.

Matthei, Charles. 1981. "Community land trusts as a resource for community economic development." In *Financing Community-Based Development.* Edited by Richard Schramm. Ithaca, NY: Cornell University, Department of City and Regional Planning. Pp. 99–106.

McClaughry, John. 1975. "Rural land banking: the Canadian experience." *North Carolina Central Law Journal* 7.

———. 1976. "Farmers, freedom, and feudalism." *South Dakota Law Review* 21 (Summer).

Moore, Barrington. 1966. *Social Origins of Dictatorship and Democracy.* Boston: Beacon Press.

Orni, Efraim. 1972. *Agrarian Reform and Social Progress in Israel.* Jerusalem: Ahva Cooperative Press.

Popper, Frank J. 1981. *The Politics of Land-Use Reform.* Madison, WI: University of Wisconsin Press.

Ross, Steven F. 1982. "Political economy for the masses: Henry George." *Democracy* 2 (July).

Salamon, Lester M. 1974. "The time dimension in policy evaluation: the case of the New Deal land reform experiments." Paper presented at the annual meeting of the American Political Science Association, Chicago, Illinois.

Scheiber, Harry N. 1975. "Property, law, expropriation and resource allocation by government: the United States, 1789-1910." *Journal of Economic History* 33.

Scott, Thane De Nimmo. 1978. "Alas in Wonderland: the impact of Penn Central upon historic preservation law and policy." *Boston College Environmental Affairs Law Review* 7.

Strong, Ann L. 1979. *Land Banking: European Reality, American Prospect.* Baltimore: Johns Hopkins University Press.

Swann, Robert (International Independence Institute). 1972. *The Community Land Trust: A Guide to a New Model for Land Tenure.* Boston: Center for Community Economic Development.

Tai, Hung-Chao. 1974. *Land Reform and Politics: A Comparative Analysis.* Berkeley: University of California Press.

U.S. Congress, House Subcommittee on the City. 1980. *Compact Cities: Energy Saving Strategies for the Eighties.* Subcommittee Report, Ninety-sixth Congress, Second Session (July). Washington, DC: U.S. Government Printing Office.

U.S. Department of Agriculture. 1981. *A Time to Choose: Summary Report on the Structure of Agriculture.* Washington, DC: U.S. Department of Agriculture.

Walker, Richard A., and Heiman, Michael K. 1981. "A Quiet revolution for whom?" *Annals of the Association of American Geographers* 71 (March).

Wiedemer, John P. 1980. *Real Estate Finance.* Third Edition. Reston, VA: Reston Publishing Co.

14

Land Ownership and
Land Reform in Appalachia

JOHN GAVENTA AND BILL HORTON

In the last decade, community groups in Appalachia have tried to battle numerous ill effects of land-ownership patterns—the wanton destruction of land by strip mining, the lack of land for housing, low tax base and poor services, flooding, loss of agricultural land, and unfair broad-form deeds and land leases. Yet until recently there had not been in the region a movement to deal with the land-ownership patterns as underlying causes of the local problems, and only limited documentation of the extent to which the local problems might be regional or national in scope.

But in the spring of 1977, major floods hit the Appalachian region and brought the people closer to a regional land reform effort. Worsened by strip mining, the floods left thousands homeless. Yet relief trailers went empty for lack of available land on which to place them, since corporations had monopolized the land. In response to a call from citizens of Mingo County, West Virginia, groups from around the region gathered to form a new coalition, the Appalachian Alliance, among whose main concerns were questions of land-ownership.

The Alliance faced serious obstacles. The Appalachian Regional Commission (ARC), the multimillion-dollar government agency concerned with Appalachian development, had never in its twelve-year history looked at land in its research or its policies. In fact, its strategies of supporting "growth centers" rather than more rural communities encouraged urbanization and the movement of people into towns—thus leaving the land open to even greater corporate exploitation. Whenever the Alliance, or other groups, attempted to confront the ARC on the issues, would be told that land-related problems were neither extensive nor severe. Without a comprehensive information base from which to argue, community groups were unable to respond effectively. The Alliance established a task force to work on land and taxation issues, and it was soon joined by a group of scholars from the Appalachian Studies Conference.

In August 1978, the task force was encouraged to learn that the ARC did plan a study on land. But in a meeting with ARC representatives, the task force learned that the study was to look primarily at settlement patterns of people on the land and would ignore the more basic question of how ownership patterns created the settlement patterns. The task force decided, with the help of its own study, to

- provide a model for citizens to do their own research, growing out of their own local needs and concerns, rather than relying on professional consulting firms with allegiances to government agencies;
- train local citizens and groups in obtaining information;
- develop a network of individuals and groups concerned with land issues and committed to using the results of the study for constructive action; and
- educate and mobilize a broader constituency of local groups for action on land-related questions in their own communities as well as at the state and regional level.

CONDUCTING THE STUDY

The logical agency to support such a study seemed to be the Appalachian Regional Commission. Citizens' groups had confronted the ARC in the past about the outcome of its research, particularly the prodevelopment strategies, that were invariably acceptable to the regional agency. But they had never challenged the research process itself. So their questioning came as something of a surprise. The allocation of millions of dollars a year in research funds was an informal, unpublicized, backroom affair among compatible technocrats, high-priced consulting firms, and politicians. Broader political questions about who controlled the creation of "legitimate" knowledge about Appalachia had never arisen before.

But after two days of meetings, it was Alliance members' turn to be surprised. The ARC's research committee not only agreed to make land-ownership research a priority, but also asked the Alliance to submit its own proposal for the study. After much discussion, the Alliance proposal outlined a decentralized, participatory research plan. In each of the six states, state task forces of citizens would decide which counties they wanted to study, what approaches should be taken, and what issues demanded concentration. Each group would choose a state coordinator, accountable to it, to implement the study. Local citizens or local students would be the field-workers. Funds would be divided equally amongst the states, except for those funds going to regional coordination and computer analysis.

Each state group had representatives on the regional task force, which also had a coordinator and a small research staff to gather regional information and assist the local groups. The task force would synthesize the local research plans, producing enough uniformity in approach to allow regional as well as local analysis. Somewhat to the surprise of the task force, the proposal was accepted in January 1979.

Recruitment of project workers was not difficult. By now the project had attracted widespread interest, and some sixty people joined in to help. By the end of the project, the number had grown to almost one hundred. Many were members of existing community groups, or individuals seeking ways to begin to address land-related problems. Others were students, recruited from Appalachian studies programs in local colleges. Several were college professors, seeking to relate their knowledge and skills to the problems of the area. Some worked for salaries; others chose to work as volunteers, thus stretching the funds further in their states.

Because most of these field-workers had not been involved before in formal research, the project put a heavy emphasis on training. The Highlander Center in New Market, Tennessee, held a three-day workshop at the beginning of the project for all participants. In each state there were periodic follow-up sessions. Skills had to be taught—where to find data, how to fill in coding forms using land books in the tax assessors' offices, conducting interviews. The training indicated a base of hard data that had to be collected in every state, but there was also latitude for open-ended case-study approaches that would allow local groups to pursue local interests.

In September 1979, at the end of much of the fieldwork, workers gathered to report their findings. As the reports were being made, it became clear that one goal of the project had been attained: a number of people, with a little training and support, had uncovered tremendous amounts of information, which they were relating to their own lives and their communities. With the sharing of the findings, connections were made between each individual's situation and that of others. Overall regional patterns began to appear, and important linkages were made among people facing common issues.

THE FINDINGS OF THE STUDY

The sheer volume of the data was enormous. With county tax rolls as a data base, over 55,000 parcels of property in eighty counties had been studied. They represented some 20 million acres of land and mineral rights in parts of Alabama, Kentucky, North Carolina, Tennessee, Virginia, and West Virginia (see map, figure 14.1). In addition, over one hundred economic and social variables had been compiled for the counties surveyed. In-depth case studies were conducted in nineteen counties. Reports were prepared on each state. The findings were presented in a regional overview and in six supporting volumes of state and local material that together amounted to over 1,800 pages.[1]

FIGURE 14.1. MAP OF EIGHTY COUNTIES INCLUDED IN THE APPALACHIAN LANDOWNERSHIP STUDY

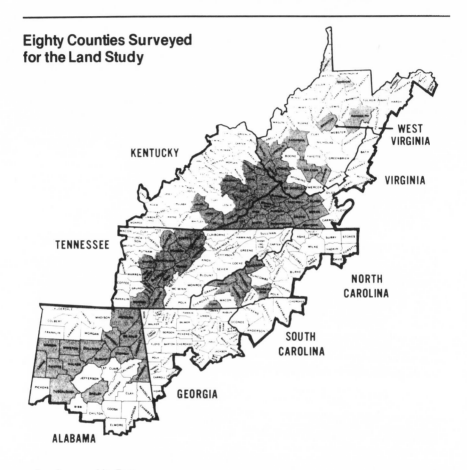

Land-ownership Patterns

The study found ownership of land and minerals in rural Appalachia to be highly concentrated among a few absentee and corporate owners. Only 1 percent of the local population, along with absentee holders, corporations, and government agencies, controls at least 53 percent of the total land surface in the eight counties.[2] Forty-one percent of the 20 million acres of land and minerals owned by 30,000 owners in the survey are held by only fifty private owners and ten government agencies. The federal government is the single largest owner in Appalachia, holding over 2 million acres.

Appalachia's land and mineral resources are absentee-owned. That is, nearly three-fourths of the surface acres surveyed are held by out-of-county or out-of-state owners. Four-fifths of the mineral acres in the survey are absentee-owned. In one-quarter of the surveyed counties, absentee-owned land in the sample represented over one-half the total land surface of the county. Contrary to expectations that absentee ownership would predominate only in the coal counties of central Appalachia, the study found a high level of absentee ownership throughout the eighty counties.

Large corporations dominate the ownership picture in much of Appalachia. Forty percent of the land in the sample and 70 percent of the mineral rights are owned by corporations. Forty-six of the top fifty private owners are corporations. Of these, nineteen are principally coal and coal-land corporations that own 1.5 million combined surface and mineral acres; eleven are oil, gas, and diversified energy companies that own 1.2 million acres; nine are timber companies with 1.0 million acres; eight are steel and metal corporations with 0.8 million acres; and four are railroads with 0.6 million acres.

As a result, little land is owned by or accessible to local people. Less than one-half of the land in the sample is owned by individuals, well under one-quarter by local individuals. Corporate ownership, bringing energy and resource exploitation, and government ownership, bringing tourism and recreation development, threaten the local population's access to land and local control over its use. These ownership patterns go a long way toward explaining patterns of inadequate local tax revenues and services, low economic development, loss of agricultural lands, lack of sufficient housing, and harmful practices of energy development and land use.

Taxation of Land and Minerals

Despite Appalachia's land and mineral wealth, the region's local governments remain poor. The counties lack revenue partly because of the failure of the property tax system to tax the region's wealth adequately and equitably. The problem occurs with both privately owned mineral and surface lands as well as with government-owned, tax-exempt properties.

Though values of Appalachian mineral properties have risen rapidly, local governments have not experienced a corresponding increase of property tax revenues. Mineral rights are greatly underassessed for property tax purposes. Over 75 percent of the mineral owners in the survey pay less than 25¢ per acre in property taxes. Eighty-six percent pay less than $1.00 per acre. In the major coal counties surveyed, the average tax per ton of known coal reserves is at most only $.0002 — or 1/50 of a cent.

The problem is particularly acute in eastern Kentucky. In the twelve counties surveyed, which include some of Appalachia's major coal-producing counties, the average property tax per acre of minerals is 1/5¢ ($.002). The total property tax received from mineral properties in 1979 was $1,500. In Alabama, the average tax per recorded acre of mineral rights is 4¢, and minerals that are part of fee-simple land are not subject to property taxation at all. A directive of the Tennessee Board of Equalization nine years ago to apply a fair market value to mineral rights has never been carried out.

Taxes paid on rural lands are low in relation to their rising market value. The amount of taxes paid per acre of surface in the survey is only 90¢. Almost a quarter of the owners in the study pay less than 25¢ per acre. The large and absentee owners tend to pay less per acre than the small or local owners have to pay.

Absentee owners often hold their property for speculation, or for the value of its minerals, and do not make improvements that would increase the value of the land. But local owners tend to build upon their land and to make valuable improvements. In Tennessee, Kentucky, and Alabama, vast tracts receive tax breaks intended for agricultural lands when, in fact, they are being held for speculative purposes or mineral development and are not farmed at all.

For example, in Martin County, which is now one of Kentucky's largest coal counties, 86 percent of the budget must come from state and federal sources because of the inadequate property tax base. The largest owner, Pocahontas-Kentucky (a subsidiary of Norfolk and Western Railroad), owns one-third of the county's surface land and mineral rights to another 81,333 acres (or 55 percent of the county's surface). Yet property taxes on Pocahontas-Kentucky's surface land hardly yield enough to buy a bus for the county school system, and the $76 the county receives as payment on the mineral rights would not buy the bus a new tire to replace the one worn out on the county's unpaved and rough coal-hauling roads. Per-pupil education expenditures in Martin County are 24 percent below the state average and 43 percent below the national average.

Tax-Exempt Lands

Many counties in the survey have substantial federal or other governmental land holdings, which are exempt from local taxes. In the case of state-owned lands, there were no programs to compensate counties for the loss of the land from the tax base. In the case of federal lands, "in lieu of tax" payments are set at a minimum of 75¢ per acre, but this amount is rarely equal to the average tax paid by private owners. In Swain County, North Carolina, over 80 percent of the land in the county is federally owned; if federal agencies paid the same amount per acre as out-of-state private owners paid, the county would receive over $150,000 annually in new revenues.

The failure to tax minerals adequately, the underassessment of surface lands, and the revenue loss from concentrated federal holdings together have a marked impact on Appalachian local government. Small land-owners are compelled to carry a disproportionate share of the tax burden; meanwhile counties must depend on federal and state funds to provide revenues, and have to deny their citizens needed services.

Economic Development

The study found that corporate ownership is greatest in those counties with the greatest coal reserves. Alternatively, government ownership is associated with tourism and recreation counties. Individual ownership is highest in the major agricultural counties.

Coal counties. In the coal counties, 50 percent of the land surveyed is corporately held, compared to 31 percent in agricultural counties and 23 percent in tourism counties. Some 72 percent of the land and 80 percent of the mineral rights are absentee-owned, and the ownership is highly concentrated in a few hands. With absentee ownership, the wealth derived from the land and mineral resources is drained from the region; with concentrated ownership a few, primarily corporate owners, can dominate the course of a county's development.

The study found that such ownership patterns limit economic diversification by lowering the amount of developable land, locally controlled capital, and local public services. Without diversification, localities become more vulnerable to the cyclical booms and busts of the coal industry.

Concentrated landownership patterns contribute to the problems produced by each turn of the cycle. Booms increase the pressures on the limited amount of land for housing and on already strained county budgets. Busts reduce the number of non-coal jobs and force many people to leave who cannot find local land to cultivate. In the coal counties surveyed, the greater the corporate ownership, the greater the percentage of the population that left the area during the 1960s' decline in the coal industry.

Tourism and recreation counties. Recreation and tourism counties have large federal holdings such as national forests and national parks as well as smaller, individual holdings (usually those of absentee owners holding the land for speculation or for second-home developments). Tourism and recreation promote a local pattern of low wages and seasonal employment. At the same time, local residents face rising prices for land, housing, and other goods because of the spending and speculation by the more affluent outsiders.

Agriculture. The study found that the traditionally important Appalachian small farm has dramatically declined: in the eighty counties surveyed, well over a million acres of farmland went out of agricultural production between 1969 and 1974, the latest year for which figures were available. Over 17,000 farmers left farming—about 26 percent of the farming population in these counties. There are a number of reasons for the decline of small-scale agriculture, both nationally and in the Appalachian region, but among them the impact of landownership patterns must be considered. The study found, for instance, that the counties with the highest proportions of land in the hands of local persons are the most likely to have the greatest use of the land for farming and the highest value of agricultural sales. Conversely, corporate, absentee, and concentrated land-ownership patterns each lead to less use of the land for farming. The decline of farmland is greatest where farmers are competing with owners who hold the land for nonfarm uses; the surveyed counties of western North Carolina, with their tourism and second-home developments, and of eastern Kentucky, with their coal developments, had the highest rate of farm decline. Each set of counties lost almost a third of its farms between 1969 and 1974.

Housing. Landownership patterns contribute to Appalachia's continuing housing crisis. In coal counties, concentrated corporate ownership of large blocks of land means that land for housing is often simply unavailable. Competition for the remaining land on the market sends prices soaring out of the reach of many low- and middle-income residents. In recreation counties, land speculation from tourism and second-home development inflates housing costs. The study found that the greater the degree of corporate ownership and the greater the degree of absentee ownership in a county, the more overcrowded the local housing stock.

Coal companies used to provide local housing in the form of coal camps. When the coal industry declined in the 1950s and 1960s, much of this housing was torn down. Now that the industry is booming again, houses are needed for miners, but housing sites are no longer available. In four southern coalfield counties of West Virginia where new housing is desperately needed, there were 12,579 fewer housing units in 1970 than in 1950. In these counties, almost 90 percent of the land sampled — amounting to well over two-thirds of the total surface of the counties — is held by corporations.

New energy developments. The study found that rapid far-reaching changes are occurring in the ownership and control of energy resources. Large energy conglomerates, primarily multinational oil and energy conglomerates, are taking over coal resources in the traditional coalfields. The new owners bring new levels of capital and technology, including strip mining on a larger scale than ever before in the region, the growth of a synthetic fuels industry, and massive pump storage facilities. Absentee and corporate ownership is expanding into new, heretofore agricultural, areas such as central and northern West Virginia, midwest Virginia, southern Tennessee, and northern Alabama. The expansion also involves the acquisition of ownership or lease rights to millions of acres of new minerals and energy sources, including oil shale, oil and gas, uranium, and gibbsite. The extraction of these minerals will have major environmental consequences.

Summary

The Appalachian Land Study found that the patterns of concentrated, absentee, and corporate ownership of land and minerals in Appalachia have major effects upon how the land is used, and to whose benefit. Systematic land-use planning and regulation are virtually nonexistent in most rural Appalachian counties. Decisions over use of Appalachian land are primarily made by the larger and more powerful land-owners in terms of their own interests. Such decisions can drastically affect an area's development, but the public has little say in how these decisions are made, and is often harmed by them.

USING THE FACTS TO PROMOTE LAND REFORM

Released on 3 April 1981, the study received publicity throughout the region. Dozens of local papers ran articles on who owned their counties, and bigger papers like the *New York Times,* the *Louisville Courier-Journal,* and the *Charleston* (West Virginia) *Gazette* ran articles summarizing the overall findings.

The report documented what many people in the region had suspected for some time, and citizen involvement in the report helped to create a climate for action. The people who had planned the study and researched, digested, and analyzed the facts were also people affected by — and ready to use — the results. Participatory, citizen-based research process had helped to gain information as well as to educate local leaders, link communities facing common problems, coalesce organizations, and serve as a spark for change.

Follow-up studies centered around the question of who benefited from existing patterns of land-ownership. Nowhere were the inequities clearer than in the patterns of taxation — where large absentee and corporate owners were hardly taxed at all, while small property owners paid much more. Angry citizens, armed with those findings, demanded that the giant corporate owners pay their fair share. This tax revolt assumes urgency as the Reagan administration slashes federal programs that have supported Appalachian schools and services since the War on Poverty. A lead editorial in the *Louisville Courier-Journal* proposed legislative action against such "economic colonialism," and the *Nashville Tennessean* called the situation "an outrage." The *Charleston Gazette* entitled its coverage, "End the Exploitation."

In Alabama, the study's release coincided with legislative debate on a bill to provide tax relief for the timber industry. With copies in hand, opponents filibustered, reading the findings into the record. The bill eventually passed. But the new tax reduction was limited to plots of less than 2,500 acres, striking an initial blow against the big timber companies. In Tennessee, Save Our Cumberland Mountains, a grass-roots group of coalfield residents, has organized several county campaigns based on study findings. One, for example, targets the Koppers Company, a Pittsburgh energy firm that owns one-third of Campbell County and plans a giant synthetic fuels plant nearby. In West Virginia, the legislature is considering a bill calling for an "excess acreage tax" on companies with large holdings. And a recent court case there — the Pauley case — has ordered the legislature to revamp the property tax structure paying special attention to taxation of land and natural resources in order to provide greater revenues for schools.

It was in Kentucky where the coal companies paid the least and where action was needed most. The study helped to crystallize a campaign as the "citizen researchers" joined hands with other groups to form the Kentucky Fair Tax Coalition. The coalition adopted the goals of maximizing local control of the taxation process, exploring new areas of mineral taxation, and monitoring how the state taxed corporately owned mineral lands. Allying with other groups concerned about federal budget cuts on local schools and services, the coalition took its case to the state legislature, proposing a new tax policy on unmined minerals which would have produced millions of dollars of new revenue from the coal owners. The bill rapidly gained support from teachers, school boards, miners, and community groups throughout the coalfields. Though voted out of the Revenue Committee by an eleven-to-one margin, the bill was quickly pigeonholed by the Speaker and the President Pro Tem of the House. Both leaders, later research showed, were attorneys whose clients included some of the major coal owners in the region, notably St. Joe Minerals and Consolidation Coal.

Other organizing efforts have concentrated on limiting the abuse of land. During the 1960s and 1970s many such efforts called for the regulation or banning of strip mining, which in Appalachia has denuded mountainsides, polluted streams, and left people homeless and jobless. In the "strip mine wars" of the 1960s, mining equipment was sabotaged, women lay down in front of the bulldozers, and mountaineers refused to leave their land. As the movement built, citizens' organizations sprang up in state after state—Save Our Kentucky, Save Our Cumberland Mountains (Tennessee), Virginia Citizens for Better Reclamation, and Save Our Mountains (West Virginia).

Some of the most bitter battles concerned the broad-form deed. Mineral rights under Appalachian land are often owned separately from the surface rights—that is, they are severed from the surface rights. The severance typically took place decades ago; and now, because of confused or lost records in the courthouse, surface owners may not know whether they own their mineral rights. If they in fact do not own them, they may not know who holds the claim. The broad-form deed gives the rights of the mineral owner precedence over the rights of the surface owner. So, with the development of strip mining in the region, families whose forefathers lost their mineral rights long before strip mining have been forced to give up their homes to the bulldozers. Some, like Widow Combs and Uncle Dan Gibson, refused; their resistance has made them folk heroes of the region. In Tennessee, Save Our Cumberland Mountains was able to push through the State Assembly a Surface Owners Rights Bill, stating that the landowners had to give permission before the mineral owner could disturb the surface. But elsewhere, as in Kentucky where similar legislation has been ruled unconstitutional, the land-owner lives in constant fear of displacement by mineral owners.

While the people in the traditional coalfields of central Appalachia have been fighting land battles for some time, those elsewhere have been less aware of the problems created by mineral extraction. However, the land study has drawn attention to the spread of corporate, absentee control of land and mineral rights. A new wave of leasing and purchasing of mineral rights is breaking on numerous counties on the periphery of the traditional coalfields, as multinationals—faced by rising nationalism in Third World countries—search for new domestic sources of energy and strategic minerals. Many of the areas in the path of new mineral development still consist of rural agricultural communities, and so have large amounts of land in the hands of small local owners. Although corporate land buyers and speculators are using their wealth and experience to gain control of land and mineral rights there—through fraudulent leases, hard-sell tactics, political manipulation—many local people in these communities do not want to see the history of central Appalachia repeat itself. They have organized to stop large-scale energy developments that threaten their way of life, and to educate other land-owners about the dangers of giving up control of their land or mineral rights to the energy corporations.

In the traditional Appalachian coalfields, where patterns of local powerlessness and dependence have been fostered by the large landlords for decades, the valiant efforts of individuals and groups to resist abuse of the land have met with limited success. But in the agricultural communities, where people own their own land, the patterns of dependency are not as strong, and citizens have won some important battles. In central Kentucky, for instance, 500 farmers who were misled into signing away their mineral rights for oil shale by false promises that strip mining would not occur have had the leases voided by the state's Consumer Protection Agency. In Brumley Gap, Virginia, citizens have delayed for several years American Electric Power Corporation plans to build a mammoth pump storage plant. In southern Tennessee, farmers and environmentalists joined to stop AMAX from developing a strip mine that would have been the largest in Appalachia.

But the citizen battles have been limited, for they have not yet challenged the legitimacy of the present ownership patterns of concentrated land. The rapid deregulation promoted by the Reagan administration has clarified the limitations of prior reforms. Citizens who for a decade fought for federal regulations of strip mining have seen their gains dissipated in eighteen months. Those who sought more equitable taxation now see corporate profits rising, while basic human needs and services suffer even more from a lack of public revenue.

One local farmer interviewed by the study summed up a growing feeling: "You know what happened in other countries when they got to where we're headed. They redistributed the land. We've got to do that." In small but significant ways, Appalachians are beginning to do just that. In Mingo County, West Virginia, angry citizens homeless after the 1977 floods persuaded Governor Rockefeller to condemn corporate land for local housing needs. While the eminent-domain action there soon grew

fallow in the courts, in eastern Kentucky several families have taken matters into their own hands. Claiming their research proved that the
companies never had obtained proper title to local land, they occupied it
for themselves. They have now been there for over two years. The coal,
timber, oil, and gas interests have never been able to prove their own
claims.

For these embryonic demands for land reform to develop in Appalachia,
as in the rest of the nation, we must have a clearer vision of what American
land reform might be. Our minds, as well as our mines and mountains,
have for too long been subject to corporate control. The patterns of concentration of Appalachian land in the hands of a few are much like those in
many countries abroad. Yet while battles rage over the land in Third
World countries, land reform has not been a serious topic of national policy in the United States for decades. In Appalachia, citizens have documented the land-ownership problem and militantly begun to deal with
some of its symptoms. We must now learn from land struggles elsewhere,
as well as from our own history and experience, to create new American
alternatives to current land-ownership patterns and practices.

NOTES

1. The project was administered by the Center for Appalachian Studies, Appalachia State
University, with research coordinated from the Highlander Research and Education Center,
New Market, Tennessee. An amended version of the summary volume is forthcoming: Appa-
lachian Land Ownership Task Force, *Land Ownership Patterns and Their Impacts on Appalachian
Communities* (Lexington: University Press of Kentucky). The supporting volumes are availa-
ble from the Appalachian Studies Center, Appalachia State University, Boone, North
Carolina.

2. Using 1978/1979 property tax records, the survey recorded all local individual owners
with holdings of more than 250 acres (representing 1 percent of the local population) and all
corporate, public, and absentee owners with holdings of more than twenty acres in the
unincorporated portions of the counties. This dual selection process reflects the task force's
specific charge of analyzing these categories of ownership in particular rather than all ownership. The survey covered 53 percent of the total land area of the eighty counties. Percentages
are based either on the total land *in the counties* or on the total land recorded *in the survey*
(specified in each case).

15

From Insurgency to Policy: Land Reform in Prince Edward Island

MARK B. LAPPING AND V. DALE FORSTER

For well over two hundred years, classical land reform issues have been the focus of much of the political and economic life of Prince Edward Island (P.E.I.). Always central have been the issues of who should own the land, to what end and uses, and for whose benefit. Primary themes of land reform in P.E.I. have been the regulation and control of foreign and absentee ownership; the concentration of ownership by corporations; land speculation and market distortion; land-use control, especially as it relates to the "public's interest" in agriculture and shorelands; and the need to create a public land base where none had existed before.

The case of Prince Edward Island is illustrative of the incremental and legalistic style of much land reform in advanced economies. As the P.E.I. land reform movement has become more pervasive, the provincial government has assumed a more substantial role in the process. In essence, land reform evolved from an insurgency issue among landless tenants to become the basis of P.E.I.'s existing "social contract." That the land reform debate continues should surprise no one, for it entails fundamental and contentious issues which have considerable historical precedent and on which cloture may not be possible.

Though important distinctions exist between Canadian and American land reform experiences, the P.E.I. case is relevant to the U.S. context in several ways. First, many American jurisdictions are just now enacting laws which seek to control foreign and absentee ownership. While these are largely symbolic, they are nonetheless indicative of a widespread concern with the locus of land tenure. Second, large corporate ownerships, especially as they relate to the structure and viability of U.S. agriculture, are coming under closer scrutiny. Third, speculation has been a concern for many decades. (Vermont, for example, uses its capital gains tax to discourage such activity.) Fourth, land-use regulation to retain farmlands has become something of a "motherhood" issue in both countries. Fifth, the nature and extent of public landownership is the focus of the Sagebrush Rebellion in the western states, though it appears to be a concern else-where, too. Just across the border, then, lie a jurisdiction and society that have wrestled with these and other land reform problems for several generations. Therein lies a story with important lessons and implications.

P.E.I.'s LAND REFORM LEGACY

Prince Edward Island, Canada's smallest province, has a gentle rolling terrain where cultivated fields are interspersed with woodlots, lakes, and small villages. The area of the province is about 1.4 million acres, of which close to 70 percent is classified as agricultural (see map, figure 15.1). The economy of the island is dependent on resource-based industries, particularly agriculture, fishing, and — more recently — tourism. However, it was the agricultural potential of the island that caused France to settle the Ile St. Jean (P.E.I.'s original name), and agriculture is still the backbone of its economy. In writing of the political structure of the province, Frank MacKinnon (1978: 22) has noted that the "dominance of agriculture on the Island assures its importance in both parties. The dependence of other industries on agriculture prevents a large gap from developing between their interests and those of farmers." Thus, in an almost unique way, the politics of Prince Edward Island are the politics of a changing agricultural land base. The island is often referred to as Canada's million-acre farm.

The management and tenure of land has been a crucial element in P.E.I.'s development since the 1760s. Foreign ownership of land, and its resultant absentee-landlord problems, retarded the development of the island for years. Not until the acceptance of confederation by the island legislature in 1873 was the landlord issue resolved.

However, in the 1960s islanders again saw considerable amounts of farmland coming under the control of foreigners. The island's beaches and bucolic landscape had always made the island the "Barbados of the St. Lawrence"; this, combined with its close proximity to large population areas, caused the island to be inundated with tourists. Many of these tourists bought property, and as a result substantial amounts of agricultural land became idle. Most of these new owners were either Canadians residing in other provinces, or Americans.

Being reminded of their earlier antipathy for absentee ownership, island residents fomented a land reform movement. They wanted to suppress the influx of nonresidents, and after much debate a land reform policy was legislated in 1972 to control nonresident purchases. In essence, nonresidents are permitted to purchase only ten acres, or 330 feet of shoreline, in aggregate, unless they receive permission from the Lieutenant-Governor-in-Council[1] to purchase more.

FIGURE 15.1. MAP OF PRINCE EDWARD ISLAND

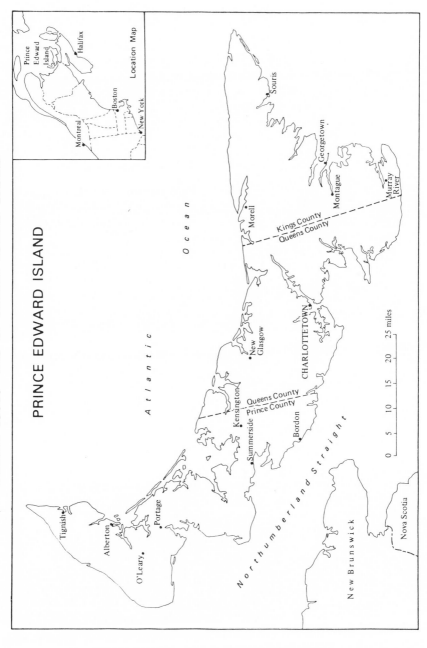

PRINCE EDWARD ISLAND

An automated landownership information system known as the Maritime Land Registration and Information Service has supported the province in its move to limit speculation and nonresident ownership of land by providing public officials and planners with information on all land transactions. The adoption of these contemporary land reform mechanisms would probably not have been possible without the island's history of more classical reform issues. An overview of the earlier problems of a landless peasantry, the insurgency over absentee landlords, and the eventual adoption of redistributive legislation is necessary for a better understanding of P.E.I.'s current land reform movement.

P.E.I. PRECONFEDERATION LANDOWNERSHIP ISSUES[2]

Alien landownership has played a dominant role in every stage of Prince Edward Island's development since its inception. As Lord Durham wrote after being sent to the colonies as Governor-General to inquire into the state of affairs, the colony's "past and present disorders are but the sad result of that fatal error which stifled its prosperity in the very cradle of its existence, by giving up the whole Island to a handful of distant proprietors." Although Lord Durham was writing in the 1830s, his statement still rings true today.

The fatal error to which Lord Durham referred was the procedure the British government followed in its attempt to settle the island after acquiring it from France in 1763. The island was surveyed and divided into sixty-seven townships of 20,000 acres each. Three townships were reserved: one of only 6,000 acres as demesne land for the crown, and the other two for groups who had been carrying on trading and fishing enterprises on the island since 1764. The remaining sixty-four townships were granted to persons deserving the patronage of the crown by means of a lottery. In this casual manner the lands of the island became privately owned.

The new proprietors were expected to fulfill certain obligations to the crown as conditions of the land grants including, among other things, the payment of quitrents (the money to be used in governing the island) and the settlement of approximately one hundred people per township over the next ten years. However, most proprietors ignored these obligations. A few proprietors moved to the island and became landlords of large estates. The other people who settled on the island were essentially landless peasants, paying rental fees to work the land while in neighboring provinces land could easily be obtained on a freehold basis.

The consequent dissatisfaction of tenants, combined with the fact that most proprietors were not paying their quitrents to the island government, led to classic requests to the crown for redistributive legislation. However, as most of the proprietors were still in England, they were more easily able to argue their case, and the crown refused to act. Tenant insurgency grew and Lord Durham was asked to investigate. As noted above, he felt the tenure system was abysmal and recommended that land be turned over to the settlers. While this marked a turning point in the island's absentee-ownership problem, resolution was far from guaranteed.

The consequent dissatisfaction of tenants, combined with the fact that most proprietors were not paying their quit rents to the island government, led to classic requests to the crown for redistributive legislation. However, as most of the proprietors were still in England, they were more easily able to argue their case, and the crown refused to act. Tenant insurgency grew and Lord Durham was asked to investigate. As noted above, he felt the tenure system was abysmal and recommended that land be turned over to the settlers. While this marked a turning point in the island's absentee-ownership problem, resolution was far from guaranteed.

Lord Durham's recommendations produced a classic land reform law in 1853 which unfortunately relied on the goodwill of the proprietors. Consequently, by 1861 the majority of the landholders were still tenants or squatters; less than half of the land was owned by land operators, and owners composed less than two-fifths of the number of farmers (Clark, 1959:132).

All of the land purchased from landlords prior to the 1860s was located in the "liberated area." This was an area, comprising most of the eastern third of the island, in which tenants had grouped together, refusing to pay rents and defending the area when land agents or sheriffs ventured near. The tenants controlled this area beginning in the 1830s, and it was their militancy which persuaded the landlords in the area to sell when they had the chance in the 1850s and 1860s, since the tenants refused to pay rent anyway.

Tenant insurgency grew, and during the 1850s and 1860s tenants began to arm themselves. The island was divided into the tenant groups, located primarily in the liberated area east of Charlottetown, and the resident landlords, who controlled the city and remaining rural area. During the 1860s the tenants organized on an island-wide basis and withheld all rents until the landlords agreed to sell land. When the insurgency grew to the point of warfare and neighboring Nova Scotian troops were brought in, all islanders and the crown realized that the land question needed to be resolved immediately.

Consequently, the land question became an important factor in the confederation discussions which commenced in 1864. Although it took almost ten years to agree on the terms of union, the island joined the confederation in 1873. In 1875 the federal Parliament passed a compulsory Land Purchase Act forcing absentee landlords and large resident landlords to sell their land to the island government at a price set by the act. The dominion government gave the island sufficient funds to buy all remaining estates.[3]

The lands obtained were to be resold, with tenants having the first opportunity to buy. In spite of the proprietors' attempt to have the act repealed, effective implementation of the act ended the land tenure question. By 1881, over 93 percent of the occupiers of the land had become owners (Clark, 1959: 132). The first land reform movement in P.E.I. had been effective in ending proprietorship. Aside from a very small amount, all of the island's land came under the control and ownership of the islanders themselves.

NONRESIDENT LAND-OWNERSHIP AND RECENT LAND USE PROBLEMS

There are many factors which have combined to make the bucolic and seaside landscape of Prince Edward Island a favorite resort haven for Canadians from other provinces and for Americans. The island is within a two-day drive for over 100 million people living in the northeastern United States and central Canada. Comparable landscapes in southern Ontario and New England have already been inundated with "hobby farmers" and recreationists. Tourism promotion has attracted many people to the island, however, and as one commentator has noted, the "Department of Tourism has unwittingly become a successful real estate agent" (Michael, 1974: 3). The relatively low land prices have induced more and more people to purchase property on the island. This inevitably has included many individuals and companies buying large tracts for speculative purposes.

In the late 1960s, a province-wide mapping program and socioeconomic survey was carried out by the Federal Economic Improvement Corporation and the Department of Energy, Mines, and Resources (Beaulieu, 1970; Bradley and Beaulieu, 1973). During the same period the introduction of the Maritime Land Registration and Information Service, a modern system of land survey, large-scale mapping, land evaluation, and land parcel registration provided up-to-date information on the extent of nonresident ownership of land. The Provincial Resources Planning Unit also undertook a study of nonresident corporations and individuals in 1971.

The results of these efforts indicated that a sizable portion of the island was owned by nonresidents — both other Canadians and Americans. As of mid-December 1970, approximately 72,000 acres or 5.13 percent of the province was held by nonresidents, including some 29,936 cleared acres of good-quality agricultural land. Of still further concern to island residents was the rapid increase in the rate of purchase which indicated that, in the absence of controls, 50 percent of the island would belong to nonresidents by the year 2000.

Other land-use issues were also surfacing. As there were no regulations concerning the location of rural recreation areas, uncontrolled subdivision of shorefront properties resulted. Cottage development along the coast reduced traditional public access to beaches, disturbing both residents and tourists.[4] This shorefront development also destroyed the advertised "unspoiled beauty" of the island of farms merging with beaches. As a result the tourist industry was threatened. Furthermore, increased demand for shorefront property caused prices to soar beyond the reach of islanders, who then put considerable pressure on provincial government to provide both public access to beaches and public parkland.

Shorefront properties were not the only real estate being affected by increased demand by nonresidents for recreational land. Farmers were finding the opportunity cost of holding large tracts too high, and as a result were selling both small cottage lots and larger parcels for summer/hobby farms. The average size of these severed parcels was 75 acres, too small to be economically viable production units,[5] but large enough to make farm consolidation difficult for farmers wanting to expand or rationalize their holdings. Also, the higher price for farmland acted as a barrier to new farmer entry.

The combination of the ownership problems and the land-use issues stimulated a movement towards land reform again, particularly among island farmers. Within the island's 200-year history of absentee-proprietorship problems, it is hardly surprising that both the public and the government were deeply concerned with the ownership issues.

THE LEGISLATIVE RESPONSE

P.E.I. has had legislation concerning alien land-ownership since 1859, when it abolished the common-law disability of aliens (non-British subjects) to hold land[6] while limiting holdings to a maximum of 200 acres. Other provinces had similar acts, although they placed no restrictions on amounts. With their legacy of foreign ownership problems, however, Prince Edward Islanders were unwilling to allow foreigners unlimited landownership. Not until 1939 was this legislation relaxed and larger parcel ownership made possible with permission of the Lieutenant-Governor-in-Council.

In 1964 the allowable alien acreage was reduced to ten acres in aggregate as a response to perceived increases in recreational land purchases by Americans. Although no real data existed concerning the extent of the problem, government felt some action was necessary and hoped that the legislation would be a deterrent. By the 1970s, government-initiated studies had made it evident that further action was necessary.

Prior to 1972, the Real Property Act restricted land-ownership by *aliens*. In 1972, as a direct result of surveys indicating that the problem was with all non-Island residents, the act was amended so as to apply to all non-P.E.I. residents, including Canadians. The 1972 legislation is not prohibitive, but regulatory. The act does not prohibit nonresidents from owning land in P.E.I., nor does it absolutely forbid the ownership of more than ten acres. Rather, it qualifies these restrictions with the statement "unless he (the purchaser) receives the permission so to do from the Lieutenant-Governor-in-Council." This is a significant distinction, particularly as the media have often been misleading on this point with headlines like "P.E.I. gets tough on land sales to outsiders" (*Financial Post,* 19 August 1972: 13). The granting of permission is discretionary and no reasons need be given when an application is denied.[7]

As with many laws, various problems surfaced in the administration of the Real Property Act, resulting in additional amendments to it. Although the act pertained to corporations as well as individuals, there were problems in differentiating between resident and nonresident companies. Furthermore, the government began to suspect that some companies, although incorporated in the province, were in fact controlled by nonresidents. There was also growing concern about the number of corporations involved in agricultural product processing, vertically integrating their operations and hence buying large tracts of land. Consequently, the act was amended in 1974 so that all corporations, both resident and nonresident, required the consent of the Lieutenant-Governor-in-Council for the acquisition of any property in excess of ten acres, or 330 feet of shore frontage, in aggregate.

An amendment in 1975 legislated the government policy of approving nonresidents' requests where a will or bequest was involved. These cases are now exempt from control if the deceased was a resident of P.E.I. at the time of death and if the beneficiaries are spouse, sons, or daughters of the deceased. As noted, this had been the policy previously, and in practice the government had allowed almost all gifts and bequests since 1972. A 1977 amendment to the act redefines "Canadian citizen" to reflect the 1975–76 changes in the Citizenship Act.[8]

Although the 1974 amendments to the act disallowed the acquisition of large landholdings by all companies or corporations without permission, it did not disallow the acquisition of shares in a company that owned large tracts of land. As a result, the Irving Corporation was able to hold 2,000 acres of land after having acquired the controlling shares of the C.M. MacLean Corporation. This loophole in the legislation was corrected in 1980 by adding a section to the act which disallowed companies with landholdings in excess of 100 acres from amalgamating with any other companies or nonresident persons without permission from the Lieutenant-Governor-in-Council. This amendment, as well as changes in the Companies Act,[9] means that the procedure used by Irving to take over MacLean and the subsequent ownership of 2,000 acres would be illegal today.

A LEGAL CHALLENGE BY ALIENS

With the legal bulwark for P.E.I.'s contemporary land reform in place in 1972, challenges to it followed immediately. Two citizens of the United States, residing in New York, attempted to purchase approximately thirty acres in Prince County.[10] When the registrar of the county refused to register the deed of conveyance because they had not obtained permission from the Lieutenant-Governor-in-Council, the two Americans challenged the validity of the amendment on Canadian constitutional grounds.

Morgan and Jacobson, the two Americans, argued that only Parliament had the right to legislate in respect to the essential attributes of citizenship and alienage, and that one of the essential attributes of citizenship was that all Canadian citizens, regardless of where they reside, have the same rights as persons residing in any province. They argued further that aliens have these same rights as a result of Section 24 of the Canadian Citizenship Act. They, too, could therefore acquire any type of real or personal property. When the Supreme Court of P.E.I. rejected their arguments, they took their case to the Supreme Court of Canada. As this case had clear implications for other provinces, all of the other nine provinces of Canada intervened in support of P.E.I. The Supreme Court of Canada unanimously upheld the legislation as within the constitutional powers of the province.[11]

The Morgan-Jacobson case is an important example of progressive land reform legislation withstanding a significant legal challenge. The P.E.I. insurgency has set a precedent for other provinces of Canada, most notably Alberta and Manitoba, which have sought to address similar problems.[12]

THE LAND USE COMMISSION AND LAND DEVELOPMENT CORPORATION

Technically, the responsibility for administering P.E.I.'s contemporary land reform laws rests with the P.E.I. Land Use Commission. This commission is a corporate body created in 1974 to review all petitions submitted and to recommend acceptance or rejection to the Lieutenant-Governor-in-Council.[13] These duties have in turn been delegated to the P.E.I. Land Use Service Centre. The centre processes all applications or petitions for land acquisition by nonresident individuals and corporations and makes recommendations, on behalf of the Land Use Commission, concerning their disposition.

The ability to deny petitions has deterred the rapid spread of nonresident landownership. Petitions have been denied for unacceptable intent of use or because the land was required for public use. Speculation, particularly rampant in the early seventies, and intensive development are also considered unacceptable uses. Even seasonal residency is often not considered acceptable. However, applicants intending to take up permanent residence and farm the land have generally received approval.

During the period from 1972 to 1979, approximately 10 percent of petitions submitted were denied, accounting for over 13,000 acres (table 15.1). Neither petition submission nor denial rates have remained constant. Denial rates were twice as high in the first two years than immediately after. This early strength, combined with the extensive publicity of the Morgan-Jacobson case, may have deterred many buyers, particularly those proposing unacceptable land uses. Other factors such as increased land prices, combined with higher fuel costs, have also undoubtedly caused nonresidents to find P.E.I. less attractive as a recreation retreat, resulting in lower submission rates during the second half of the decade.

TABLE 15.1.   DISPOSITION OF NONRESIDENT APPLICATIONS FOR LAND
ACQUISITION UNDER THE REAL PROPERTY ACT, 1972-79

Year	Disposition	Applications	Percent	Acreage	Percent
1972	APPROVED	173	82.4	10,934	74.0
	DENIED	37	17.6	3,835	26.0
	CANCELLED	—	—	—	—
	TOTAL	210	100.0	14,769	100.0
1973	APPROVED	187	77.0	12,944	76.0
	DENIED	50	20.5	3,843	22.6
	CANCELLED	6	2.5	246	1.4
	TOTAL	243	100.0	17,033	100.0
1974	APPROVED	208	88.9	11,391	87.7
	DENIED	26	11.1	2,601	12.3
	CANCELLED	—	—	—	—
	TOTAL	234	100.0	12,992	100.0
1975	APPROVED	137	89.0	7,418	64.5
	DENIED	14	9.1	2,501	21.8
	CANCELLED	3	2.0	1,591	13.9
	TOTAL	154	100.1	11,510	100.2
1976	APPROVED	169	93.9	9,779	91.7
	DENIED	9	5.0	613	5.8
	CANCELLED	2	1.2	273	2.6
	TOTAL	180	100.1	10,665	100.1
1977	APPROVED	139	90.9	8,345	79.4
	DENIED	6	4.0	277	2.7
	CANCELLED	8	5.3	1,900	18.1
	TOTAL	153	100.2	10,522	100.2
1978	APPROVED	130	87.3	7,007	84.1
	DENIED	4	2.7	202	2.5
	CANCELLED	15	10.1	1,131	13.6
	TOTAL	149	100.1	8,340	100.2
1979	APPROVED	113	98.3	8,029	95.7
	DENIED	1	0.9	194	3.5
	CANCELLED	1	0.9	70	0.9
	TOTAL	115	100.1	8,393	100.1
TOTAL 1972- 1979	TOTAL APPROVED	1,256	87.3	75,847	80.5
	TOTAL DENIED	147	10.2	13,166	13.9
	TOTAL CANCELLED	35	2.4	5,211	5.5
	GRAND TOTAL	1,438	99.9	94,224	99.9

Source: Compiled from Land Use Commission data sheets

These same factors have probably deterred prospective speculators and seasonal residents most, resulting in less need for petition denial.

The type of transaction is another factor considered carefully during petition review. Gifts, bequests, or sales to persons with family connections in P.E.I. have been nearly always approved; these represented almost 36 percent of all approvals between 1972 and 1976. Although the Real Property Act was amended in 1975, bequest cases have continued to be submitted. The proportion of purchase cases submitted relative to gifts or bequests has declined noticeably since 1975. This helps to explain the increase in approved petitions, as almost all gifts (98 percent from 1972 to 1976) and bequests (100 percent from 1972 to 1976) received approval.

Although the intended use of the property was very important in assessment, there was no mechanism to ensure that applicants were in fact carrying out their stated intent. Local farmers discovered many properties were being subdivided after the application had been approved for farming purposes. After the government was made aware of this problem, the Land Identification Program was introduced in 1977 to ensure that identified land would not be subdivided but would, where applicable, remain in agricultural use. This voluntary identification program applies to nonresident and corporate purchases for a minimum of ten years; at the end of this period, it is automatically renewed unless the property owner has applied for termination.

The identification program does not yet possess a mechanism to ensure that land is being farmed, but it does help to restrict subdivision. However, the program is voluntary and, since it places restrictions on owners, the acceptance rate has not been high. For example, during 1979, the Land Use Commission made recommendations on 190 nonresident and corporate petitions; land identification agreements were signed for only 51 properties. The only incentive to sign an identification agreement is that it indicates the sincerity of the purchaser's land-use intent and predisposes the commission toward approval of the application. For this program to be truly effective, it must become compulsory on all approved petitions.

When a petition is denied and it is desirable that the public acquire the land, the petition is given to the Land Development Corporation. The corporation requests an appraisal from the Land Valuation and Assessment Branch of the Department of Finance. That office provides the corporation with a fair market value of the property, and the corporation is instructed to make an offer of purchase. If the fair market value of the property, and hence the price the corporation is able to offer, is much lower than the price offered by the nonresident, the application by the nonresident may be resubmitted and the decision may be reversed.[14] This government policy arose out of a desire that no seller should suffer because of the new legislation. However, strict adherence to this policy has led to more approvals than may have been desired from the land reform point of view. Still, over 13,000 acres (see table 15.1) have successfully been kept from nonresident ownership during the period from 1972 to 1979, and this is a significant achievement for the land reform movement in P.E.I.

THE MARITIME LAND REGISTRATION AND
INFORMATION SERVICE (M.L.R.I.S.)

Land reform in P.E.I. has been closely tied to information reform regarding ownership. It was not until a modern system of land survey and land parcel registration was instituted that the full extent of the nonresident ownership issue became known. Prior to the late 1960s, information concerning landownership was most often gathered in an informal, intuitive fashion. No rigorous land survey existed, and property boundaries were defined by local landmarks. Although the move towards a formal, systematic process for the gathering of information was independent of the landownership issue in P.E.I., the two became closely intertwined.

The M.L.R.I.S. is a modern, computerized information system developed in 1968 jointly by the provinces of New Brunswick, Nova Scotia, and P.E.I. After instituting an elaborate survey network, the government could produce a series of resource, urban, and property maps. Implementation of an improved system of land registration provided information for the first time on land titles for each property. Since P.E.I. was selected as a test case for the system, data became available quite early in the 1970s. Although the system is not yet entirely computerized, it is still important for providing information about landownership, parcel size, and distribution. It has also been of assistance to the Land Development Corporation in providing key information such as precise location, present land use by type and acreage, type of buildings, and appraised value on parcels the province wishes to purchase. As the system becomes completely operational, it will become increasingly important in land-use control on P.E.I.

THE LAND DEVELOPMENT CORPORATION (L.D.C.)

In addition to the nonresident problems unearthed by studies during the late 1960s (Beaulieu, 1970; Bradley and Beaulieu, 1973; Raymond and Rayburn, 1963), other problems were seen as impediments to raising provincial and national levels of agricultural productivity and efficiency. Sizable amounts of potentially productive land were not being used. Furthermore, landownership patterns, land tenure arrangements, and land management techniques were likewise perceived as obstacles to progress by both federal and provincial governments.

Thus, the Land Development Corporation was established as a crown corporation in 1969, with its primary purpose to assist farmers and the agricultural industry so as to add to the value of the agricultural sector in the provincial economy. This was to be accomplished through the judicious acquisition and release of land to farmers to enable consolidation and enlargement of farms. At the same time, land unsuited to agriculture was to be acquired and managed for other purposes such as forestry, fish and wildlife habitat, outdoor recreation, or watershed production. On

Prince Edward Island, the L.D.C. was to become, at least partially, the institutional core of land reform, responsible for a comprehensive land management program which would enable optimum development of the island's land resources. As such, the agency has become a land bank. In order to fulfill this role, the L.D.C. established a number of programs related primarily to land acquisition and dispersal.

As mentioned previously, the corporation receives all nonresident petitions which are denied cabinet approval, and must act on them. Second, the corporation acts as the purchasing agent for all provincial departments, except for the Department of Public Works. There are two methods by which the corporation may acquire land—the annuity program and cash purchase. The annuity program was designed to benefit older farmers near retirement age who, for one reason or another, wished to sell their land. Farmers were able to retain a life interest in the home on the property and to receive monthly payments. However, the program has lost popularity in recent years, mainly because rising land values have made cash transactions more attractive to the landowner. In the period from 1976 to 1980, no annuity purchases were completed, and as a result the program is being phased out. Greater than 90 percent of all purchases are cash transactions.

Conforming to the Land Development Corporation's policy of not competing with the real estate market, the corporation does not actively seek land to purchase; people must apply to sell land to the Land Development Corporation. The exception to this policy occurs when the corporation has received a request for the acquisition of a particular piece of land from a government department.

Although anyone may apply to sell land, not all applications are accepted. For example, the corporation does not usually purchase viable farm units. Exceptions are made in those cases where the seller wishes to leave the farm business because of age, poor health, or financial reasons. Once an application to sell land to the corporation is accepted, the land and buildings are appraised by the Land Assessment and Valuation Division of the Department of Finance. Every reasonable effort is made to maintain and reflect the current land-market situation so that the corporation neither pushes land values up nor lags behind. The land is also appraised for its agricultural, forestry, or recreational capability. If the land is suitable and a price can be negotiated, the sale takes place.

Between 1972 and 1975, 41 percent of all nonresident petitions that were denied were acquired by the Land Development Corporation (table 15.2). Comparing tables 15.2 and 15.3, the acreage acquired as a result of petition denials accounts for less than 50 percent of corporation purchases; however, from a land reform point of view, these purchases are significant. Although one of the primary purposes of the corporation is to assist farmers by acquiring land and making it available for farm expansion and consolidation purposes, few of the properties acquired through petition denial are for agricultural purposes (table 15.2). This is because the corporation

TABLE 15.2. NONRESIDENT PETITIONS DENIED AND PROPERTIES ACQUIRED
BY LAND DEVELOPMENT CORPORATION

Action	1972	1973	1974	1975	Total
Total Petitions Denied	46	54	35	12	147
Total Acreage Denied	4,565	4,050	2,495	850	11,960
Total Shore Frontage* Denied	230	487	528	272	1,517
Total Value of Par- cels Denied	$274,400	$318,900	$323,600	$113,200	$1,030,100
Total Petitions Acquired	22	18	14	6	60
Total Acreage Acquired	2,321	1,442	1,051	521	5,335
Total Shore Frontage* Acquired	151	234	127	25	537
Total Value of Par- cels Acquired	$192,500	$113,800	$ 84,000	$ 64,900	$ 455,200
AGRICULTURAL PURPOSES					
Petitions Acquired	7	2	3	1	13
Acreage Acquired	634	50	258	85	1,027
Shore Frontage* Acquired	40	—	10	15	65
Value of Parcels Acquired	$ 40,700	$ 4,500	$ 11,900	$ 1,000	$ 58,100
FISH AND WILDLIFE PURPOSES					
Petitions Acquired	—	1	3	—	4
Acreage Acquired	—	52	265	—	317
Shore Frontage* Acquired	—	10	94	—	104
Value of Parcels Acquired	—	$ 7,500	$ 29,400	—	$ 36,900
FORESTRY PURPOSES					
Petitions Acquired	10	9	7	4	30
Acreage Acquired	918	674	481	426	2,499
Shore Frontage* Acquired	—	5	8	—	13
Value of Parcels Acquired	$ 17,800	$ 24,900	$ 19,200	$ 48,900	$ 110,800
RECREATION PURPOSES					
Petitions Acquired	5	6	1	1	13
Acreage Acquired	769	666	47	10	1,492
Shore Frontage* Acquired	111	219	15	10	355
Value of Parcels Acquired	$134,000	$ 76,900	$ 23,500	$ 15,000	$ 249,400

Source: Lands Directorate, Non-Resident Landownership Legislation and
Administration in Prince Edward Island Land Use in Canada
Series No. 12, p. 52. Ottawa: Environment Canada, 1978.
*Shore frontage given in chains

can only offer a price within the agricultural market value, while nonresidents are usually willing and able to pay higher prices which often exceed the appaised market value.

In these cases, although the petition is denied originally, if the corporation cannot afford to purchase the property, the petition is reconsidered and usually approved. This difference in prices has probably increased as property values have risen more rapidly outside of the province, and as a result appears to have contributed to the drop in denied petitions, particularly in 1975 (table 15.2). Although more recent data were not available, no properties have been acquired by L.D.C. as a result of cabinet denial since 1978.[15]

The number of properties purchased has dropped over the decade, with 1979–80 levels being about half of the 1970–71 levels (table 15.3). This decline is attributable primarily to three factors. First, during the first part of the decade, the land market was very active, with many properties for sale. During the latter part of the decade the market stabilized, creating less absolute demand for corporation purchase. Corporation purchase as a proportion of the market may not have declined, but no data were available to test this possibility.

TABLE 15.3. LAND DEVELOPMENT CORPORATION PURCHASES,
1970–1980

Fiscal Year	Total No. of Acres	Average Acres per Property	Total Cost*	Average Cost per Property
1970–71	16,854	130	$ 887,861	$ 7,063
1971–72	23,448	113	1,507,776	7,368
1972–73	21,194	88	1,681,473	7,327
1973–74	14,687	81	1,374,445	7,722
1974–75	12,760	83	2,354,406	15,447
1975–76	15,230	77	2,574,565	12,947
1976–77	12,023	79	2,223,843	14,535
1977–78	10,083	82	2,323,193	19,529
1978–79	7,239	82	2,172,970	24,693
1979–80	5,727	87	1,694,503	25,674

Source: Compiled from Land Development Corporation
annual reports
*Excluding building improvements

Rising land prices were a second factor in the decline. Although table 15.3 indicates that the cost of land rose drastically over the decade, this was not unique to P.E.I. In Canada, the per-acre value of farmland increased 160.3 percent between 1971 and 1976 (Lands Directorate, 1979b). Farmland-value increases greatly exceeded the inflation rate during the entire period from 1961 to 1976. It is not surprising that this trend continued throughout the seventies and resulted in fewer land sales/purchases.

The third factor accounting for the decline in purchases is related to the corporation's function as purchasing agent for other provincial departments. As mentioned previously, there was very little public land in P.E.I. prior to the establishment of the Land Development Corporation. As the corporation provided the mechanism, and as the federally assisted Comprehensive Development Plan provided 90 percent of the cost, many provincial departments requested land. Consequently, many of L.D.C.'s earlier purchases were for other departments. As those departments built up their land-holdings to the desired levels, demand for more provincial land naturally fell.

Besides acquiring land for provincial purposes, L.D.C. also acquires property for national parkland. Unlike other Canadian provinces, P.E.I. had no provision for crown land in its original land dispersal. In 1932, a national park was established at Cavendish, though it proved to be much too small for current demand. As a result, Parks Canada entered into an agreement in 1973 which enabled the Land Development Corporation to act as a land purchasing agent of the province for Parks Canada. Some land had been acquired previously as national parkland, but the negotiation period between landowners and Parks Canada was much too long, and potential parkland was being sold elsewhere.

By March 1980, 1,859 acres had been purchased for Parks Canada. However, no land was purchased during 1980, as Parks Canada and P.E.I. began debating the mineral rights to parkland. The federal government wants the mineral rights to all Parks Canada land, but P.E.I. wants to retain such rights. This is an issue being debated in many provinces. Until this issue is decided, P.E.I. is not purchasing land for national parks.

L.D.C.'s LAND DISPERSAL PROGRAMS

In fulfilling the corporation's role of making land available to farmers and enabling consolidation of farms, L.D.C. sells or leases suitable agricultural land.[16] Only land with genuine agricultural capability is released to the farm sector. Persons eligible to acquire these lands are farmers wishing to expand their operations, or qualified younger persons who wish to enter farming. These people are evaluated according to their need, their training and experience in agriculture, the proposed use of the land, and the location of the land relative both to other land owned by the applicant and to other resources.

Although the small family farm and the new farmer receive highest priority, producer cooperatives and farm corporations are also considered. In all cases, the gross assets of the farm operation must be less than $300,000; this level is adjusted every year to reflect inflation rates. For a cooperative or corporation to be accepted, it must be involved primarily in production of agricultural products and have the major portion of its assets invested in agriculture. Also, it should not have sufficient capital at its disposal to be eligible for other sources of credit. In 1980–81, only five family farm corporations leased L.D.C. lands, and no cooperative or nonfamily corporations applied.

Land sales can be by cash arrangements, mortgage, or agreement of sale. The latter two methods are offered to a maximum of thirty years. If the land is sold by the corporation within the year that it was purchased, farmers pay the cost price; if land is held beyond that year, the price is adjusted to reflect market value. In cases where land has been held for more than three years, financial assistance for agricultural improvements is provided to the farmer who acquires it.

The most common method of acquiring corporation land is the five-year-renewal lease with an option to purchase. If a lessee decides to purchase the property under lease, he pays the value of the property when the lease was first signed five years earlier. It is beneficial for a farmer to lease the property before buying it since the rent payments are less than mortgage payments would be. The rent charged is the cost of the money used by L.D.C. to purchase the land; this interest rate is usually below the market rate. Short-term leases of one to three years are also available. Properties available under short-term leases are those which are awaiting sale and those which L.D.C. has purchased for another department's future needs. These short-term leases enable a farmer to supplement his holdings and at the same time keep L.D.C. land in production. Many of these short-term leases are used for pasture. In all cases, L.D.C. makes specific demands concerning cropping and proper soil conservation. For example, when lands are leased to potato farmers, the farmer is required to grow another crop specified by the corporation, not potatoes, in the last year of the lease. In longer-term leases, "mining" of the land (i.e., exhausting the land's productivity by means of intensive use) is not a problem, since most farmers buy the land at the termination of the lease.

In 1980, there were 337 leases in effect, covering slightly more than 16,000 acres.[17] Table 15.4 indicates the number of lease agreements signed each year. The performance of leases has been fairly stable. While the number of sales varies more from year to year, the largest percentage of land released has either been sold or leased to farmers. This is consistent with the primary aim of making good agricultural land available to farmers at fair market value.

For the first five years of L.D.C.'s operation, leases exceeded sales. In 1976–77, leases and sales were almost equal in numbers. Since 1977–78, sales have slightly exceeded leases. This trend may be a result of farmers taking advantage of the "five-year lease with option to purchase" plan. As

TABLE 15.4. LAND DEVELOPMENT CORPORATION
LAND DISPERSALS

Fiscal Year	Leases		Sales	
	Properties	Acres	Properties	Acres
1971–72	24	2,586	15	1,357
1972–73	65	4,637	22	2,181
1973–74	111	8,946	96	5,480
1974–75	110	7,742	70	4,235
1975–76	122	6,800	57	4,049
1976–77	112	6,052	105	6,042
1977–78	68	3,290	93	3,508
1978–79	100	5,158	128	8,622
1979–80	99	5,121	102	4,837

Source: Compiled from Land Development Corporation
annual reports

their five-year leases expire, they are buying the land they had been leasing.

Besides acquiring land for its own programs, L.D.C. also acquires land for other departments. This land must then be dispersed, and L.D.C. does this through its Land Leakage Program. "Leaking" land to other departments means that the management rights of the land become vested in the appropriate provincial department or the Community Pasture Program, but ownership remains with L.D.C. The corporation is the only provincial entity other than Public Works legally able to own lands.

By 31 March 1980, L.D.C. had transferred 46,688 acres to Forestry, 6,580 acres to Tourism, 8,334 acres to Fish and Wildlife, and 7,241 acres to the Community Pastures Program. These lands include properties that have been specifically requested by individual departments as well as portions of properties the L.D.C. has acquired which are unsuitable for agricultural purposes. The number of acres "leaked" each year is shown in table 15.5. As noted previously, demand for land by provincial departments has declined dramatically in recent years, resulting in lower "leakage" rates. These acreages are scattered over the province, rarely in a pattern. For example, about half of the Forestry lands are located in twelve general areas that are semicontiguous; the remaining acreage is scattered in small parcels. Much of the Forestry land has been acquired as a result of subdivided parcels; if a 100-acre parcel had 60 acres cleared and 40 acres wooded, a farmer might apply to purchase the cleared land, and Forestry would buy the woodlands. This has resulted in a scattering of parcels.

COMMUNITY PASTURE PROGRAM

The Community Pasture Program directly benefits the agricultural community through the consolidation and improvement of underutilized and idle land. Community pastures were first established in the 1960s under the federal Agricultural and Rural Development Act (A.R.D.A.) Program. At that time they were administered and managed by cooperatives. In the early 1970s, the provincial government requested that the Land Development Corporation take an active role in creating, developing, and managing the community pastures, and in 1972 L.D.C. assumed responsibility for the program's administration and management.

Users of community pasture must be bona fide farmers and are selected on the basis of proximity, need, and previous use. The selection process is carried out by a Patrons' Committee consisting of elected local users. The Patrons' Committee is also responsible for animal loss claims, the breed of bulls used, and presentation to the L.D.C. of recommendations on policy and operational functions.

Farmers with operations too large for them to be eligible for the land-purchase assistance program may still be eligible to use community pas-

TABLE 15.5. LAND DEVELOPMENT CORPORATION
LEAKAGE PROGRAM ACTIVITIES

Fiscal Year	Land Leaked to Other Departments	
	Properties	Acres
1971–72	125	10,418
1972–73	156	10,769
1973–74	116	8,145
1974–75	—	11,531
1975–76	—	9,314
1976–77	—	8,904
1977–78	—	4,686
1978–79	—	2,975
1979–80	—	2,791

Source: Compiled from Land Development
Corporation annual reports

ture. This can occur when the farmer is close to the community pasture, and when smaller farmers are either too far away or not in need of pasture. For all farmers using the pasture, there are strict requirements concerning herd health, dehorning, castration, and identification. Regulations are monitored by pasture managers, usually local residents with a good knowledge of livestock management, who are hired on a seasonal basis.

The operation costs, including the wages of a manager and part-time help, are covered by the grazing rates. In 1979–80, the cost to farmers was 18¢ per head per day. Community pasture lands have risen from 2,242 acres with 400 head of cattle in 1973, to 7,241 acres and 2,382 head of cattle in 1980 (table 15.6). The average daily weight gain in the herds appears to have stabilized at about 1.67 lbs/day.

The Land Development Corporation maintains that the current acreage in community pasture is sufficient. Of the 7,241 acres, approximately 4,000 acres have been cleared. If more cleared acreage is required, it would be possible to clear and seed some of the land already owned by L.D.C. There are five community pastures and, as with forest lands, these are scattered throughout the province.

LAND INVENTORY PROGRAM AND
SOCIAL HOUSING PROGRAM

One of the ways in which the Land Development Corporation is to aid the agricultural sector is by providing a stable market for land in P.E.I. In years when there is a low demand for land, as was the case in the corporation's early years of development, there is not necessarily a low supply. As a result, more land is purchased than released. This system is of benefit to the farmer, who, if he or she wishes to sell land, need not wait for the market to improve to be assured of a good price. Such land is then held in inventory until such time as the market improves and farmers are better able to expand their operations. In the early years, this inventory amounted to more than 36,000 acres. Recently L.D.C. has been able to keep its land inventory at less than 10,000 acres. This is desirable due to the high costs associated with holding the land.

L.D.C. carries out essential maintenance on inventory properties, including upkeep of fences, removal of weeds, erosion control, fire insurance, and winterizing of buildings. As noted previously, if the land is in inventory for three or more years, financial assistance may be provided to the lessee for land or building improvements.

Clearly, many of the properties held in inventory contain unoccupied houses. During 1972 and 1973, L.D.C. entered into agreements with the provincial housing authority and a volunteer housing association. Houses which were structurally sound and met federal standards were offered to the Provincial Housing Authority, while those that did not meet federal standards but did adequately supply safe shelter were offered to volunteer groups. These housing groups lease these houses for a nominal sum and

TABLE 15.6. COMMUNITY PASTURE PROGRAM

Fiscal Year	Number of Acres	Number of Farmers	Number of Cattle	Average Weight Gain/Day (lbs.)
1972–73	2,242	—	400	—
1973–74	2,242	25	600	1.5
1974–75	4,026	60	950	1.9
1975–76	4,026	59	1,215	1.78
1976–77	5,630	68	1,711	1.9
1977–78	6,357	98	1,853	1.67
1978–79	7,241	137	2,275	1.68
1979–80	7,241	160	2,382	1.67

Source: Compiled from Land Development Corporation annual reports

are responsible for their regular care and maintenance. The housing groups make these houses available to low-income rural families. Houses that do not meet federal standards are improved by volunteer associations.

This program allows a further public service, while at the same time the corporation is released from maintenance of these buildings. At one point L.D.C. had about thirty such houses, but many of these houses deteriorated substantially and had to be demolished. As a result, only seven or eight are still being used.

SUMMARY OF L.D.C. PROGRAMS

The Land Development Corporation has developed a number of programs in order to fulfill its objectives. The farm sector has benefited directly and indirectly from at least four of the programs. The Land Acquisition Program enables retiring farmers and those with marginal units to sell their land when they wish, without being subject to the vagaries of the market. Small portions of land of little value to the farmer may also be sold and the capital used to improve the productivity of the remaining land. The Land Inventory Program is also important here, as it is the corporation's ability to hold inventory properties that permits land sales even during low demand periods.

Farmers are also able to lease or buy land of good agricultural capability through the Land Dispersal Program. Land that is not suited to agriculture is leaked to other programs or provincial departments. The

Community Pasture Program enables marginally productive land to be used and also permits many of the patrons to diversify production and to make more complete use of their own land resources.

The dispersal program also assists the agricultural sector by promoting farm consolidation and scale increases. The consolidation of farm units is a slow process, but as preference is continually given to farmers who live closest to available fields, benefits will accrue. The leasing policy allows farmers to increase their scale of operation with minimal capital outlay.

Thus the Land Development Corporation allows for more effective use of land. Land is leaked to the department which will use the land in a manner more closely related to its inherent natural capabilities. Management and use of land resources are much more rational due to the corporation's activities.[18]

CONCLUSION

Historical proprietorship problems, the lack of a public land base, and the importance of the family farm have sharpened the edge of land issues in Prince Edward Island. Land reform in P.E.I. may be divided into two distinct periods: an early era wherein insurgency over absenteeism led to the redistribution of lands, and a more contemporary era whose centerpiece has been a legalistic, comprehensive land-use planning process. The modern themes have again come to focus on absenteeism and foreign ownership, together with corporate concentration, land speculation, and land-use control. So ubiquitous are these issues as public concerns that they are tacitly accepted as constituting elements of the "social contract" which all political parties support. This has provided the rationale for the institutionalization of the land reforms in a variety of recent laws.

P.E.I.'s strategy is bifurcated. First, there exists a Land Use Commission which administers a legal system that successfully deters land purchases by nonresidents. Second, a Land Development Corporation has been created which conducts technical studies and monitors use and tenure characteristics (which are fundamental to modern land reform); operates an acquisition program to help rationalize family farms; creates a public land base (community pastures, forests, and recreational sites and parks); and generally "organizes" the land economy throughout the province given its significant role and substantial resources. When combined, these programs create an organic land reform which is mutually supportive and which fulfills many objectives islanders believe are appropriate.

The question invariably arises as to the transferability of the P.E.I. model elsewhere. As noted previously, P.E.I.'s innovative amendments to its Real Property Act, which restricts nonresident landownership, were supported by all other provinces in Canada. It has become the precedent upon which all similar controls throughout the country now operate. The land registration and information system, which monitors the land market, is becoming a component of many provincial land-use systems. Public land banking has long been a feature of provincial policy and now operates in different forms on both the federal and provincial levels. Likewise, approaches to the rationalization of farm units and efforts to retain farmlands also exist across Canada. Though P.E.I.'s approaches did not pioneer in some of these areas, they do provide a link in an emerging national system which is characterized by regionally integrated laws and programs.

In any discussion of the relevance of P.E.I.'s approach to conditions in the United States, it becomes abundantly clear at the very outset that the systems operative in Canada and the United States, legal and otherwise, are so markedly different that comparison is difficult. Moreover, P.E.I.'s scale — 110,000 inhabitants and 1.4 million acres — is also unique. Still, valuable lessons may be drawn and derived which should be pursued elsewhere.

First, any program to control foreign or absentee ownerships should not outlaw such practices. Rather, jurisdictions should regulate this activity, assuming that such ownerships constitute a problem in the first place. Second, experience in P.E.I. strongly supports the notion that information reform is vital to modern land reform. Nothing short of a cadastral revolution may be required in some states. The promulgation of the Agricultural Foreign Investment Disclosure Act (1978)[19] was an important first step toward such an end, at least from the federal perspective, and many state or local counterparts could be imagined. Third, the issue of the concentration of ownership, especially important in terms of energy and agricultural lands, should be a matter of public discussion and reform. Corporate ownership of land resources can be made subject to public scrutiny, and methods for regulation can be fashioned. If P.E.I.'s history demonstrates anything, it is that land tenure is as important an issue as is land use and that there is nothing sacrosanct about ownership and information about it. Such information should be public and easily acccessible.

Fourth, farmland policy in the province has focused not only on the need to retain agricultural land, but also on the need to enhance the economic viability of family farms and to ease new farmer entry. The vast majority of jurisdictions in the United States still maintain the official mythology that these concerns can be addressed independently of one another (e.g., rural housing, new farmer assistance programs, and farm structure research). Fifth, the public land base of the province has been kept at extremely modest levels. In some cases, notably forest lands, the province is seeking to further divest itself of some of its holdings. In a place where landownership is widely dispersed — and this clearly constitutes a social objective with broad endorsement — large governmental ownerships and overcentralization may be as dangerous as vertical integration, corporate ownerships, or substantial absentee control.

Sixth, and perhaps most important, is the fact that over the generations a unique land ethic has evolved in the province. Certainly the early insurgency reflected this, and the more contemporary elements of land policy further amplify the importance of land to Prince Edward Islanders. In accepting the province's premiership, Conservative James Lee recently echoed this when he vowed that islanders will "never again be tenants in our own native province." Moreover, as noted in the press, Lee stated that

> he won't allow K. C. Irving or any other large corporate interest to control the Island's economy by controlling P.E.I.'s land — a clear indication that the Irving processing company, Cavendish Farms, won't be allowed to obtain 6,000 acres of farmland it has made application to purchase. *Mr. Lee's comments on land use drew the largest applause of the evening.* (Harris, 9 November 1981, p. 10, emphasis added)

That land still matters as much as it does in P.E.I. is a reflection on the maturation of this ethic and its centrality at nearly all levels of society. In a rural economy, land is understood to be the means of production, to use a classical term of reference. Without achieving such a consensus on the importance of land use and tenure, which transcends the generations, all else may be meaningless. In this sense, land policy in Prince Edward Island is an awfully "big deal" in a small place.

NOTES

1. The Lieutenant-Governor-in-Council is the personal representative of the Queen in the province. He/she is appointed by the Governor-General of Canada, and is the head of the executive branch of the government. He/she is advised by members of the cabinet, and assents to all measures or bills passed by the legislature before they become law.

2. This discussion of the history of the land issue in P.E.I. draws on the research of Bolger (1973), Clark (1959), MacKinnon (1951), and Sharpe (1976).

3. The P.E.I. government borrowed a total of $782,402 from the Dominion, but never repaid the loan. Instead, the Dominion reduced the subsidy in lieu of public lands (Bolger, 1973).

4. Numerous public access routes to beaches exist at road endings, but most of these are not known by the general public. Furthermore, many of these access routes are through farmers' properties and do not appear to be public property. As a result, even though the access points exist, public awareness of them is very poor (Griswold, Dept. of Agriculture and Forestry planner, personal communication, 24 June 1981).

5. It has been estimated that in P.E.I. a farmer today requires between 250 and 300 acres in order to remain competitive with mixed operations of livestock and potatoes (Bradley and Beaulieu, 1973, p. 11).

6. In British common law, and consequently as applied in the colonies, aliens could "take" land, but not "hold" it. This meant that the title was good against everyone except the crown. The crown could forfeit the land at any time. Furthermore, an alien could not even "take" land through inheritance. For a complete discussion of the alien landowner in common law, see Spencer (1973).

7. Whereas there was no mechanism for enforcing the 1964 amendment to the Real Property Act, another central piece of legislation, the Registry Act, was also amended in 1972 to check for compliance. Now deeds of properties conveyed to nonresidents that exceed the above-mentioned limits would be registered only if a copy of the order granting the approval of the Lieutenant-Governor-in-Council was provided. Also, under the provisions of the Frustrated Contracts Act, all contracts or agreements entered into between a vendor and a nonresident purchaser are null and void if the petition is denied.

8. The changes in the Citizenship Act came about as a result of the P.E.I. amendments to the Real Property Act. This is discussed further in the next section.

9. To allow for enforcement of this amendment, the Companies Act was amended in 1980 as well. It now requires that membership shares in all companies be disclosed.

10. This section draws on the work of Young (1975) and Jones (1976).

11. The court realized that there was some ambiguity in the Canadian Citizenship Act, and as a result it was amended in 1975–76 to uphold the right of provinces to control ownership of real property by aliens. The federal government did, however, reserve the right to reconsider the matter and to enact further legislation in the future if it deems such action appropriate.

12. See Mage and Lapping (1982), pp. 364–89.

13. The Land Use Commission was created by An Act to Establish the Land Use Commission, 23 Eliz II (1974) Cap 22. Nonresident applications must include a legal description of the property, an air photo showing its location, information on the vendors and their residency, the purchaser's citizenship and residency, acreage of the property and other parcels owned, shore frontage, sale price, nature of transaction, and intended use.

14. There is no monitor to check to see if the price quoted on the petition is the actual price paid to the owner. Clearly, this allows for possible misuse of the system, although there does not appear to be any evidence of misuse occurring.

15. W. Stanhope Moore, general manager, Land Development Corporation, personal communication, June 1981.

16. Once a property is sold, the L.D.C. no longer retains files on that property.

17. Data providing a breakdown of long- and short-term leases were not available.

18. The corporation helps other sectors. Public land acquisition has allowed increases in forestry, wildlife, and tourism lands. In addition, because of the agreement with Parks Canada, the island now has substantial parklands.

19. Agricultural Foreign Investment Disclosure Act, Pub. Law No. 95–460, 92 Stat 1263 (1979).

REFERENCES

Beaulieu, A. 1970. *Land Adjustment Problems in Prince Edward Island.* Geographical Paper No. 45. Ottawa: Policy Research and Coordination Branch, Department of Energy, Mines and Resources.

Bolger, Francis W. P. 1973. *Canada's Smallest Province.* Toronto: John Deyell Co.

Bradley, L. F., and Beaulieu, A. 1973. *Social and Geographical Aspects of Agricultural Land Use in Prince Edward Island.* Geographical Paper No. 54. Ottawa: Policy Research and Coordination Branch, Department of Mines and Resources.

Clark, A. H. 1959. *Three Centuries and the Island.* Toronto: University of Toronto Press.

Financial Post. 1972. "P.E.I. gets tough on land sales to outsiders." *Financial Post,* Toronto. (August 19): 13.

Harris, Michael. 1981. "P.E.I. Tories decide Health Minister will be Premier." *Toronto Globe and Mail* (November 9): 10.

Jones, David Phillip. 1976. "Comments: constitutional law-rights of Canadian citizens - aliens - non-residents - discrimination - role of Supreme Court of Canada - stare decisis." *The Canadian Bar Review* LIV: 381–91.

Lands Directorate, Environment Canada. 1978. *Non-Resident Land Ownership Legislation and Administration in Prince Edward Island.* Land Use in Canada Series No. 12. Ottawa: Environment Canada.

———. 1979a. *Prince Edward Island Land Development Corporation: Activities and Impact 1970–1977.* Land Use in Canada Series No. 16. Ottawa: Environment Canada.

———. 1979b. *The Changing Value of Canada's Farmland 1961–76.* Land Use in Canada Series No. 17. Ottawa: Environment Canada.

———. 1980. *The Land-Use Impacts of Recent Legislation in P.E.I.: An Analysis of the Land Development Corporation and Non-Resident Ownership.* Land Use in Canada Series No. 18. Ottawa: Environment Canada.

MacKinnon, Frank. 1951. *The Government of Prince Edward Island.* Toronto: University of Toronto Press.

————. 1978. "Prince Edward Island: big engine, little body." In *Canadian Provincial Politics*. Edited by Martin Robin. Englewoodd Cliffs, NJ: Prentice-Hall. Pp. 222–47.

Mage, J. A., and Lapping, M. B. 1982. "Legislation related to absentee foreign landowner-ship in Canada." *Agricultural Law Journal* 4 (Fall): 364–89.

Michael, Paul. 1974. "The non-resident problem on Prince Edward Island." *Community Planning Review* 24(ii): 3–6.

P.E.I. 1973. *Report of the Royal Commission on Land Ownership and Land Use.* Charlottetown: Queen's Printer.

P.E.I. Land Use Commission. 1980. *Report to Executive Council on Non-Resident and Corporate Land Ownership.* Mimeo.

Raymond, Charles W., and Rayburn, S. A. 1963. "Land abandonment in P.E.I." *Geograph-ical Bulletin* 19: 78–86.

Spencer, John. 1973. "The alien landowner in Canada." *The Canadian Bar Review* 51(3): 389–418.

Young, David. 1975. "Jurisdiction over aliens: does Morgan clarify the law?" *Osgoode Hall Law Journal* 13(2): 354–67.

PART SIX

Land Reform and Urban Communities

16

Condominium Conversions: A Reform in Need of Reform

DANIEL LAUBER

When creating the condominium form of ownership, state legislators across the country imagined they were instituting a major reform. Families that could not afford to buy a single-family house could now realize the American dream and own a home of their own. Buildings constructed as condominiums produced few adverse impacts. But when developers started to convert existing rental buildings, already in short supply, to higher-cost condominium ownership, the reform began to sour. "The first bill I got through the legislature was the condominium act, which we thought would be a boon for low- and moderate-income families," recalls Michael Dukakis, former governor of Massachusetts. "Now we have a conversion problem."[1]

By the middle 1970s demographic factors, the shortage of affordable rental and ownership housing, and the peculiar psychology of inflation had created the panic situation newspapers called condomania. And with condomania came gentrification, displacement, worsening shortages of rental housing, housing-cost inflation of about $18 billion,[2] overcapitalized housing, increased need for subsidized housing, increased rents in the remaining rentals, and a general tightening of the market of low-, moderate-, and even middle-income housing. By the end of 1979, with 366,000 apartments converted to condominiums and another 1.1 million expected to be converted before 1986 (U.S. Department of Housing and Urban Development, 1980), the reform itself was badly in need of reform.

ORIGINS

The conversion of a rental apartment building to condominium ownership is much like the subdivision of land into separate parcels. But instead of

---

dividing land, a conversion divides airspace, and instead of one deed or title for the apartment building, conversion generates a separate one for each unit within the building. Condominium buyers purchase their unit and a proportion of common elements such as the hallways, roof, heating and electrical systems, and basement. Each owner is a member of the condominium association that governs the common elements, prepares a budget, and levies a monthly assessment of each unit owner to cover maintenance and insurance of the common elements and keep a reserve fund for repairs.

Nobody is absolutely certain how the condominium form of ownership began in the United States. A delegation from Puerto Rico, which had enacted laws permitting condominium ownership in 1951 and 1958, successfully urged Congress to enact Section 234 of the National Housing Act of 1961, which extended Federal Housing Administration (FHA) mortgage benefits to condominiums. The FHA proceeded to draft and publish a model Horizontal Property Act as a guide for state legislatures. By 1968, in response to pressure from the real estate industry, forty-nine states had enacted legislation to create the condominium form of property ownership. Such acts were needed because, under the common law, property owned in fee simple consists of not only your home, but also the land under it to the center of the earth, and the airspace above it. Consequently, a multiple-story building could not be a condominium unless state legislatures enacted legislation to create this different form of ownership.

But in its 1973 book, *How to Convert Apartments to Condominiums,* the California Association of Realtors reports that the first condo-like project was a nine-unit building turned into individual ownership units by Clayton Thompson in 1955 as part of an "own your own" campaign that started slow and eventually petered out. Jan van Weesup, associate professor of urban geography at the Free University of Amsterdam, who has been researching the condominium phenomenon in the United States for three years, reports that the idea for condominium conversion was imported to California by a developer who learned about condominiums while vacationing in Mexico City. *California Builder* ran a series of articles on condominiums in the early 1960s, and someone from New Jersey who sat in on the meetings which generated the articles took the idea back to the east coast. At the same time, the condominium idea independently reached Florida via Puerto Rico.[3]

Whatever the origins of the condominium, it did not come about due to overwhelming public demand for it. Condominium laws were not the product of reform-minded legislators in the early 1960s. Instead, it was the prime beneficiaries of conversion — the middlemen profiteers — who provided the impetus for the condominium acts in many states.

THE ILLINOIS EXPERIENCE

In Illinois, for instance, "Chicago Title and Trust Company was among the first to promote condominium conversions," reports Chicago real estate attorney Julius Yacker. "A rental project may change hands every ten or twelve years and there's only one title for the building to be insured. However, if you convert the building to condominiums, the units change hands more frequently. As condos there are now perhaps hundreds of little title insurance policies to be issued, one for each unit, where there was only one prior to conversion. So at least from the business point of view, this has been an exceptionally good thing for the title company. They did a great deal of promotion on it" (Lauber, 1979).

One of the most important promotional pieces Chicago Title and Trust produced was *Condominium: The New Look in Co-ops: Practical and Legal Problems* (Ramsey, 1961). This 29-page book detailed the condominium model in Puerto Rico and explained the relevant provisions of the National Housing Act of 1961. Charles Ramsey, the book's author and now retired in Arizona, sums up the company's interest in condominiums: "They just thought it was a good way to make money. The whole idea was that condominiums would create more business for the title company. There was one policy on a lot on Sheridan Road. They tore down the building there and put up a condominium with 550 units, which meant 549 more titles for us to insure. And there were a lot of cooperatives converted to condominiums for the same reason, too."[4]

Chicago Title and Trust had a near-monopoly — 90 percent of the title business in Chicago's Cook County. Even before the Illinois General Assembly passed the Condominium Property Act in 1963, Chicago Title and Trust was known to be ready to insure titles on condos. At the same time, the Chicago Real Estate Board began to hold seminars on converting existing rentals to condominium ownership. Chicago realtors and developers, educated at these seminars, took a stab at the condo business in 1964 and 1965. But they found few takers.

A NATIONAL VIEW

Chicago's experience was typical of most real estate markets. The 1970 Census of Housing found only 60,000 first-home condominiums (there were another 20,000 second-home units), nearly all new. Condominiums amounted to less than 0.1 percent of the nation's total housing stock. But over 92 percent of all condominiums were in cities, mostly in the South and West, usually in retirement communities. In the Fort Lauderdale/Hollywood area, they constituted 9 percent of the total housing stock (not just multifamily buildings). They accounted for 6.9 percent in West Palm Beach, Florida; 3 percent in Miami; 4.7 percent in Anaheim/Santa Ana/Garden Grove, California; and 2.9 percent in Honolulu. Outside the South and West, condominiums (and market-rate cooperatives, for which financing is readily available only in New York State) were significant only in New York City, where they accounted for 3 percent of the total housing stock, and in Bridgeport, Connecticut, where they constituted 2.5 percent (U.S. Department of Housing and Urban Development, 1980:IV–7). In these early years prices were relatively cheap. Fifteen percent of the condominiums were priced below $20,000; 48 percent were in the $20,000 to $35,000 price range.

Between 1970 and 1975, over one million units were built, still mostly in the South and West. The recession of 1973–74 slowed down all new construction, and condominium production fell from 218,000 units in 1974 to 40,000 in 1975. The high production figures of the early 1970s have not been matched since. Developers turned to the quicker, less risky, more profitable conversion of existing rentals to condominiums. Between 1970 and 1975, only 85,000 rental units were converted to condominiums. But in 1976, 20,000 conversions took place; in 1977, 43,000; in 1978, nearly 75,000; and in 1979, over 145,000. Officials at the U.S. Department of Housing and Urban Development predicted that another 1.1 million units would be converted before 1986 and that half the population will live in condominiums by 1990 (U.S.Department of Housing and Urban Development, 1980:IV–5). These estimates, however, look excessive.

Seventy-six percent of all conversions have occurred in the 37 largest metropolitan areas. The twelve most active cities accounted for 59 percent of all conversions. These included Miami, Tampa, Los Angeles, Chicago, Boston, Denver, Minneapolis, New York, San Francisco, the District of Columbia, and Seattle. In some cities virtually every desirable building has been converted. By 1980 less than five high-rise rental buildings remained in Chicago, the nation's condo conversion capital. Nationally, 49 percent of all conversions have been in suburban communities, seriously depleting their already short supplies of affordable rental housing (U.S. Department of Housing and Urban Development, 1980:IV–8). Today developers have turned their attention to smaller cities such as Mobile, Alabama.

Converted units account for 1.3 percent of the country's rental stock. But national figures tend to mask the local significance of conversions. Evanston and Oak Park, Illinois, have both seen over 15 percent of their rentals converted to condominiums (Fremming and Howery, 1978; Community Relations Department, 1979). More than 10 percent of Chicago's rentals have been converted. Over 12 percent of the District of Columbia's rental stock has gone condo, while over 20 percent of the rentals in some District suburbs have been converted, as has also happened in Boulder, Colorado. Two Connecticut municipalities had 36 and 29 percent of their rental stock, respectively, converted before 1979. Walnut Creek, California, has seen the conversion of more than 18 percent of its rentals, mostly in 1979 (U.S. Department of Housing and Urban Development, 1980:IV–9–10).

But as recently as 1975, condominiums were not as lucrative as the real estate industry had anticipated. Conversion magnate Harold Miller, who later put together the most expensive condominium conversion in the country — the $110 million purchase of the 2,650-unit Sandburg Village in Chicago — actually lost money on his first conversion.[5] During the 1973–74 recession, condo resale prices actually fell in Chicago. Prospects were so bleak, the public so disinterested, that one ever-tasteful developer tried to attract attention by advertising his units as "condom-iniums." What happened between 1974 and 1980?

FROM CONDOM-INIUMS TO CONDO-MANIA

A collision between two immovable forces, coupled with the peculiar psychology of inflation, produced the condomania the real estate industry loves and tenants hate. By the late 1970s, a rapidly accelerating rate of household formation collided head-on with an acute shortage of affordable ownership and rental housing.

While the population grew at an annual rate of just 1 percent in the last decade, the number of new households grew at an annual rate of 2 to 3 percent. By 1980 there were 80.4 million households in America, an increase of 27 percent over 1970. It is the number of households that determines the need for housing, not the size of the population.

The baby boom had come of age. Those four million-plus persons born each year between 1945 and 1964 started to leave the nest, form their own households, and reach home-buying age. But rather than get married right away, they stayed single longer than previous generations. Between 1973 and 1978 the median age for first marriages rose from 23.2 to 24.2 for men, and 21.0 to 21.8 for women. More stayed single. In 1970, 19 percent of the men and 14 percent of American women were single; by 1980 those figures had risen to 23 and 17 percent, respectively. The proportion of women never married was 48 percent in 1978 for the 20- to 24-year-old bracket and 18 percent for the 25- to 29-year bracket.

Adding to the number of single-person households was the rising divorce rate. In 1970, 3.5 out of every 100 Americans were divorced; by 1980 that figure had risen to 5.3 percent. In addition, greater longevity increased the number of single-person households. By the end of the decade, women were outliving their mates by an average of about eight years. Widows are more likely than widowers to maintain a separate housing unit. Thus there was unprecedented growth in single-person households. To meet their housing needs, the nation would have to produce 2.5 million new housing units annually, including 300,000 mobile homes, just to keep supply and demand roughly in balance (Schechter, 1980).

This is precisely what America's builders have failed to do. New housing starts dropped from 2.02 million in 1978 to 1.74 million in 1979. The housing shortage is indicated by disastrously low rental vacancy rates. Housing experts believe that a rental vacancy rate of 5 to 8 percent allows for reasonable mobility within a community. When the rate falls below 5 percent, low- and moderate-income households have a difficult time finding replacement housing. Tenants must pay higher rents than they can afford, accept housing below previous standards, or move to another community with a higher vacancy rate. Below 3 percent, all households encounter these difficulties (U.S. Department of Housing and Urban

Development, 1975). Nationally, the rental vacancy rate fell to less than 5 percent in 1979, "the nation's lowest recorded rental housing vacancy rate" according to a report by the General Accounting Office (General Accounting Office, 1979).

But, again, national figures mask worse local situations. The rental vacancy rate in Chicago was 4.8 percent in the mid-1970s, and less than 2 percent in the areas in which condo conversion took off. Suburban Evanston's rental vacancy rate has hovered around 0.5 percent for years. Oak Park's was last estimated to be 0.9 percent (Federal Home Loan Bank of Chicago, 1982). The rental vacancy rate in the District of Columbia was just 1.8 percent in the mid-1970s. San Francisco's planning department estimates a rental vacancy rate of less than 2 percent. Denver's stood at 3.6 percent in 1979 (U.S. Department of Housing and Urban Development, 1980).

There was no way to meet the enormous demand for multiple-family rental housing. The proportion of newly constructed, unfurnished and furnished apartments that were rented within three months of completion rose to 86 percent by the first quarter of 1979. Vacancy data for the last quarter of 1979 revealed that 37 percent of all vacant units available for rent had been vacant for less than one month, and only 27 percent for more than four months (General Accounting Office, 1979).

Meanwhile rents continued to rise faster than incomes. Median rents rose an average of 9.6 percent annually between 1973 and 1979, while average renter income increased 5.6 percent annually. By 1977 over 30 percent of the nation's tenants paid more than 35 percent of their income for rent, and over 18 percent of tenants paid between 25 and 34 percent (Schechter, 1980). Many renter households are spending too much on housing: budgets developed by the Bureau of Labor Statistics suggest that a lower-income urban household of four should not spend more than 19 percent of its income for housing to allow for other necessities (Feins and Lane, 1981:62). These hardships were borne because, with exceedingly low vacancy rates, there really was no alternative. These households could not afford to buy a single-family house.

Doubling up increased. Between 1973 and 1979, the number of occupied units that contained nonrelatives and relatives other than the spouse or children of the household head increased from 6.2 million to 9.9 million. Another jump of 16 percent occurred between 1977 and 1979 (Schechter, 1980). Today housing experts anticipate even greater increases in doubling up (Galano, 1982). Newly built apartments are frequently built for roommates rather than single-person or family households.

It is not surprising that under these circumstances there would be a wave of conversions of rental housing to individual ownership. According to a 1979 report by Mid-America Appraisal & Research Corporation, "Historically, individual ownership of what might be termed multi-family residential structures accelerates in times of short housing supply. Unquestionably, this is a condition which exists in the country today, as housing vacancy rates have declined to their lowest levels since the end of World War II" (Mid-America Appraisal & Research Corp., 1979:2).

THE POST-SHELTER SOCIETY

It took still another ingredient to create condomania: the peculiar psychology of inflation spurred by federal tax policy. "A generation ago, it made economic sense to save up for a down payment on a home, borrow as little as possible, and expect to eventually pay off the mortgage," writes Rolf Goetze, formerly of the Boston Redevelopment Authority. "The pot of gold at the end of the 20-year mortgage term was the result of paying off the mortgage. The ethic involved getting free of debt" (Goetze, 1981).

But today the American ethic is debt. People are expected to borrow as much as possible to invest in what they hope will be rapidly appreciating real estate. Borrowing produces tax deductions. Small down payments maximize appreciation. Property appreciation beats inflation. The buyer of multiple properties with small down payments beats inflation more.

According to Kenneth Kidwell, chairman of the board and president of Eureka Federal Savings and Loan Association of San Francisco, "Since the 1974–75 recession the general public has been buying properties at an unprecedented pace in an effort to combat inflation or to become overnight millionaires. One of the consequences of over-demand is that, without reason, property values escalate at a rate that is inflationary in and by itself. Buyers believe that it doesn't make any difference what they pay for a piece of property, as the price escalation can't stop" (Kidwell, 1980).

For many small households, the condominium was the perfect vehicle for home ownership. They did not need the space a single-family house offered; they could also remain in popular residential areas while enjoying tax shelters. Households flocked to purchase condominiums before the price of condos rose beyond their reach as single-family houses had done. They had witnessed rapid increase in the price of single-family houses and could not help but hear how the first condo buyers enjoyed appreciation of as much as 20 percent in just a few weeks. As Professor van Weesup writes, "The rapid increase in housing prices drives people to buy now, even at unreasonable expense, because there is a widespread fear that the market will be completely out of reach within one or two years" (van Weesup, 1980). And as one condo buyer said, "In my city, the condominium craze is so bad that if you want to live in a decent area near your work, you've got to buy a condo. I hope the market keeps going up 30 percent a year, like it has the past few years. Because with the price I had to pay for the place we bought, I need inflation to make my purchase seem sensible" (Baber, 1979:204).

Thus housing is now an investment rather than just a shelter. "Ours is now a post-shelter society and this is perhaps a condition unique in its depth to our own time," write James W. Hughes and George Sternlieb of the Center for Urban Policy Research at Rutgers University. "Housing in

America is much more important as a form of investment, and of forced savings (and tax savings), and as a refuge from inflation, than as a refuge from the elements" (Sternlieb and Hughes, 1980:100).

WHO BUYS CONDOMINIUMS?

Industry spokesmen privately admit that 366,000 rentals annually could not have been converted to condominiums through 1979 without artificial demand by speculators and investors. The natural market for condominium ownership was insufficient. Twice as many apartments have been converted to condominiums as there was demand for them from households that wanted to own and live in a condominium. Purchasers of converted condominiums fall into three categories.

Natural Demand

These are the households that genuinely and voluntarily wish to live in and own a condominium. These buyers constitute the natural market for condominiums and are a "classic expression of demand, i.e., consumers with given preferences and resources freely entering the market to purchase" (Larvo, 1981). Of those who purchased a condominium, 91 percent were looking to buy some form of housing and for 87 percent a condominium was the form they desired (U.S. Department of Housing and Urban Development, 1980:Appendix I–III:23). Buying a condominium was an act of free will on their part.

The housing industry claims that conversions open the ownership market to households that cannot afford to buy single-family houses, but research shows that condominium purchasers generally are as affluent as those who buy a single-family house. The U.S. League of Savings Associations found that 1981 condominium purchasers were a wealthier group than all home buyers. Their monthly housing costs were as high as those for other home buyers (U.S. League of Savings Associations, 1982).

Reluctant Tenant Purchasers

There is a vast market of reluctant tenant purchasers who already live in the converted buildings; they have little choice but to buy. Their demand is quite different from the classic definition of demand. "It cannot be assumed that the demand of tenant buyers existed apart from their situation because many were offered purchasing incentives from developers, and because, in the absence of a purchase, they would most likely have had to find other housing" (Larvo, 1981). Some renter households are happy to buy, but others purchase at financial hardship to avoid an unwanted move. They buy primarily because they fear they cannot find affordable replacement housing in the same community, or if they do, it too will be converted — assumptions borne out by planning research. Elderly residents are often afraid to move for physical or health reasons. Long-term tenants do not want to move for emotional reasons. Many tenants simply feel hemmed in (U.S. Department of Housing and Urban Development, 1975; Beal, 1981; Adels, 1979; Palo Alto Planning Department, 1974). With record low rental vacancy rates, many tenants feel they must purchase or else move out of their neighborhood or community.

Planners for Palo Alto, California, found that 72 percent of the purchasing tenants fell into this category (Palo Alto Planning Department, 1974). Researchers in Chicago's Hyde Park neighborhood around the University of Chicago (rental vacancy rate: 0.25 percent) found that 70 percent of the tenants who bought did so most reluctantly; the figure was even higher for elderly tenants (Adels, 1979). A 1980 study by the U.S. Department of Housing and Urban Development found that half the purchasing tenants in its limited sample would have preferred to continue to rent (a finding not reported in any of HUD's many press releases on the study) (U.S. Department of Housing and Urban Development, 1980:Appendix I–III:23). In Philadelphia, 62 percent of buyers said they preferred to rent; 82 percent of elderly purchasers agreed (Garz et al., 1981:65, 89). To the real estate industry, these buyers represent "demand" for converted condominiums. To the makers of public policy, these buyers should instead represent artificial demand.

Every community that has experienced widespread conversions has a very low rental vacancy rate, usually below 3 percent (U.S. Department of Housing and Urban Development, 1980:V–15). The low rates induce tenants to purchase, since tenants know they will probably not find comparably priced housing in the same neighborhood that is safe from conversion (Garz et al., 1981; Beal, 1981). Without reluctant tenant purchasers, conversions could not flourish. The typical developer hopes to sell 35 percent of the units in any conversion to existing tenants so he can reduce marketing costs and start repaying his conversion loan. However, the studies cited above show that about 70 percent of the tenant purchasers are buying reluctantly. So if a developer reaches his 35 percent tenant sales goal, only 10.5 percent of the units are actually sold to willing tenants. If reluctant tenant purchasers did not exist, the market for a quarter of all converted condominiums would disappear.

Nonoccupant Investors

The third group of purchasers produce the most artificial demand imaginable, providing the money that creates condomania. Speculators and investors benefited in the early days of conversion, especially during periods of high inflation, by deducting high interest payments and paying the low tax rate on their capital gains when they sold their units. They also had the tax benefits of mortgage-interest, property-tax, and depreciation deductions, as well as the appreciation they realized at sales time (Larvo, 1981). "The natural demand was insufficient to keep the tremendous pace of conversions going," reports Richard Helms, attorney for many of Chicago's biggest converters. "In one building we had over 500 individual mortgage closings in five days. There just aren't enough owner-occupants around to sell that fast."[6]

Estimates of the number of nonoccupant purchases vary. Researchers at Harbridge House in Boston estimate that "probably a majority of converted units in Chicago were purchased by speculative investors" (Dinkelspiel et al., 1981:14). One Chicago developer estimates that nonoccupants own as many as 60 percent of the converted units there. Other Chicago sources claim that speculators own 30 to 50 percent.[7] A study by the government of Montgomery County, Maryland, outside the District of Columbia, found that nonoccupants owned 17 percent of all converted units (Task Force on Condominium Conversion, 1979). San Francisco's Planning Department reports that nonoccupants bought 59 percent of the converted units sold between 1 January 1979 and 31 March 1981 (Backer, 1981). The U.S. Department of Housing and Urban Development estimates that, nationally, nonoccupants own 37 percent of all converted units (U.S. Department of Housing and Urban Development, 1980:VI–11–12). On the average, these units are rented out for 175 percent of the preconversion rent (Palo Alto Planning Department, 1974; U.S. Department of Housing and Urban Development, 1975).

Nonoccupants tend to hold onto their units for eighteen to twenty-four months in a good market, according to Chicago investment broker Peter Arnold of U.S. Investors Resources, Inc.[8] Many investors follow a developer around the country, purchasing from one to ten units in each of his conversions, according to Helms.

Nonoccupants have created a false market for converted condominiums, which is now falling. "I think speculation has done a tremendous disservice to the American dream," says Chicago-based developer Alex Bruni. "It's artificially inflated the cost of condos as the time of conversion and today it's helping to depress prices by putting so many units on the resale market."[9] Since 1980, investors generally have been unable to charge rents high enough to cover ownership and operating costs. Hence they suffer a negative cash flow. Though many have made an annual profit after taking tax benefits into account, for others the negative cash flow became unbearable, and they rushed to unload their units even before mortgage interest rates skyrocketed. Investors who bought condos with personal loans whose interest rate floats daily a few points over the prime rate have suffered the most from high prime rates in the early 1980s.

The collapse of the condominium market in such heavily converted areas as Chicago, New York, the District of Columbia, and Philadelphia shows up in the longer average length of time needed to sell units. Once it had taken four to seven weeks to sell a unit; by 1981 it took four to seven months, according to Dun and Bradstreet (*Chicago Sun-Times,* 1981a). Resale prices declined. By May 1982, initial prices for Chicago condominiums had fallen 20 to 30 percent below the peak period of 1979 (*Chicago*

Sun-Times, 1982b). Growing numbers of conversions are failing (*Chicago Sun-Times,* 1981b; *Chicago Tribune,* 1982; *Washington Post,* 1982a, 1982b). Resale prices started falling even before interest rates rose high (*Chicago Sun-Times,* 1982a). Real estate office manager Barbara Novak of Chicago's Baird and Warner describes the sales history of an illustrative condo unit: "At Hemingway House a one-bedroom unit with a good view on the upper floors sold for $50,000 when converted in 1978. A year later it resold for $79,000. By 1981 you could not even get $79,000 for the unit. The cause is oversaturation of the marketplace."[10]

THE SOCIAL COST OF CONDOMINIUM CONVERSION

All told, conversions completed through 1979 have generated between $3.47 and $7.13 billion in costs to buyers, and tied up $15 to $18 billion in mortgage money, that would have been free for other uses had condominium conversion never existed. If, as HUD estimates, another 1.1 million units are converted through 1986, they will create another $19.5 billion in costs and tie up another $44 to $55 billion in mortgage funds by the end of the decade. As table 16.1, "Estimates of Earnings from Condominium

TABLE 16.1. ESTIMATES OF EARNINGS FROM CONDOMINIUM CONVERSION

Profession	Earnings from Initial Sale of Units Converted through 1979, and Resales, 1970–1981 (in millions of dollars)	Earnings on Initial Sales of Units Converted, 1980–1985, and Resales of These Units through 1990 (in millions of dollars)
Converters	$1,800 – 3,900	$9,000
Appraisers	$58 – 104	$135 – 270
Attorneys	$250 – 500	$906
Surveyors	$36	$110
Title insurers	$170 – 210	$458 – 530
Realtor commissions	$975 – 1,900	$7,080
Lenders – end loan origination fees only	$272 – 465	$1,830

Source: Daniel Lauber, original research

Note: Due to inadequate data, it is impossible to reliably estimate the earnings from conversions for engineers, landlords, apartment developers, promotion and marketing firms, media advertising, renovators, or accountants. Many real estate professionals estimate that conversions have allowed landlords to raise prices for their buildings 35 to 50 percent above what they would have sold for if they had remained rental.

Conversions," shows, developers, realtors, appraisers, attorneys, title insurers, surveyors, and lenders all have a substantial stake in condominium conversion.

The housing consumer is footing the bill. Eight years ago HUD found that the monthly carrying costs of owning a condominium — mortgage payment, property tax, and condominium association assessment — were, on the average, 30 to 35 percent greater than preconversion rents (U.S. Department of Housing and Urban Development, 1975). Using a very limited and questionably selected nonrandom sample, HUD's 1980 study reports an increase of 36 percent (U.S. Department of Housing and Urban Development, 1980:IX–27). But as tables 16.2, 16.3, and 16.4 show, vir-

TABLE 16.2. MONTHLY HOUSING COSTS AFTER CONVERSION
IN 33 CALIFORNIA PROJECTS

Percentage Increase in Housing Costs	Number of Projects	Percent of Total Sample
Less than 50 percent	0	0%
50–100 percent	10	30%
101 – 200 percent	13	40%
201 – 300 percent	6	18%
301 percent or more	4	12%
Total	33	100%

Assumptions:
Postconversion costs include principal, interest, and property tax payments. They do not include monthly assessments. Hence these figures under-estimate the increase in monthly housing costs.

Mortgage basis: 10% downpayment, 12% interest, 30-year term

Potential tax deductions were not subtracted. They cannot be calculated except on an individual basis.

Cost of insurance and possible cost of borrowing a downpayment were not included.

Source: Jennifer Soloway, Condos, Co-ops, and Conversions: A Guide on Rental Conversions for Local Officials. Sacramento: Office of Planning and Research, November 1979, p. 8.

TABLE 16.3. EFFECTS OF CONVERSION IN BROOKLINE, MASSACHUSETTS

Household Income	Current Average Gross Monthly Rent		Estimated Average After-Tax Monthly Cost of Owning Unit as a Condominium	
	Rent	% of Income	Cost	% of Income
Under $10,000	$280	45%	$506–520	81–83%
$10,000–19,999	330	26%	479–494	38–39%
$20,000–29,999	375	18%	478–501	23–24%
$30,000–39,999	425	15%	474–504	16–17%
$40,000–49,999	455	12%	455–485	12–13%
$50,000 or more	$500+	——	——	——

Mean gross monthly rent: $345, 24% of monthly income
Mean monthly carrying cost: from $481 to $498, 33–34% of income
Mean income: $17,490
Sample size: 705

Source: John R. Dinkelspiel, et al., Condominiums: The Effects of Conversion on a Community. Boston: Auburn House Publishing Company, 1981, p. 112.

tually every study conducted at the local level reports increases of 60 to 100 percent or more.

Specific examples from these studies bring these figures to life. For example, in the District of Columbia, if the typical elderly household in a converting building bought its unit, it would have to increase its monthly outlay for housing from 26 to 53 percent of its monthly income. The typical nonelderly household would have to increase its monthly housing expenditures from 26 to more than 70 percent of income to buy its converted unit (District of Columbia, 1976:7, 8).

While the studies in table 16.4 show the general inflationary effects of conversions, the two studies summarized in tables 16.2 and 16.3 make the point much more specifically. In California, conversion to condominiums usually increased housing costs at least 50 percent. Table 16.2 shows that conversion more than doubled monthly housing costs in 70 percent of thirty-three projects around the state. Table 16.3 shows that for all but the highest-income tenants in Brookline, Massachusetts, conversions substantially increased monthly costs and the proportion of income tenants paid, even after counting tax benefits.

The increases were somewhat less for wealthier purchasers, whose high tax brackets allow them to deduct as much as half of their mortgage interest and property tax payments. But for the vast majority of purchasers, the deductions either amount to less than the standard deduction or result in only a few hundred dollars in annual tax savings. For many tenants caught in a conversion, the tax benefits do not come close to making up the cost of increased monthly payments. HUD's 1980 study found that the income of

TABLE 16.4. FINDINGS OF STUDIES ON

Study	Proportion of Tenants Not Purchasing Converted Units (Displacement Rate)	Proportion of Displaced Tenants Who Move from Community or City
Condominium–Cooperative Conversion Housing Study: City of Philadelphia, 1981	65–71%	35–42%
Condominiums: The Effects of Conversion on a Community, 1981 (Brookline, MA)	67%	Not reported
Condominium Conversion and Displacement as It Affects the Elderly in the District of Columbia, 1981	Not reported	17%
Preliminary Progress Report, Condominium Research, 1981 (San Francisco, CA)	86%	Not reported
Twin City Conversions of the Real Estate Kind, 1981 (Minneapolis, St. Paul, MN)	72%	Not reported
Condominium Conversion Survey Report, 1980 (Evanston, IL)	88%	Not reported
The Conversion of Rental Housing to Condominiums and Cooperatives, HUD, 1980	58–69%	Not reported
Condominium Conversion in Hyde Park, 1965–1979, (Chicago), Peter Adels	61%	33%
Condominium and Cooperative Conversions in the District of Columbia, 1979 (developer-financed)	76%	25–33%
Final Report of the Emergency Condominium and Cooperative Conversion Commission to the Council of the District of Columbia, 1979	Not reported	52%

THE EFFECTS OF CONDOMINIUM CONVERSIONS

Increase in Monthly Carrying Costs of Unit When Converted from Rental to Condominium Ownership, Average	Proportion of Tenant Purchasers Who Buy Reluctantly	Proportion of Units Purchased by Nonoccupant Investors
84%	50–59%	24%
71%	61%	Not reported
196%	93%	Not reported
Not reported	Not reported	59%
54–79%	Not reported	Not reported
Not reported	Not reported	Not reported
36%	50%	37%
Not reported	70.7%	Not reported
Not reported	Not reported	Not reported
Not reported	Not reported	Not reported

TABLE 16.4 (continued). FINDINGS OF STUDIES ON

Study	Proportion of Tenants Not Purchasing Converted Units (Displacement Rate)	Proportion of Displaced Tenants Who Move from Community or City
Condos, Co—ops, and Conversions: A Guide on Rental Conversions for Local Officials, 1979 (State of California)	75%	Not reported
Condominium Survey Questionnaire Report, Oak Park, Illinois, 1979	90%	Not reported
Effects of Condominium Conversions on Tenants, Tenants Organization of Evanston, 1978	95%	55–73%
Condominium Conversions in the City of Evanston, Human Relations Commission, 1978	80–88%	Not reported
Condominium Conversions in Cambridge, Massachusetts, 1978	80%	29+%
Condominium Conversions in San Francisco, 1978 (conducted by city and industry)	72–83%	10%
Condominium Housing: A New Home Ownership Alternative for Metropolitan Washington, WASHCOG, 1976	82.3%	Not reported
District of Columbia Housing Market Analysis, 1976	76%	Not reported
HUD Condominium/Cooperative Study, 1975	75–85%	Not reported
Palo Alto, California, Condominium Conversion Study, 1974	82%	Not reported

THE EFFECTS OF CONDOMINIUM CONVERSIONS

Increase in Monthly Carrying Costs of Unit When Converted from Rental to Condominium Ownership, Average	Proportion of Tenant Purchasers Who Buy Reluctantly	Proportion of Units Purchased by Nonoccupant Investors
53–301%	Not reported	Not reported
60%	Not reported	Not reported
60–100%	Not reported	Not reported
100%	Not reported	Not reported
Not reported	Not reported	Not reported
153%	Not reported	11%
Not reported	Not reported	Not reported
Not reported	Not reported	Not reported
30–35%	Not reported	Not reported
Not reported	70%	Not reported

42 percent of the tenants in its sample of already converted buildings (largely more expensive high-rises) could not have qualified them for new mortgages even at single-digit interest rates (U.S. Department of Housing and Urban Development, 1980).

Given the increases in monthly costs, is it any wonder that relatively few tenants actually purchase? A joint study by the San Francisco Planning Department and local realtors concluded that 33 percent of tenants simply could not afford their units (San Francisco City Planning Department, 1978:47). HUD's 1980 survey found that more than 40 percent of tenants could not afford to buy them (U.S. Department of Housing and Urban Development, 1980). Therefore, many tenants are displaced, as was found in the studies summarized in table 16.4. HUD's 1975 study candidly noted that displacement "is an unavoidable by-product of the conversion process. . . . In a city where rental [vacancy] rates are low and where rental units are occupied by the elderly, who are often on fixed incomes, and by low- and moderate-income families, the displacement potential of this conversion process appears awesome" (U.S. Department of Housing and Urban Development, 1975).

Thus conversions threaten a community's stock of affordable housing. Oak Park's *Condominium Survey Questionnaire Report* concluded:

> Oak Park's supply of middle-, moderate-, and low-income housing is being depleted directly, and perhaps indirectly, due to condominium conversions. Rentals found in this study ranged from $200 a month to $375, definitely within the range of low- to middle-income housing. Clearly condominium conversion is not restricted to higher rent units in Oak Park. (Community Relations Department, 1979).

Similarly, Evanston's Human Relations Commission reached the following conclusion about this traditionally diverse community:

> The continued availability of housing affordable, on a rental basis, by low- and moderate-income families and the fixed-income elderly cannot be assured by operation of the real estate marketplace. Thus the city must act . . . to prevent condominium conversion from erecting an economic wall that forecloses the entry into the Evanston community of upwardly mobile young families of diverse backgrounds and [from causing] displacement of present low- and moderate-income families and the fixed-income elderly. (Fremming and Howery, 1978:ii–iii)

After noting that at least 12 percent of the rental housing in Washington, D.C., had already been converted by the beginning of 1979, and that conversions underway threatened another 9 percent, a city commission concluded, "There is a clear and present danger to the continued existence of much of the city's low- and moderate-income housing" due to condominium conversion (Emergency Condominium and Cooperative Commission, 1979:52).

As long as condo units appreciated in value faster than inflation, they proved a prudent investment. But once the resale market started to collapse, condominiums did not prove to be a hedge against inflation.

All home purchasers feel the effect of conversions in the interest rates they pay. Converting rentals to condominiums invariably doubles the amount of money tied up in a building. Typical is the conversion of the Promenade Apartments in Bethesda, Maryland, by the controversial conversion pioneer American Invsco (AI). AI purchased the apartments for $49 million (the previous owner held a mortgage of $29 million). The purchase prices of the units were so great that, had the conversion succeeded, more than $100 million would have gone into mortgages on the individual units (U.S. Congress, 1981). Conversions through 1979 tied up around $15 billion more in mortgage money than the preconversion mortgages of the buildings. As Goetze notes, "It is no surprise that the cost of mortgage money is bid up" (Goetze, 1981). With more people competing for limited mortgage funds and seeking larger amounts due to the high prices of condominiums, interest rates have naturally risen precipitously in recent years. Even without the tight money policies of the Federal Reserve, increased competition for limited mortgage funds because of conversions would have helped increase mortgage interest rates well into double digits.

These increased mortgage interest rates, according to Goetze, produce "bigger tax deductions (over $19 billion in 1981 for all housing), resulting in bigger federal deficits, and increases in the housing component of the consumer price index. This in turn triggers higher social security checks, still bigger deficits, and largely futile demand for more direct housing subsidies to the poor — who are the only ones left off the bandwagon" (Goetze, 1981). All these factors help trigger still more inflation. Economists at the Purdue School of Management estimate that without the tax benefits of home ownership, 4.5 to 5 million fewer of the nation's 77 million households would have been home owners at the end of 1978 (Goetze, 1981). James Poterba of the National Bureau of Economic Research concludes that the interaction of tax policy and the inflation it supports could be responsible for as much as 30 percent of the increase in housing prices (Poterba, 1980).

For the remaining renters, the effects of conversion have been devastating. In a 1979 report to clients, Mid-America Appraisal & Research Corporation said, "The condominium ownership concept has probably contributed the greatest to reducing the supply of rental apartments and driving up rents, and hence, the value of the remaining units (Mid-America Appraisal & Research Corp., 1979:4). Further conversion becomes inevitable as many remaining apartment buildings are priced too high to continue as rentals. Once the price of a rental building rises above a threshold, mortgage payments become so great that the rents go too high to attract tenants. But the profit generated by conversion allows the higher prices to be paid for buildings. Only recently, as the demand for buildings to convert has faltered, have prices begun to return to reasonable levels.

New construction has done little or nothing to ease the crunch on tenants. The small amount has not kept pace with the spiralling demand created by the formation of new households. The high cost of new construction also results in rents much higher than in existing rentals. For example, in 1981 a typical one-bedroom apartment in an old building in a "good" Chicago neighborhood rented for $300 a month. Newly built apartments in comparable neighborhoods generally rented for $540 to $800 a month, largely due to high construction costs.

Thus the overall cost of housing rises, and tenants have few alternatives but to pay. Americans are spending a greater proportion of their incomes on housing than ever before. Real estate speculator Samuel Zell, president of Equity & Financial Management Company of Chicago, who warns that tenants may soon become extinct, says that instead of paying 25 percent of our income on housing, we should expect to pay 40 to 50 percent as in Europe (McKelvy, 1979). As noted elsewhere in this chapter, such high expenditures for housing are becoming increasingly common in the United States already (see also Feins and Lane, 1981).

REFORMING THE REFORM

Somewhere along the line, the reform went sour. Condominiums did not improve the overall housing picture, reconcile supply and demand, or adjust the housing stock to meet housing needs. Instead, they turned housing that low-, moderate-, and middle-income households could afford without government subsidies into costly housing they could no longer afford. By reducing the supply of rental housing further, condominium conversions also increased rents and threatened the future of rental housing. The overall result has been an increase in housing costs for all households.

Most laws on condominium conversions treat surrogate issues rather than the central issue of preserving affordable housing. By treating surrogate issues — for instance, consumer and tenant protections — local and state officials are usually able to quiet protesting tenants and buyers and not upset politically powerful developers. While conversion has affected hundreds of municipalities, only a few dozen have adopted laws that deal with affordable housing. Part of the reason is the bias toward homeownership.

But the bottom line has generally been politics. For example, Philadelphia tenants successfully pressured their city council into adopting an eighteen-month moratorium on conversions in September 1979. In less than a year, the development industry got the moratorium eradicated by getting the state legislature to adopt the Uniform Condominium Act (UCA), which preempts local ordinances, literally wiping out Philadelphia's moratorium and any other local condominium ordinances in the state (*Philadelphia Inquirer,* 1980). The UCA has also been adopted in

Minnesota, West Virginia, and, with substantial amendments, Louisiana.

State preemption, primarily through the Uniform Condominium Act, is the cornerstone of the industry's efforts against condominium-conversion legislation (Craig, 1981:20). Preemption has been used successfully to rescind conversion moratoriums in New Jersey and Maryland, to terminate local condo laws in Massachusetts and Maryland, and to prevent passage of local ordinances in Wisconsin and Virginia. The National Association of Realtors and the National Multi-Housing Council, a group representing developers and landlords, have made adoption of the UCA their main goal in Arizona, Colorado, Connecticut, Idaho, Illinois, Massachusetts, Missouri, Tennessee, Vermont, and Wyoming (Uniform Law Commissioners, 1980:4). Efforts to preempt local legislation in California have failed only due to a strong tenant lobby and local government lobby.

The industry seeks exclusive state regulation of conversions because it is much easier for the industry to prevent passage of restrictive laws at the state level. Condomania strikes communities at different times. Hence most state legislators have no permanent constituency that opposes conversions and have no interest in curtailing the phenomenon. People directly affected by conversions have greater access to local officials than to state officials. Among the states, only New York has adopted moderately stringent conversion legislation. Otherwise the most demanding laws are at the local level.

In addition, it may be easier for the development industry to use campaign contributions to control state legislators than local officials. In Illinois, for example, legislators report that the Illinois Association of Realtors, the state's principal sponsor of the UCA, has been making massive campaign contributions to most legislators for the last two years to promote the UCA. So far the UCA languishes in committee as local government officials fight to retain their ability to legislate on condominiums. Several legislators report that the only thing keeping the UCA alive in Illinois is campaign contributions.[11]

CONDO LAWS ADDRESSING THE AFFORDABLE-HOUSING ISSUE

A number of communities have passed laws which directly address the central condominium-conversion issue of preserving affordable housing. Most of these laws have been adopted by California municipalities, which often have extremely active, high-priced real estate markets. California and Colorado both treat condominium conversion as a subdivision; hence conversions must be approved by a jurisdiction's planning commission and comply with its comprehensive plan. State law also requires California communities to consider the housing needs of all their residents, particularly low- and moderate-income ones.

Automatic Moratorium

Since a low rental vacancy rate indicates a shortage of rental housing, some communities prohibit conversions whenever the rental vacancy rate falls below a specified threshold level, usually 3 or 5 percent. Most of these communities will exempt a building from this moratorium if the conversion would result in little displacement. The lack of heavy displacement is usually demonstrated by a specified percentage of tenants agreeing to exempt the building or agreeing to purchase their apartments. This method in effect attempts to limit conversions to the number that would satisfy natural demand.

Cities with this type of law appear below. The first figure in parentheses is the vacancy rate threshold; the second, if any, indicates the percentage of tenants in a building that must approve an exemption. These jurisdictions are:

District of Columbia (3%; 51%)   Marin County, CA (5%)
Cambridge, MA (4%)   Montclair, CA (3%)
Vail, CO (3%)   Newport Beach, CA (5%; 67%)
Claremont, CA (3%)   Orange County, CA (5%)
Cupertino, CA (5%)   Palo Alto, CA (5%; 67%)
Fremont, CA (3%)   San Bernadino, CA (6%; 67%)
Gardena, CA (3%)   San Diego, CA (5%)
Hayward, CA (5%)   Santa Monica, CA (5%; 80% of
Los Angeles, CA (5%)   tenants must agree to buy)

Tenant Approval

Conversion is permitted only if a certain percentage of tenants vote to approve the conversion or agree to purchase their units. This approach amounts to the exemption procedure used in the automatic moratorium law. Enforcement can be a problem. San Francisco officials have found massive fraud by developers in obtaining tenant signatures. Cities with this type of law are New York (35 percent must agree to purchase if evictions are allowed, 15 percent if there are to be no evictions); Newport Beach, California (30 percent vote); Thousand Oaks, California (50 percent vote); San Francisco (51 percent must sign a city-supplied "intent to purchase" form).

Numerical Limits

Some cities limit the number of conversions each year to the number of new rental units built during a specified time period, such as the previous two years. Such laws maintain the same number of rental units. But since the rents in the new units are invariably higher than the preconversion rents of the older ones, the overall cost of housing still rises. This type of law is in effect in these California cities: Albany, La Mesa, Mountain View, Oakland, Riverside, San Francisco, Walnut Creek.

Balanced Housing Stock

A conversion is allowed only if it does not adversely affect the balance of a community's housing stock. Communities using this approach usually proscribe a conversion if it would reduce the supply of affordable rental units. Jurisdictions using this moderately effective method include Lynnwood, Washington; Cambridge, Massachusetts; Vail, Colorado; and in California: Belmont, Concord, Gardena, Marin County, Mountain View, Oceanside, and Thousand Oaks.

Displacement Potential

A number of municipalities consider a conversion's potential to displace tenants or specific classes of tenants such as the elderly, handicapped, or households with children. The potential for displacement is usually evaluated in light of the community's goals and objectives as contained in its comprehensive plan. Communities employing this fairly effective approach include Aspen, Colorado; and in California, Albany, Concord, Duarte, Gardena, Mountain View, San Francisco, and Thousand Oaks.

Retention of Low- and Moderate-Income Units

Some jurisdictions require a developer to retain units for low- or moderate-income tenants. Marin County, California, for example, has required developers to make available as many as 40 percent of the units at prices modest-income households can afford. San Francisco requires that any unit affordable to low- or moderate-income households before conversion must be kept affordable to them after conversion as well. At least 10 percent of the units in any conversion of fifty or more units must be for low- or moderate-income households. These units may be rented or sold. Resale prices are limited so later purchasers in the same income category can buy them.

This method is reasonably effective as long as it allows no loopholes and is vigorously enforced. It works best with moderate rent controls that prevent a landlord from evicting all low- and moderate-income tenants before applying for a conversion permit. In the absence of rent controls, enforceable laws requiring proof of just cause for eviction and prohibiting arbitrary lease nonrenewals will help. Writing the law to take into account rent levels for the previous five years could also help prevent abuse.

Right of First Refusal to Buy Building

Perhaps the most effective approach of all is used by the District of Columbia. Under its "Rental Housing Conversion and Sale Act of 1980,"[12] tenants are given the right of first refusal to purchase their entire building or complex. If tenants decide to convert the building to limited-equity cooperatives, the city provides technical and financial assistance through a variety of revolving loan funds. The law establishes a timetable for tenants to organize into a tenants' association capable of owning property and for the association to inspect the building, make an offer, and obtain financing, usually on the private market. Through July 1980, tenants had used this law to purchase twenty-seven buildings with 2,714 units. In the meantime, developers converted another 4,300 units to condominiums. Obviously this law does not eliminate conversions, but it tends to limit them to those needed to meet natural demand.

TOWARD A SOLUTION: LOW-EQUITY COOPERATIVES

The key to the District of Columbia law is the low-equity cooperative, which may be the most effective way to preserve affordable housing in America. The residents of a low-equity cooperative do not own their individual units. Each owns a share in the nonprofit corporation, which in turn owns the building and underlying land through a single mortgage and deed. In a conventional market-rate cooperative, the cost of these shares is what the market will bear. In a limited-equity cooperative, the increase in resale price of shares is limited by the cooperative's bylaws or charter to some lesser rate of increase. In some cases — those of no-yield cooperatives — this rate is zero. In others the increase may be held to 5 percent annually or $100 a year. By restraining the resale price of shares, the cooperative guarantees that low- and moderate-income households will be able to afford shares. It also breaks the speculative resale cycle and returns housing to its original function as shelter from the elements.

The key reason the resale price of shares can be kept relatively low is the cooperative's single fixed mortgage, also called debt service. Debt service generally constitutes at least 30 to 50 percent of the total cost of owning and operating a residential property. When such a building is sold, the debt service nearly always rises, either because the new mortgage is for a greater amount or because the interest rate is higher. But when a low-equity cooperative changes hands, only the share in the cooperative is sold. The debt service on the building stays the same since the building itself is not being sold and does not have to be refinanced. Only the operational costs, insurance, and taxes can increase. Figure 16.1 illustrates the difference by comparing the mortgage payments and monthly tenant costs for two identical buildings — one a limited-equity cooperative, the other a rental property that is sold every five years, a typical practice.

Residents of a low-equity cooperative pay a monthly fee much like the rent a tenant pays. It covers the resident's proportional share of the mortgage payment on the building, taxes, insurance, reserve funds, and all operating costs. But unlike the renter, the owner of a low-equity cooperative is able to deduct from his income taxes the part of the monthly payment that covers his share of the property tax and interest on the mortgage principal. Since the debt service does not have to be refinanced each time a unit is sold, increases in monthly charges are limited to actual in-

FIGURE 16.1. COMPARISON OF COST BETWEEN LIMITED-EQUITY COOPERATIVE AND RENTAL OWNERSHIP

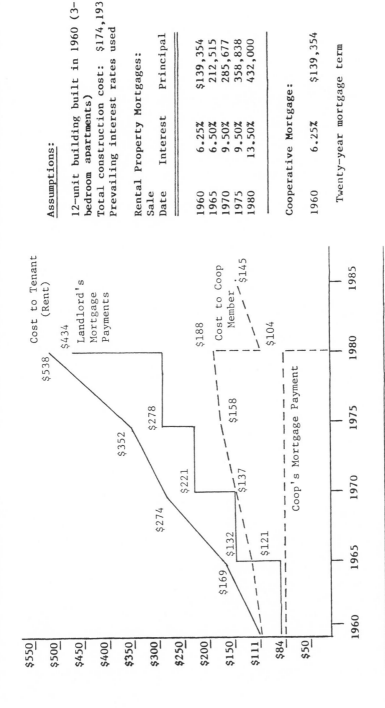

Assumptions:

12-unit building built in 1960 (3-bedroom apartments)
Total construction cost: $174,193
Prevailing interest rates used

Rental Property Mortgages:

Sale Date	Interest	Principal
1960	6.25%	$139,354
1965	6.50%	212,515
1970	9.50%	285,677
1975	9.50%	358,838
1980	13.50%	432,000

Cooperative Mortgage:

1960	6.25%	$139,354

Twenty-year mortgage term

Source: John Gilderbloom, et al., Rent Control: A Source Book, Santa Barbara, California: Foundation for National Progress, Inc., 1981, p. 242.

creases in operating costs. By the time the building in figure 16.1 is twenty years old as a rental, the debt service has more than quadrupled because of its frequent resale. But the debt service for the limited-equity cooperative has remained the same.

Residents of a limited-equity cooperative cannot use their housing for investment purposes, as the rest of the post-shelter society does. Instead, their housing returns to its original purpose — to provide physical shelter and a home. Since the resale price of a share is limited (initial shares usually run anywhere from $500 to $3,500), the unit will also be affordable to its original income group for generations. The residents will have control over their housing costs, and many will be able to save enough money to eventually purchase a conventional home.

Limited-equity cooperatives are not new. Programs supporting them have been the most successful of all federal multifamily housing programs. While federal programs that directly subsidize developers or subsidize rents have produced a large number of defaults, the Federal Housing Administration's Section 213 market-rate low-equity cooperative housing program returned over $32 billion in mortgage insurance dividends to the cooperatives it financed since 1970, because of the lack of defaults (National Association of Housing Cooperatives, 1977:8). That program financed 2,033 projects with 115,976 units and a combined mortgage value of more than $1.5 billion (Zimmer, 1977:22). The program enabled cooperative associations to secure 97-percent financing and forty-year mortgages, both of which helped minimize the cost of shares and monthly payments, even though the interest was market rate. This program remains on the books and could work well again when interest rates decline. In 1961, Congress established the FHA 221(d)(3) *below*-market-rate program that made up to 100 percent financing available at interest rates as low as 3 percent. The rate was related to the average cost of federal treasury bonds at the time. More than 22,000 units were financed under this successful program. Section 236 of the 1968 Housing Act provided up to 100 percent financing at interest rates as low as 1 percent because of a federal subsidy. The Section 202 program lends funds at 3 percent for cooperative housing for the elderly (Zimmer, 1977:22–23). Since the 1973 Nixon moratorium on housing programs, these programs have fallen into disuse.

Officials in the District of Columbia report that its right-of-first-refusal program has subsidized low-equity cooperatives at a cost of $3,000 per unit (staff time and grants).[13] This is a one-time expenditure, in contrast with Section 8 subsidies that can come to more than $3,000 per unit annually. Such outlays are much cheaper than building new rentals at a cost of $35,000 to $42,500 per unit and then subsidizing rents.

CONCLUSION

Condominium conversion was originally touted as a reform that would enhance home ownership opportunities for households of modest incomes.

It has failed to live up to its notices. Instead, it has primarily increased housing costs across the board and exacerbated an already serious rate of inflation in housing costs.

The District of Columbia experiment with limited-equity cooperatives has shown that there is an alternative to condominium conversion. It provides an affordable ownership opportunity even to low-income households, without the massive and continuing subsidies of so many other federal housing programs. America cannot afford to continue to treat housing, particularly low- and moderate-income housing, as a speculative commodity. We cannot afford to continue to sink billions of dollars into financing resales of existing housing. Tying up so much money only forces interest rates higher. Above all, we cannot afford to remain a post-shelter society. Condominium conversion has become a reform that must be reformed.

NOTES

1. Interview with Michael Dukakis by author on 11 October 1979 in Boston.
2. Original research by author.
3. Interviews with Jan van Weesup by author in 1980 and 1981.
4. Telephone interview with Charles Ramsey by author on 10 August 1981.
5. Interview with Harold Miller by author in September 1981.
6. Interview of Richard Helms by author on 4 August 1981.
7. Interviews by author of Chicago developers who wish to remain anonymous, in August and September 1981.
8. Interview with Peter Arnold by author on 22 September 1981.
9. Interview with Alex Bruni by author on 4 September 1981.
10. Interview with Barbara Novak by author on 22 September 1981.
11. Interviews by author of Illinois state legislators who wish to remain anonymous, in January 1982.
12. D.C. Act 3-204.
13. Interview with Marie Nahikian, program administrator, by author on 3 April 1981.

REFERENCES

Adels, Peter. 1979. "Condominium conversion in Hyde Park, 1965–1979." B.A. thesis, University of Chicago.

Baber, Asa. 1979. "The condominium conspiracy." *Playboy,* November: 167–258.

Backer, Richard. 1981. *Preliminary Progress Report, Condominium Research.* San Francisco, CA: San Francisco City Planning Department.

Beal, Kathleen. 1981. *Condominium Conversion and Displacement as It Affects the Elderly in the District of Columbia.* Washington, DC: City-Wide Housing Foundation.

Chicago Sun-Times. 1981a. "Home digest." *Chicago Sun-Times,* Homelife Section, 18 October: 25.

———. 1981b. "Some condos fizzle . . ." *Chicago Sun-Times,* Homelife Section, 4 December: 2.

———. 1982a. "Condo crunch: value of studio units declining." *Chicago Sun-Times,* Homelife Section, 9 April: 1.

———. 1982b. "Is the condo market dying? Not yet, says wary housing expert." *Chicago Sun-Times,* Homelife Section, 1 May: 1.

Chicago Tribune. 1982. "Condo plans seemed blessed until economy cursed them." *Chicago Tribune,* Sect. 14, 2 May: 1.

Community Relations Department. 1979. *Condominium Survey Questionnaire Report.* Oak Park, IL: Community Relations Department.

Craig, Pat. 1981. "Fighting condominium regulations: what's being done." *Real Estate Today,* February.

Dinkelspiel, John R., Uchenick, Joel, and Slesnick, Herbert. 1981. *Condominiums: The Effects of Conversion on a Community.* Boston: Auburn House.

District of Columbia. 1976. *District of Columbia Housing Market Analysis.* Washington, DC: District of Columbia Government.

Emergency Condominium and Cooperative Commission. 1979. *Final Report of the Emergency Condominium and Cooperative Commission to the Council of the District of Columbia.* Washington, DC: Emergency Condominium and Cooperative Commission, September.

Federal Home Loan Bank of Chicago. 1979 to 1982. *Housing Vacancy Survey* (Series 1979, 1980, 1981, 1982). Chicago: Federal Home Loan Bank of Chicago.

Feins, Judith D., and Lane, Terry Saunders. 1981. *How Much for Housing?* Cambridge, MA: Abt Books.

Fremming, James L., and Howery, Carla B. 1978. *Condominium Conversions in the City of Evanston.* Evanston, IL: Evanston Human Relations Commission.

Galano, Robert. 1982. "Doubling up is a sign of the times." *Washington Post,* 19 June: E1, E24.

Garz, Sandra, Frankel, Susan, and Jastrzab, Gary. 1981. *Condominium-Cooperative Conversion Housing Study: City of Philadelphia.* Philadelphia, PA: Philadelphia City Planning Commission.

General Accounting Office. 1979. *Rental Housing: A National Problem that Needs Immediate Attention.* Washington, DC: U.S. General Accounting Office.

Gilderbloom, John, et al. 1981. *Rent Control: A Source Book.* Santa Barbara, CA: Foundation for National Progress, Inc.

Goetze, Rolf. 1981. "The housing bubble." *Working Papers* VIII, January/February: 44–52.

Kidwell, Kenneth. 1980. "Housing forecast for the 1980s." *San Francisco Examiner,* Spring Real Estate Review, 4 May: 29.

Larvo, Jean. 1981. "Demand for converted condominiums and cooperatives." Paper presented at the Annual Meeting of the Eastern Economic Association, Philadelphia.

Lauber, Daniel. 1979. "How and why condo boom altered Chicago." *Chicago Sun-Times,* Homes/apartments/condos, 10 August: 3, 6, 25.

McKelvy, Natalie. 1979. "Renters to become extinct, investor says." *Chicago Tribune,* Sect. 14, 24 June: 1E.

Mid-America Appraisal & Research Corporation. 1979. *Memorandum to Clients, February 1979.* Chicago: Mid-America Appraisal & Research Corporation.

National Association of Housing Cooperatives. 1977. *Cooperative Housing: People Helping Each Other.* Washington, DC: National Association of Housing Cooperatives.

Palo Alto Planning Department. 1974. *Palo Alto Condominium Conversion Study.* Palo Alto:, CA: Palo Alto Planning Department.

Philadelphia Inquirer. 1980. "Thornburgh should veto the condominium sell-out." *Philadelphia Inquirer,* 25 June: 12–A.

Poterba, James M. 1980. *Inflation, Income Taxes and Owner-Occupied Housing.* Working Paper No. 552. Cambridge, MA: National Bureau of Economic Research, September.

Ramsey, Charles. 1961. *Condominiums: The New Look in Co-ops: Practical and Legal Problems.* Chicago: Chicago Title and Trust Company.

San Francisco City Planning Department, and Members of the Real Estate Industry. 1978. *Condominium Conversions in San Francisco.* San Francisco: City Planning Department, November.

Schechter, Henry B. 1980. "Economic squeeze pinches the future of housing." *Journal of Housing* 37(4): 192–97.

Soloway, Jennifer. 1979. *Condos, Co-ops, and Conversions: A Guide on Rental Conversions for Local Officials.* Sacramento, CA: Office of Planning and Research, November.

Sternlieb, George, and Hughes, James W. 1980. "The post-shelter society." In *America's Housing: Prospects and Problems.* Edited by George Sternlieb and James W. Hughes. New Brunswick, NJ: Center for Urban Policy Research. Pp. 93–102.

Task Force on Condominium Conversion. 1979. Report of the Task Force on Condominium Conversion. Rockville, MD: Montgomery County Government.

Uniform Law Commissioners. 1980. Uniform Condominium Act (1980). Chicago: National Conference of Commissioners on Uniform State Laws.

U.S. Congress, House Subcommittee on Commerce, Consumer, and Monetary Affairs. 1981. *Condominium and Cooperative Conversion: The Federal Response.* Washington, DC: U.S. Government Printing Office.

U.S. Department of Housing and Urban Development. 1975. *HUD Condominium/Cooperative Study.* Washington, DC: U.S. Department of Housing and Urban Development.

———. 1980. *The Conversion of Rental Housing to Condominiums and Cooperatives: A National Study of Scope, Causes and Impacts.* Washington, DC: U.S. Department of Housing and Urban Development.

U.S. League of Savings Associations. 1982. *Homeownership: The American Dream Adrift.* Chicago: Economics Department, U.S. League of Savings Associations.

van Weesup, Jan. 1980. "Condominiums in large U.S. cities." Paper presented at the Seventy-sixth Annual Meeting of the Association of American Geographers, Louisville, KY.

Washington Post. 1982a. "Beached whales: Miami's luxury condo market is floundering on speculation." *Washington Post,* 24 April: F1.

———. 1982b. "Foreclosure begun on complex." *Washington Post,* 15 May: 1.

Zimmer, Jonathan E. 1977. *From Rental to Cooperative: Improving Low and Moderate Income Housing.* Beverly Hills, CA: Sage Publications.

17

The Right to Stay Put

CHESTER HARTMAN

Residential stability engenders a host of personal and social benefits. Long-term residence brings safety of person and property ("eyes on the street," people looking out for each other and each other's homes), helpful and satisfying social ties to neighbors and local commercial establishments, greater care for public and private space, and lower housing costs (Fried, 1973; Gans, 1962). This is not to say that mobility is to be avoided. Change of residence may be necessary and advisable to meet changing space needs and preferences, to take advantage of employment opportunities, to satisfy shifting personal consumption preferences, to escape what is perceived to be a confining social or physical environment, to secure change for change's sake, or for other reasons. The distinction between involuntary and voluntary change of residence is, however, crucial. Shifts of residence that are sought—for which people are financially and socially prepared—clearly are nondetrimental to society. But changes of residence which are foisted on people, which they did not seek out or propose, for which they may lack the social and economic coping resources—these are detrimental to the individuals and families involved, and produce social costs as well.

In theory, the economic, political, and social forces that trigger these involuntary moves may be associated with societal benefits that outweigh the costs to those forced to move (a point that will be explored in greater detail below). But, aside from those rare instances in which the person forcibly displaced winds up retrospectively grateful for what was initially perceived as a catastrophe, we can safely say that from the displacee's perspective forced displacement is most often a severely damaging experience.

Quantitatively, the problem of forced displacement is substantial and probably growing. A recent study by the Legal Services Anti-Displacement Project concludes that "2.5 million persons a year in the

United States is a conservative estimate of the magnitude of displacement at the present time" (LeGates and Hartman, 1981). The proximate cause of most displacement is private-sector rather than public-sector action. This has been true for the last decade and represents a shift from the 1950s and 1960s, when government programs, particularly urban renewal and construction of the interstate highway system, were the primary displacing forces.

Government still has a substantial role in the displacement process today. Some direct government-initiated displacement still occurs for a wide variety of public-works projects — highways and roads, dams, public buildings, airports. And a great deal of ostensibly private-sector displacement is supported by or the indirect result of government policies, programs, or action. Examples are private-market ripple effects caused by government investment in downtown redevelopment, public transit, or housing rehabilitation; tax policies that foster home ownership and thus encourage conversion of rental units into condominiums, or that encourage luxury renovation of historic properties; policies of federal financial-institution regulatory bodies that permit and encourage a shift from fixed- to variable-rate interest mortgages; and state and local landlord-tenant laws that permit easy evictions (Roisman, 1981). But in the vast proportion of cases today, the direct displacing agent is in the private sector.

Forced displacement produced by the private sector may be divided roughly into that related to *revitalization* forces in the private market and that related to *disinvestment* forces in the private market.

DISPLACEMENT GENERATED BY REVITALIZATION

Home owners as well as renters (although overwhelmingly the latter) may be forced out by actions associated with increasing investment in and attractiveness of an area — what has commonly been referred to by the British term "gentrification." Older structures may be rehabilitated by new or existing owners in order to take advantage of an area's new market attractiveness, due in turn to location, inherent structural or historic qualities, taste and fad, or other factors.

Where the work is done by an investor/developer, such rehabilitation often requires removal of the current residents in order to allow the work to be done efficiently. The rehab work itself may result in higher rental costs which current residents cannot afford or do not choose to bear. A change in unit sizes following rehab — conversion of large units into smaller ones, or vice versa — may make unworkable the former fit between space and occupants. Or a desired change in the social character of the area may make the rehabber unwilling to allow former residents to continue living in the renovated unit. New owner-occupants, whether or not they undertake renovation work, will displace the existing residents of the units they wish to occupy.

Gentrification probably will lead to overall rent increases in an area, even if no or only cosmetic improvements are made in a building located there; and these increases, too, will cause existing residents to move. Property tax increases can also be expected as an area is upgraded, and these also cause rent increases, as well as increased tax bills for home owners, who then may be forced to move. Such "house-rich" but otherwise lower-income persons can reap the windfall benefits of increased property values when they sell, of course, but the social and personal disruption in their lives caused by their inability to pay sharply increased tax bills may be severe, especially since their "windfall" may have to be used to pay higher housing costs elsewhere. Gentrification also is associated with speculative buying and selling of properties, conversion of housing into office and other commercial use, and condominium conversion, all of which are leading causes of displacement.

DISPLACEMENT GENERATED BY DISINVESTMENT

The disinvestment process sets in motion an opposite set of forces, for the most part similarly rooted in the profit considerations of those who own and control property. At the extreme, owners simply abandon, or walk away from, properties they no longer regard as profitable or potentially profitable, leaving unpaid mortgages, property taxes, and utility bills in their wake. A final touch may be "selling out to the insurance company" — that is, arson. A less extreme version of this response is under-maintenance, investing little or nothing in upkeep and repairs, in an effort to keep up profits. "Disinvestment" of this type often is followed shortly by abandonment.

Obviously, such processes cause displacement, when a building is made unfit for habitation or so dangerous and unpleasant that seeking out another place is preferable to staying. A public version of the disinvestment process is withdrawal of municipal services, such as fire stations, street cleaning and repairs, hospitals and clinics, and police protection. Sometimes the disinvestment is a result of inadequate local political power to compel the city to serve the area properly; at other times it may represent a city's conscious policy of "planned shrinkage" or "triage" to induce people to move as a way of preparing the area for some form of redevelopment without the necessity of eminent domain and formal relocation services. As with the revitalization phenomenon, owners as well as renters may be forced out, although the latter predominate. The concept of a "forced" move means not just the legally enforceable decision by someone who owns and controls the property to evict those living there as tenants; it also involves a decision by an occupant to sell or depart because external forces have made continued residence undesirable or impossible.

IS DISPLACEMENT EVER IN THE PUBLIC INTEREST?

Given the undeniable magnitude of the nation's displacement problem (U.S. Dept. of Housing and Urban Development, 1981) and the severity of its impacts on those displaced, what can be said about the competing claims of the public- and private-sector actors involved? At present, an entire legal, political, and economic structure undergirds the displacement process. Generally speaking, those who own property have the legal right, within some broad constraints, to decide how and by whom that property will be used. Those who own property obviously tend to be persons and institutions with wealth and political power. As the data below on housing tenure by income show (see table 17.1), far fewer lower-income residents than upper-income residents live in their own homes. Lower-income home owners tend to be the elderly, who are most vulnerable to the rising costs of home ownership in revitalizing areas. They are therefore most likely to have to take their equity and run when the inevitable reassessments occur.

No national data exist on who owns the rental properties that tenants occupy, but it is unlikely that a substantial proportion of renters have incomes or wealth positions higher than their landlords'. Also, owners of rental property have in recent years been able to organize themselves into effective local and state trade associations, lobbying groups, and political action committees. These owners have exercised their influence over politicians and the political process by electing candidates, affecting legislation, and defeating local housing-reform initiatives (Hartman, 1979).

Virtually every case study of displacement (see the summaries of existing studies in Hartman, 1964; Hartman, 1971; LeGates and Hartman, 1982) arrives at a similar conclusion: those displaced are poor, with disproportionate numbers of nonwhites, elderly, and large households among them. In seeking a new place to live, the displaced tend to move as short a distance as possible, in an effort to retain existing personal, commercial, and institutional ties and because of the economically and racially biased housing-market constraints they face. What they find

TABLE 17.1. HOME OWNERSHIP RATES AND INCOME (1980)

Annual Income	Percent Home Owner Households	Percent Tenant Households
Under $7,000	45%	55%
$7,000–9,999	53%	47%
$10,000–14,999	56%	44%
$15,000–24,999	70%	30%
$25,000–49,999	86%	14%
Over $50,000	92%	8%

Source: Census Bureau/HUD, Annual Housing Survey for 1980

usually costs more, has less adequate space, and is of inferior quality. Involuntary residential changes also produce a considerable amount of psychosocial stress, which in its more extreme form has been found analogous to the clinical description of grief (Fried, 1963).

Some variations from these patterns have been found in particular types of displacement — condominium conversions to date have affected mainly moderate- and middle-income whites, and the gentrification process up to this point seems to have hit fewer nonwhite neighborhoods than were affected by earlier public displacement programs. Yet the overall pattern described above has been remarkably persistent for several decades, regardless of who was displaced or displacing and for what reasons the displacement occurred.

The motivations of the displacers almost invariably are tied to their profit calculations, or at times to their own class-based residential needs and preferences. For instance, when a gentrifying family returns from the suburbs with the resources and desire to restore an older Victorian house to its original middle-class single-family use, it may empty the house of the several low-income households currently occupying the units that the house was cut up into years back. In the less frequent instances when a government agency is doing the displacing, some version of the "public interest" may be involved. But when subjected to scrutiny, it usually emerges that the public interest to be served is class-biased toward the same interests that undertake private displacement.

The philosophical and political question then becomes: whose rights are paramount, those of the displacer or those of the displacee? Under current conditions the answer is clear. Almost any owner of residential property in the United States can force out a nonowning resident, even though on occasion some trouble and time are required. There are some exceptions, to be discussed below. But the "right to displace" is an overwhelming fact of life, which is why over 1 percent of the population is kicked out of their homes each year (LeGates and Hartman, 1981) and several times that number live under the very real threat that displacement is only a short time off.

In opposition to this "right to displace," I would like to put forth a "right to stay put," a kind of tenure guarantee for those who do not own their own homes. This right would allow them to stay as long as they want, so long as they meet certain fundamental obligations as tenants. While there are some legal underpinnings for such a right, which will be discussed, the fundamental arena for creating it — as with the assertion of new rights generally — is political. In the course of, or following, the political struggle to achieve such a right, the appropriate legal theories and mechanisms will be fashioned and accepted.

DEVELOPING A "RIGHT TO STAY PUT"

In establishing the concept of a "right to stay put," it is useful to itemize the many ways in which the absolute right of the owner of a piece of property to do with it as he/she sees fit already has been breached. Many of these are relatively new developments in law and public acceptance; others have a long history:

- Zoning regulations put considerable limits on an owner's free use of property. Type, intensity, timing, and many other elements of use are controlled in the public interest, even when these regulations limit the owner's profit and freedom.
- Housing and building codes setting minimum construction, rehabilitation, and occupancy standards must be met, even though they are quite costly for the owner. These minimum legal standards have been strengthened by court decisions and state legislation establishing a "warranty of habitability"—consumer protection that someone holding out residential property for rent guarantees it to be habitable. Breach of this warranty becomes a legal basis for withholding rent, resisting eviction, and bringing damage claims. Legalized rent withholding and court appointment of receivers to make needed repairs that landlords refuse to perform have provided tenants with self-help remedies to facilitate compliance with these codes (Blumberg and Robbins, 1976).
- Eminent-domain laws give governments the power to appropriate land and buildings altogether for public purposes, with compensation that may not meet the owner's expectations or claims.
- A wide variety of uses may be prohibited via restrictive covenants.
- Uses of property that are illegal or that create a nuisance can be banned.
- The owner's freedom to set rents and evict occupants is subject to legal limits in many localities.
- Short-term buying and selling of housing is discouraged by antispeculation ordinances or high capital-gains taxes.
- Conversion of residential units to nonresidential uses, removal of units from the market, and conversion of rental units to condominiums all are limited or banned in some localities.
- Property owners who do displace occupants are required in some areas to provide home-finding assistance and monetary compensation to those they move out.

Some of these restrictions on the absolute rights of property owners relate solely to the owner and his/her use of the property: eminent-domain and nuisance laws, sales-profit limits, conversion restrictions, and use restrictions based on covenants. Others restrict the owners' rights with respect to nonowning users of the property, who thereby are invested with a set of rights. Rent and eviction controls and required relocation compensation and aids, for example, give to those who by choice or necessity do not own the place they live in a shield against self-interested or arbitrary behavior by the legal owners. The controls may properly be described as a form of property or tenure right.

We need to begin to distinguish between ownership of property that is someone's home and ownership of other kinds of property. The property someone lives in but does not own engenders a special relationship between user and property, consisting of ties built up around that residency. Breaking these ties — destroying the bonds built up through usage (often long-term usage) — produces large individual and social costs. An extreme (but by no means unheard-of) example: although a family may have lived in a rental unit for thirty years, a decision by the legal owner to end that tenancy or sell the property can often require the family to move out in thirty days, or at the end of the lease period, should there be a lease. The financial and psychological costs of such a move, as well as the difficulties of obtaining alternative accommodations, are in most cases deemed legally irrelevant.

Is it not reasonable to assert that such costs are a concern for public policy? The importance of property as residence and the realities of the housing market warrant legal protection for nonowners. Such considerations are often more socially meritorious than the legal owner's right to maximize profits, ignoring all other considerations and rights.

The arguments for the right to stay put in part derive from a concept of the public interest. (Additionally, Paul Davidoff has recently put forth the notion that a legal argument for a right not to be displaced might be fashioned based on the right to travel that the Supreme Court has found implicit in the Constitution [Davidoff, 1983].) More stable communities are likely to produce greater care of property and a lower incidence of crime. There will be fewer antisocial acts related to the anger and impotence experienced by those who are forcibly displaced. The rate at which housing costs are inflating will be reduced. Individual misery will decrease. But the underlying motivation for asserting and supporting such a right is primarily an interest in securing greater equity: more rights and benefits for those in the society who fall at the lower end of the spectrum of resources and power.

Let us look at what this right might mean in detail, how it could be instituted, and what specific instances there have been of such a right in action. The issue breaks down differently depending on whether the persons being protected against forced displacement own or rent their homes.

Protecting Home Owners

The case of home owners is easier to handle (and unfortunately involves far fewer people), since it does not require intervening in the rights and expectations of another actor — the owner of the property — but merely altering those external conditions that are forcing the home owner to sell and move.

These changed external conditions usually involve one of several situations. Property-tax assessments and bills may increase beyond the household's ability to pay. Mortgage-payment costs may increase due to general inflation that in turn triggers an increase in the interest rate under the new variable-rate mortgage instruments now being widely introduced. The quality of public services may deteriorate so as to make the neighborhood less desirable or less suited to the household's needs. The owner's home may deteriorate due to inadequate resources to maintain and repair the building. Mortgage funds to undertake needed rehabilitation may be unavailable. Illegal practices or "scams" related to mortgage financing and home repairs may be perpetrated that deprive home owners of their property. Ways of protecting home owners against each of these threats are suggested below.

Property-tax increases. To handle the problem of increased property taxes in an area that is experiencing rapid gentrification, enactment of a version of some of the more progressive features of California's Proposition 13 would be a relatively simple and effective reform. That is, assessment increases could be limited — in California the cap is 2 percent annually — so long as there is no transfer of property ownership. Only when ownership is transferred can reassessment take place. The reform would effectively insulate existing home owners who wish to remain in an area from the economic forces swirling around them.

A variation of this Proposition 13 feature might be to postpone collection of increased property taxes until title is transferred, rather than having the city entirely forgo the revenue increases. This variation would perhaps better balance the public's and the home owner's interests. The city would recapture the tax based on the increased value upon sale, or it would acquire a lien on the home owner's estate upon death. Eventual repayment of the increased tax obligation thus would be required, without interfering with the owner's current status or plans. Another possibility would be some form of full or partial purchase of the home by the city in exchange for reduction, elimination, or forgiving of property-tax payments.

Mortgage-payment increases. The displacement effects of the new inflation-sensitive mortgage instruments are yet to be felt, but it is inevitable that the mortgages will turn into a major source of displacement. They have indisputably been introduced as an attempt to solve the problems of savings institutions rather than those of housing consumers. Under the traditional level-payment mortgage, the home owner was assured that for the length of the mortgage (usually twenty-five to thirty years), principal and interest payments — the central element in housing costs — were fixed and predictable. Under some of the new mortgage forms — the graduated-payment mortgage, for example — payments rise over the course of the mortgage, but at rates and to levels that are laid out in advance. Under others — the variable-rate mortgage, for instance — the rate and level of increase are not known in advance; they rise (and in theory can fall as well) according to some inflation index, usually with a built-in ceiling.

Consumers desperate to become home owners or to trade up enter into these arrangements; they hope their payment capacities will rise at least as fast as inflation. Many of these owners seem unrealistically optimistic, and some will default as their monthly payments rise. These effects are not neighborhood-specific, but society-wide. The only way to prevent this type of displacement — other than expensive "gap" subsidies to individual households — is to reverse the trend away from fixed-interest-rate mortgages. Possibilities range from consumer and political demands to retain the traditional mortgage instrument to more radical proposals to eliminate mortgage costs entirely in favor of outright housing construction and rehabilitation grants (Hartman and Stone, 1980).

Deterioration in public services. Public disinvestment in basic services, a problem that leads to displacement of owners and renters alike, is an issue that must be aggressively exposed and fought politically, as it was by a community group in the Northside section of Brooklyn, New York. This neighborhood of 12,000 people, an area the city wanted for new industrial development, began to see its sanitation, police, and health services gradually cut back during the mid-1970s. When the city announced it was closing Engine Company #212, located for 114 years in Northside, the neighborhood knew it had to act. The dense wood-frame tenements, nearby paint and chemical factories, and other combustibles made good fire services a must — to close the station was to sign the neighborhood's death warrant. The day before the scheduled closing, hundreds of neighborhood residents surrounded the firehouse and held it hostage. For sixteen months they ran it as "People's Firehouse #1," collecting information to back their claim for reopening the station, researching shortcomings in the area's fire protection system, and running community programs from the building. They also mounted a series of dramatic public protests, including a rush-hour sit-in on the Brooklyn-Queens Expressway following a destructive fire that would have been far less damaging had equipment from Engine Company #212 been able to respond.

In the end, the city finally gave in, restoring services in two stages. The various residential and commercial revitalization projects begun by the residents in People's Firehouse #1 have started to reverse the trend of decline and population loss. Recent firehouse closings in Massachusetts mandated by Proposition 2½ have led to establishment of parallel "people's firehouses" in four communities there, the first of which was aided by "how-to-do-it" lessons given by their Brooklyn predecessors. [1]

Redlining. Unavailability of rehabilitation loans in a given area — a practice termed "redlining" — is a problem Congress addressed when it passed the Home Mortgage Disclosure Act (HMDA) of 1975 and the Community Reinvestment Act (CRA) of 1977. In effect, the HMDA provides a data base to ascertain whether a particular lending institution in fact is redlining, while the CRA provides a tool for community groups to use in fighting this practice. The CRA adds to a lending institution's service obligation the obligation to provide credit within its service area, and permits community groups to present negative information to the federal financial regulatory bodies when lending institutions seek permission to expand, merge, acquire, or close branches.

While few instances exist of actual denial of permission to lending institutions based on their redlining practices, the few cases that do exist are sufficiently frightening to the institutions that they are willing to go to considerable lengths to avoid the possibility of highly lucrative moves being barred. Community groups have found that the main utility of the CRA has been as a threat to induce lenders to negotiate concessions (Center for Community Change, 1979, 1981; National Training and Information Center, 1979). In order to be a truly effective antidisplacement tool, the CRA needs to be strengthened, and community groups need clear antidisplacement demands to bring to the negotiating table.[2]

Criminal practices. Home owners may be displaced by shady practitioners who prey on ill-informed persons needing help with mortgage-loan management or home repairs. Often they use a device known as a "lien sale contract," under which home owners who fail to meet payments can lose their homes. Such practices are rife where owner-occupied single-family homes in stable, moderate-income neighborhoods are rapidly appreciating in value. In Los Angeles, where such scams have been notorious, they were effectively countered by a combination of good investigative reporting by the *Los Angeles Times,* subsequent prosecution by state and local agencies, establishment of home owner fraud-prevention projects by city and county governments, and passage of new state laws.

Protecting Renters

As noted, the problem of tenant displacement is far more complex than that of home owner displacement, since it springs from the competing rights of owner and user of a given property. To the extent a landlord is denied the traditional prerogatives and expectations of property ownership, the owner may withdraw. Fewer persons may be willing to own residential rental property. Thus the assertion of a tenure right for renters necessarily means developing alternatives to the present mode of owning and managing property.

More precisely, if tenants are to avoid displacement, they need protection from eviction, from rent increases beyond their ability to pay, and from removal of their units through demolition or conversion. Yet the concept that the landlord has a right to evict tenants for virtually any reason, with but thirty days' notice or upon termination of the lease period, still dominates relations between the vast majority of American tenants and landlords. Federal, state, and local antidiscrimination laws can on occasion alter this dominance, but discrimination is terribly hard to prove, particularly in a tight housing market where there may be many competitors for any available unit. Landlords rarely are foolish enough to announce—in the presence of witnesses—that illegal prejudices have motivated a decision to evict a tenant or reject an applicant for a vacancy. Eviction in retaliation for assertion of legal rights—particularly the right to have the housing code enforced or to otherwise ensure habitable conditions—also is barred in many jurisdictions. But again motivation is hard to prove. Given the wide range of legally acceptable reasons for eviction — including the absence of a requirement that a reason be offered at all — it is the equally rare landlord who will announce in public a motive of spiteful retaliation when presenting an eviction notice.

"Just-cause" eviction. So-called "just-cause" or "good-cause" eviction statutes may represent a fundamental change in the one-sided landlord-tenant relationship. Such statutes now apply to most federally assisted housing, to every tenant in the state of New Jersey and the District of Columbia, and to certain segments of the renter population in many other states and cities. Residents of mobile homes — usually owners of their home but renters of the lot on which the home stands, and therefore particularly vulnerable to eviction threats — are protected by "just-cause" eviction statutes in Florida, and to some extent in California. Similar protection is offered as part of rent-control laws — to prevent circumvention by means of eviction — in New York City, Los Angeles, San Francisco, San Jose, and over a dozen other municipalities in Connecticut, Massachusetts, California, Virginia, Maryland, and the Virgin Islands. In theory, "just-cause" eviction statutes reverse the tenant-landlord relationship; instead of a landlord having a right to kick a tenant out for virtually any (or no) stated reason, a set of allowable reasons for eviction is stipulated in the law. Only these reasons may be the basis for a court-ordered eviction. A tenant has a secure right of tenure so long as one or more of these conditions is not violated. If the tenant challenges the eviction notice, the burden of proof falls on the landlord to demonstrate that the cause for eviction is one permitted by the statute.

Yet in practice the range of stipulated just causes for eviction is so broad — with many lying outside the tenant's control — that no meaningful right of tenure is created. Nonpayment of rent, violating lease conditions, creating a nuisance, or destroying property — all just causes for eviction in most of these ordinances — can be avoided by most tenants. But the landlord's desire to recover possession for his/her own use or use by a close relative, or to remodel or demolish the property, are matters over which the tenant has no control; most ordinances consider these reasons just causes for eviction.

The greater the number of just causes, the larger the loopholes. If the owner is permitted eviction to allow a relative to move in, how does one protect against the fraudulent use of this reason? The law can include penalties to deter this behavior. But once the tenant is gone, follow-up to ascertain whether the relative actually moved in is unlikely. Even if the relative does not move in, how can one distinguish a genuine change of plans from intentional, collusive misuse of the just cause?

If just-cause eviction statutes are to grant tenants effective security of tenure, they must be written so as to apply to tenant behavior only. This means depriving the property owner of the freedom to evict because he or she wants the unit for personal use or use by a relative, or because the owner wants to remodel the unit, or because the owner wants to remove the unit from the market. Such use or occupancy changes would not necessarily be barred, but they would have to take place only between tenancies, after a truly voluntary move-out of the current occupant.

These are not radical concepts. A unanimous Massachusetts Supreme Court decision recently upheld a Cambridge ordinance that gives the city discretion to grant or withhold eviction permits when the purchaser of a condominium unit wants to evict the current occupant so a new purchaser can move into the unit. The court held that the right to own property did not automatically grant the right to occupy it, that there was a legitimate public interest to be served in government regulation of evictions.[3]

If such rights can be invoked against would-be owner-occupants, obviously they can be invoked against owners whose personal interest is more remote. Controls over removal of units from the rental stock through demolition or conversion to condominiums already appear in several local rent-control ordinances, such as those of Santa Monica and Berkeley, California, and New York City. These cities regard preservation of the rental-housing stock as in the public interest, given the shortage of such housing, the threats to it from profit-seeking developers, the low rates of new construction, and the low incomes and limited choice that renters have.

Thus an important step in guaranteeing a right to stay put is to enact a "just-cause" eviction statute that permits eviction only for a very few tenant-caused reasons — that is, nonpayment of rent, persistent disorderly conduct that neighbors regard as a nuisance, willful or grossly negligent behavior that is destructive of property, or persistent breach of reasonable written rules. It should be noted that in some instances evictions, even for just cause, are now forbidden during extremely cold weather, because of the health consequences of putting families out in such weather. A recent amendment to the District of Columbia Landlord-Tenant Act stipulates that "no landlord shall evict a tenant on any day when the National Weather Service predicts at 8 a.m. that the temperature at the National Airport Weather Station will not exceed twenty degrees Fahrenheit within the next twenty-four hours."[4] Relatedly, the Secretary of Housing and Urban Development issued a telegram in February of 1977 ("Subject: Weather/Fuel Shortage Problems") to all HUD regional and area offices enunciating a policy that "no persons will be evicted from HUD-owned property unless you are certain that the persons evicted are able to move into decent, safe, sanitary and satisfactorily heated housing. Absent such assurances, no occupants will be evicted" (National Housing Law Project, 1977).

Rent controls. Control over arbitrary and inflationary rent increases is another key element of a tenant's right to stay put. In a situation where the demand for decent rental housing far exceeds the supply — the case in nearly every part of the U.S. today — the free market system works to the detriment of consumers. Unlike most other commodities, an excess of demand over supply in housing does not quickly result in increased production to meet the demand or to restore market equilibrium. The short-age and high cost of construction financing and permanent financing, the fear and reality of regulation, high land costs and restrictive land-use reg-ulations, difficulties in managing rental property, and greater available profits from other forms of real-estate development and manipulation — these all combine to retard the market response, which at a minimum occurs over several years. If renters — a disproportionate number of whom are low-income, elderly, nonwhite, or large households — are to be pro-tected from injurious market forces, government regulation of landlords' profit drives is mandatory. Difficulties have appeared in some rent-control ordinances: partial circumvention through black-market practices; the cost of establishing the necessary regulatory mechanisms; reduced attract-iveness of owning, maintaining, and improving rental property. But these defects often result from passing weak, compromised legislation designed to minimize offense to property-owning interests, or from neglecting to fashion the needed array of mechanisms that will produce a combination of controlled rents, adequate property maintenance, and protection and expansion of the rental-housing supply.

A well-designed rent-control ordinance must:
- Keep rent increases to a level that reflects only real and unavoidable cost increases to the landlord.
- Forbid landlords from escaping controls by converting housing to uncontrolled uses (condominiums, commercial activities, new construction).
- Cover as much of the rental-housing stock as possible.
- Regulate rents for the unit regardless of continuity of a specific tenancy.
- Have adequate enforcement mechanisms.

No rent-control ordinance currently in force in the U.S. adequately meets all these criteria. (For an example of the specific provisions such an ordinance might contain, see Hartman, Keating, and LeGates, 1982). But such an ordinance, along with the strong "just-cause" eviction statute outlined above (which also does not currently exist in the United States), would go a long way towards creating truly secure tenure for those who cannot afford or do not wish to own their homes. It cannot, of course, make housing affordable for those who have extremely low incomes. Nor will the ordinance be much help to those with incomes that are not keeping up with inflation. Nor will it help with the housing costs that landlords can legitimately pass on to tenants even under a strong rent-control ordinance — for instance, increases in property taxes, utility costs where these are paid by the landlord, maintenance costs, and mortgage-interest costs where the landlord does not have a fixed-interest-rate mortgage. Rent control can at best only help keep housing affordable. It cannot cre-ate universally affordable housing.

To create truly secure tenure, a well-crafted rent-control ordinance would have to be supplemented by a program of housing subsidies to those who need them. If, even under rent control, a tenant household cannot afford the allowable rent increase, or cannot afford the rent level altogether without paying an unacceptable portion of its income, then adequate government subsidies must be forthcoming. This is a crucial element of any meaningful right to stay put.

THE RIGHT TO DECENT HOUSING

The right to stay put is but a short step from a right to be decently housed. Effective antidisplacement measures are an integral part of a comprehensive housing-reform program. A right not to be displaced implies a right to have been housed satisfactorily in the first place. The same social, political, and moral considerations that condemn the displacement of 2½ million Americans each year so that landlords and developers can make profits also apply to the tens of millions of Americans who are inadequately housed today.

Existing constitutional theories and statutes do not offer a strong basis for asserting that there is a "right to housing" (Michelman, 1970). None of our housing programs has been regarded as vesting an "entitlement" to receive benefits on the entire class of persons eligible for these benefits. (Ironically, the home owners' deduction, although not commonly regarded as a housing program *per se,* grants to all owners who itemize their deductions an entitlement to deduct from their taxable income base all mortgage- interest and property-tax payments. This set of benefits — estimated by the Congressional Budget Office to be $48 billion in fiscal 1983, $57 billion in fiscal 1984 — accrues overwhelmingly to upper-income taxpayers.) But the policies and rights — and above all, political action — outlined above can move us toward some more solid legal underpinnings. Aggressive, carefully designed litigation can advance the day when such a right will be upheld in the courts.

Recent developments around the problem of "homelessness" suggest some promising precedents. A class-action suit brought against the City and State of New York on behalf of men without shelter led to a court-ordered consent judgment in August 1981. Under the consent decree, the city guarantees to provide a shelter, with minimum standards, for any homeless man requesting it (*New York Times,* 1981). The agreement has subsequently been extended to include homeless women (*New York Times,* 1983b). The men's case relied on a provision of the New York State Constitution that made the state responsible for providing "aid, care, and support of the needy," as well as for other statutory obligations to the indigent. The government's acknowledgment of a statutory obligation to house its homeless, at least to a minimum standard, may be regarded as establishing a limited right to housing.

In addition, the District of Columbia government was recently enjoined from closing its men's shelters. The decision was based on a set of rights deriving from the city's policy on homelessness, its past practice of providing these shelters, and its failure to observe due process in arbitrarily attempting to close the shelters without sufficient notice or the opportunity of the shelter residents to challenge the proposed closing.[5]

The homelessness problem, and the nation's awareness of it, are likely to grow. Cuts in federal and state social-welfare programs, decreasing vacancy rates, skyrocketing rents and utility rates, rising unemployment, deinstitutionalization of people with mental disabilities, and the weakening of central-city welfare agencies because of fiscal pressures are likely to lead to increased homelessness (*New York Times,* 1982; *San Francisco Examiner,* 1982; *Washington Post,* 1982). The obligation of government to provide decent housing for the homeless may be extended to other populations, including those who are inadequately housed and those who can find housing only by paying proportions of their income that make impossible the provision of other household necessities.

The recent rise in organized "squatting" also warrants mention here. In Philadelphia, Tulsa, Atlanta, St. Louis, Houston, and other cities, successful campaigns have been organized to move people without adequate housing into empty, often abandoned buildings. Much of this activity has been led by ACORN (the Association of Community Organizations for Reform Now), a nationwide community-organizing group.

Such actions provide housing for those who need it, build strong popular organizations and movements, and bring to light the contradiction of having empty houses at a time when people need housing. Some of these campaigns are aimed at publicly owned properties, in particular housing that has come into HUD's possession as mortgage insurer when the owner/developer abandoned a property or defaulted; others are aimed at privately owned buildings.

While these campaigns have not housed great numbers of people, they highlight the issue of housing/human rights vs. property rights. The response from the public and media has been extraordinarily supportive. A major "Walk-In Urban Homesteading" campaign in Philadelphia, organized by Milton Street, now a state senator, forced HUD to turn over title to 150 homes occupied by "do-it-yourself" homesteaders. While government officials railed against "violation of property rights" and "anarchy," the major Philadelphia newspapers supported the squatters. For example, a *Philadelphia Daily News* (August 8, 1977) editorial, headed "Squatters' Rights," stated:

> Milton Street seems to be an expert at what no other government agency —
> city or federal — is very good at. And he is doing it without miles of red tape,
> bureaucratic forms, administrators, inspectors, lawyers and all the other
> things that make bureaucracy the monster it is. He is putting people who
> need homes into houses that have stood vacant for far too long.
> . . . Rather than doing battle with Street, the [Mayor] Rizzo administration
> and HUD should get behind the man and help him.

ACORN's dozen recent squatting campaigns have received similar media support, with sympathetic "human-interest" news accounts, editorials (*St. Louis Post-Dispatch,* 1982; Brashear, 1982), and columns. Neal Peirce's column in the May 15, 1982, *Washington Post,* " 'Squatter' Housing Is Sign of Times," concluded:

> Oddly enough, housing squatters may be doing a big favor for Europe and North America. Though their actions are technically illegal, they are occupying only long-deserted buildings. In a colorful, compelling way they underscore the blindness of governments that fail — by defective national economic policies and by sluggish local housing bureaucracies — to provide affordable housing and protect the treasure that a nation's old housing stock represents.

This encouraging sign — that common sense and common decency about meeting people's housing needs may transcend formal, legal precepts regarding ownership of property — suggests that carefully prepared publicity and organizing campaigns can be important building blocks toward political and legal acceptance of a "right to housing."

Additionally, litigation over exclusionary zoning is moving toward establishment of a set of housing rights. In the most recent and far-reaching in this line of cases, the New Jersey Supreme Court, in its unanimous "Mt. Laurel II" decision, ordered all of the state's municipalities to take steps to insure housing opportunities for low- and moderate-income households — a decision the state's public advocate characterized as "the most dramatic opinion handed down by any court anywhere in the United States since the one-man, one-vote decision" (*New York Times,* 1983a).

We are increasingly seeing that the profit system is incompatible with the national housing goal of "a decent home and suitable living environment for every American family" that Congress first promulgated in the 1949 Housing Act and reasserted in the 1968 Housing Act. This goal is impossible if people have to pay more than they can afford to reach it or if people constantly are faced with the threat and reality of forced uprooting. For American society the displacement problem raises land reform issues of the profoundest sort.

NOTES

1. A detailed account of this and other specific antidisplacement strategies actually undertaken by community groups can be found in Hartman, Keating, and LeGates (1982).

2. Further information on proposals for strengthening the HMDA and CRA can be obtained through National People's Action, 954 West Washington Blvd., Chicago, IL 60607.

3. See *Flynn* v. *City of Cambridge,* 418 N.E. 2d 335 (1981).

4. Sec. 2, D.C. Act 4-143, new Sec. 501a.

5. See *Williams* v. *Barry,* 490 F. Supp. 941 (1980).

REFERENCES

Blumberg, Richard, and Robbins, Brian Quinn. 1976. "Beyond URLTA: a program for achieving real tenant goals." *Harvard Civil Rights - Civil Liberties Law Review* 11: 1-47.

Brashear, Bob. 1982. "Housing Tulsa's other 'refugees'." *Tulsa* (Oklahoma) *Tribune* (May 14).

Center for Community Change. 1981. *The Community Reinvestment Act: A Citizens' Action Guide.* Washington, DC: Center for Community Change.

Center for Community Change, Neighborhood Revitalization Project. 1979. *Neighborhood Based Reinvestment Strategies: A CRA Guidebook.* Washington, DC: Center for Community Change.

Davidoff, Paul. 1983. "Decent housing for all: an agenda." In *America's Housing Crisis: What Is To Be Done?* Edited by Chester Hartman. Boston: Routledge and Kegan Paul.

Fried, Marc. 1963. "Grieving for a lost home." In *The Urban Condition.* Edited by Leonard Duhl. New York: Basic Books.

Fried, Marc, et al. 1973. *The World of the Urban Working Class.* Cambridge, MA: Harvard University Press.

Gans, Herbert. 1962. *The Urban Villagers.* Glencoe, IL: Free Press.

Hartman, Chester. 1964. "The housing of relocated families." *Journal of the American Institute of Planners* (November): 266–86.

―――. 1971. "Relocation: illusory promises and no relief." *Virginia Law Review* 57: 745–817.

―――. 1979. "Landlord money defeats rent control in San Francisco." *Shelterforce* (Fall).

Hartman, Chester, Keating, Dennis, and LeGates, Richard. 1982. *Displacement: How to Fight It.* Berkeley: National Housing Law Project.

Hartman, Chester, and Stone, Michael. 1980. "A socialist housing program for the United States." In *Urban and Regional Planning in an Age of Austerity.* Edited by Pierre Clavel, John Forester and William Goldsmith. New York: Pergamon Press.

LeGates, Richard, and Hartman, Chester. 1981. "Displacement." *Clearinghouse Review* 15 (July): 207–49.

―――. 1982. "Gentrification-caused displacement." *The Urban Lawyer* 14: 31–55.

Michelman, Frank I. 1970. "The advent of a right to housing: a current appraisal." *Harvard Civil Rights - Civil Liberties Law Review* 5: 207–26.

National Housing Law Project. 1977. *Law Project Bulletin.* Berkeley: National Housing Law Project VII (January-February): 1.

National Training and Information Center. 1979. *Home Mortgage Disclosure Act and Reinvestment Strategies: A Guidebook.* Chicago: National Training and Information Center.

New York Times 1981. "Pact requires city to shelter homeless men." (August 27).

―――. 1982. "Increase in homeless people tests U.S. cities' will to cope." (May 3).

―――. 1983a. "Jersey ruling aids housing for the poor." (January 21).

―――. 1983b. "Equality in shelters." (February 9).

Peirce, Neal. 1982. " 'Squatter' housing is sign of times." *Washington Post* (May 15).

Roisman, Florence Wagman. 1981. *Combatting Private Displacement.* Available from National Clearinghouse for Legal Services, 500 N. Michigan Ave., Suite 1940, Chicago, IL 60611.

San Francisco Examiner. 1982. "Hard times for new homeless." (August 29).

St. Louis Post-Dispatch. 1982. "Toward homesteading?" (April 5).

U.S. Department of Housing and Urban Development. 1981. *Residential Displacement: An Update - Report to Congress.* Washington, DC: HUD Office of Policy Development and Research.

Washington Post. 1982. "1982's homeless: Americans adrift in tents, autos." (August 14).

18

Private Neighborhoods:
A New Direction for the
Neighborhood Movement

ROBERT H. NELSON

The neighborhood movement is nothing new. A leading zoning historian reports that the first zoning ordinance in the United States, adopted in New York City in 1916, had the objective of ensuring that "today's neighborhood will be a neighborhood tomorrow" (Toll, 1969:186). Traditional patterns of American suburban development amounted to the implementation of a neighborhood movement on a massive scale. Many individual communities in the suburbs — each possessing its own spending and taxing authority — are no larger than a single neighborhood. Some analysts have even characterized the American suburban system as a revival of a feudal social organization, with the neighborhood the new equivalent of the feudal district — that is, a manor (McClaughry, 1975).

A more apt analogy, however, is the private club, home owners' association, or condominium. The evolution of suburban land-use controls has effectively transformed the suburban neighborhood into a new form of collectively owned private property.[1] Most private property is defended by the exercise of individual property rights. In the suburban neighborhood, this function is filled instead by zoning; for most practical purposes, zoning has become a collective private property right to the neighborhood environment.

These developments have occurred behind a curtain of legal fictions and myths. Such a disguised evolution, however, is typical of the development of property rights — indeed, perhaps of most social institutions. Historically, most property rights have been recognized only after the fact — reflected in the saying that "possession is nine-tenths of the law." An eminent nineteenth-century student of English land law once commented that "the history of our land laws, it cannot be too often repeated, is a history of legal fictions and evasions, with which the legislature vainly endeavored to keep pace until their results . . . were perforce acquiesced in as a settled part of the law itself" (Pollock, 1883:62).

Although the twentieth century has been characterized by a strong faith in the powers of rational planning and social engineering, in practice the designs of planners have often borne only a slight relationship to the final results. The law of unintended consequences has come to command much greater appreciation in recent years, although it frequently takes a long time before the full gap between plans and consequences can be widely and explicitly acknowledged. Zoning history provides a good case study in these themes.

A NEW COLLECTIVE PROPERTY RIGHT

The essence of a private property right is the power to control the use of the property. Government backs up this power with the coercive instruments of the state available under the police power. Zoning meets these requirements in that it provides direct control over use of land in a neighborhood, enforced by means of the police power. As a property right, zoning is somewhat unusual in that it is collectively exercised and deals only with the exterior elements of otherwise individually owned property. Thus it closely resembles the private rights of home owners' associations or condominium members to control their "common elements."

Zoning rights are exercised not by groups of private individuals, but by the local city council. Use of zoning referenda — approved in principle by the U.S. Supreme Court in 1976 — is the equivalent of polling all the members of the condominium.[2] Local property taxes correspond to assessments imposed on condominium owners based on relative property shares. In most cases, city councils closely follow the wishes of neighborhood residents in administering neighborhood zoning controls, perhaps no less than would a condominium board of directors.

Zoning has provoked controversies similar to much wider battles over the social legitimacy of any private property rights. Arthur Okun described "the big trade-off" with respect to the capitalist system based on private property rights: on the one hand, capitalism provides a marvelous engine of efficiency and productivity; on the other, it promotes widespread social inequality (Okun, 1975). Zoning imposes a similar trade-off. If neighborhood residents create an attractive environment, no one else can capture the benefits of their labors. Zoning thus sustains the incentive to build and maintain such desirable neighborhoods, much as ordinary private property rights sustain productive incentives for the economy as a whole. However, by excluding housing for people with low and moderate incomes, zoning also promotes wide inequalities in levels of neighborhood amenity. Much as the rich drive more expensive cars or eat in better restaurants under a system of private property rights, zoning allows the rich to live in better neighborhoods as well.

Attacks on "exclusionary zoning" essentially challenge the basic right of neighborhood property owners to exclude other uses as they wish. Making the neighborhood a form of privately owned property is blamed for increasing social inequality and, in some cases, causing racial segregation as well. Although not usually recognized as such, this controversy is really a recurrence in a limited sphere of the long-time property-rights debate between capitalism and socialism.

Because of the deep American attachment to private property, challenges to exclusionary zoning have generally proven unavailing (Sager, 1979). Indeed, the role of zoning in protecting neighborhood quality has received wide acceptance, even among many critics of other aspects of zoning. The National Commission on Urban Problems in 1968 commented that

> regulations still do their best job when they deal with the type of situation for which many of them were first intended; when the objective is to protect established character and when that established character is uniformly residential. It is in the "nice" neighborhoods, where the regulatory job is easiest, that regulations do their best job. (National Commission on Urban Problems, 1969:219)

In 1974, the Supreme Court delivered a ringing endorsement, written by Justice William Douglas, of both neighborhoods and the walls for them erected by zoning.

> A quiet place where yards are wide, people few, and motor vehicles restricted are legitimate guidelines in a land use project addressed to family needs. This goal is a permissible one. . . . The police power is not confined to elimination of filth, stench, and unhealthy places. It is ample to lay out zones where family values, youth values, and the blessings of quiet seclusion and clean air make the area a sanctuary for people.[3]

While zoning is analogous to a private property right, direct government involvement was still necessary in its initial creation. Most private property owners could not band together to establish ordinary private property rights to their neighborhood environment — although such rights are established in many large developments where condominium or other forms of collective ownership exists. In neighborhoods already existing under separate ownership, prohibitively large negotiation and other transaction costs would be incurred in trying to form voluntary private agreements among the residents — agreements which would have to be unanimous. By use of government coercive powers, however, zoning can short-circuit these costs. Zoning's legal fictions have been necessary because there is no explicit provision in American legal tradition for government redistribution of private property rights by fiat. If the true function of zoning had originally been made more explicit, zoning in all likelihood would not have survived its early legal challenges. Instead, zoning was portrayed as a new device for controlling nuisances or, even more misleadingly, as a necessary instrument for implementing public land-use plans.

Zoning authority is employed not only to protect an existing neighborhood environment, but also by many suburban municipalities to exclude most new uses altogether from currently undeveloped neighborhoods. This use of zoning has much less justification in public policy or law, since it mainly aims to preserve open spaces and a rural municipal environment at little cost to municipal residents. Indeed, I have argued elsewhere that the authority for municipal zoning actions of this kind should be revoked.[4]

To be sure, zoning still lacks some important elements of a property right. Most critically, as will be discussed later, transfers of zoning rights (that is, zoning changes) cannot be accomplished by direct sale — at least, not legally. Zoning also does not grant complete discretion to private owners to control use of neighborhood property. The courts, for example, limit the ability of zoning to control fine details of use that affect only the aesthetic character of a neighborhood. The creation of historic districts in many cases represents an effort to escape this limitation under a fiction of historic significance.

For the most part, broader zoning issues — if not specific zoning changes — have been debated and decided out of public view by a narrow segment of the legal profession. In recent years, however, neighborhoods have become a popular cause (Boyte, 1980). While the neighborhood movement thus far has generated more talk than action, it could yet prove more substantial. The neighborhood movement is moving in a direction that provides an intellectual legitimacy to the "privatizing" of zoning, a legitimacy that so far has been lacking.

THE NEIGHBORHOOD MOVEMENT

In March 1979 the National Commission on Neighborhoods conveyed its final report to the president. The commission enthusiastically endorsed a greater social role for neighborhoods, giving a high-level official blessing to a growing neighborhood movement. The commission reported that "the neighborhood movement represents a demand for self-government in the daily lives of people as well as in the dry abstractions of law. It represents a demand for returning to the residents of neighborhoods the capacity for effective influence in policymaking. It represents a demand for debureaucratizing America" (National Commission on Neighborhoods, 1979:10).

The emergence in the 1970s of a vigorous neighborhood movement was in many ways a remarkable development. In the 1960s most urban experts decried the fragmentation of the suburbs into small municipalities, some even of neighborhood scale. Indeed, for most of this century the refrain of urban professionals has been the excessive decentralization of local government. In a well-known study of the New York metropolitan region, *1400 Governments,* political scientist Robert Wood lamented the social divisions and lack of policy coordination resulting from so much division of responsibility. Wood considered that "the individual strategies of individual municipalities are condemned to frustration because of the sheer number of their neighbors."[5] Although mostly unsuccessful, a long tradition of municipal reform sought the formation of metropolitan governments. The local neighborhood stood for parochialism and resistance to modern social currents. Nonlocal governments sought to break down neighborhood distinctions in the interests of a more fully homogeneous and equal society.

Thus, the emergence of a neighborhood movement shows shifting tides of public opinion. In the pursuit of efficiency and equality, modern society may have taken for granted other critical dimensions. The neighborhood is now seen as attractive because it seems to offer virtues that are threatened by modern life — close personal ties, strong moral values, mutual trust, permanence, and stability.

The critical black box in modern social science has been the creation of values. No one can doubt that a solid structure of values is fundamentally important to a well-functioning society. Yet the social sciences generally offer little if any guidance on how to build values. Indeed, science is supposed to be value-free. The main body of economics is erected on the assumption that values are given, and economic analysis begins only after that point. In this respect, economic science, along with other social sciences, can be accused of myopia. For example, the act of competing in a market in itself has a critical influence on the formation of personal values. Deeper social thinkers such as de Tocqueville and Max Weber have emphasized the inextricable linkages among cultural, religious, and economic institutions. Proximity may make it more difficult for us to recognize these linkages in the current era, but there is no reason to believe them less important.

THE NEIGHBORHOOD AS COMMUNITY

During the nineteenth century the state, the local community, and private associations and organizations were the prime objects of American communal attachments. De Tocqueville found that

> Americans of all ages, all stations in life, and all types of disposition are forever forming associations. There are not only commercial and industrial associations in which all take part, but others of a thousand different types — religious, moral, serious, futile, very general and very limited, immensely large and very minute. Americans combine to give fetes, found seminaries, build churches, distribute books, and send missionaries to the antipodes. Hospitals, prisons, and schools take shape in that way. Finally, if they want to proclaim a truth or propagate some feeling by the encouragement of a great example, they form an association. (de Tocqueville, 1969:513)

De Tocqueville felt that "nothing . . . deserves more attention than the intellectual and moral associations in America." He even went so far as to say that "among laws controlling human societies there is one more precise and clearer it seems to me, than all the others. If men are to remain civilized or to become civilized, the art of association must develop and improve among them at the same speed as equality of conditions spreads" (de Tocqueville 1969:517). De Tocqueville considered that the voluntary association in America filled a need for social leadership and continuity that in Europe had traditionally been met by a native aristocracy.

In Europe the old aristocratic order was gradually being destroyed by the market forces of capitalism. The growth of nationalism substituted a new national community for old local ties. Socialism went the furthest in exalting the nation, proposing to put all key responsibilities in the hands of a government acting in the name of a single national (ideally, international) community. Many prominent students of socialism, including Keynes and Schumpeter, have noted its critical role in providing a system of basic values and beliefs — in essence, a new form of religion.[6]

A similar longing for national community characterized the Progressive movement in the U.S. early in this century. Many of its leaders considered that a "powerful central government was but the instrument of a far larger project: the creation of a true national community, within which Americans would transcend self-interest altogether and bind themselves to the purposes of the nation" (Schambra, 1982:39). A sense of community was seen as an antidote to the alienation of the individual who has no other goal than his own interest. As a leading Progressive theorist, Herbert Croly, put it, "The promise of American life is to be fulfilled — not merely by a maximum of economic freedom, but by a certain measure of discipline; not merely . . . by the satisfaction of individual desires, but by a large measure of individual subordination and self-denial." This would be accomplished by Americans who understand the "necessity of subordinating the satisfaction of individual desires to the fulfillment of a national purpose."[7]

There is no longer the automatic confidence today, however, that the nation is capable of fulfilling this role. It may be, according to Schambra, a realistic possibility during dire crises such as World War II, but "self-transcendent, nation forging moments are truly extraordinary, . . . requiring extraordinary circumstances (such as war), which are not often desirable, and extraordinary leaders (such as Lincoln and Roosevelt), who are not often at hand." In Schambra's perspective, the accrual of power and responsibility at the federal level after World War II represented a fundamental misjudgment. It was workable only with a strong sense of national community, which, while it may have existed for a while, could not be sustained over the long run. In short, "it seeks to make permanent and ordinary a kind and degree of community possible only in transitory and extraordinary circumstances" (Schambra, 1982:41).

Providing evidence of a declining sense of national community, interest is instead reviving in the nineteenth-century local and private forms of community association found by de Tocqueville to be so attractive in American life. A 1977 study focused on the role of mediating structures in public policy—church, family, union, and other private institutions that stand between the individual and the state. Mediating structures were seen as performing a critical function because they "are the value-generating and value-maintaining agencies in society." Of particular note is the authors' view that "the neighborhood should be seen as a key mediating structure in the reordering of our national life" (Berger and Neuhaus, 1977:6 and 8).

Such new mediating structures are considered necessary partly to offset the excessive individualism fostered by the market—a conclusion found frequently in the writings of conservationists as well as liberals. Market-fostered individualism, in Schambra's view, "has meant the unleashing of the productive and acquisitive energies of millions of people, creating in America a prosperity beyond the wildest fantasies of earlier men." Yet Schambra maintains it is also possible to "prize the liberty and prosperity bequeathed to us by the founders without being complacent about some of the uglier, and perhaps even dangerous, aspects of American self-interest. A regime grounded in self-interest does tend to be less generous or compassionate (at least in its official pronouncements) than, say, a Christian or socialist commonwealth founded on selfless ideals such as charity, benevolence, or universal brotherhood" (Schambra, 1982:37). The neighborhood might provide a socialist commonwealth on a small scale—indeed, probably the only scale at which the vision is not purely utopian. It has often been said that true democracy is probably practical only at the level of the city-state.

Showing the wide reach of such thinking, the National Commission on Neighborhoods conferred an official blessing on a concept of the neighborhood as a key "mediating structure":

> If city, state, and federal governments are to effectively respond to people's needs, and if the natural resource of every person is to be converted into energy for the common good, then healthy neighborhoods are essential. Neighborhoods are human in scale, and they are immediate in people's experience. Since their scale is manageable, they nurture confidence and a sense of control over the environment. Neighborhoods have built-in "coping mechanisms" in the form of churches, voluntary associations, formal and informal networks. The neighborhood is a place where one's physical surroundings become a focus for community and a sense of belonging. (National Commission on Neighborhoods, 1979:276)

A new major role for neighborhoods would require a wide diversity of neighborhood types; tastes in neighborhood values and environments are far too varied to think of enforcing any single communal model across the nation. Diversity makes acceptable collective restrictions on personal behavior at the neighborhood level that would be wholly unacceptable at the national level. As long as a wide latitude exists for people to choose a neighborhood, no one would be forced to bow to community values he or she finds strongly objectionable. To the contrary, each individual would join together with other neighborhood residents of similar values to sustain a particular social environment to their liking. As Peter Berger and Richard Neuhaus put it,

> the whole point, however, is the dramatic difference between a nation and a neighborhood. One is citizen of a nation and lays claim to the rights by which that nation is constituted. Within that nation there are numerous associations such as neighborhoods — more or less freely chosen — and membership in those associations is usually related to affinity. This nation is constituted as an exercise in pluralism, as the *unum* within which myriad *plures* are sustained. (Berger and Neuhaus, 1977:12-13)

This model of a plurality of neighborhoods, many perhaps enforcing rigid restraints on their own residents, requires some rethinking of traditional attitudes concerning local powers to restrict civil liberties. The establishment of a desirable neighborhood environment includes not only the physical environment but also the social environment. Neighborhood control would thus extend beyond property to some kinds of social behavior. Neighborhoods might, for example, adopt dress codes for public places. A neighborhood of members of a particular religious sect might require specific garb prescribed by the religion. A colony of nudists, on the other hand, might ban the wearing of clothes in certain gathering-places. Some neighborhoods might prohibit X-rated movies, while others would have no objection.

A few strict libertarians may oppose any steps to legitimize or sanction tight neighborhood authority — private or public. They will regard almost any kind of neighborhood controls as an unacceptable infringement on personal liberty. However, it is equally an infringement on individual freedom to deny a person the opportunity to live in a social environment of his choice. Full individual freedom requires that a motorcyclist be free not to wear a helmet, however foolish this may seem; it also requires that the individual have the right to affiliate with a group and to subject himself to group authority, however foolish others may regard this action. Of course, it is also essential that each individual be able freely to reverse this decision — that there be no barriers to leaving the group. Each individual should also have the freedom to live in a group that rejects most social controls.

THE NEIGHBORHOOD AS ANTIDOTE TO BUREAUCRACY

While the neighborhood movement has reflected a discontent with the alienating character of the market, it has also reflected an equally strong discontent with big government and big bureaucracy. Bureaucratic government in its impersonality and unresponsiveness offers little if any improvement on the market, similarly eroding critical social values. The National Commission on Neighborhoods commented that

> people do not live as numbers in an economic report, as the disembodied statistics that distant bureaucracies deal with as though they were the reality rather than a mere representation of it. Middle income, working, and poor neighborhoods alike experience the frustration of government that does too little, costs too much, and denies meaningful influence to the vast majority. Power has been more centralized; people have become more alienated. More Americans live together, yet feel alone. Increasingly government deals with Americans as clients, not citizens; as sources of revenue, but not of authority. (National Commission on Neighborhoods, 1979:7)

The commission considered that an enhanced neighborhood role would spur much greater sensitivity to the widely varying needs and values of individual neighborhoods.

> The diversity of neighborhood groups, which may seem to be a weakness, in fact is an important strength. They can respond flexibly, with different organizational structures, across a range of issues from sanitation services to discriminatory insurance rates. Community development organizations and advocacy groups are best suited to certain tasks; neighborhood government can deal better with problems such as juvenile crime with which larger social institutions deal badly, if at all. (National Commission on Neighborhoods, 1979:9)

One of the undesired consequences of the growth of big government has been to divide the public into more numerous interest-group factions, each competing to influence government actions to its own advantage (Lowi, 1969). The foremost victims of this system of interest-group competition have often been the poor; in a system where political power is typically exercised in groups, the lack of social organization of the poor has been a particular handicap. Thus, in big cities it is often the poorest neighborhoods which receive the lowest quality of service delivery. On close inspection, many government programs to aid the poor turn out to be of much greater benefit to the middle class. In recent years Social Security recipients and other middle-class beneficiaries of government income transfers have resisted budget cuts much more effectively than the poor.

One of the main objectives of the neighborhood movement has been to organize the poor to participate more effectively in political life. By developing a much greater social cohesiveness at the neighborhood level, the level of voting of the poor might be raised. The leadership of the neighborhood could speak for residents in city and metropolitan political contests. The experience gained in political activity in the neighborhood might develop the skills needed in much wider political arenas. In general, a neighborhood organization might provide an effective mechanism whereby the poor could marshal their own resources to help themselves.

Perhaps without realizing it, the neighborhood movement effectively seeks to bring suburban government patterns into the central city itself. Rather than the time-honored recommendation of the central city expanding by annexations to envelop the suburbs, the recommendation is now reversed—the suburban pattern of small local jurisdictions should move into the central city.

A NEW LEGITIMACY FOR PRIVATE NEIGHBORHOODS

The new intellectual respectability of the neighborhood, combined with long-standing popular support for neighborhoods already shown in suburban settings, suggests a promising future for the neighborhood. The neighborhood movement may provide an intellectual legitimacy that will make it possible for the private neighborhood to receive formal acknowledgment. The legal fictions that have surrounded zoning thus might be dropped. New collective private property rights similar to those exercised by home owners' associations and condominium owners might formally replace zoning. At a minimum, the change would be an advance for intellectual clarity and honesty.

The goals of the neighborhood movement—stronger personal values, longer-term stability, a firmer sense of belonging and community identity—are more typically associated with private institutions. The church and the family have been the foundation for these needs in most societies. Americans expect government to show characteristics such as objectivity, neutrality, efficiency, and equity. The new neighborhood role would often give greater latitude to be subjective, emotional, arbitrary, value-laden, discriminating, and perhaps discriminatory. Neighborhoods cannot achieve significant independence unless—for better or worse—they actually have considerable scope to decide their own fate. If the neighborhood is to play a growing part in American life, it is probably better accomplished in a private context.

Feudal society was centered on small social units of neighborhood size. In recent years proposals reminiscent of feudalism have been heard with surprising frequency. A recent polemic advocates the dissolution of the United States into independent nation-states (Cummins, 1980). The popular novel, *Ecotopia,* portraying an environmentalist utopian vision, describes what amounts to a revived feudalism in the Pacific Northwest, which has seceded from the rest of the U.S. (Callenbach, 1977). Yet modern society must provide wide scope for economic growth and development—current concerns about alienation and lack of values arise partly because material needs are already so well satisfied. Romantic pastoral notions to the contrary, there would be few volunteers for a feudal system that also promised a feudal standard of living.

The modern requirement thus is for a balance between forces for stability and forces for change. Zoning protection of suburban neighborhoods has provided a great deal of stability. However, zoning has fared poorly in offering flexibility and the possibility of necessary change. These features could be achieved by allowing the right of entry into neighborhoods to become a normal marketable commodity, subject to normal market forces. Such a step would be a logical accompaniment to the formal recognition of zoning as a private property right.

SALE OF ENTRY RIGHTS INTO NEIGHBORHOODS

Land use is constantly evolving. A new highway interchange or new mass-transit stop can create strong demands for higher-density, more intensive development. Such demands raise questions as to the willingness of a neighborhood to accept any new uses, the speed with which new uses might be introduced, the particular sites for the new uses, and the impacts on neighbors who want to remain after the neighborhood has begun to change character. However, the implicit assumption of most neighborhood residents, reflected in the design of zoning and other neighborhood institutions, is that the neighborhood will always stay as it is. Anthony Downs has commented that "local residents naturally tend to be partisans of their particular areas. They are also very conservative about major changes in existing institutions, no matter how bad, and are much more interested in immediate local improvements" (Downs, 1981:10–11).

In the post–World War II period there have been two main areas of land-use transition — the farming fringes of metropolitan areas and poor inner-city neighborhoods. Indeed, these two areas have been closely linked; the expansion of the suburbs has drawn the population from the center cities, causing neighborhoods there to change as well. In the future, however, this direction may be reversed, reflecting a shift back to the city caused by higher energy prices and a greatly reduced pace of highway construction. The strongest development pressures may occur in existing central-city neighborhoods — the "gentrification" process. The society as a whole has a strong interest in finding ways to channel and accommodate demands for new uses that arise. It is possible that neighborhood exclusions in central cities could pose an obstacle to the future housing supply in much the way that past suburban zoning exclusions hindered development of suburban land.

As matters now stand, only the immediate land-owner in a neighborhood benefits from entry of a new use. This leaves the rest of the neighborhood to suffer any undesirable consequences, causing the neighbors to try to deny most new entry. In the face of growing demands for neighborhood land, however, even the most resistant neighborhood is likely to be overcome eventually by economic pressures. The precipitating event for suburban land-use change has often been corruption or other unsavory zoning practices. Sale of development rights thus is actually commonplace under the current zoning system; however, the sale has had to occur through extralegal rather than institutionally provided channels. In addition to its

ethical corrosiveness, this practice has had many other undesirable consequences, not the least being a tendency towards piecemeal, uncoordinated
development.

Under an alternative system, just as most private rights are salable, the
right of entry into a private neighborhood would be salable. The neighborhood as a collective unit would undertake the transaction and distribute the financial rewards. If this were the case, neighborhood residents
could then jointly make a decision that balanced their own desires for stability and continuity with outside needs for use of neighborhood land.
These outside needs would be represented by the prices for neighborhood
entry that potential new users were willing to pay. Acceptance of an offer
would show that the neighbors collectively were compensated adequately
for any disruptions imposed on them or for other adverse impacts on new
neighborhood development.

Left to its own devices, the market is a powerful engine for change.
When property becomes more valuable in one use than another, market
incentives lead to its sale to the user who values it most highly. As long as
the transaction is voluntary on both sides, both the buyer and seller benefit. The new buyer receives a property more valuable than alternative uses
of the money; the seller, on the other hand, prefers receipt of the payment
and the purchasing power it conveys. Currently, neighborhood institutions not only fail to utilize such market virtues, but actively obstruct their
functioning.

The rigidity of current zoning also inhibits small-scale use changes that
might well enhance existing neighborhood character. A convenience store,
small restaurant, drugstore, or other such facility, attractively designed,
could be an asset to many neighborhoods. Zoning generally poses a barrier
to the mixing of uses, partly because such mixing would require broad exercise of regulatory discretion. The courts, fearing that arbitrary and ca-
pricious actions might result, have traditionally held that government
powers should not be wielded in a highly discretionary fashion. Yet, at
least since the writings of Jane Jacobs, many urban analysts have con-
tended that neighborhoods of mixed uses are the most satisfactory (Jacobs,
1961). Sale of entry into neighborhoods would make such mixing possible,
again leaving the final use of neighborhood land in the hands of neighborhood residents themselves.

The American world of business was shaped by the development in the
nineteenth century of the corporate form of collective private ownership of
business property. Collective ownership of private residential property
could similarly exert a great influence on the future living environment
for Americans. In some places private communities under condominium
or other collective ownership forms are now assuming many of the functions formerly performed by municipalities. They not only regulate land
use, but provide private police, sanitation, and other community services.
The appropriate interrelationships among public and private institutions

at the local level are generally in a state of flux and seem certain to become a major issue.

A BRIEF PROSPECTUS

The full realization of private neighborhoods would constitute a major American land reform at the neighborhood level. Achieving this objective would require devising brand-new forms of land tenure that formally established collective private property rights as a replacement for existing zoning. Property rights within the private neighborhood would be divided into individual and collective rights, the latter including control over the "common elements" of the neighborhood, such as trees, shrubbery, and fencing, as well as control over more substantial changes. The decision to substitute private rights for zoning would occur by vote of the neighborhood residents — perhaps by a 66 percent, 75 percent, or even higher-proportion vote, but not requiring absolute unanimity. The neighborhood residents would exercise their new private property right through a neighborhood association or other suitable collective instrument.[8]

As a private entity, the neighborhood association would be able to negotiate with potential new users over financial terms of entry into the neighborhood. A retail or business facility desiring a neighborhood location would need to offer a price high enough to secure neighborhood agreement. For example, agreement might be reached to pay the neighborhood $100,000 for permission to modify a neighborhood property for use as a restaurant. This money could be distributed among neighborhood residents according to their relative shareholdings in the neighborhood. It might also be appropriate to provide disproportionately higher payments to those neighbors located closest to the new use.

Shareholdings in the neighborhood would be determined according to the value of property owned in the neighborhood. Renters and others not owning property thus would not normally have a vote, although they might vote on some limited matters.

It is possible that portions — or even all — of a privately owned neighborhood would be sold lock, stock, and barrel to a new developer. For example, a neighborhood located adjacent to a new highway interchange might make way for a new shopping center, allowing the neighborhood residents collectively to reap a large windfall for their troubles. Neighborhood residents would vote on such a prospect, again requiring a high percentage in favor but not unanimity. Analogous to such a vote would be a decision of corporate stockholders to accept a takeover bid by another company, perhaps putting the corporate assets to a whole new use.

There would be wide flexibility in the type of private controls exercised over neighborhood property. Some neighborhoods might well prefer that there be no neighborhood controls on use of property — a solution that a neighborhood of libertarians might find appealing. Farm neighborhoods, for instance, might prefer minimal neighborhood control over farmland use (Nelson, 1981). However, other neighborhoods might prefer tight controls over even fine details of architectural design, or over matters such as paint color. New uses would have to conform precisely to the neighborhood historical context and culture. The key point is that, in keeping with the neighborhood movement's aspiration toward local autonomy, each neighborhood could determine its own private controls. Home buyers could then select a neighborhood which maintained the sort of collective controls they preferred. The result would be a wide individual choice in neighborhood designs and types.

Under the current zoning system, municipal administration of zoning relieves individual neighborhoods of the burden of administering collective controls. This is a significant advantage for many neighborhoods which lack legal and other skills. With the creation of private neighborhoods, this administrative function would not necessarily shift to the neighborhood. Instead, law firms or other private service firms could be expected to arise which specialized in assisting the exercise of neighborhood property rights. They would call neighborhood meetings, supervise agenda- and decision-making procedures, and otherwise aid in exercise of neighborhood rights. Their presence would help to assure that neighborhood decision making treated all parties fairly and equitably.

SOME NEWLY FORMED PRIVATE NEIGHBORHOODS

Existing models for such tenure include home owners' associations, condominiums, and other forms of private collective ownership of property rights which have been widely adopted in the past fifteen years for large-scale developments. There are also a few instances where separately owned properties have later been brought together under private collective ownership. The best-known instance is the conversion of existing public streets into private streets in the St. Louis area — by now involving more than one thousand streets. This case has been closely studied by the community planner, Oscar Newman:

> For many students of the dilemma of American cities, the decline of St. Louis, Missouri, has come to epitomize the impotence of federal, state, and local resources in coping with the consequences of large-scale population change. Yet buried within those very areas of St. Louis which have been experiencing the most radical turnover of population are a series of streets where residents have adopted a program to stabilize their communities, to deter crime, and to guarantee the necessities of a middle-class lifestyle. These residents have been able to create and maintain for themselves what their city was no longer able to provide: low crime rates, stable property values, and a sense of community. Even though the areas surrounding them are experiencing significant socioeconomic change, high crime rates, physical deterioration, and abandonment, these streets are still characterized by

middle-class owner-occupied residency—both black and white. The distinguishing characteristic of these streets is that they have been deeded back from the city to the residents and are now legally owned and maintained by the residents themselves. (Newman, 1980:124)

The private streets are closed off to through traffic, helping to create a well-defined neighborhood area free of vehicular disruption. According to Newman, "residents claim that the physical closure of streets and their legal association together act to create social cohesion, stability and security. The private association provides a legal framework which structures this cohesion, and the physical closure provides an effective tool for allowing residents to control the activities on their street" (Newman, 1980:126).

Residents of a private street have literally had the street conveyed from the city to themselves. They are assessed a yearly fee to cover street maintenance and other joint responsibilities. Covenants are attached to the properties providing for neighborhood control over the uses of homes and property. Originally, creation of a private street required 100 percent agreement from street residents, but Newman reports that St. Louis has examined lowering the requirement to 95 percent (Newman, 1980:155).

Study of the St. Louis experience has shown that the existence of private ownership in itself plays a key role in the stabilization of neighborhoods. If a street remains publicly owned, even its closing "is unlikely, in itself, to provide the social and legal reinforcement necessary to resist change." Moreover, according to Newman, "the evidence indicates that public block associations do not provide residents with the same protections as private associations." The effect of the conversion to private ownership is to enhance greatly the sense of neighborhood identity. Newman found that "when asked by our interviewers to delimit the boundaries of their neighborhood, residents of private streets almost invariably defined it as congruent with their private street. By contrast, residents on public streets rarely equated the boundary of their neighborhood with that of their street." One private-street resident enthusiastically reported, "When I come through those gates onto Cabanne Place, it is like coming into another world. . . . There's a spirit here to keep things going. Closing the street gives the area a different feeling. If it is closed, you have the feeling of control and that you are living on your own turf" (Newman, 1980:153–54, 132–33).

SOME PARTIAL MODELS

While there are only a few instances of the full creation of a private neighborhood from separately owned properties, there are many other situations that contain partial elements of this approach to urban land reform.

In some cases, new private neighborhoods have been formed by individual renters or lessees taking over properties which the original developer wished to abandon. Because the properties have never been individually owned, it is easier to form such a private neighborhood. This procedure is being followed, for example, in Austinville, Virginia, where the lead and zinc mines recently closed after 225 years of operation. The newly formed corporation of New Town, Inc., will take over sixty-seven homes from the mining company, assess fees against each home owner for sewer, utilities, and other common facilities, and manage the jointly owned properties.

A similar procedure was followed in David, Kentucky, where coal mining stopped in 1968. The residents eventually joined together to form the David Community Development Corporation, which raised $110,000 to buy the whole town — a move that was credited with saving it. One corporation member, demonstrating a new high morale, reports that "the real story of David is the story of its people. Every person over eighteen in this town is a member of this corporation. The Planning Committee and the Board of Directors meet more than twice a week on planning and to make decisions. . . . We now own our own town and own our own homes, and we keep both of them up. We have a water system now and a sewer system and a day care center, and we know exactly where we are going (HUD, 1979:79).

The Institute for Community Economics in Greenfield, Massachusetts, has pioneered the conept of a "community land trust" (Institute for Community Economics, 1982). This approach may involve the formation of a neighborhood organization by means of acquisition or donation of separately owned properties. The trust then owns all the land and property, much like a cooperative. However, members of a community land trust receive a lifetime lease which is also heritable. Members elect a board of trustees to manage community affairs. The most distinctive feature of community land trusts is the effort to promote economic integration in such communities. The leaseholdings are not intended to be salable for their market value; rather, their price is controlled by the trust at the original acquisition cost plus the value of any improvements made. In this way it is hoped that entry of low- and moderate-income groups into the neighborhood can be maintained. The community land trust thus far has seen only limited application, but demonstrates the appeal of collective property rights within the neighborhood movement. (CLTs are examined more closely in chapter 13 of the present volume.)

The goals of community land trusts could be facilitated by the new institutions for neighborhood property rights described above. The neighborhood concept required would be one of the many neighborhood types made feasible by a wider social role for private neighborhoods. The residents of any given neighborhood would need only to adopt the specific concept of a neighborhood that they desired.

The Sabre Foundation in Washington, DC, has sought to promote establishment of "neighborhood enterprise associations." Initially, these associations might be formed within the urban enterprise zones proposed by the Reagan administration and several members of Congress. Neighborhood enterprise associations would receive, at nominal prices, long-term leases to existing government land and other properties which they could later sublet at going market prices — in this way creating a powerful financial incentive to improve the area. Tax benefits would also be available where an association took over municipal services, thereby relieving public service burdens. The associations in general would be expected to serve as a stabilizing influence in poorer areas, promoting neighborhood loyalties and identity (Frazier, 1980).

If private neighborhoods are to be widely created, a less than unanimous vote will have to be sufficient. This procedure may raise some legal issues, such as the fairness of forcing unwilling property owners to join a private collective organization — even though property owners are now subject to equivalent compulsions under zoning. In Connecticut, creation of historic-district zoning can be accomplished if 75 percent of residents vote favorably — considerably less than unanimous agreement. A similar issue is faced in the creation of special service districts. Such districts have been widely established in many parts of the country for a variety of purposes, including fire, sanitation, water supply, and police provision. In Connecticut, special tax districts can be established by majority approval of as few as twenty voters. About two hundred such Connecticut districts have been created, ranging from a few acres to several hundred.

Service districts have a formal public status but operate in many respects as a private enterprise. For example, the provision of services is often financed by a direct pricing scheme in the form of user charges and fees. Creation of special districts occurs by vote of district residents and normally does not require unanimous consent. The minority of unwilling residents are nevertheless required to pay special assessments and user fees and otherwise to accept the terms of membership in the district. The imposition of new private neighborhood controls on property use seems no more severe an infringement on property rights than the creation of a special tax district.

A business precedent for compelling a minority of unwilling property owners to join a private collective ownership is provided by oil and gas "unitization" laws. These laws — enacted in twenty-eight states — require that separately owned private properties above a common oil pool must be developed jointly, thereby preventing individual property owners from draining the pool to the detriment of fellow owners. In most states the consent of a majority or more of the oil and gas interests involved — ranging from 50 to 85 percent in different state statutes — is needed to form a unit agreement.

The National Conference of Commissioners on Uniform State Laws has recently published proposals for uniform state statutes for condominium, home owner association, and cooperative forms of private property ownership (National Conference of Commissioners on Uniform State Laws, 1980a, 1980b, 1981). Under the proposed uniform statutes, it appears that private owners of collective property could jointly enter into transactions involving sale and purchase of entry rights into the neighborhood. However, there is no provision for establishing a new neighborhood ownership with less than unanimous consent of existing neighborhood residents. Once a private collective ownership is established, it is standard practice to operate on a basis of less than unanimous agreement of the members.

The issue of the morally and philosophically legitimate uses of government coercive powers has attracted considerable attention in recent years (Nozick, 1974). On the one hand, the initial creation of private neighborhoods would necessitate wide use of such powers. On the other hand, once private neighborhoods were created, many responsibilities could be decentralized to small, homogeneous neighborhoods. The necessity to override minority preferences in large governmental units with diverse populations would be greatly reduced.

CONCLUSION

The neighborhood movement does not offer a carefully crafted and fully developed view of the world. Its objectives are not always compatible. Perhaps the greatest significance of the neighborhood movement lies in the challenge it poses to some widely accepted beliefs.

The neighborhood movement shows a deep distrust of market institutions. The market is regarded as a destabilizing influence which erodes rather than sustains important social values. However, unlike traditional market antagonists, the neighborhood movement also shows a great distrust for governmental solutions. Large bureaucracies are seen as little better — perhaps no better — than the market in their effects on the human spirit and human values. The institution of the neighborhood is attractive precisely because it seems to offer a communal alternative that could shield its residents both from the forces of the market and from large bureaucracies.

However, neighborhoods insulated from the market and from government would be isolated from the primary forces for change in modern society. Like the environmental movement, the neighborhood movement reflects a wide loss of faith in the possibilities for social progress. There is no longer a broad conviction that scientific advance — translated into goods and services by profit-making incentives — is leading inexorably towards great future abundance and well-being. Rather, the current utopian visions portray autonomous communities of neighborhood scale in a pastoral setting, insulated from forces for change.

The need is for a better compromise between the ideals of community stability and vitality on the one hand and technocratic efficiency and social progress on the other. Achieving such compromises may well require the design of new social institutions. The proposal made in this paper for private neighborhoods offers a possible approach. By making the neighborhood a private institution, neighborhood residents acquire firm internal control over their own neighborhood environment, promoting the desired stability. But by also allowing neighborhood residents to sell entry rights, a desirable flexibility is introduced to accommodate socially beneficial changes in the use of neighborhood land. The neighborhood residents themselves would decide whether social benefits resulting from neighborhood use changes exceeded the costs of disruption.

Finally, if neighborhoods are to maintain greater autonomy, they will require formal protections. The neighborhood movement thus far has stirred strong popular enthusiasm, but its aims will have a much more lasting impact if they are codified in and supported by new legal institutions. There are two basic models under which neighborhood autonomy could be sustained: the neighborhood as sovereign state or the neighborhood as private property. American traditions of respect for private property, the existence of many incremental steps already taken toward private neighborhoods, and the greater ability to accommodate social change all point toward the private neighborhood rather than the sovereign neighborhood as the preferred institutional framework.

NOTES

1. For a full review of this evolution, see Nelson (1977). A summary is given in Nelson (1979). Similar interpretations of zoning are developed by Tarlock in Bangs (1972); Ellickson (1977); Fischel (1978, 1979, 1980).
2. *City of Eastlake* v. *Forest City Enterprises, Inc.,* 426 U.S. 668 (1976).
3. *Village of Belle Terre* v. *Boraas,* 416 U.S. at 9 (1974).
4. See Nelson (1977), especially chapters 2 and 8.
5. Wood in Chinitz (1964), p. 153. This chapter is excerpted from Wood with Almendinger (1961).
6. See especially Schumpeter (1950), original edition 1942.
7. Croly (1965), p. 22 (original edition 1909). Quoted in Schambra (1982), p. 39.
8. For details on forming a homeowners' association, see Urban Land Institute (1970).

REFERENCES

Berger, Peter L., and Neuhaus, Richard John. 1977. *To Empower People: The Role of Mediating Structures in Public Policy.* Washington, DC: American Enterprise Institute.
Boyte, Harry C. 1980. *The Backyard Revolution: Understanding the New Citizen Movement.* Philadelphia: Temple University Press.
Callenbach, Ernest. 1977. *Ecotopia.* New York: Bantam Books.
Croly, Herbert. 1965. *The Promise of American Life.* Cambridge, MA: Harvard University Press.
Cummins, Richard. 1980. *Proposition Fourteen: A Secessionist Remedy.* New York: Grove Press.
de Tocqueville, Alexis. 1969. *Democracy in America.* Edited by J. P. Mayer. Garden City, NY: Anchor.
Downs, Anthony. 1981. *Neighborhoods and Urban Development.* Washington, DC: Brookings Institution.
Ellickson, Robert. 1977. "Suburban growth controls: an economic and legal analysis." *Yale Law Journal* (January).
Fischel, William A. 1979. "Equity and efficiency aspects of zoning reform." *Public Policy* (Summer).
———. 1978. "A property rights approach to municipal zoning." *Land Economics* (February).
———. 1980. "Zoning and land use reform: a property rights perspective." *Virginia Journal of Natural Resources Law.* Volume I.

Frazier, Mark. 1980. "Privatizing the city." *Policy Review* (Spring).

Institute for Community Economics. 1982. *The Community Land Trust Handbook.* Emmaus, PA: Rodale Press.

Jacobs, Jane. 1961. *The Death and Life of Great American Cities.* New York: Vintage Books.

Lowi, Theodore J. 1969. *The End of Liberalism: Ideology, Policy and the Crisis of Public Authority.* New York: Norton. Second edition 1979.

McClaughry, John. 1975. "The new feudalism — state land use controls." *No Land Is an Island: Individual Rights and Government Control of Land Use.* San Francisco: Institute for Contemporary Studies.

National Commission on Neighborhoods. 1979. *People, Building Neighborhoods: Final Report to the President and the Congress of the United States.* Washington, DC: U.S. Government Printing Office.

National Commission on Urban Problems. 1969. *Building the American City.* New York: Praeger.

National Conference of Commissioners on Uniform State Laws. 1980a. *The Uniform Condominium Act.* Chicago, IL: N.C.C.U.S.L.

———. 1980b. *The Uniform Planned Community Act.* Chicago, IL: N.C.C.U.S.L.

———. 1981. *The Model Real Estate Cooperative Act.* Chicago,IL: N.C.C.U.S.L.

Nelson, Robert H. 1977. *Zoning and Property Rights: An Analysis of the American System of Land Use Regulation.* Cambridge, MA: M.I.T. Press. Paperback edition 1980.

———. 1979. "A private property right theory of zoning." *The Urban Lawyer* (Fall).

———. 1981. "Agricultural zoning: a case study in the purposes, consequences and alternatives to zoning." Paper prepared for presentation at the Conference on "Agricultural Land Preservation: Economics or Politics," Bozeman, Montana, December 2–6.

Newman, Oscar. 1980. *Community of Interest.* Garden City, NY: Anchor.

Nozick, Robert. 1974. *Anarchy, State and Utopia.* New York: Basic Books.

Okun, Arthur M. 1975. *Equality and Efficiency: The Big Tradeoff.* Washington,DC: Brookings Institution.

Pollock, Frederick. 1883. *The Land Laws.* London: Macmillan and Company.

Sager, Lawrence G. 1979. "Questions I wish I had never asked: the Burger Court in exclusionary zoning." *Southwestern University Law Review* 11:2: 509–44.

Schambra, William A. 1982. "From self-interest to social obligation: local communities v. the national community. In *Meeting Human Needs: Towards a New Public Philosophy.* Edited by Jack A. Meyer. Washington, DC: American Enterprise Institute.

Schumpeter, Joseph A. 1950. *Capitalism, Socialism and Democracy.* New York: Harper Brothers.

Tarlock, A. Dan. 1972. "Toward a revised theory of zoning." In *Land Use Controls Annual.* Edited by F. S. Bangs. Chicago: American Society of Planning Officials.

Toll, Seymour I. 1969. *Zoned American.* New York: Grossman Publishers.

United States Department of Housing and Urban Development. 1979. *Neighborhoods: A Self-Help Sampler.* Office of Neighborhoods, Voluntary Associations and Consumer Protection. Washington, DC: U.S. Government Printing Office (October).

United States Supreme Court. 1974. *Village of Belle Terre* v. *Boraas.* 416 U.S. at 9.

———. 1976. *City of Eastlake* v. *Forest City Enterprises, Inc.* 426 U.S. 668.

Urban Land Institute. 1970. *The Homes Association Handbook.* Technical Bulletin Number 50 of the Urban Land Institute, Washington, DC.

Wood, Robert C. 1964. "The political economy of the future." In *City and Suburb: The Economics of Metropolitan Growth.* Edited by Benjamin Chinitz. Englewood Cliffs, NJ: Prentice-Hall.

Wood, Robert C., with Vladimir V. Almendinger. 1961. *1400 Governments: The Political Economy of the New York Metropolitan Region.* Cambridge, MA: Harvard University Press.

Index

Absentee ownership: agricultural, 59; in Appalachia, 236–37, 238, 239, 240, 243; on Prince Edward Island, 245, 246, 248, 250–53, 254, 255, 257–59, 267

Acreage limitations: under Homestead Act, 11, 13; in large-scale farming, 36–38; in small-scale farming, 36

Agribusiness: agricultural research by, 65; water district land owned by, 18. *See also* Corporate farms

Agricultural Adjustment Administration, 22, 178–79

Agricultural exports, 63–64

Agricultural labor: cooperative farms and, 69–70; on large-scale farms, 58, 59, 68, 69; migrant, 68–69; Roman Catholic Church's statement on, 83; on small-scale farms, 58, 59, 68; unionization of, 68, 69

Agricultural land: land speculation and, 213; market regulation of, 67–68; ownership patterns of, 8; preservation of, 63–64; taxation of, 63, 65, 67

Agricultural land reform, 55–72; agricultural land preservation in, 63–64; commodity policies and, 65; community land trusts and, 68; cooperative farms in, 69–70; corporate farming restrictions in, 62–63; current options in, 66; family farms in, 56–66, 67, 69, 70; land-grant colleges and, 64–65; land market regulation in, 67–68; neopopulism and, 66; public assistance in, 61–62; tax policies and, 65, 67; in Third World, 55

Agricultural Reform in the United States (Black), 22

Agricultural research, 64–65

Agricultural sales: by large-scale farms, 56, 59; by small-scale farms, 56, 59, 60, 62

Agricultural technology, 64–65

Agriculture: absentee ownership in, 59; alternative agricultural movement in, 64, 88, 96; capital-intensive nature of, 64; democratization of, 66; dualistic structure of, 60; energy use in, 88–97; family basis of, 57; food production costs in, 89–90; fuel shortages and, 93–94, 95; hired labor in, 58, 59; mechanization of, 57, 91–92; public subsidies for, 65; rented land in, 57–58. *See also* specific types of farms

Alabama: mineral rights taxation in, 237, 238; Yazoo land fraud in, 10

Alaska, reservation lands in, 153

Alaska Purchase, 120

Alternative agricultural movement, 88, 96; small-scale farming and, 64

Amana Society, 19

American Farm Bureau Federation, 65

American Indian Movement, 159–60, 167

Anderson, Osborne, 173

Apartments. *See* Rental housing

Appalachia: absentee ownership in, 236–37, 238, 239, 240, 243; agriculture in, 239–40; coal counties of, 239; corporate ownership in, 236–37, 240–41; economic development in, 239; energy development in, 101–6, 237, 240; federal land in, 103; foreign ownership in, 104; housing in, 240; land reform in 102, 106–14, 233–44; land redistribution in, 112–13; landownership patterns in, 102, 103, 104–5, 106–7, 112, 233, 236–37, 239, 240–41, 244; landownership study of, 233–44; mineral resources in, 236–37; mineral rights in, 112–13, 241–42; property taxes in, 105, 109–12, 237–38; recreational counties in, 239; Roman Catholic bishops' statement on, 80–81; strip mining in, 107–8, 242, 243; tax-exempt lands in, 238; taxation system in, 237–38; tourism counties in, 239; urbanization in, 233; water supply projects in, 108–9

Appalachian Alliance, 106, 233–34

Notes on the Contributors

CHARLES C. GEISLER teaches in the Department of Rural Sociology at Cornell University, where he does research on national landownership patterns, the political and economic context of land-use planning, and the role of alternative property institutions in local community development. He has edited and coauthored several books, including *The Community Land Trust Handbook, The Social Consequences and Challenges of New Agricultural Technologies,* and *The Social Impacts of Rapid Resource Development on Native Peoples.*

FRANK J. POPPER is a Gilbert White Fellow at Resources for the Future and Associate Professor in the Urban Studies Department at Rutgers University. He is author of *The Politics of Land-Use Reform* and *The President's Commissions;* coauthor of *Urban Nongrowth;* and author of the forthcoming *The LULU: Coping with Locally Unwanted Land Uses.* He has served as a consultant for many government agencies and private corporations.

FREDERICK H. BUTTEL, of the N.Y. State College of Agriculture and Life Sciences, Cornell University, is primarily interested in environmental sociology, the sociology of agricultural systems, and the sociology of economic change in developed and underdeveloped nations. His major publications are *The Rural Sociology of the Advanced Societies; Environment, Energy, and Society,* and a forthcoming reader entitled *The Political Economy of Food and Agriculture in Advanced Industrial Societies.*

JOHN EMMEUS DAVIS has worked as a community organizer and neighborhood planner in east Tennessee, upstate New York, and Cincinnati. He joined the staff of the Institute for Community Economics in Greenfield, Massachusetts, in 1981. Among other writings on land, housing, and community-based development, he is coauthor of *The Community Land Trust Handbook.*

V. DALE FORSTER, a specialist in geography and housing studies, is Research Associate in the University School of Rural Planning and Development, University of Guelph, Ontario. She has been a planner with the Greater Vancouver Regional District and a research analyst with the Wyoming Research Corporation.

JOHN GAVENTA served with Bill Horton as a co-coordinator of the Appalachian Land Ownership Project and as an author of the summary volume of the Appalachian Land Ownership Study. He currently works at the Highlander Research and Education Center in New Market, Tennessee. His first book, *Power and Powerlessness: Quiescence and Rebellion in an Appalachian Valley,* has won numerous awards, including the 1981 Woodrow Wilson Award of the American Political Science Association.

JOHN HART was until recently Director of the Heartland Project of the Catholic Bishops of twelve midwestern states, and principal author of their *Strangers and Guests* land statement. He has also worked with migrant farmworkers in Texas and with the American Indian Treaty Council. He is the Administrator of the Live Oak Fund for Change in Austin, Texas.

CHESTER HARTMAN is a Visiting Fellow at the Institute for Policy Studies in Washington, DC. He has taught at Cornell, and Harvard, Yale, the Universities of California at Berkeley and North Carolina. His books include *Housing and Social Policy, Housing Urban America, Yerba Buena: Land Grab and Community Resistance in San Francisco,* and *Displacement: How to Fight It.* He chairs the Planners Network, a national organization of progressive planners.

DAVID HOLLAND is Associate Professor in the Department of Agricultural Economics, Washington State University. He does research on the development of United States agriculture, especially the relation between structural change in agriculture and the use of renewable energy.

BILL HORTON taught at Drew University and at Davis and Elkins College, where he also served as Coordinator of Appalachian Studies. Currently he is the Director of the Appalachian Alliance, a coalition working for social, political, and economic change in Appalachian land and natural resources. He co-coordinated the Appalachian Land Ownership Project, was an author of the regional volume of the Appalachian Land Ownership Study, and has written other articles on community and natural resources.

MARK B. LAPPING is Professor and Director of the University School of Rural Planning and Development, University of Guelph, Ontario. He has taught at the universities of Vermont and Missouri and at SUNY, and has served as a consultant to local, regional, and national planning and development bodies. His research, teaching, and activist interests are land reform in advanced economies, rural planning, and rural social development.

WENDY U. LARSEN is a partner in the Chicago law firm of Ross & Hardies, where she practices land-use law for private-sector and government clients. She recently assisted in the preparation of regulations for the Pinelands Commission in New Jersey and the Dade County [Florida] East Everglades Management Plan. Her publications focus on land use, public utilities, and planning topics. She is now lecturer in land-use planning law at the DePaul University College of Law.

DANIEL LAUBER is President of Planning/Communications, a consulting firm in Evanston, Illinois. A director of the American Planning Association, Lauber is a housing expert and author of dozens of articles and monographs on condominium conversion, limited-equity cooperatives, zoning for family and group homes, and socially informed planning. He created "Condo-watch," the first regular newspaper column in the country exclusively devoted to condominium issues, for the *Chicago Sun-Times.* He has been Senior Planner for Oak Park, Illinois, Principal Contributing Consultant to the American Bar Association's Advisory Commission on Housing and Urban Growth, and Research Associate for the American Society of Planning Officials.

DAVID LIDEN was West Virginia Coordinator for the Appalachian Land Ownership Study, done under the direction of the Appalachian Alliance and with the support of the Appalachian Regional Commission. He now works with Rural Resources in Murphy, North Carolina, where he provides technical assistance and organizing support for progressive organizations concerned with land use, mineral development, and property taxation. He also works with community groups across the Appalachian region in conjunction with the Institute for Southern Studies and the Appalachian Alliance. He has written community education guides and journalistic pieces on land and mineral development.

GUILLERMO LUX is Professor of Southwestern History at New Mexico Highlands University in Las Vegas, New Mexico. He is a native New Mexican from a rural background and has published on developmental problems in the Southwest and Latin America. He has worked with rural community development programs in Guatemala, Paraguay, and Colombia. He lives in Santa Fe, New Mexico.

DEAN MACCANNELL is Professor of Applied Behavioral Science and rural sociologist in the Experiment Station at the University of California, Davis, where he serves as Chair of the Graduate Program in Community Studies and Director of the Macrosocial Accounting Project. He was consultant to the U.S. Secretary of Agriculture's *Structure of Agriculture* project and the Department of the Interior's *Environmental Impact Statement on Acreage Limitation.* In addition to his research on the effects of agriculture on communities, Dr. MacCannell has published books and articles on social theory and the structure of modern society. He is currently analyzing 1980 census tract data in the Westlands area as a sequel to the present chapter.

HAROLD A. MCDOUGALL is an Attorney/Professor at the Antioch School of Law. He began his involvement in the Black Movement for Liberation at nineteen as a field-worker in Alabama for the Student Nonviolent Coordinating Committee. He is the author of articles on land issues and black liberation.

ROBERT H. NELSON is a member of the Office of Policy Analysis, U.S. Department of the Interior. He has written on zoning and the public lands, including *Zoning and Property Rights* and *The Making of Federal Coal Policy.* He has taught at City College of the City University of New York. The views expressed in his paper do not necessarily represent those of the Interior Department.

ROXANNE DUNBAR ORTIZ is Associate Professor in Native American Studies at California State University, Hayward. Among her publications are *Roots of Resistance: History of Land Tenure in New Mexico, The Great Sioux Nation,* and *Economic Development in American Indian Reservations.* She is an American Indian and is active in the work of the International Indian Treaty Council, a U.N.-affiliated nongovernmental organization.

KEVIN J. RIELLEY practices with the Chicago law firm of Ross & Hardies, where he counsels public-sector clients. His work has involved drafting major land-use regulations for the New Jersey Pinelands Commission, land-use litigation in Illinois, litigation for the enforcement of municipal ordinances and contracts, and work as special counsel on the implementation of new energy technology.

CLIFFORD L. WEAVER is a partner in the Chicago law firm of Ross & Hardies, where he counsels clients in both the public and private sectors on government regulation, especially land use and development. He has also practices in intergovernmental relations and administrative proceedings, regulation of the nuclear industry, and implementation of new energy technology. He has drafted major land-use regulations, including those for the New Jersey Pinelands Commission, and consulted on problems of neighborhood and downtown preservation and redevelopment. His publications include *City Zoning: The Once and Future Frontier* and *New Approaches to Residential Takings.* He is now Adjunct Professor in the Graduate School of Urban Sciences, University of Illinois, Chicago Circle Campus.

JERRY WHITE, a doctoral candidate in geography, is a lecturer at Solano College. He grew up on a farm in Fresno County, California, and has done extensive research in agricultural geography. He is a postgraduate researcher with the Macrosocial Accounting Project and served with Dean MacCannell as consultant to the Department of the Interior's *Environmental Impact Statement on Acreage Limitation.*